Intermedia, Fluxus and the Something Else Press

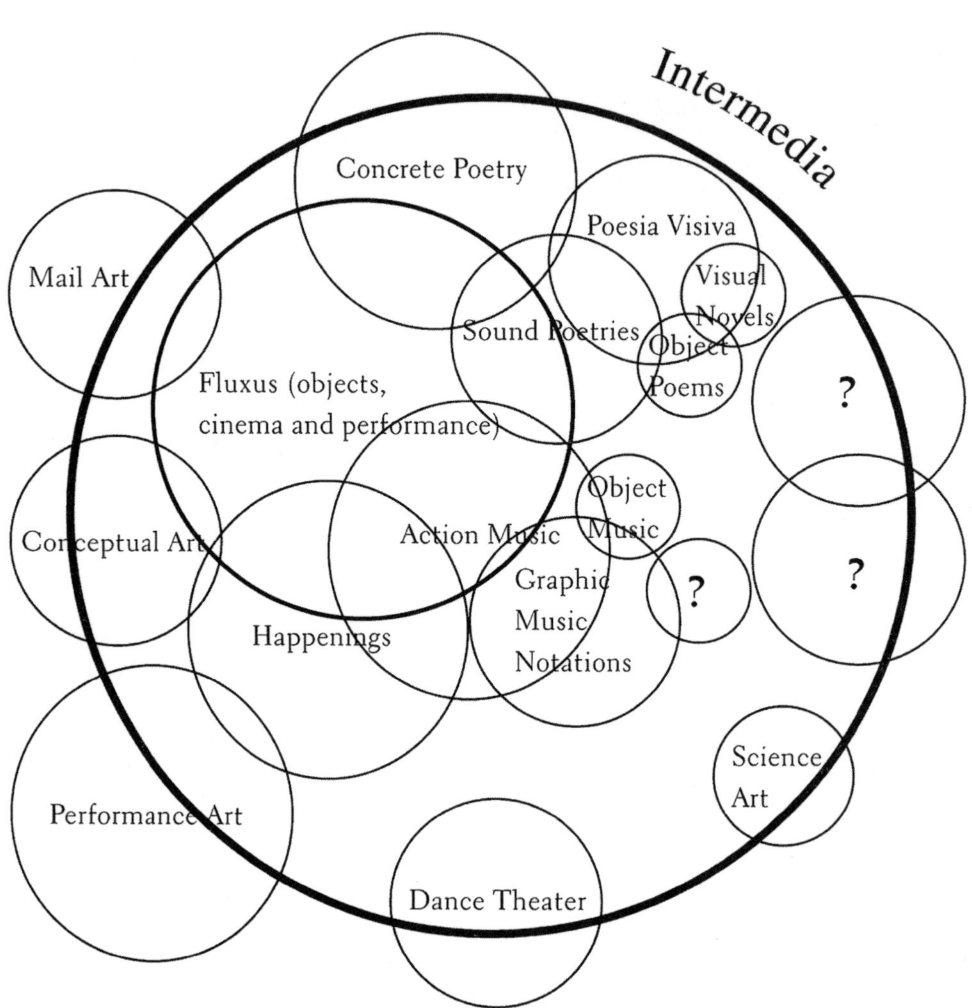

Intermedia
Concrete Poetry
Poesia Visiva
Visual Novels
Mail Art
Sound Poetries
Object Poems
Fluxus (objects, cinema and performance)
?
Object Music
Conceptual Art
Action Music
Graphic Music Notations
?
?
Happenings
Science Art
Performance Art
Dance Theater

Intermedia, Fluxus *and the* Something Else Press

SELECTED WRITINGS BY DICK HIGGINS

edited by
STEVE CLAY and KEN FRIEDMAN

siglio   2018   CATSKILL, NEW YORK

Acknowledgments

First and foremost, I wish to extend thanks to Christian Xatrec and Alice Centamore of the Emily Harvey Foundation. Both were extremely encouraging of the project from the start and more than generous with their knowledge and resources, particularly with respect to the Something Else Press. I offer appreciation to Peter Frank for his groundbreaking work in writing the first Something Else Press bibliography in 1983 and thanks for answering my questions in 2018; compiling the Something Else Press Checklist would have been a much more difficult job without Peter's pioneering model. Julie Harrison continues to be my biggest supporter and her steadfast enthusiasm for the project together with editorial and design suggestions have been, as always, an invaluable contribution. Thanks as well to Jan Herman, editor at the Press 1972–74, who tirelessly answered my stream of picky queries. Others have helped in ways large and small: My sincere thanks to David Abel, Victoria Baker, Brian Cassidy, John Corbett, John Giorno, Hannah Higgins, Emily Gross, Jon Hendricks, James Hoff, Andrea Latham, Jeff Maser, Mark Melnikov, Richard Milazzo, Barbara Moore, Lisa Pearson, George Quasha, Richard Kostelanetz, Michael von Uchtrup, and Elizabeth Zuba. —SC

In great part, my acknowledgments overlap with those of Steve Clay. My thanks and gratitude to Christian Xatrec and Alice Centamore of the Emily Harvey Foundation. Christian and I have been talking together about the Press since the early 1980s. I also thank the late Emily Harvey—Emily Harvey Gallery represented Dick Higgins's work and mine, along with many other Fluxus artists and composers. Emily left the legacy of her work and her galleries in New York and Venice to the Emily Harvey Foundation—for which we are all grateful. Peter Frank's 1983 book, *Something Else Press: An Annotated Bibliography*, was the first comprehensive study of the Press. Peter and I have been talking and thinking together about the Press and about Dick's work since we first met in 1976. I owe thanks to Jon Hendricks, Jan Herman, Hannah Higgins, Barbara Moore, and George Quasha, whose advice and assistance helped to make this book possible. I also owe a debt of intellectual gratitude to David Doris, Natasha Lushetich, Roger Rothman, and Owen Smith. Their pioneering work on Fluxus helps to place Dick Higgins's thinking in perspective. So, too, my thanks to Bengt af Klintberg—Dick's friend and colleague in Fluxus, and mine. Bengt and I have been thinking together about Dick for many years. I thank Tongji University College of Design and Innovation in Shanghai for supporting my research on this book, and our dean, Lou Yongqi, whose approach to design and architecture capture the intermedia spirit. I also thank Swinburne University of Technology of Melbourne. Vice-chancellor Linda Kristjanson and pro vice-chancellor Scott Thompson-Whiteside supported my research on Fluxus that contributed to this book. Finally, I thank Lisa Pearson of Siglio, a publisher whose work continues the spirit of Something Else Press, carrying the legacy of the Press into the current era. —KF

Contents

Introduction
STEVE CLAY

Dick Higgins was born in 1938 and by the time he was twenty-seven, he had co-invented Happenings, co-founded Fluxus, named, practiced, and theorized the concept of intermedia and founded the Something Else Press. He was the quintessential proto-hyphenated artist: poet-writer-painter-performer-composer-editor-filmmaker-designer-typographer-publisher-critic-scholar—and more. Coming of age at exactly the right time and place—New York City in the late fifties and early sixties—Higgins incited, nurtured, and chronicled an emerging complex of cultural tendencies that have influenced the experimental art of the past half century. In 1998, he died of a heart attack at the age of sixty following a performance in Quebec City, Canada, but the projects and processes he set in motion reverberate today.

Intermedia, Fluxus and the Something Else Press is a long-overdue survey of Higgins's theoretical writings from throughout his prolific career. Our intention is to inspire and renew interest in Higgins's insights, attitudes, and methods—not simply as historical example (although that's important)—but as a model of inquiry and expression for immediate use.

Dick Higgins was a consummate explainer. Unlike most artists who bury their failures, Higgins was equally scrupulous in documenting and analyzing both his failures as well as his successes. An early book, *Jefferson's Birthday*, consisted of all the things he "wrote, composed, or invented between April 13, 1962 and April 13, 1963 . . . on the assumption that the bad work that one does is just as valuable as the interesting work."

Jefferson's Birthday was accompanied by *Postface*, a strident yet remarkably prescient eighty-six-page treatise (a large portion of which we include in facsimile) on what Higgins would later call the "arts of the new mentality." Written to give the reader some context for his collection of scores, events, theater pieces, and more, *Postface* became an important work in its own right. It is, in effect, the first outline of the origins of Happenings and Fluxus, and vividly describes the work of a specific generation of international avant-garde artists, many of whom would soon be published by the Something Else Press, including Al Hansen, George Brecht, Benjamin Patterson, Alison Knowles, and Wolf Vostell, among many others. Higgins wrote about *Postface*: "It is necessary to have an art which creates a tough, uncompromising, revolutionary mentality capable of expressing, handling, and extending scientifically the great tendencies of our times." This is exactly what he did in the four decades of his career.

Postface was also an instance of Higgins's lifelong exercise of critical engagement, his ongoing self-dialogue encompassing theory and practice, which is vividly exemplified in the essay "The Strategy of Each of My Books." Here he makes an analytical inventory of his published work from *What Are Legends?*, designed, illustrated, and published by Bern Porter in 1960 when Higgins was twenty-two, to *Variations on a Natural Theme*, a large orchestral work published in 1982 by Printed Editions, a small press directly descended from Something Else Press. When he reprinted "A Something Else Manifesto" in *A Dialectic of Centuries* (1978), which was originally published on the inside of the dust jacket of *Jefferson's Birthday/Postface* in 1964, he added a note: "This manifesto was used to define the editorial position of the Something Else Press—itself not just an avant-garde publishing house but, cumulatively, a critical statement."

Higgins's essays on Fluxus and intermedia range over a period of nearly thirty-five years, from the urgency of *Postface* (1964) to the well-considered backward glance of "Fluxus: Theory and Reception" (1987, 1998). He explores the interdependence of Fluxus and Something Else in "Two Sides of a Coin: Fluxus and Something Else Press," published in 1992. We also include the little known though essential history of the Press, "The Something Else Press Notes for a History to be Written Some Day." This honest, straightforward, and necessary piece was published in two issues of the short-lived *New Lazarus Review* in 1979–80.

Something Else Press: An Annotated Bibliography by Peter Frank was published by McPherson & Company in 1983 and has been the single indispensable resource for information on the Press for thirty-five years. We stand on the shoulders of Peter Frank and include a revised and illustrated Something Else Press checklist with annotations derived from Press-generated jacket copy, catalogs, prospectuses, and newsletters to provide a descriptive critical context for the making and selling of the books in the words of Dick Higgins, whenever possible. For those with an archival interest, we've accumulated and included a list of titles announced or mused about in print yet never published, which we find to be a fascinating glimpse of what almost was or might have been.

Our selection continues with essays concerning visual poetry ("A Short History of Pattern Poetry"), sound poetry ("Points Toward a Taxonomy of Sound Poetry"), correspondence (a four-page letter to poet/scholar Steve McCaffery in facsimile), and reproductions of posters (including "Some Poetry Intermedia" and "Five Traditions of Art History, an Essay") before ending with Hannah Higgins's exemplary portrait of her father, "Eleven Snapshots of Dick Higgins." We have retained the idiosyncrasies of the original publications as well as certain narrative redundancies, particularly with respect to Higgins's history with George Maciunas and the foundational story of the Something Else Press. We do so to preserve the internal integrity of each of the essays.

Dick Higgins was an intermedia artist of and for his time, on the proverbial cutting edge of new paradigms within and between poetry, painting, performance, and more. In a 1991 interview he described the publication list of the Something Else Press as "love letters to the future." We offer the current selection to another future, particularly to young artists, poets, and publishers, that through the works of Dick Higgins they might find new possibilities for their own.

Thinking About Dick Higgins
KEN FRIEDMAN

Pioneer and Catalyst

Dick Higgins was a pioneering figure in the arts of the new mentality. With Allan Kaprow, Al Hansen, Claes Oldenburg and others, he invented happenings. With George Maciunas, George Brecht, Alison Knowles, and Nam June Paik, he co-founded Fluxus. As an artist and composer, his work influenced the experimental art of the past half century. As publisher of Something Else Press and a theorist of art, he helped to generate new ways to think about art, literature, and music. Higgins was born in 1938 in Jesus Pieces, England. He died in 1998 following a performance in Quebec City, Canada, only sixty years old.

Over the last four decades of those six, he became a major figure in twentieth-century culture. Higgins's role as an influential presence in the arts of the century compares with that of Marcel Duchamp or John Cage. While he was less famous, Higgins abstracted and concretized the profound artistic and intellectual ferment of an era as Duchamp and Cage did. Higgins was a bold experimental artist. He was also a quiet, tireless contributor to the world of ideas. By shaping an innovative stream of exhibitions, projects, and publications, he became a pivotal figure in the network of idea-based artists whom he attracted and with whom he interacted. For many, Higgins personified and exemplified these issues from the 1960s through the last days of the twentieth century.

Higgins's art explored the issues that attracted his attention. In European terms, one can say that he also problematized them. His exemplative works functioned as the demonstration of larger theories in the framework of intermedia, and his theories shaped the crucial framework within which much of the artistic thinking of our era emerged. While the art world is often driven by intellectual fashion, it is often unaware of its own history. Many of the artists and composers whom Dick Higgins influenced have little or no knowledge of Higgins as a source of their ideas and work. One reason for this book is restoring Higgins's writings and ideas to visibility. A proper historical appraisal is overdue.

Higgins's intellectual program was astonishing in scope and scale, encyclopedic in perspective. His work ranged across painting, performance, and poetry; happenings, intermedia, and film; typography, book art, and publishing. Beyond this, he shaped a theory of the arts for our times, and he explained his theory in an extraordinary series of books and essays. His explanations opened an artistic territory for those around him. At different times, Higgins described these worlds under the various rubrics of experimental art and the arts of the new mentality. The most expressive term, and the one that Higgins most durably gave to the English language, was the word "intermedia."

He coined the term "intermedia" in the mid-1960s to describe the tendency of the most interesting and best work in the new art to cross the boundaries of recognized media or even to fuse the boundaries of art with media that had not previously been considered art forms. With characteristic modesty, he often noted that Samuel Taylor Coleridge had first used the term. Higgins was too modest. Coleridge used the term "intermedium" in the singular, using it once (and apparently once only) in referring to a specific issue in the work of Edmund Spenser. Coleridge's "Lecture Three: On Spenser" bears a distant kinship to Higgins's construction of the term, but Coleridge's use was different and distinct in meaning and form. Coleridge referred to a point between two kinds of meaning in a single art medium. Coleridge's "intermedium" was a singular term, used almost as an adjectival noun. Higgins's "intermedia" referred to a tendency in the arts that became both a range of art forms and a way of approaching the arts. Higgins said that he may have read the Coleridge essay in his years as a student at Yale or Columbia, subconsciously taking it in. This may be so, but Dick Higgins coined a new word in the current form and contemporary meaning of the term "intermedia." He went on to elaborate the issues and ideas involved in this term in a program of artistic research and writing that spanned over four decades.

Higgins was an artist as well as a theorist. He approached experimental art in a genuinely experimental spirit. In essence, he constructed an extensive research program of ideas and issues ripe for exploration. He then posited cases and examples to explore them. These cases and examples formed the body of his work. To comprehend the radical and experimental nature of Higgins's work, we must compare his studio program with a scientific research program. He was interested in the operation of chance, but he did not rely on chance effects. Quite the contrary. One of his famous one-sentence manifestos was, "If you haven't done it twice, you haven't done it." He also placed great emphasis on learning and mastering the specific artistic skills needed to undertake his experiments. In some cases, he only put these skills to use once or twice, but he felt the mastery of skills essential if art works were to fulfill the experimental goals for which he shaped them. He was equally rigorous in documenting his results. He accepted and critically analyzed the failed results of his experiments as well as the successes. Rather than bury his failures, as most artists do, he published or exhibited them when he felt it appropriate to a larger program of ideas. More important, he challenged the scope of an art world that insisted on artists who confine themselves to the limits of a single discipline or medium.

While intellectuals and critics admired Higgins's extraordinary experimental spirit and his rigorous integrity, these virtues hardly suited him to an art world interested in the repeatable production of recognizable and salable physical artifacts. Dealers market art works under brand names, much like soap, perfume, or automobiles, and the collectors who buy those works expect their purchases to embody brand values. Many critics and curators who oppose market mechanisms and corporate branding prefer art in readily identifiable formats and branded value packages. While this is a mild irony, it is easy to understand. Criticism and curating are both linked to an art world that is, in turn, driven by the art market. The market subjects art to a range of forces that are as powerful in this sector of the economy as the military-industrial complex is in the larger, general economy. It is nevertheless sad that scholars and critics accede to and reinforce this aspect of the system. While Higgins's work may not have suited dealers and collectors, things should have been different for critics, scholars, and curators. The work should have excited them, especially given the fact that the ideas and range of meanings he helped to shape influenced work that they often admired. In his last book, *Modernism Since Postmodernism*, Higgins considers some of the reasons for the systematic exclusion of Fluxus artists from the art market at the very moment they had become increasingly famous. One imagines that independent thinking by critics and curators who understand the intellectual foundations of experimental art might have made a difference. But Higgins effectively poses a corollary question. Do enough critics and curators understand the intellectual foundations of experimental art?

Higgins was concerned with far more than his own work. He was engaged in the work and ideas of the colleagues he respected. This was an important reason for his work as a publisher and public thinker. This role, in fact, was a key reason for Higgins's great influence, and he helped to shape an international community of inquiry through two major forums for intellectual dialogue and artistic interaction. These were Fluxus and Something Else Press. Higgins played an important personal role in shaping the laboratory of ideas that swirled around Fluxus and Something Else Press. These became a meeting-point and breeding ground for some of the best and most innovative experimental art of our era, in music and performance, in visual art and intermedia.

Thus it is that comparing Higgins with Cage and Duchamp has become common for a knowledgeable few, and Higgins holds his own in this comparison. But if he holds his own, it is because there are important differences between his career and theirs. As an artist, far fewer of Higgins's works are known than Duchamp's. His work as an artist was incomplete, and it will remain incomplete. He will never complete the program of works he planned to undertake. As a result, his true stature as an artist will never be known. There are no works in Higgins's body of work that rank with Duchamp's acknowledged masterpieces. This is partly so because Higgins was not given to the memorable single gesture. This is also the case because times have changed, and times have changed in great part because of Duchamp's influence and Cage's, not to mention the influence that Higgins himself exerted. Even so, Higgins's standing as an artist may be subject to reconsideration. I still recall the time in 1968 that a friend offered to sell me a Duchamp for $300. Duchamp's reputation wasn't always what it is now. But then, Joseph Beuys was just an eccentric art teacher in those days and you could still buy a copy of George Brecht's *Water Yam* for $5.00.

If it is not yet possible to evaluate Higgins's work as a visual artist, few dispute the power of his ideas. In intellectual rigor and depth, he was one of the few artists since Duchamp who had the capacity to plan and complete a comprehensive program of idea-based art. And unlike Duchamp, whose program is expressed in enigmatic notes and elliptical comments, Higgins was a skilled theorist who presented his ideas and concerns in an expansive, thorough body of sophisticated, articulate publications. Unlike Cage, Higgins was not old enough when he died to have been forgotten and rediscovered. Like Higgins, Cage lived in genteel poverty until he was quite old. Despite the differences that might eventually have been rectified by time and a longer life, however, those who had a deep knowledge of the two legendary figures with whom he forms a triumvirate hold Higgins in high esteem. The reason rests on qualities that make Dick Higgins unique among the artists of the twentieth century. To understand these qualities, one must look back in history, neither to the composers of the Romantic era nor to the artists of the Renaissance, but to the humanists who transformed the Middle Ages into the modern world. To find Dick Higgins's proper comparison, one must look to Erasmus of Rotterdam.

Like Erasmus in philosophy, theology, and the humanities, Higgins's work attracted many of the best minds of his era in art, music, and literature. His thinking and his work ranged wide and deep over several fields. He exchanged letters and correspondence with a wide circle of colleagues. And, in notable similarity to Erasmus, Higgins harnessed the power of the printing press in the service of his theories. Time and context gave Higgins's works different meaning. He never achieved the popular success of Erasmus: in 1520, Erasmus's work alone comprised nearly one third of all books sold by one Oxford bookseller. When Milton studied at Cambridge a century later, Erasmus's works were still in wide use. While Higgins's works never achieved this kind of success, Higgins himself viewed life and learning in the broadest perspective. Much as Erasmus did, Higgins read widely, aided by a near-photographic memory, and he could have said, as Erasmus did, "My home is where I have my library." Even more significant, principles held a prime place in Higgins's life, and principles informed his art, his intellectual activities, and the way he conducted his life. Simply put, he was the kind of human being whose greatness rests on the natural dignity of moral grandeur, a dignity that combined with talent to make him admirable in the deepest sense of the word.

Like Erasmus, Higgins was also committed to a knowledge that bridged past times and present moments, classical issues and modern concerns, prehistoric structures and postmodern phenomena. His books outline the broad range of his interests. Among them, we find the first major historical study of pattern poetry, essays and monographs on a sixteenth-century Italian philosopher, a seventeenth-century English theologian-poet, a pair of eighteenth-century German historian-critics, and several major modern composers and poets. More recently, Higgins completed a massive study on an influential twentieth-century book designer. As publisher of Something Else Press, Higgins was also responsible for a major revival of interest in the work of Gertrude Stein with the publication of a wide range of her books, including the first complete edition of her enormous masterpiece, *The Making of Americans*.

Higgins was cut of the same cloth as the great humanists who gave voice to the intellectual and spiritual upheaval bridging medieval times and the early modern era, an Erasmus or a Montaigne. And like Desiderius Erasmus, Dick Higgins was a model of everything one may aspire to be as an intellectual, as a person of dignity. It was never necessary to agree with Dick on everything for this to be the case. That's not the role of a model. When minds meet in difference, they learn and grow as much or more than when they meet in similarity. That's one of the things we loved best about Dick Higgins. It was always possible to debate freely with Dick, trading ideas, sources, and suggestions for reading and thoughts for the next debate. He played a role in many lives because he cherished the life of the mind and the life of ideas. That is why he seems well compared with Erasmus.

As an intellectual presence, Dick Higgins is still alive for us, towering, and grand, an embodiment of ideas and issues, a mind engaged in the virtue and value of ideas without consideration of personal advantage. Like Erasmus, he is still here through the living presence of his work in the life of the mind. He was a friend, a colleague, and an exemplar. He was an explorer of new worlds, a pilgrim, a catalyst. He helped to shape the era in which he lived.

In the 1960s, it would have been impossible to envision the world of 2018. That's always the way it is. Whoever said, "The future isn't what it used to be" was quite right. Nevertheless, the past is still with us—and an opportunity to recover the past is also an opportunity to reshape the future. Dick would have liked that—and he would be happy to see the past restored—and with it, the new future that appears with a new understanding of the past.

Designer of Books, Designer of Worlds

To understand Higgins's influence on art, music, and literature, one must understand the Something Else Press and especially the Great Bear Pamphlets. At the beginning of Fluxus, Fluxus co-founder and impresario George Maciunas announced his intention to publish an encyclopedic series of works by the other Fluxus artists and composers. His idea, at one point, was to serve as the comprehensive publisher of all work by the core Fluxus artists. One of these projects was a collection of work by Higgins titled *Jefferson's Birthday*, a collection of all the works that Higgins composed between April 13,

1962 and April 13, 1963. Coincidentally, this was the birthday of Thomas Jefferson.

Maciunas never realized his original publishing program. He worked a day job in graphic design to pay for Fluxus projects. It was Maciunas's idea that there would be a market for his innovative, low cost Fluxus products and editions. While the massive collection of well-known Fluxus boxes and editions visible in Jon Hendricks's *Fluxus Codex* appears to be a series of industrial production runs, these projects were all assembled by hand. They were intended for mass production, but Maciunas never produced them on an industrial basis. They were, in reality, prototypes. They had no market, and no one bought them. During the year that Maciunas maintained a Fluxshop on Canal Street in New York, he did not manage to sell a single thing. Instead, he funded all the Fluxus products himself. One result of this was that many more Fluxus editions were planned and announced than Maciunas actually realized. One of these was Dick Higgins's *Jefferson's Birthday*, and its companion volume, *Postface*.

After waiting far too long for Maciunas to publish the book, Higgins grew impatient. He retrieved his manuscript from Maciunas, brought it home, and announced to Fluxus artist Alison Knowles that he was founding a publishing house to produce the kinds of book that this project represented. When Knowles asked him what he planned to call it, he said, "Shirtsleeves Press."

"That's terrible," she replied. "Call it something else." At that moment, Something Else Press got its name.

But Dick Higgins's concept of publishing was different to that of George Maciunas. Maciunas produced small art works in multiple editions. While he intended that they should eventually achieve industrial scale, they never did. Higgins understood that a medium for publishing art work on an industrial scale already existed. This medium was the book. To communicate the new art to a large public, Higgins established a publishing house rather than an avant-garde artist's outlet. He planned to publish experimental and radical work along with avant-garde classics and he wanted to make them visible. Higgins did not publish limited editions aimed at the tiny population of the downtown New York art scene. He aimed his publishing house at the international book trade, seeking an audience among the broad, book-buying public. While he could not compete with Doubleday, Random House, or the other trade giants, he was a trade publisher. He intended Something Else Press to be the smallest and most experimental of the big houses. And—unlike Maciunas—Higgins had financial resources. In the early 1960s, he was the beneficiary of a substantial inheritance. He put this money to work, investing it in his new publishing firm.

Most Something Else Press books appeared in standard trade formats as cloth-bound editions suitable for libraries and scholars with a few paperback editions for students and artists. The Press distributed its books internationally through established firms rather than Fluxus-style committees. The Press published most editions in runs of three thousand to five thousand copies.

With a characteristic mix of bold insight and practical naiveté, Higgins launched a business venture to promote experimental intermedia and contemporary art. Early on, he decided that the books would not carry the message far enough, so he created the Great Bear Pamphlets, a series of small, inexpensive pamphlets designed for the widest possible audience. The roster of Great Bear authors reads like a *Who's Who* of the international avant-garde. Higgins included material by Ay-O, George Brecht, Robert Filliou, Allan Kaprow, Bengt af Klintberg, Alison Knowles, Claes Oldenburg, Nam June Paik, Jerome Rothenberg, Dieter Roth, Emmett Williams, and many more. The pamphlets made an important contribution to the literature of the avant-garde. While the Great Bear Pamphlets have long been out of print, they are now available in a series of free digital editions on UbuWeb. But this does not explain the radical impact of the Great Bear Pamphlets in the art world of the 1960s. Higgins's technological genius does.

The Great Bear Pamphlets generally ran between sixteen and thirty-two pages in length. Higgins intended these pamphlets for wide circulation. He wanted them to convey and proselytize the excitement of what he called "the arts of the new mentality." This involved more than building a market for the larger and more expensive Something Else Press book volumes. In a sense, he hoped to generate and further an artistic reformation, much as the pamphlets of Martin Luther spread the religious Reformation in the early 1500s. In the 1500s, what was then the new technology of the printing press brought the words of Luther and his colleagues to a wide audience through a kind of transmission that we would now call "viral." Local printers generally produced pamphlets in small press runs. An edition might consist of several hundred examples; a large edition might be a thousand. The pamphlet revolution took place in a simple way. As traveling merchant-booksellers went from city to city and town to town, they would buy pamphlets in one place, taking them to another, much like animals spreading seeds in an ecosphere. When printers got hold of pamphlets that had market potential, they would set type on their own press to launch a new edition. In an era before copyright, every printer had the potential to become an independent publisher. In this way, popular texts and books spread from place to place without the author's involvement. The books of Erasmus spread in much the same way. While Erasmus earned money from authorized editions of his work, many more books appeared in workaday editions from publishers who copied Erasmus's works.

The early 1960s saw the birth of a new technology that offered individuals an opportunity to share the printed word in a way that resembled the first era of the printing press. This was the photocopy process, and this was the era in which the new Xerox machines were coming into wide use for the first time. Higgins published the Great Bear

Pamphlets in a size just right for copying. Each two-page spread fit a standard sheet of the 8 ½ by 11 inch paper used in the photocopy process. People copied the Great Bear Pamphlets in colleges and universities around the nation, as well as in libraries and museums. Artists, poets, and composers built useful libraries of experimental art for the cost of copies. On one hand, copying the booklets in their entirety was a violation of copyright and widespread copying meant that Something Else Press lost sales revenue. On the other hand, it was the 1960s, and Higgins implicitly encouraged wide copying—even pirate editions—by producing in a format that would spread the word. As an evangelist of Fluxus and intermedia, Higgins was always more eager to spread ideas than to make money, and Something Else Press was far better at spreading ideas than turning a profit. Profitable or not, Higgins understood how to influence the era through contemporary print technology, and he used several formats that encouraged widespread copying. The Great Bear Pamphlets were the first.

Following the success of the Great Bears, he launched the *Something Else Newsletter*. The newsletter was free. The printing technology was simple offset lithography. Higgins used direct mail distribution in a sophisticated direct mail marketing program applied to intellectual and artistic debate. It was the main tool in a long-term campaign. While scholars and critics were the primary audience for the *Something Else Newsletter*, it was particularly influential among artists, as it helped to define what Robert Filliou termed "the eternal network." It linked like-minded souls together in a web of discourse, serving as an important precursor to the phenomenon of artist magazines and periodicals.

Higgins built a strong intellectual constituency through Something Else Press, and he achieved an impact rivaled by few small publishers. The technology of an era helps to redefine its art. Printing technology led to the emblemata of the Middle Ages. The successive developments of woodcut, etching, lithography, silk-screen, photography, desk-top computing, and the internet, each influenced the published artistic production of their times. Like George Maciunas and Dieter Roth, Dick Higgins eagerly exploited the use of new technology to carry multiple messages. The major difference was that Higgins developed a way to distribute the messages that he put into print. In its decade of active production, Something Else Press had an extraordinary impact on the world of ideas. The Press books reached a circle of connoisseurs, scholars, and advanced artists. The books became an intellectual and historical resource used and studied for decades after the press closed in 1974. The Great Bears and the *Something Else Newsletter* were evangelical projects, designed to spread the Fluxus gospel.

George Maciunas's multiple Fluxus editions, and such small Fluxus publishers as Beau Geste Press, represented the experimental workshop tradition of intermedia publishing. Something Else Press became the public face of this tradition. Many Fluxus artists theorized inviting a large public audience to participate in art, music, performance, and design—erasing the border between art and life while dissolving the boundary between artist and spectator, performer and audience. Something Else Press brought this idea from studio and workshop to the larger world. It became a central part of the borderless international laboratory of experimental art. The books of the Something Else Press were a central contribution to the arts of the new mentality. Where most small presses produced limited editions at high prices, Higgins produced high quality mass market editions at the lowest possible price he could afford. While the books were vital, the Great Bear Pamphlets and the *Something Else Newsletters* were decisive in spreading the ideas exemplified in the books. Higgins's own ideas traveled from city to city and nation to nation in the essays he published in the newsletter. His voluminous correspondence—and these essays—made him an Erasmus for the twentieth century avant-garde.

I

Fluxus,
Happenings,
Intermedia

Intermedia

Originally published in the *Something Else Newsletter,* vol. 1, no. 1, 1966.

the something else
NEWSLETTER

Volume 1, Number 1   February, 1966   40¢

INTERMEDIA

by Dick Higgins

Much of the best work being produced today seems to fall between media. This is no accident. The concept of the separation between media arose in the renaissance. The idea that a painting is made of paint on canvas or that a sculpture should not be painted seems characteristic of the kind of social thought—categorizing and dividing society into nobility with its various subdivisions, untitled gentry, artisans, serfs and landless workers—which we call the feudal conception of the Great Chain of Being. This essentially mechanistic approach continued to be relevant throughout the first two industrial revolutions, just concluded, and into the present era of automation, which constitutes, in fact, a third industrial revolution.

However, the social problems that characterize our time, as opposed to the political ones, no longer allow a compartmentalized approach. We are approaching the dawn of a classless society, to which separation into rigid categories is absolutely irrelevant. This shift does not relate more to East than West or vice-versa. Castro works in the cane fields. New York's Mayor Lindsay walks to work during the subway strike. The millionaires eat their lunches at Horn and Hardart's. This sort of populism is a growing tendency rather than a shrinking one.

We sense this in viewing art which seems to belong unnecessarily rigidly to one or another form. We view paintings. What are they, after all? Expensive, handmade objects, intended to ornament the walls of the rich or, through their (or their government's) munificence, to be shared with the large numbers of people and give them a sense of grandeur. But they do not allow of any sense of dialogue.

Pop art? How could it play a part in the art of the future? It is bland. It is pure. It uses elements of common life without comment, and so, by accepting the misery of this life and its aridity so mutely, it condones them. Pop and Op are both dead, however, because they confine themselves, through the media which they employ, to the older functions of art, of decorating and suggesting grandeur, whatever their detailed content or their artists' intentions. None of the ingenious theories of the Mr. Ivan Geldoway combine can prevent them from being colossally boring and irrelevant. Milord runs his Mad Avenue gallery, in which he displays his pretty wares. He is protected by a handful of rude footmen who seem to feel that this is the way Life will always be. At his beck and call is Sir Fretful Callous, a moderately well-informed high priest, who apparently despises the Flame he is supposed to tend and therefore prefers anything which titillates him. However, Milord needs his services, since he, poor thing, hasn't the time or the energy to contribute more than his name and perhaps his dollars; getting information and finding out what's going on are simply tooooo exhausting. So, well protected and advised, he goes blissfully through the streets in proper Louis XIV style.

This scene is not just characteristic of the painting world as an institution, however. It is absolutely natural to (and inevitable in) the concept of the pure medium, the painting or precious object of any kind. That is the way such objects are marketed since that is the world to which they belong and to which they relate. The sense of "I am the state," however, will shortly be replaced by "After me the deluge," and, in fact, if the High Art world were better informed, it would realize that the deluge has already begun.

Who knows when it began? There is no reason for us to go into history in any detail. Part of the reason that Duchamp's objects are fascinating while Picasso's voice is fading is that the Duchamp pieces are truly between media, between sculpture and something else, while Picasso is readily classifiable as a painted ornament. Similarly, by invading the land between collage and photography, the German John Heartfield produced what are probably the greatest graphics of our century, surely the most powerful political art that has been done to date.

The ready-made or found object, in a sense an in-

A spiritual blast-off—

A Primer of Happenings & Time / Space Art
by Al Hansen

160 pages, with over 100 illustrations: $4.50

A collection of intermedial art—

The Four Suits
by Philip Corner, Alison Knowles, Benjamin Patterson and Tomas Schmit

208 pages, with graphics and notations: $5.00

Available from Something Else Press, Inc. or from the Gotham Book Mart, the 8th Street Bookshop, or Wittenborn & Company in New York, or through your favorite bookdealer anywhere.

termedium since it was not intended to conform to the pure medium, usually suggests this, and therefore suggests a location in the field between the general area of art media and those of life media. However, at this time, the locations of this sort are relatively unexplored, as compared with media between the arts. I cannot, for example, name work which has consciously been placed in the intermedium between painting and shoes. The closest thing would seem to be the sculpture of Claes Oldenburg, which falls between sculpture and hamburgers or Eskimo Pies, yet it is not the sources of these images which his sculpture resembles so much as the images themselves. An Oldenburg Eskimo Pie may look something like an Eskimo Pie, yet it is neither edible nor cold. There is still a great deal to be done in this direction in the way of opening up aesthetically rewarding possibilities.

In the middle 1950's many painters began to realize the fundamental irrelevance of Abstract Expressionism, which was the dominant mode at the time. Such painters as Allan Kaprow and Robert Rauschenberg in the United States and Wolf Vostell in Germany turned to collage or, in the latter's case, dé-collage in the sense of making work by adding or removing, replacing and substituting or altering components of a visual work. They began to include increasingly incongruous objects in their work. Rauschenberg called his constructions "combines" and went so far as to place a stuffed goat—spattered with paint and with a rubber tire around its neck-onto one. Kaprow, more philosophical and restless, meditated on the relationship of the spectator and the work. He put mirrors into his things so the spectator could feel included in them. That wasn't physical enough, so he made enveloping collages which surrounded the spectator. These he called "environments." Finally, in the Spring of 1958, he began to include live people as part of the collage, and this he called a "happening."

The proscenium theater is the outgrowth of seventeenth century ideals of social order. Yet there is remarkably little structural difference between the dramas of D'Avenant and those of Edward Albee, certainly nothing comparable to the difference in pump construction or means of mass transportation. It would seem that the technological and social implications of the first two industrial revolutions have been evaded completely. The drama is still mechanistically divided: there are performers, production people, a separate audience and an explicit script. Once started, like Frankenstein's monster, the course of affairs is unalterable, perhaps damned by its inability to reflect its surroundings. With our populistic mentality today, it is difficult to attach importance—other than what we have been taught to attach—to this traditional theater. Nor do minor innovations do more than provide dinner conversation: this theater is round instead of square, in that one the stage revolves, here the play is relatively senseless and whimsical (Pinter is, after all, our modern J. M. Barrie—unless the honor belongs more properly to Beckett). Every year fewer attend the professional Broadway theaters. The shows get sillier and sillier, showing the producers' estimate of our mentality (or is it their own that is revealed?). Even the best of the traditional theater is no longer found on Broadway but at the Judson Memorial Church, some miles away. Yet our theater schools grind out thousands on thousands of performing and production personnel, for whom jobs will simply not exist in twenty years. Can we blame the unions? Or rents and real estate taxes? Of course not. The subsidized productions, sponsored at such museums as New York's Lincoln Center, are not building up a new audience so much as re-cultivating an old one, since the medium of such drama seems weird and artificial in our new social milieu. We need more portability and flexibility, and this the traditional theater cannot provide. It was made for Versailles and for the sedentary Milords, not for motorized life-demons, who travel six hundred miles a week. Versailles no longer speaks very loudly to us, since we think at eighty-five miles an hour.

In the other direction, starting from the idea of theater itself, others such as myself declared war on the script as a set of sequential events. Improvisation was no help: performers merely acted in imitation of a script. So I began to work as if time and sequence could be utterly suspended, not by ignoring them (which would simply be illogical) but by systematically replacing them as structural elements with change. Lack of change would cause my pieces to stop. In 1958 I wrote a piece, *Stacked Deck,* in which any event can take place at any time, as long as its cue appears. The cues are produced by colored lights. Since the colored lights could be used wherever they were put and audience reactions were also cuing situations, the performer-audience separation was removed and a happening situation was established, though less visually-oriented in its use of its environment and imagery. At the same time, Al Hansen moved into the area from graphic notation experiments, and Nam June Paik and Benjamin Patterson (both in Germany at the time) moved in from varieties of music in which specifically musical events were frequently replaced by non-musical actions.

Thus the happening developed as an intermedium, an uncharted land that lies between collage, music and the theater. It is not goverened by rules; each work determines its own medium and form according to its needs. The concept itself is better understood by what it is not, rather than what it is. Approaching it, we are pioneers again, and shall continue to be so as long as there's plenty of elbow room and no neighbors around for a few miles. Of course a concept like this is very disturbing to those whose mentality is compartmentalized. *Time, Life* and the High Priests have been announcing the death of happenings regularly since the movement gained momentum in the late fifties, but this says more about the accuracy of their information than about the liveliness of the movement.

We have noted the intermedia in the theater and in the visual arts, the happening and certain varieties of physical constructions. For reasons of space we cannot take up here the intermedia between other areas. However, I would like to suggest that the use of intermedia is more or less universal throughout the fine arts, since continuity rather than categorization is the hallmark of our new mentality. There are parallels to the happening in music, for example, in the work of such composers as Philip Corner and John Cage, who explore the intermedia between music and philosophy, or Joe Jones, whose self-playing musical instruments fall into the intermedium between music and sculpture. The constructed poems of Emmett Williams and Robert Filliou certainly constitute an intermedium between poetry and sculpture. Is it possible to speak of the use of intermedia as a huge and inclusive movement of which Dada, Futurism and Surrealism are early phases preceding the huge groundswell that is taking place now? Or is it more reasonable to regard the use of intermedia instead of traditional compartments as an inevitable and irreversible historical innovation, more comparable, for example, to the development of instrumental music than, for example, to the development of Romanticism?

From time to time, when articles come our way that seem to justify it, we will replace our newscards with a Something Else Newsletter, of which this is the first. There will be no advance scheduling on this and no paid subscriptions, although we will accept advance orders. We cannot accept responsibility for unsolicited manuscripts, nor will these be returned unless accompanied by a stamped, self-addressed envelope. However, we hope you will enjoy our Newsletter, and we will welcome any comments on how we can improve it.

Emmett Williams will arrive in the States in the middle of February. Readers of these newscards and of Spoerri's Anecdoted Topography may be anxious to meet him. If so, please send in your name, address and telephone number. These will be listed in an address book which will be given to him on his arrival.

In the Spring we are going to open the Something Else Gallery to show work which falls between media, which is by amateurs, or which otherwise would normally be considered unshowable. Our first show will be of art-objects by poets and composers. The Gallery expects to present a program of five shows—each lasting a week and a half—and then go on an indefinite vacation, until such time as it seems necessary to open again.

Something Else Press, Inc.
160 Fifth Avenue
New York, N. Y. 10010

Return Requested

Games of Art

Originally published in the *Something Else Newsletter,* vol. 1, no. 2, 1966.

the something else
NEWSLETTER

Volume 1, Number 2   March, 1966   40¢

Games of Art

by Dick Higgins

Starting with nothing is a good way to get somewhere. As anyone who has studied Set Theory knows, the whole Real Number system is based on the empty set. Nothing worked for Descartes and Sartre, and perhaps it works in art too.

On the other hand, there are those for whom the beauty of Nothing is simply an inherent thing, for whom it needs no function, like the old man in the famous cartoon, smiling over his desk while two younger men in the foreground say, gesturing to him, "He started at the bottom, liked it and stayed there." The apparent unassumingness of emptiness is what gives it its charm. Yet this charm is very fragile. Put something in an empty room and it is no longer empty.

Perhaps we can conceive then of an assumed nothingness, rather than of some absolute. Of a table just waiting for something to be on it, of a mind just waiting to think about supper. We might call this somethingness. Or anythingness (a very dangerous thought). Or maybe invitingness. The last term is the one I will use. It is clumsy but clear.

Some things having a quality of invitingness seem to invite almost anything. The mind is an example of this in its relation to ideas. Almost any idea available to a person may pop into his head at one time or another. Other things seem to be more specifically directed toward something. For example, one does not normally expect to pick up a coffee pot and discover that it is a table lamp, that it would be dangerous to make coffee in it. Not that one cannot be delighted and surprised, like the child Ray Johnson once wrote about, who opened a wardrobe in an unused room of her house and found not clothes but hundreds of mushrooms growing inside.

Taking these two sorts of invitingness as points of reference, we may conceive of a whole arc of degrees between them. In art, every time an artist makes a choice, this choice is implicitly projected onto this arc in various ways. But normally this is automatic. What the artist does is unambiguous, at least in its physical manifestations, whether we are speaking of a painter, a pianist, a composer, etc.

But suppose we conceive next of an Intermedium between this arc and the arts, which consists in the artist being extremely conscious about the projection of his artistic choices onto this arc of invitingness, perhaps even to the point where this concern becomes primary. We then reach a point where the rules become paramount. If we are clear where we are, there is no problem. If we are not, there is. The Eighteenth Century composer Fux was primarily concerned with the rules of his fugues, but insisted on embedding them in musical compositions which, since they were not his prime concern, suffered from neglect and were perfectly awful. The same observation can be applied, with devastating effect, to the work of such composers as Karlheinz Stockhausen and Milton Babbitt. Why not simply give the rules if, for the moment, that's the point? Then let the individual performer work out his own performance, since he, more than the composer, knows his strong and weak points.

This is, of course, precisely what athletes do. And because of the parallels to any card game or sport, we could call such works Art-Games. But in order to keep the emphasis on Art, let's call them Games of Art. The artist, then, might be likened to a carpenter who puts together a table. If he does a bad job, coffee cups will upset on it. If it is a beautiful and polished one, it will invite the possibility of many fine meals being enjoyed on it. Thus, there is a connection between the not-cookery of making a table and the cookery of preparing a fine meal. In the same way, in preparing the rules of his game, like commedia dell'arte, will have an of possibilities. He may make this range very large, in which case the performance of the game, like commedia dell' arte, will have an essentially improvisational character. Or there may be a limited scope of possibilities, con-

trolled and limited by the physical demands on the performers, or by the narrow scope of specified subject matter which, for example, may be limited to love or to politics (this last in my own **The Quill Game**). The game may even be unperformable (for example, my **Fleischenlieder**), at which point we might suggest it establishes an Intermedium between Games and Poetry.

But few games are played because of the charm of the rules. Most are played for the joy that is involved in them, or for the catharsis (in the case of rough games).

Even so, there are a few observations we can make about the nature of these rules. One, they do have social implications. Normally, in a concert situation we are not too shocked by the dictatorial relationship between the conductor and the performers. However, when a work belongs both to the Game of Art and Happenings Intermedia, we are extremely conscious of all details of this sort. Therefore the artist has to be extremely careful, in working with things like this, that the social situation he establishes is something that he really means. Such a piece as Tomas Schmit's **Zyklus** is unfortunately arrogant in its use of time. In this piece the performer is surrounded by bottles or buckets, one of which contains water or some other liquid. He pours the water from one to the next until it has all evaporated. The point of the piece is its concentration and the transformation of a meaningless act into an interesting one through repetition. But the unfortunate, extreme length of the piece— which is inherent in it—seems to be saying: look how much richer in time I am than you, look how much more patient, how I can afford to do this endlessly. The moment a spectator becomes restless, this problem appears with such force that is it difficult to put it away. We would like to note, however, that this piece is unique among the otherwise fascinating works of this composer.

Two, these rules establish a community of participants who are more conscious of behaving in similar ways than they would be if they were acting in a drama. This community aspect has its dangers and its blessings. In being conscious of the other participants, an individual may become self-conscious and decide to reject them, grandstanding and damaging the spirit of the piece in a much more uncontrolled way than if he had not been given the responsibility of making his own use of the rules. The artist has to make certain decisions then about how best to promote a team spirit. On the other hand, in Games of Art the team spirit and cooperation among the participants can be much more beautiful than in other media. For example, the community of madness which develops in Al Hansen's comic Game of Art, **Car Bibbe**, a Happening involving seven automobiles and a great many participants in each, is as interesting as what the participants actually do.

Three, an element of fascination, about just which rule will be followed when, can be very useful. In looking at a fountain, we know that the water will come from a point and go to a point, but the details of how this happens constantly shift. People playing bridge hope to be surprised by the hands they are dealt, and too much good luck is as dull as too much bad luck. Therefore the artist can, if he chooses, build variety and surprises into his game. In many sorts of Games of Art—particularly such rough and cathartic ones as those of Wolf Vostell, such concentrated ritual-image ones as those of Allan Kaprow, and such even-textured ones as most of my own—surprises are best confined to the detail, like the playing of a fountain, rather than allowed to be major

structural exceptions. Kaprow, in such pieces as his **Calling**, has even gone out of his way to insure that no participant or spectator will be surprised by 1., eliminating the spectators altogether and 2., giving each participant a detailed script describing precisely what will happen and in what order.

A critical remark might be made at this point, that perhaps Games of Art depend too much on the creative abilities of the participants to fill in the blanks. One answer to this could be that other kinds of art depend too much on the omniscience of their creators. Another, to return to the analogy of sports, is that few people are interested in knowing who invented ice hockey and why, when the game is being played and there's plenty of action to watch.

To summarize then, Games of Art are a medium which can be used to produce a great variety of art works. Most media imply their game as soon as the artist makes a choice what to do. For example, the composers and performers of romantic symphonies are all playing one game. By shifting the emphasis to the game, the situation is transformed and other situations become possible, with other emphases. Three of these we highlighted. We did not take up the questions of art and anti-art, since the latter depends on the former even to be conceived and is therefore merely a branch of the former. The question of classifying such open phenomena as the group dances of certain American Indians, for example the Robin Dance of the Iroquois, strikes us as rather artificial, since, while they are certainly games as we have described what we mean, we have not been concerned with the other question of whether Games of Art are, themselves, art.

Second of three articles

Newscard #11

Wolf Vostell arrives in New York on Friday, March 4th at Pier 86 (West 46th Street). Call us to find out the time of arrival (212-WA 9-2699). Dick Higgins will perform his **Welcome Event** for the occasion. Please bring musical instruments if you have them. Does anybody know any bagpipers? Important: black tie. Incidentally, it's disgraceful but true that this finest (and one of the best-known) of German artists has no New York gallery.

Claes Oldenburg's **Injun & Other Histories**, our newest and most Rabelaisian Great Bear Pamphlet, consists of scenarios from the late 1950's in which some of the central Oldenburg images first appear. $1.00, plus 10¢ postage (New York residents please don't forget the sales tax).

Emmett Williams has joined the Press as an editor. He is arranging to execute his **Ultimate Poem #1** on an IBM machine because, executed by all the people in the world, even if they worked throughout their complete lifetimes, it could still not be completed. Also he plans appearances in Boston and Philadelphia in March.

Charles Ives' birthplace is going under the wrecker's ball this Spring unless funds can be found to rescue it. Persons interested in contributing to save it can do so by sending checks or money orders to The Ives Homestead Fund, c/o The Fairfield County Trust Co., 210 Main, Danbury, Conn. 06811.

Marta Minujin's **El Batacazo**, an environment which becomes a happening when the spectator enters it, has just closed at the Bianchini Gallery in New York. On February 25th it opens at the Yale Art Gallery in New Haven. A unique show: don't miss it for anything. Robert Watts follows at the Bianchini (50 West 57th Street), from February 22 till March 19. Larry Loonin's **Our First Gobi Fossils** happens February 26th at 9 PM and February 27th at 6 and 9 PM at the Spencer Memorial Church in Brooklyn Heights (phone MA 5-3512 for reservations). We asked him to describe it. He did: "Quantum theater (pockets of energy)."

Something Else Press, Inc.
160 Fifth Avenue
New York, N. Y. 10010

Return Requested

Intending

Originally published in the *Something Else Newsletter,* vol. 1, no. 3, 1966.

the something else
NEWSLETTER

Volume 1, Number 3   April, 1966   40¢

INTENDING
by Dick Higgins

Back in the days of pure media, when pictures were painted in paint on cloth, before the best artists became more interested in the intermedia between painting and sculpture, between music and theater, etc., there was no particular value attached to intention. A work, finished, was essentially an entity. The painting was hung, noticed, and ignored. The script ruled the life of a few actors for a couple of hours, then was placed aside and forgotten until its next moment of dominance. It lasted, as opposed to the reality of shoes. Shoes serve and wear out. From the moment they are put on the feet, they are always changing, until the time when their change makes them less serviceable, irreversibly so, and they are discarded.

So many of the artists became unhappy about this eternal, unyielding quality in their art, and they began to wish their work were more like shoes, more temporary, more human, more able to admit of the possibility of change. The fixed-finished work began to be supplemented by the idea of a work as a process, constantly becoming something else, tentative, allowing more than one interpretation. We see it in literature in the controlled ambiguities of Joyce, William Carlos Williams, Abraham Lincoln Gillespie, Kurt Schwitters. In music we see the tendency from Wagner, of whom a very small variety of definitive performances is possible, through Ives, of whom a rather enormous possibility of definitive performances can coexist, through Cage, where the emphasis is on variety and the expanded experience rather than on any sort of definitiveness, to Philip Corner (and, perhaps, beyond?), in whose work the only definitive quality of the performance becomes the negative one of not only being fascinating itself, but of suggesting as many as possible other interpretations within the context of the piece.

The composition then consists less of providing performers with explicit materials to work with than of fixing boundaries and kinds of images within which the performers operate. The reasoning which makes this attractive to the composer or playwright we shall get to shortly. But first I would like to take up a few historical observations and contrasts about the period in which this way of working originated.

The late 1950's was typified by Abstract Expressionism (called "*tachisme*" in Europe) in painting, and by the International Style (Stockhausen, Koenig, Boulez, Nono, Nilsson, etc.) in music, so called because of its very close parallels, aesthetically and technically, to the post-Bauhaus International Style in architecture. The International Style and Abstract Expressionism both emphasized working with very specific materials in an abstract(i.e., uncrystallized-into-clearly-semantic-details) manner. The reasons for this we will not take up here. However, the clarity and the vividness of certain of the painters' viewpoints, those of Pollock, Kline, and de Kooning, gave a certain prestige to painting over all the other arts, greater than it had previously had in recent times. As a result, some of the younger painters began to feel that their work should include other media, and began to extend toward them. This is specifically true of Rauschenberg and Kaprow, and their experiments resulted in environments and happenings. On the other hand, people involved in the other arts began to feel that painting was much more advanced, much more filled with exciting implications. And so they tried to associate themselves with painting. This brings us to the work of John Cage.

Cage was always involved in both formal and acoustic experimentation. In fact, the implications of such an early piece as *Construction in Metal* (1937)* have never been followed up. However, in the early 1950's his work began to parallel that of the best Abstract Expressionists. At the time, he seemed anxious to avoid the responsibility of trying to mean something semantic in his work, but now it begins to look more like trying to develop a structural principle that was an alternative to the typical willed-structural-imposition of the International Stylists, which began to be seen as both arbitrary and requiring the subservience of the performer's own knowledge to the composer's will, and therefore implicitly fascistic and undesirable. Whether or not it was Cage's view, it is certainly my own, that serial music, in fact, is a neo-feudal tendency, characteristic, socially, of the McCarthy era in which it flourished, and quite without relevance to the rather different problems of our own times. However, a sense of this problem was certainly implicit in Cage's attempt to find more realistic structural means of composing music; and he developed the idea of working by chance operation, or what is known in Europe as "aleatropic methodology."

Chance meant fixing a set of possibilities and allowing a system of relationships between dice, coins, etc., to determine the details of material. It was on the one hand a practical structural method of giving materials to performers, and on the other a distinct reaction against the International Style's habit of applying arbitrary subforms to even the most minute of details.

But of course it meant much more than this. It meant accepting certain risks. By accepting the validity of this randomized material, one no longer was willing to accept the necessity of a clearly-defined willful imposition over the details. This was implicit in the whole procedure. A major part of the responsibility for the piece now lay in the system of relating the chance operation to the materials that were to be used. In other words, the composer could talk all he wanted about abdicating certain of these responsibilities. In fact, this was not what he did (nor am I certain it was what he would want to do, since in order to randomize a piece completely, wouldn't one have to give up responsibility for the system? And wouldn't this mean giving up thinking itself? And who wants to do that? Any

*This piece is recorded in *The 25-Year Retrospective Concert of the Music of John Cage*, recorded in New York in May 1958. Please make check payable to George Avakian, and mail it to him at 285 Central Park West (8S), New York 10024. The album costs $25 in mono or stereo, and consists of three LP's with a 38-page booklet which includes various manifestos, writings by Cage, and photographs, some by Robert Rauschenberg.

serious artist? Surely not Cage.) What he did was to place the material at one remove from the composer, by allowing it to be determined by a system he determined. And the real innovation lies in this emphasis on the creation of a system.

I am not going to take up, here, Cage's concept of indeterminacy, since it strikes me as an essentially defensive argument that leaving the system open to the performers' contributions is valid, which I not only agree with but assume. Neither do I intend at this time to describe (or attack) the kind of art work which was sometimes done on the basis of this attitude, which gave materials to a performer, which he would then interpret according to his own system. This work depended for its interest on the performer becoming a composer and developing his own system of interpretation. It is therefore another story, really, and a very interesting one. Perhaps it is a point of further development. I suspect it is not, that it is a reason why La Monte Young turned to what I have called "Balkan Jazz" after doing such developments of Cageian indeterminacy as simply presenting would-be performers with the proposition, "Little whirlpools in the middle of the ocean," and letting them take it from there. To depend on someone else's ingenuity, as this piece does, leaves any artist little scope to be relevant in. Since Young has more imagination than this scope allowed, it is inevitable that he should have turned to something else.

Another way to approach the idea of an art work as the projection of a system is to forego the idea of giving materials to the performer (or to the spectator). Jackson Mac Low, myself, and Philip Corner (all independently) began to do this kind of piece about 1960. This is the origin of the idea of composing (or writing, or—unfinished business—working in the visual arts) by emphasizing intentions and systems rather than the particularizations that most materials produce.

Now, obviously, it is impossible to see anything except in its physical manifestations. On the other hand, what one sees is irrelevant unless one is able to see it in the context of one's experience or to interpret it in some way. So what does this new emphasis have to offer?

The question disappears the moment the illusory contradiction is resolved: by giving blank forms, the most relevant materials for a given time and mentality can be filled in, thus avoiding the appalling irrelevance of perishable materials that are no longer current (e.g., O'Neill's emphasis on the need for a more honest sexuality, Sartre's interpretation of the alienation problem, Ionesco's interpretation of the same problem).

What the idea of working with blank forms really offers is the opportunity of working with unperishable materials and (implicitly) a field of renewable ones.

The composer, writer, artist defines the scope of the work. What falls within it is the piece.

This brings us to the point of this kind of emphasis on the artist's intention: he is no longer completely ruled by the specifics of his particular corner of history. The entire material of a piece can be worked completely in terms of local problems of the moment. A production which realizes a particular piece during the New York subway strike can be followed, shortly afterwards, by a production that relates to general labor problems in Sweden or to the interrelations between the two Germanies, the two Viet Nams, the two Chinas or Koreas. And it remains the same piece. The field is open to realization in terms of the most perishable materials, the political, social, or economic tendencies that are most current at the moment of production. This releases the artist from the kind of datedness that makes it almost impossible to appreciate an older political play, such as *Waiting for Lefty,* without a very conscious (and annoying) effort to compensate.

Again, it eliminates the problems that result from the limitations of one's own artistic experience. For example, writing a piece by Intention allows a composer to use the complete skills of a particular instrumentalist without his having known what specialties this performer has. Some trombonists, for example, are able to produce the effect of certain slides which any "well-trained" composer knows are impossible, and therefore doesn't call for. Only in this way can certain technical potentials be allowed to exist.

Finally, and probably most important, in composing music and choreography by Intention, the composer is able to concentrate the broad outlines and forms of his piece into an integrated whole. Frequently (I have Stockhausen and Balanchine in mind) a composition will make perfectly good sense in its details, but the whole won't have any clarity or sense whatever. By specifying clearly procedures and processes which have sense imbedded into them, this problem can be avoided. By this, of course, I do not mean simply to say, "Be sensible," since that doesn't really mean anything specific. I mean that the composer, choreographer, playwright, happenings-man, what have you, merely says, specifically, what he has in mind, not in its material, but in the basis for the material. This has very great appeal for artists, and is, in a way, a greater departure from the boringness of a "classical art" that has become irrelevant in the sense of becoming discontinuous from our daily lives, than simply finding

ingeniously new sorts of cut-and-dried materials which do not, in themselves, imply new processes.

Just a moment ago we mentioned the key word in evaluating any work in this general field of possibilities: "specific." The specificity of the artist's intentions has to be passed along if the work is to suggest anything to think about, which is normally a requisite for comprehensibility and impact, whether visual or sensuous or emotional. If the artist is sufficiently specific about what he intends, work which is written by describing intentions is capable of implying a very high moral stature in the community which it creates among performers and audience, and the emotional impact can be very great indeed. For example, in Philip Corner's musical composition, published in *The Four Suits,* "4th Finale," one would have to be very insensitive indeed not to appreciate the emotional community which this game of art creates. The success of the piece is clearly to be attributed to its specificity. Everyone knows just what he is to do, and in the course of performing he experiences why as well.

Specificity can therefore be used as a factor to look for in evaluating the new music, happenings, and other works which present formal innovations of this kind. Once noted, the piece, if it has anything in it, will open up. If not, better luck next time. But what kind of value is specificity? For one thing, it's a relative one. There are certainly degrees of specificity, and being as specific as possible is not necessarily a guarantee of the quality of a piece. One would have to be demented to attach much artistic value to the suggestion, "Bark loud like a dog." Yet it could be a very interesting situation if one hundred people would all do just that together. In other words, the first instance, presented in isolation, is specific enough, but by simply being presented as an imperative, one is more conscious of the sort of person who might ask that this be done. A hundred people doing the same thing together could create a mood of absolute terror. The second possibility, with the hundred people, might therefore be said to have greater specificity in that it leaves less open: who is to do the barking is specified, and the image becomes clarified. In so doing, it becomes more possible to comprehend the artist's intentions meaningfully. In the first case, one is told what to do and one asks, Why? In the second, one gets the picture and joins the fun. Obviously this is a very simple instance, but the point holds true even in the more complex pieces of Corner and Mac Low. The specificity which is of value, then, is whatever most efficiently defines the artist's intentions in as many ways as possible.

Last of three articles

The Something Else Gallery, 238 West 22 Street (behind the Chelsea Hotel), will open its first show, *Object Poems,* at 8:00 PM, Friday, April 15. Included will be works by Robert Filliou, Emmett Williams, Wolf Vostell, Carl Fernbach-Flarsheim, Daniel Spoerri, Dick Higgins, Alison Knowles and many others. Come along and help launch the Gallery. After the inaugural show, the Gallery will be open 10:00 AM til 5:00 PM, Tuesday through Saturday. Other Something Else Gallery openings: Friday, April 29, *Intermedia,* with works by Alison Knowles, George Brecht and Joe Jones; Friday, May 13, *The Arts in Fusion,* which explores the convergences of painting, typography and poetry; and Friday, May 27, *Dé-Collage-Happenings,* which will display Wolf Vostell's originals and notations for his book of the same name, to be published by the Press this summer.

Robert Filliou arrives in New York shortly. He can be reached through the Press. Wolf Vostell is living at the Chelsea Hotel and doing giant scores for his book in the cellar of the building in which the Gallery is located. Camille Gordon was killed on Route 1 when her car smashed into a chicken truck. When the feathers settle we will do her novel, *The Golden Armadillo.* Any recent arrivals from Czechoslovakia: we would be very interested in knowing what happened at the Prague Festival of Happenings that Chalupecky and Knizak organized in March.

We have a new distributor for Germany and Holland. It's Typos Verlag, 6000 Frankfurt am Main, Grünebergweg 118, West Germany. Now our books will be easier to obtain in those countries. We're also going to distribute Typos publications here, but we'll announce that in more detail on the next newscard. Europeans please note: Typos' accounts are: Postscheck Frankfurt am Main 17523, and Frankfurter Sparkasse von 1822 Konto-Nr. 50-251 542.

John Cage is already at work on *Notations,* a profusely illustrated 400-odd-page monster, with reproductions of manuscripts and notations by most of the important composers of music and performance pieces of the last three decades, which will create a context for the new experimental forms of notation. We should have the book ready early in the Fall. Also in the Fall: Alison Knowles' *Big Book,* a book so large that it contains collapsible rooms in which, if only there were plumbing and cooking facilities, one could live for quite a while.

The liveliest of the book newspapers around is Jerome Agel's *Books.* Ask around for it. Much more open and forward-looking than others of its sort, its 15-column article last September was the first major feature on Marshall McLuhan in the U. S. That's long before *Fortune, Life,* the *SatEvePost, Time* and the other booky-papers hopped on the M-M bandwagon.

Do you have all our **Great Bear** pamphlets yet? There's Claes Oldenburg's *Injun & Other Histories,* $1; Alison Knowles' *By Alison Knowles,* 40¢; Dick Higgins' *A Book About Love & War & Death, Canto One,* 60¢; George Brecht's *Chance-Imagery,* 80¢; and, about April 11th, Allan Kaprow's *Some Recent Happenings* (which includes the most recent definition of the word by this inventor of the concept), 60¢. These are the least expensive major documents in the new art forms; without them it costs a fortune to be informed. New York residents please remember sales tax, and postage for each pamphlet is 10¢. Something Else Press, Inc., 160 Fifth Avenue, New York, N.Y. 10010.

Something Else Press, Inc.
160 Fifth Avenue
New York, N. Y. 10010

Return Requested

JEROME ROTHENBERG
SOME-THING
600 WEST 163 STREET
NEW YORK N Y   10032

Postface (excerpt)

Originally published in *Jefferson's Birthday/Postface*, New York: Something Else Press, 1965.

POSTFACE

by Dick Higgins

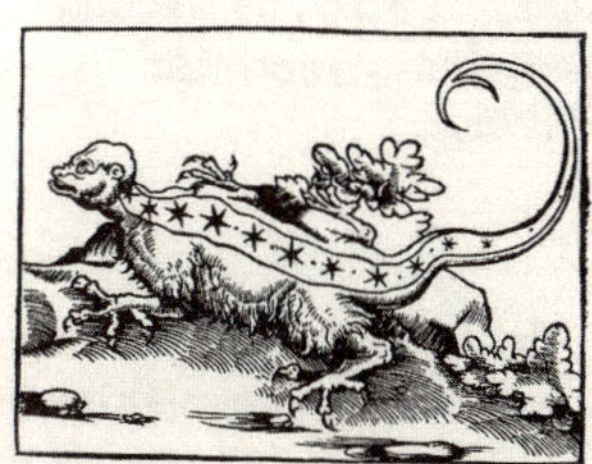

SOMETHING ELSE PRESS
New York   Nice   Cologne

POSTFACE

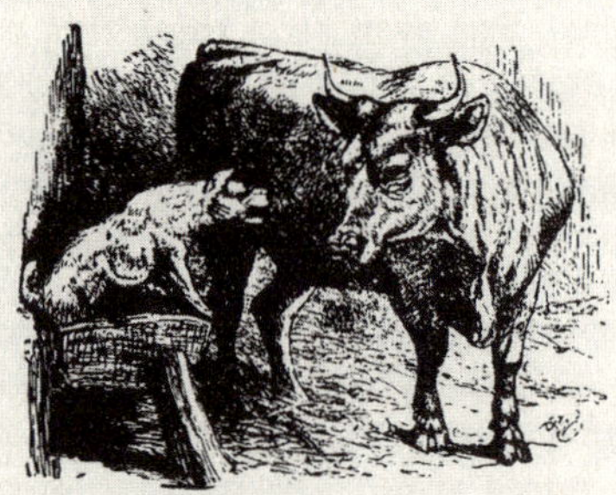

At that time Al Hansen, George Brecht, and myself met in John Cage's composition class at the New School for Social Research. The year was 1958. Kaprow had studied with him the previous year. For us, it was an odd coming together from many ways of many very different people.

Hansen was – and is – a most striking individual. I think of him as a soldier for whom the wars will never end until every man is articulate. He sometimes is the soldier on leave and sometimes the soldier fighting. But the only reason I can find evidence of in his work is his love of articulateness. This gives him a great deal in com-

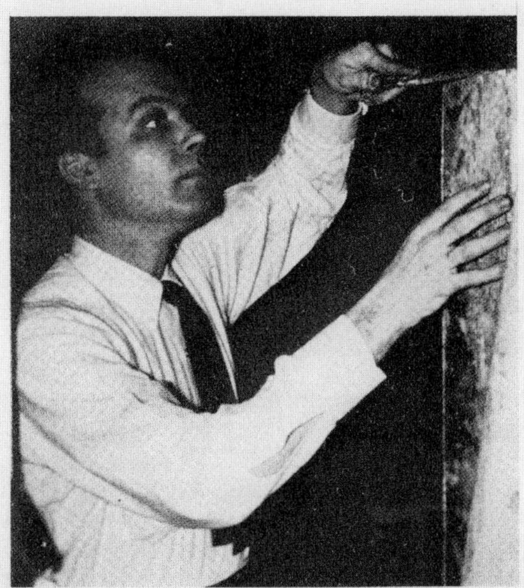

mon with all non-artists. But it is the real core of his work, as I
see it. In fact he got into the army at the tag end of World War II,
saw duty overseas, came home, and had a good many adventures,
in the course of which he began his drift into art and acquired his
lovely little daughter Bibbe for whom "Bibbe's Tao" and "Car Bibbe"
are named. He reentered the armed forces, this time the Air Force,
and became an exhibition paratrooper. When Hansen becomes nos-
talgic, it is parachute jumping that he talks about. When he came
out he went to Pratt Institute, married, and began to be not merely
an artist but a very serious artist. When I first knew him he was
living in a loathesome middle-class housing project, one of those
Palaces of Poverty, in Queens, making a living as a commercial
artist, and trying hard to enjoy it. Of course it could not last, considering the personality of the people involved. One day at Pratt
somebody played him a Cage composition. Its anarchy appealed. "It
was just a mess, a racket. It made no sense. I loved it," and,
totally undeterred by the fact that to this day he cannot read a note
of music, he seriously took up musical composition with Cage.

Brecht, at that time, still described himself as "you might say, a
painter," though most of his work was already marvelous objects,
usually with moving parts, things for adults to play with. He made
a living as a scientist in the suburbs in New Jersey, in Metuchen,

and his life and his aesthetic seemed connected with that. For hours in class he would talk with Cage about the need for spiritual virtu-

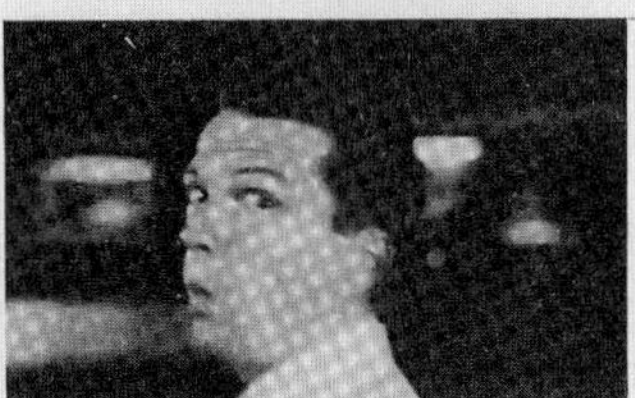

osity and abdication from technical virtuosity, both of which were very attractive to Cage.

I was a skeptic from New England, fat and nervous. I had fled the north in order to see what goes on down on earth. I wanted to make a career in musical theater, which was to be based on calypso. For the moment I was working for a Public Relations firm which I felt was a little immoral. I could write my quadruple fugues with any textures or affections desired. I wanted to synthesize within my-self all the techniques I couldmaster to make an art form along the lines of Brecht-Eisler or Brecht-Weill, but based, as I have men-tioned, on more indigenous materials from calypso to rock-and-roll. My own ideas bored even me, so I became restless. I had, a few years before, experimented with hoisting many many hunks of iron and metal up in the trees on either side of a valley in Vermont and raising one hell of a ruckus at five o'clock one afternoon. Once I had put on a crazy set of goings-on in a barn, amid a mess of hung cloth and animals (it would be called a happening today). But these were essentially entertainments and I felt no great urgency about them. However I had begun my habit of taking notes and developing them into pieces, compressing them back into notes, expanding these, and so on. My whole output consists of workings of a mass that is constantly on the back of my stove. I had discovered the old Galli-mard edition of Artaud, -not the translation (which is excellent but not Artaud) - and had, as a result, begun a play about people with horrible diseases wearing diving costumes, and some surrealistic farces that consisted of collaged fragments. Some of this stuff wound up in Stacked Deck, The Ladder to the Moon, and 27 Episodes for the Aquarian Theater.[11] I came to take Cage's course because I couldn't think what else to do. What I got from it was a sense of general activity and a taste for my own direction, to which previously my own skepticism had been very unkind. I agreed with much of Cage's aesthetic, but not with his taste. When he and Brecht took off for spirit and nobilities yet uncharted, I made wisecracks that there was no difference between spiritual virtuosity and any other kind of virtuosity.

But Cage used to talk about a lot of things going on at once and having nothing to do with each other. He called it the autonomous behavior of simultaneous events: I called it independence.

In fact, the beauty about studying with Cage was that he brought out what you already knew and helped you become conscious of the essence of what you were doing, whether or not it was noble (and, thus, acceptible to him). Though my own inclinations were always rather antithetical to Cage, I was able, through him, to become conscious of my love of autonomy, variety, some sorts of inconsistency, rationalism, etc.

In the same way Brecht picked up from Cage an understanding of his love of complete anonymity, simplicity, and non-involvement with what he does. And Hansen got his anarchy enforced and accepted his own love of letting people be just as they are. Is Hansen the ultimate in philanthropists?

To us, Cage's ideas about indeterminancy and all that seemed very democratic and just fine, because we had each other and all of us seemed to think a little the same way. We even took indeterminacy farther than Cage without his ever having told us about it. About the second meeting of class Cage, who had previously written down all aspects of performances he could think of, passed out pencils and paper and asked us to write pieces, since none of us had done our homework and brought pieces to class. The pieces we wrote were done with words. Perhaps they were about the first notationless non-improvisatory music. They were all different and all left something unsaid except me, I was not indeterminate. I lined up adjectives opposite Cage's list of aspects of performances, which made him tell me that nothing had any inherent qualities other than physical ones and that therefore psychology was an illusion: this led to my 17th-century-cum-Artaud book of characters, Stacked Deck.

POSTFACE 52

Cage had to go on tour, so he turned over his class for two meetings to Feldman, who said taste was everything, and Maxfield, who had just completed his first electronic pieces. Maxfield was then very lively – he was interested in really using all aspects of the electronic media. Later he went metaphysical, and became obsessed by the idea of notationless music per se; but first he just did what he made, mixed his cut pieces of tape in a salad bowl, spliced them together, and did any superimposing that seemed necessary. I thought it was a very natural way to do things, and so I invited Maxfield to do Stacked Deck with me. It was to be the first electronic opera, and I think it was, though I wouldn't swear to it. Maxfield liked to be an electronic composer because there was no separation between the composer and the performance. The original score was the most gorgeous electronic music I have ever heard. In later scores he allowed theoretical notions to win out – besides, he was suspicious of the beautiful aspects of the early score – so he mixed them all up together and got a piece with too much unity and universality and compromise to it. He wound up with a justification rather than a manifestation. But nobody else has ever done such interesting electronic music. Only Maxfield has succeeded in doing electronic music in which one is conscious of the latter word rather than the former. In such more recent music as Night Music and Italian Folk Music he just suggests sounds with sounds, and he rapes the very basis of the Feldman-Stockhausen International Style. If only there were more of his pieces! But the economics of electronic composition are very harsh, and such resources as are available in the field are taken up by those who specialize in getting them rather than by composers.

In that fall of '58 not much seemed to be going on. In the theater one hoped that the Living Theater would open (it opened many months late). I had so much hope for the operation that I painted the ladies' room myself to help speed things up. Hansen did some obscene geometrical items and a portrait in which he worked weeks painting each hair but never did paint in the face. Brecht stayed in New Jersey. But we were all up to doing things. I wrote six hours a day and began most of the things in 100 Plays. Also there was my unpublished novel, Orpheus Snorts, and a series of graphic notations for theater and music (or either) called Graphis, each a separate work, which by now numbers nearly 120. I also filled up two notebooks with ideas and notions which have since turned out to be lectures, praphisses, poems, constellations, concertos, and the like. Hansen, late that fall, cut out a bunch of holes in pieces of card stock, wrote numbers on them in verticle and horizontal lines, and did his first really Hansen-ish piece by handing the performers these cards and just telling them to use them as notations for events. A week or so later he did Alice Denham in 48 Seconds which was the result of an interesting accident: he found three or four sets of numbers on the street all of which happened to add up to 48. He wrote them on a piece of paper in a square. In his hand he had a magazine. It had a pretty nude in it, a red-head by the name of Alice Denham. It also had a very fine short story in it by her. This piece has been done a good many times now, forty or fifty. Once I answered the phone: it was Alice Denham. She'd read that this piece was being performed and wanted to know what was going on, had Hansen used her name or was it a coincidence? Poor girl. But she finally did catch up with Hansen, they got along fine, and I've never met her but I understand she comes to his things from time to time. The whole affair, the titling of this piece, is itself a Hansen composition.

Hansen wrote the numbers on the wall, and he wrote an arbitrary set of numbers on the diagonal. He gave everybody toys to use as instruments - guns, battleships, whirlers, helicopters, etc. It was one of the good things, this first Alice Denham.

But that winter Hansen began his way of life that he has since held to and it seems very appropriate to his work.

Every winter when the rich go to Florida, Hansen lives in the subways for a month. It is his vacation. He knows which latrines he

POSTFACE   54

can be locked into, and what places will give him something to eat.
In the spring there is a knock on the door, and you open it, and there
is this vile-smelling, unshaven man, and you say, "Hello, Al."
He shaves and he showers, and he goes and gets some clothes, and
he looks great. He gets a job, and there are any number of places
that will hire him since he's a wonderful worker. But then, spring
ends. He does his pieces, they don't interfere with his activities,
which in turn don't interfere with his job, but when summer comes,
Hansen takes one look at the blue sky and one breath in the hot air,
and it is time for the beach. So he goes to the beach from time to
time till he loses his job. When he has lost his job it is fall, and
he has done his performing for the year. He writes some new pieces,
but mostly he just takes apart whatever studio he has acquired,
leaves his things here and there, and, when the snow falls, Al disappears. And you know that somewhere under the city Al Hansen is
riding, dreaming about his new activities and maybe smiling a little.

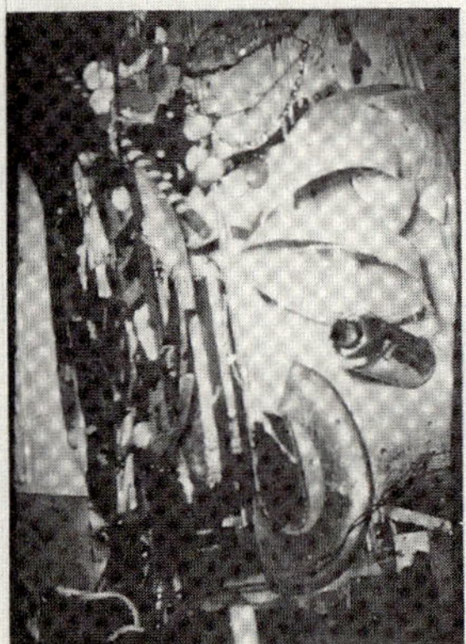

The way I am writing this might be mentioned at this point. I have
over a hundred and fifty pages of notes, indexed by number, to relate to an outline. I have a quart of beer. And everything I write,
I say out loud. I don't mind using lots of jargon and slang, because the written language of tomorrow will probably have more to
do with our spoken language than with our written one. And this is
a well-outlined conversational ramble. If only the typewriter were
a tape recorder and there would be no separation between the intoned
sentence and the odd-looking sentences that appear. I go on swig-

ging and collating my notes and reflecting in an organized way, knowing where I am heading but taking my own sweet time about getting there.

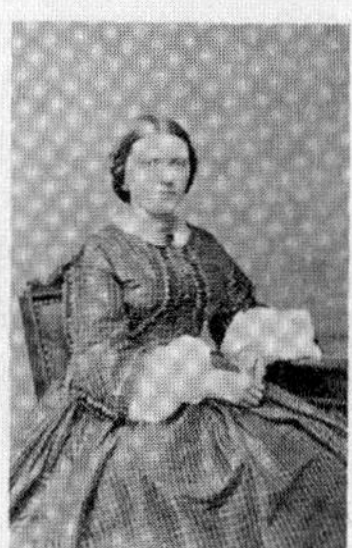

That winter the Epitome coffee shop opened up. Lawrence Poons, the painter, took care of it, though he had two nudnik partners. All three were painters, but Poons was the rough diamond of the lot, and they all did a sort of geometric iconoclasm, but the other two wound up showing swastiskas in Greenwich Village while Poons developed the notion of read painting. This coffee shop became a good display place for work that was not the Going Thing, although for commercial reasons the Epitome had Joel Oppenheimer, Allen Ginsberg, and others to attract tourists - Ray Bremser, Ted Joans, etc. Hansen read his poem, "A Requiem for W.C. Fields," there, and a Hansen movie that included lots of W.C. Fields materials was projected on his chest. I did various concertos and read from Orpheus Snorts and Machines in the Wind and various of my poems. We gave a concert there at five in the morning and others at night. We did lectures and read dada, lettriste, and Iliazd texts. In the spring I gave my first New York performances; Al Hansen did my last instrumental piece there (his only appearance, so far as I know, as a conductor) To Everything Its Season,[12] and we did Alice Denham, along with some of my Aquarian Episodes.[11] David Tudor did a Wolff piece and Cage's Music of Changes. My pieces were very badly performed, but the music critics said nothing about that, one just said it sounded like a flea typing the collected works of Macrobius and Paul Henry Lang, more seriously, said it was a rejection of all music since the beginning of the Christian Era. Hansen's piece was attributed to the BBC (Broken Bottle Chorus) Orchestra and we were surprised that we didn't get an irate letter from London. Also that Spring we did a television performance for Henry Morgan on which I, who climbed out of a bathtub and stomped ink on rolls of paper, was compared to Charles Chaplin, which was very nice but very incongruous flattery. All summer long things were quiet. In the fall the Happenings began, and in December Hansen exhibited his "Hep Amazon," a 200 lb. monster of tiny motors that slowly got cued in and out, provoking blinking lights, turning wheels, even a vaccuum that seemed like a fellatio machine. That was the end of Hansen's geometric and neoplastic work. Brecht had his Toward Events show, where he displayed medicine chests, card games, pingpong ball drop-boxes, and so on. That was very exciting. And in February the Judson Church had its Ray-Gun happenings, presented by Oldenburg with Dine helping, at which Dine's Smiling Workman, Oldenburg's Snapshots from the City, Hansen's multiple projector collage movie of parachutes and pursuits, a Kaprow happening about football, a Whitman rag-happening, and my own Cabarets, Contributions, Einschlusz,[11] and a collaboration intermission piece all were done. That was the end of something: it made the people involved well-known in a young-man-to-watch-sense, and for two of us it started a success syndrome that drove their work away from any danger, experiment, or imagination.

Shortly afterwards I did Saint Joan at Beaurevoir at a little theater on MacDougall Street, which I still think of as Beaurevoir. The play is about almost nothing, it avoids anything relevant to the performance situation, any articulate sequence of sentences, words, or, occasionally, phonemes, any purposeful activity, anything in its usual context. It suggests that history is non-sequential when it is considered at any moment in an orderly way, and that random examination of the past gives sufficient understanding of the present. Except for this historicism it was an experiment in gratuitousness. But I was not interested in historicism so I went on and wrote Design Plays, which is a large mechanical nothing, about nothing, for nothing, and good for nothing, although rather attractive to look at in an innocuous way. Therefore it is my favorite of the pieces I wrote of that sort. I'd sure like to see it. That spring Stacked Deck was finally done, but as a very messy melodrama, which raised issues I had not intended. At the end of the Spring I married Alison Knowles, who did wonderful paintings, silk screen work of all kinds, and, more recently, extremely concrete performance pieces.

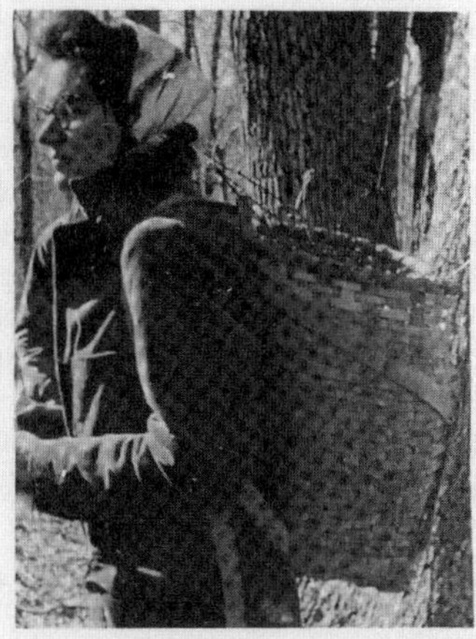

Around May of 1960 I began to be conscious of La Monte Young's activities out on the west coast. He sent copies of A Vision and Poem for Tables, Chairs, and Benches. A Vision was very technically involved, but easy to hear. I liked his lengthiness, and suggested he expand the piece enormously. I would like to see it published burned into sheets of lead. However, La Monte complained that it was boring: this suggests something very interesting in him. He is fascinated by a lot coming from a little. The Poem is very concrete. One drags the objects over the performance area at given rates, as described in the text. La Monte answered a remark I sent him, that everybody ought to do the Poem pretty often, with the reply that everybody was doing the Poem, did I know anyone who wasn't but that it was too entertaining and so he wasn't interested any more.

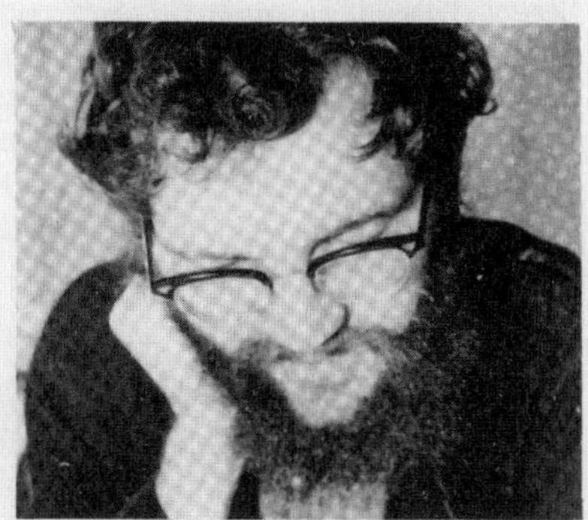

Postface   58

These pieces were followed by the best-known pieces, clear-cut sentences that are simply provocations for events, usually reflecting a taste for the most poetic sorts of imagery and almost always implying an orientation towards either useless or extraordinary activities. Throughout 1961 the same piece, "Draw a straight line and follow it," was written over and over twenty-nine times, and also a sort of jazz that he liked, indian ornaments and modal effects over extremely monotonous rhythmic patterns, usually a triple time of some kind, and a drone; this sort of jazz has almost completely taken over his attention. Except for new ways of looking at the earlier pieces and the "Death Chant" I do not know of anything new he has been doing for a couple of years now. He cooks, and he plays his jazz with a drone and a drum-player and a sopranino saxophone. This music seems part of his life, which is deliberately alienated, if not outside, the social environment of our times. My only objection to his work is that it makes a body feel insulated against the world, which is a sensation I do not care for.

There is just enough of his work to give you a taste for it. Then it stops.

We in the states didn't know that already at that time Benjamin Patterson was beginning to do marvelous pieces in Koln, such as the "Paper Piece for Five Performers," the "Sextet" from Lemons, and the pieces in Methods and Processes. Patterson's pieces are the most concrete of dissociated pieces, the most dissociated of concrete pieces. You get nothing out of doing any of them that doesn't disappear afterwards. While they happen, they are a joy to do, but afterwards, who knows why? I remember liking a piece called "Stand Erect," doing it several times, writing to Patterson that it made me feel religious, and then I forgot about it. Last winter I wrote a piece called "Gångsång." It turned out to be nearly a duplication of "Stand Erect." Occasionally Patterson makes pieces that are simply entertaining, such as the "Variations for Contrabass Viol," in which the

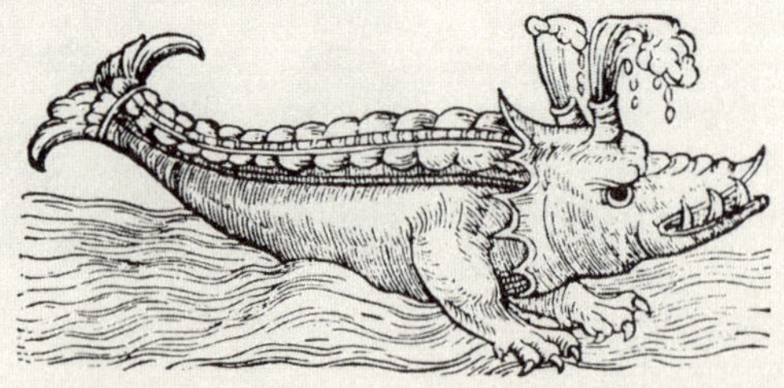

performer, working with a bass viol, attaches things (eg. clothes-pins) to it, shoots with it, and writes a letter, among other things. A piece like this has some appeal to one's sense of the fantastic, but since it depends primarily on the visual aspects of the actions, no matter how short, it always seems too long, since the ideal length of time for any of the particular events would be no longer than it takes to recognize what is going on, and any longer amount of time is not very economical.

Appeals to surprise, shock value, the audience's sense of amazement, or of iconoclasm, these are not things which endure. If there is any weak aspect in Patterson's work, it is this kind of appeal. So much depends on surprises, and the effect is sometimes like a joke told in too many words. Often it is not necessary to see or perform the piece, merely to hear about it suffices.

But Patterson, more than hardly any other composer, seems to understand that for a composer to divide activities into musical and non-musical, what-I-do and what-I-do-not-do is to accept the dualism of good and evil, of black and white, and, ultimately, to place one's work on a level of purely theoretical relevance. Patterson goes for the grey, and he seems to accept, even to encourage, the non-memorable, disappearing aspect of his work. In pieces such as "A Lawful Dance," where you follow the directions of a traffic light from corner to corner, back and forth, ad lib, till you are through performing, Patterson gets somewhere that nobody else is. Marvelous things happen to you while you cross the street. The last time I performed this piece at Times Square I met and was, briefly, joined by Bea, Lindy, and Shirley, three overdeveloped young ladies with colossal hairdoes. They saw me (and a group of others) crossing back and forth, and it occurred to them that it would be fun to join in. So they did, no questions asked.

And afterwards the piece blurs, crossing the street is remembered as crossing Times Square, it is inexorably connected with Bea, Lindy, and Shirley. Or was Lindy really Jackie? Have I forgotten their names?

So far we are from Germany. Patterson did these things for maybe two years before any of us heard about them. Cage and Brown made their trips there, and I asked them what was going on, but it was always officially Stockhausen and the International Stylists: Cage never told about Paik till I had read about him and asked specifically. And very few people had any idea at all what Patterson was doing. Only Paik and Vostell really cared. And so Patterson married and went to France, as he had gone from the U.S. before, where he did not want to be a "negro artist" but just one Hell of a good one and, among other things, a negro. Only James Baldwin and Benjamin Patterson have ever attained that proportion. Actually Patterson's way of using periodic repeats and the blues feeling that this produced being so ingrained and natural struck me so much that when he first sent me a copy of methods and processes I wrote to him and guessed he was a negro. But considering this does not get one very far with what he does. The main thing is that his work acquires a remarkable unity with our lives as we absorb it and forget it. It seems oddly ethical, oddly concrete.

Paik and Patterson: Faust and Schweik. Paik is the legitimate school of Schoenberg and Artaud. For him his work seems to come as a revelation. When it is not being expressionistic, it is still at least expressing him, in a most personal way.

Around 1959 or 1960 Paik began to do those pieces where he chops John Cage's necktie off or knocks the piano over and operates on it. In 1961 he began to think about moving the audience around, visiting this or that display of sounds. He did – or began to talk about (which for him, like Spoerri, is about the same thing) – his "Symphony for Twenty Rooms," and his "Omnibus Music No. 1" in which the sounds sit down and the audience visits them.

These things have to do with the phenomenon that fascinates La Monte Young too – that you can really get inside a sound. In the same way, I used to say, when I played bridge, that I liked to get inside the cards. It is all the same phenomenon, and it is very much in the air.

In 1961 he did his last big performance piece, "Simple," for Stockhausen's Originale. Here he peeps, covers himself with shaving cream, works with an ancient Norwegian phonograph, and dumps water over himself in an old tin bathtub. Also he did a piece – is it called "Solo for Violin?" – where a violin is raised very slowly above his head – then it is suddenly smashed onto a table and shat-

tered. In 1962 he worked on "Bagatelles Americaines" which were
a set of pieces in what he thought of as the american spirit, implicitly unimpressive, uninspiring, unentertaining, perhaps very boring,
and with specific relationships to the work of Brecht, Young, Patterson, and myself. Hansen, of course, is not known in Europe.

The only two examples I have of this series are these, his impres-
sion of what I was doing: "Danger Music No. 1 for Dick Higgins," -
"Creep into the VAGINA of a living WHALE!" and (written when I
remarked that there was no real danger when there was no risk that
I might be able to do this) "Danger Music No. 2 for Dick Higgins," -
"Walk the Metro-Tunnel of PARIS from Franklin Roosevelt till
Stalingrad. If you feel suffocated, think of WARSAWA-Resistance."
What he has done since these pieces, or, more accurately, since
Fluxus, I will get to later.

Actually what he has done is to achieve a lot of the spirit of action
painting in the medium of performance. The work is almost the exact opposite of Patterson. For Paik, art is a gnostic mystery that
is revealed, the complete antithesis of daily activities. He tells a
story that is very revealing: he saw Cage's Music Walk, which is
a dancerly event-piece, and he loved it and began to think about
indeterminacy. Then, taking this very seriously, he decided to
meet Cage. He visited Cage at his hotel room. Cage was polishing
his shoes, Paik was shocked that Cage was not above such things.
And from that moment he has been opposed to indeterminacy and
dailiness which, for him, is the source of the best of current activities, and the intellectual pool from which all our ideas are supposed to some. Most European critics, of course, feel that way -
they do not see that only Hansen and Brecht have anything at all to
do with indeterminacy, that I am a moralist in the school of Bunyan
and perhaps Genet and that my techniques have nothing to do with
indeterminacy, that Patterson's medium is experience and his style
is, like his message, disappearance, that Young takes things aesthetically and avoids anything at all mechanistic. As an observer
and thinker Paik is totally commonplace with a bizarre style and a
joy in the perverse, a German outlook on the current scene and a
fascination for himself, the Artist, imposing Platonic ideals on implicitly hostile (or is the word "philistine"?) society.

If you assume to impress and assume shock, secrecy, and hostil-

POSTFACE

ity as your tools what do you do when your audience understands you? And, horrors, when it approves and is delighted? Do you kill yourself or pretend you didn't hear? There is no need to answer the question, all answers come out the same.

Of course, Paik knows all this. Once he wrote to me that he was old-fashioned inasmuch as he felt like Schiller and Delacroix, that his ideal was the same, that he liked Beethoven more than anybody else, (and, incidentally, hated Schubert).

In Paik, as in abstract art, art (or anti-art) becomes not just a way of life but a form of suggestion, necessary to bring up short those who might otherwise be very complacent. At best this turns people on. At worst it makes enemies of those who might have been persuaded by other means. In the middle between these ends lies the typical, - newspaper articles appear which pretend to be shocked (even when the reporter knows better), word gets around, the sort of activity becomes typed (thus blinding observers to what is actually going on), - and so the artist who does this kind of thing finds

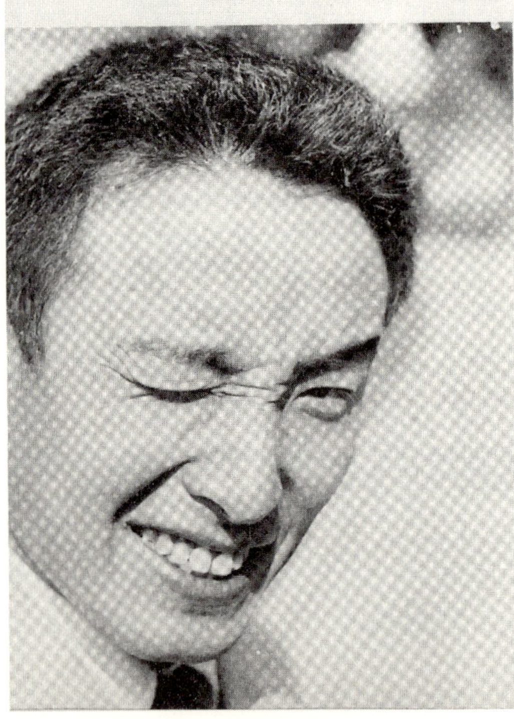

himself merely being exploited in his most bizarre aspects for his newspaper-selling ability.

Nevertheless it is a very strong tendency and might almost be said to characterize many of the best artists of this day, many of the Fluxus people, and certainly Paik. Everything in art which suggests this tendency – or function – is viewed almost exclusively this way. For example, an ideal is created of disorder, deliberately opposed to rational order. This led Paik, in building his great Wuppertal exhibition, to break up and renail objects which had, as a matter of economy or speed, been nailed too symmetrically, too thriftily, or too strongly. It is this tendency which leads some observers, such as Hans Helms, a semantic letterist in Cologne who is the poet laureate of the International Stylists, to feel that this kind of work tends to fascism, through its love of violence for its own sake and through its implicit hostility towards daily chores and the earning of daily bread. Of course, a critique like that is like the blind man's description of an elephant as a kind of large snake with a hollow head. Nevertheless, the necessity to view this tendency in perspective is very great.

Another little story, as an example of something or other: once when I worte Paik a letter that didn't mean much but which I thought was pretty funny, Paik wrote back that I was very Platonic. Perhaps I had implied some of the above-described tendencies. But Paik's remark was very surprising to me.

Once somebody, Jackson Mac Low, I think, explained that "Plato" means "broad one" in Greek, while my name, "Dick," means "fat" in German – and therefore I sometimes like to become very fat and really be Dick. So I have this one thing in common with Plato anyway. But my point is that because of Paik's concern with this tendency, he sees it whether it is present or not.

And so one sits in the audience, and one observes. One may or may not be annoyed by the self-consciousness of the presentation, by its slickness (they are the same thing). For all his messiness, is Paik any different from Tudor? There is so much ballyhoo, so many people writing down what is going on, there are so many photographers, big-wig Herr Doktors, document-makers, etc. But the orthodox will be denied, possibly without useful implications, but surely in an inspiring way. Something ordinarily secret will be revealed. A new way of looking at something may be suggested. The presentation will be at least unorthodox, and possibly cathartic.

But we didn't know much about Paik or Patterson. Starting in 1961 we knew only of their existence, and descriptions we knew of Paik's performance which Earle Brown used to tell us. La Monte Young contacted Paik for his Anthology. I knew about Spoerri's Material and put Young in touch with Rot, Williams, and Bremer. But none of us knew, as yet, anything about Spoerri. That came later.

Aroung this time, Al Hansen composed his Bibbe's Tao and his piece with a thirty-word name known as "Hi-Ho Jack Paar Moon." These are completely simultaneous pieces in which the performers just do what they can with the physical materials available and the environment. Since Hansen does not write out his pieces I am not sure what the difference is, although I have seen both twice. They are super-duper Hellzapoppin blow-ups of life in a busy city inhabited by cruel and lovable perverts. A special piece of this sort was performed in Brooklyn, where Hansen was living for a while, in the back yards of the ring of houses on Hansen's block.

Hansen hung the back yard of his particular house with huge sheets of polyethylene. He built a throne, and set pieces of furniture behind some of the sheets of polyethylene. Once these preparations were made he went looking for performers and rehearsed them. When they were ready, the performance was announced. About a thousand people were sitting on their roofs and in their windows, many swigging away at a bottle, some playing cards while they watched, and so on. During the performance, a very pretty chinese girl sat on her throne reading aloud from time to time from a chinese newspaper. A couple of girls made lesbian love on a sofa while a man yelled Maoist slogans. A girl tried to get the audience to eat dirt and grass, offering it as very good for one. Occasionally a light flashed on the roof of Hansen's studio, a sort of shed behind the audience's backs, and a girl danced a peculiarly violent belly dance. Phonographs flicked on and off. A group painted with spray paint on the polyethylene sheets from both sides - "Zap" and "Zowee," the traditional sounds of childrens' space-man ray guns, were the most frequently written words. The solvents in the paint dissolved the polyethylene, which tore and hung in shreds, exposing the lesbians and the maoist, who stopped their activities and indulged in an extraordinary Pepsi-Cola fest. Finally, when the polyethylene artists had retreated about as far as they could go, with a loud clatter the belly dancer fell through the skylight of Hansen's studio. "I'm hurt, I'm hurt," she screamed, but nobody believed her. We all thought it was part of the piece, till Hansen, looking in his window, saw the girl was lying in a pool of blood. He called an ambulance, which came, together with the police. The audience could not leave, since we would have to go through the studio. To keep us quiet, Lawrence Poons began to yell, "Roar! Roar! Roar!," Tzara's best piece. The people in the windows and on the roofs took up the cry and roared back. The end of the piece - after one hundred seventy-six roars, one asks, "Who still considers himself quite charming," a characteristically Narcissid statement for Tzara the Pseudo-anything-ist, was completely drowned out. When we left, nearly an hour later, the children were still roaring "Roar" at each other over the fences. My own feeling about this piece, I might add, is that it was the most exciting expression of nihilism I have ever seen. It was very actual, concrete, even moving, though I felt it was a little thin on hope, and therefore it struck me that for all its excellence, its total effect was not quite salutory. But I cannot deny that this was unquestionably the most brilliant happening that has ever been done, that it came perilously close to going to pieces, and therefore risked all, and thus was able to succeed where the more facile venturers crack their noggins open in falling.

Another Hansen happening might be described here, a less baroque piece called "Car Bibbe." A hundred cars came to the beach at twilight, when people might well be going home. They filled up the beach parking lot. They flashed lights, and honked horns, drove forward and back again rapidly and jerkily, now ten feet forward, now five feet back, now ten feet forward, now twenty-five feet back, wherever there was room to go. To one puppeteer, a teacher whom I know, it was the most maddening thing he had ever seen. He ran up and down the dunes screaming. In the midst of the cars there was a single car with twenty-five people on and in it, all singing and having a fine old time. On the roof one of the people had a broken leg. He feel off and cracked his cast and rebroke his leg. There is almost always plenty of physical danger in a Hansen piece as well as intellectual danger. I love his riskiness. Perhaps fools walk in where angels fear to tread, but I think not. "Nothing ventured,

POSTFACE   66

nothing gained." I have heard that attributed to everyone from Benjamin Franklin to J. Rockefeller Sr. to the brothers Gracchi to Maxim Gorki. All I know about the line is that more and more as I live I find it to be true. It is our only answer to the intellectual critics of our own activities, from Raoul Hausmann to Morton Feldman to Henry Flynt. We cannot answer them directly, since we do not think so fast and cannot match their subtlety. But there is no question that limiting the risk limits also the potential. Better to come up with a magnificent flub than a charming nothing.

And that is why one prefers a Hansen, none of whose things will ever be perfect, to a Robert Sheff, to name one who is no International Stylist but who still plays it safe, and who is all with but no wits.

In the spring of 1961 George Maciunas turned up. He had an art gallery on Madison Avenue, where terrible modern art was shown, but he wanted a good series of goings-on, and people put him in touch with other people, who put him in touch with still others, till he wound up presenting the most interesting performances I have ever heard of, and he has never stopped. Eventually he got stuck with the debts from his gallery and fled to Europe, which is why Fluxus began there. As I will tell in a while, Fluxus was quite an interesting and wonderful experience there, and I like it that it developed out of economic necessity.

At the AG Gallery, Maciunas did concerts of Maxfield, Mac Low, Flynt, myself, and Ray Johnson, among others.

Ray Johnson I haven't yet talked about. He is the thoughtful collagist, also he does synthetic dramas and some poems, which very often make use of the mails. He knows all about things like knives and poisons, rats and clocks, air and packages, glue and ink, Brooklyn and belly-dancers. For his "Nothing" concert at the AG, Johnson covered the stair-case up to the gallery with cut-up dowels, and he turned the lights off. People came, tried to climb the stairs, and were rolled down. It was unlikely, that anyone would stay at the top, once he fought his way up, since the gallery was shut, there was no light, no anything to do, and only one way to go - down. It was a parable, just as most of Ray Johnson's things, no matter how carelessly tossed-off they seem (he meticulously hides his earnestness) are really parables or at least ironic comments on something. Many

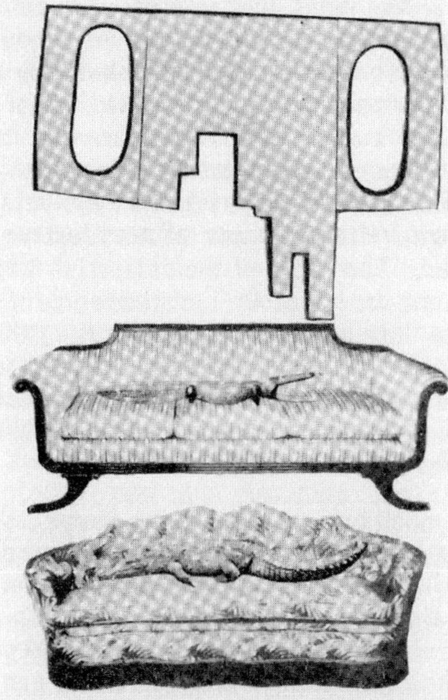

of his collages were once brightly colored, but he has ripped the colored materials, the paint, the words off, till only a half-rough grey sheet remains. He has nothing left to sell. And many of his pieces are blank. Not one, a four minute thirty-two second hymn, as in Cage's case, but many many, many of them pre-dating Cage and there is some possibility that is was he who first taught Cage about empty things. Johnson is conscious that a hole in the ground, a hole in the doughnut, and a hole between the walls of a room are not the same thing. He is actively conscious that the emptiness of a sheet of paper makes it useful for writing on. He is conscious that it is stupid to say something when you don't want to or when you have nothing to say, and some of his blank pieces seem to be memos to that effect. Perhaps Ray Johnson runs deeper than any other living artist.

Around that same time Young was invited to guest edit an issue of a magazine, in which he decided to collect those in New York plus those in Europe who were moving along allied lines. The magazine went broke, but Young had recruited lots of material, which he de-

POSTFACE   68

cided to turn into An Anthology. Maciunas was interested in publishing it. He worked very hard on the Anthology, but he did not
want to see it all end there. So he began to think about building a
magazine, to be called Fluxus, to appear irregularly. Not long afterwards, Maciunas had to flee the country. The structure that he
left behind for performances collapsed. He went to Wiesbaden,
Germany. Here he planned the first of the various Fluxus Festivals,
or more properly, Festa Fluxorum. His idea was of a collective,
doing festivals and publications. The basis of the collective was
that the work had to be realistic and concrete. On both these grounds
it was implicitly opposed to the International Style in music, the
Going Thing in poetry, Abstract Expressionism in painting, and so
on. There was no creed, no possibility of a "Fluxus Group" – which
would probably have driven every one of us away – nothing but the
rostrum and the material. We were very excited about this.

Brecht's work had changed very much by now. He was no longer using directions and making spiritual processes. He had begun to merely isolate things that appealed to him or particularly occurred to him.
These were usually very daily things, and they took a very simple
form. I used to say, a propos of some of my more involved directions, that lots of things looked complicated on paper but were simple in practice. But Brecht said that depended on what you meant.
If you meant something simple, it was simple, in every respect. I
liked that, and since then I don't do things that look complicated very
much, even on paper.

I wanted to get out of New York, mostly to see what was going on.
I had done a lot of performing and had finished my movie, The Flaming City. I wanted to perform in Europe, and also I was a little a-
fraid of what performers with "professional instincts" might do to my
pieces (and Brecht's, Young's, etc.). So Alison Knowles and I went.

Alison Knowles and I got to Germany, met Patterson, Williams, Paik,
and Vostell; and the Wiesbaden Fluxus had already begun. The previous week-end, in line with his ideal of Fluxus being a united front,
Maciunas had invited a bunch of International Stylists to perform:
Von Biel, Rose, and a couple of others. But they did not like some
of the pieces Maciunas was doing and quarrelled with him, and they
had a style of living that was too self-indulgent to be concrete with
the lively aspects of Fluxus. So he kicked Von Biel's crowd out and
Rose left.

The Wiesbaden Fluxus was the most ambitious of all. It lasted a
month, with three, four, or five performances each week-end. The
other festivals were smaller. The beauty of the Wiesbaden festival
was that we had no worry for time – we could do many terrific long
pieces that could not be fitted into other festivals. We did Emmett
Williams's german opera, "Ja, es war noch da" in English: it was
the longest three-quarters of an hour I have ever spent, since it is
mostly tapping on a pan in regular rhythms a prescrived number of
times. We did a one-hour version of La Monte Young's B-F sharp
held, unvarying, sung and accompanied by Benjamin Patterson's
bass viol. We invented a piece by a mythical Japanese and improvised it for an hour (on the same program as the Young) – it became
very beautiful. Vostell came down from Köln – a gigantic blond potato, three hundred pounds, with the tiniest feet in the world, so
that he glided lightly. He said, "Arghh," hammered some toys to
pieces, erased a magazine, broke some light bulbs on a piece of
glass, and heaved cake at the glass. Finis Sahnetortis, and he
went right back to Köln. It was a beautiful mess. We did lots of
old things of mine – I avoided the new ones mostly, for no particular reason – and we did Brecht, Watts, Patterson, Young, Williams,
Corner, all galore. We did Danger Music No. 3 by shaving my head
and heaving political pamphlets into the audience and Danger Music
No. 16 by "working with butter and eggs for a while" so as to make
an inedible waste instead of an omelette. I felt that was what Wiesbaden needed. For a while eggs were flying through the air every
couple of minutes. A very smartalec sculptor named Viebig reached
out his hand to dare me to throw egg – I did (splat) up his arm to his
face. During Emmett Williams' opera some college boys came up
out of the audience and stood, holding pine bows, singing college
songs. We did Maciunas' metronome-rhythmic "In Memoriam Adriano
Olivetti" by raising hats, popping fingers, gasping, sitting up and
down, waving heads, and so on. For three weeks this went on. We
did Corner's "Piano Activities" by taking apart a grand piano and
auctioning off the parts. Most of my "Requiem for Wagner the Criminal Mayor" was done, to the delight of the house super, who left
in the middle and came back with his whole family, they liked the
goings-on so much. Paik did "Simple" and Patterson did his "Variations for Contrabass."

Because fo its scope, difficult to duplicate elsewhere since Maciunas'
facilities were at Wiesbaden, the Wiesbaden Fluxus was all that

POSTFACE   70

might be hoped for such a series. Our audiences varied from enormous to tiny, from explosive (we had two riots) to docile and indifferent to sympathetic.

There was talk about other Fluxus festivals happening immediately after Wiesbaden, but they did not seem very promising. Vostell was invited to have a show at Amsterdam of his Decollages, and the resulting situation, while not done by Fluxus, was relevant to it, since it included so many Fluxus people.

Vostell's work is mostly decollages. These are the opposite of collages. They involve ripping off or erasing, they suggest dying and metamorphosis. Their quality is dependent on Vostell's artistic eye, which is excellent. The result is not dissimilar to good painting in the sense that Rauschenberg's combines are paintings. Vostell also edits Decollage magazine, which is the best forum for avant garde ideas in Europe- by default, in the world. It appears irregularly, is ordinarily given away rather than sold, and is a newsletter in that Vostell likes to keep Decollage appearing and on the move. Since Fluxus is organized on an international basis but each issue is a national anthology, there is no real basis for conflict with Decollage, which is international in every issue and much more limited in scope, even though Vostell publishes some of the same people. The first issue of Fluxus, for example, has been in the works for two years, contains only American materials, is about four hundred pages long, and is not yet in circulation. No Decollage is more than fifty pages long, and no really major works are included. However, a fight simmered between Vostell and Maciunas from the beginning, occasionally breaking out into the open (for example, a crisis was provoked when Henry Flynt, whose complete works were planned for publication by Fluxus, submitted an essay to Decollage, not realizing that Fluxus does not reprint anything), and leading to a final rupture, the details of which I do not know, at Düsseldorf.

At Amsterdam, in connection with Vostell's show, the gallery owner invited Vostell to arrange a program of happenings, so Vostell announced performances of Busotti, Cage, Brecht, Caspari, Patterson, Paik, Williams, Riley, himself, Maciunas, myself, Young, Knowles, Hulsmann, and Gosewitz. Maciunas and Patterson withdrew immediately, Cage, Brecht, and Riley were not consulted, and only Cage was performed, of these: I did his "Solo for Voice." Caspari was at Amsterdam, but he seems to have been frightened away. Gerd Stahl and a couple more Germans were added to the program to make up the lacks. And Tomas Schmit appeared for the first time, not to do a piece of his own, because so far as I know he had not yet written any, but to perform Paik's "Moving Theater No. 1." Willem de Ridder and Jac K. Spek were listed on the program, from Holland, but I do not remember that either did anything. First Jean-Pierre Wilhelm introduced us all. Then I sang the Cage, and next Diter Hülsmann began to read some shove-it-into-him pornography. The audience was all jammed into a little tiny art gallery, with German art on the walls, and with all this blatant pornography they began to get a little restless. It was all so German. Then Alison Knowles came and did Paik's "Serenade for Alison," a melodramatic striptease for amateurs only, which relieved the air. But when Stahl dragged in a bed, and began a very very very very long meta-physical-erotic tape played on the bed, the dutchmen became very upset. "How can you do this in Holland?" one asked me. The jittery room was too much, by now. The remaining pieces that were to be done inside were cancelled, and the audience went outside, where I did my american-accent french cabarets, "Cabarets Exotiques et Sentimentaux. While this was going on a man showed up with a small crane for Vostell's piece - a juke box playing rock-and-roll was to be listed high into the air and dropped. This was too much for the audience. A large pile of papers that someone had brought were ignited. Alison Knowles tried to do her street paintings. The head of the gallery became very upset and retired to nurse his poor little nerves, while his wife, who was the brains of the outfit, tried to get the fire put out. The juke box was hoisted up, but it wouldn't come detached from the crane: Vostell kept yelling "Arghh!" but the jukebox was only slowly lowered. I tried to get the audience to stop feeding the bonfire, but a group of students had decided this was a demonstration against German art and they would not stop. A girl shoved a burning paper at me, I slugged her, and was told that in Holland men don't hit ladies (I suppose they get their moustaches burned off instead?), that I should go back to Germany (to Berlin in 1933 perhaps? there are parallels), and if I hadn't gotten rough there would have been real trouble. But I did, and Paik and two others backed me up, so we kept the students at bay. Now the cops showed up. They cancelled the rest of the performance. Our m.c., whose name I don't recall, was drunk and tried to measure the angles of the cop's head with a protractor. He was jailed and then

POSTFACE

72

given twelve hours to leave Holland. Vostell had planned to make a large decollage: he had brought a twenty-foot billboard from Germany with posters, thirty deep on it. The cops told him to remove it immediately to wherever he had found it. All the while the gallery director was wiping his forehead while his wife tried to calm everybody. At last we took off across the back streets, chanting something a little Tibetan. When we crossed one canal, Paik floated a flaming violin with a radio on it down the canal. At another canal, Tomas Schmit took a swim. Later on, Emmett Williams measured the bridge that I mentioned before with inflationary marks in such a way as to simultaneously perform his composition for millionaire and one-eyed poet (Filliou has only one eye). Williams was the millionaire and Jed Curtis was the one-eyed poet (wearing an eyepatch). I did "Danger Music No. 17." All in all, it was an amazing collage of pieces and all too concrete with Dutch nationalism. However, it started me thinking about nationalism and how I hated its blindness: therefore I wrote my series of Vanity Fair, Germania Unveiled, and the rest.

In London Williams, Spoerri, Køpcke, Filliou, Page, Metzger, and Ben Vautier were cooperating on the show where Filliou did the pieces I described. Ben (he does not use the Vautier) exhibited himself as a work of art. He is the master of the Nice Academy, whose members are their work. They do not produce objects or aesthetic interest except by interesting (to them) viological processes. A baby might be considered a masterpiece of Ben, especially if the baby dies.

And so, in London, and in Mayfair in particular, where the Down-With-The-Bombers marched (since it was not made in Her Majestie's Angellonde) and the Rolls Royces purred and the overdressed Elite ran galleries of pornography, Ben showed himself, Køpcke set up things to steal (called "presents"), Spoerri made a labyrinth in which you stumbled among textures in the dark, Page did some moveable junk pieces, Metzger made objections (he is a dogmatist for auto-destructive art) and slowly withdrew, Køpcke glued books together and sprinkled pigment around, Williams attached rubber stamps to a white wall (by means of chains) and, instead of stamping on the wall himself, invited the spectator to do so, leaving stamp pads of colored ink around – I was interested that he assumed that people would not tie up the chains or write with lipstick on the walls (which they did do) – perhaps he thought such noble thoughts about what people might

do reflected well on him (which they did) and hated to appeal to anything but the best in people (which he did). Spoerri arranged for a
series of performances to happen, and everyone, even Metzger, did
something. Metzger made things fluoresce, dissolved nylon with hy-
drochloric acid while wearing a gas mask, and removed items with
magnets that would have been more easily removed by hand. I performed my "Fourth Symphony." Spoerri had a sculpture contest. Emmett Williams did his Alphabet Symphony. Køpcke put Scotch Tape
on a record, played it, and cleaned up the mess left over from Patterson's Paper Piece." Every time the needle hit the tape, Køpcke
stopped picking up, began the record again, and then went back to
work. When the stage was all clean, the piece was over. Outside,
the Cuba crisis was on. Peace Marchers ran up and down the street,
chased by bobbies with clubs who knocked them down with theoretically un-English violence. Inside, Alison Knowles performed her
Proposition, in which she made a salad for two hundred people.
Schweik. Robin Page kicked a guitar around the block.

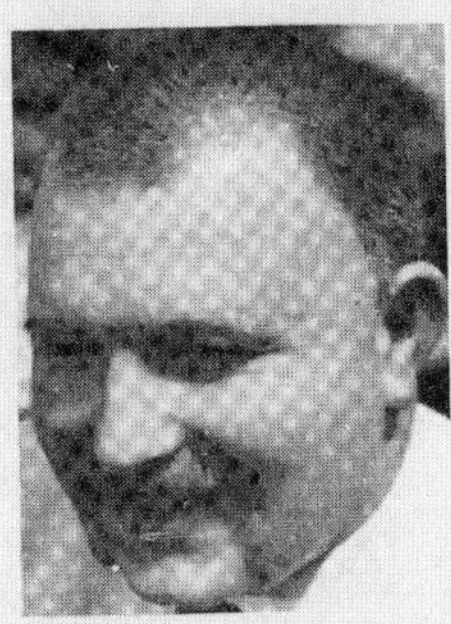

I did a performance of some of my pieces at Köln not long afterwards.
Tomas Schmit performed, with Jed Curtis, Frank Trowbridge, Agna
Redemann, and Paik and Vostell. Schmit mentioned writing pieces
but he did not show me any. In London I had bought a notebook, in
which I began to write down copious notes on pieces to put together
when I got back to the USA. Pieces in Jefferson's Birthday written
before September 1962 were written outright, while I was working
on the movie. I simply thought along and when I came to something
that seemed important I wrote it down. But the ones written after
September were written into this notebook, usually with supplementary notes, then collected and organized when I came home. That
was March. Now it is September, and I have yet to finish the last

POSTFACE   74

of these note-organizings. Because I travelled so much it seemed like the thing to do to sit and ride and think and speculate. Ordinarily I do not think so much, and so I don't come up with so many pieces in so little time.

The next big thing that happened was the Fluxus Festival at Copenpagen. It took place in the Nikolaikirke, a sixteenth century church. As it happened, the Danes were very glad to have us there, and we had audiences of four and five hundred every night. Resources; seemed to be unlimited: – we were given fine rooms in fine hotels. When items needed for performance were difficult to get, one of our danish friends went and helped us. The result was that the Copenhagen Fluxus was extraordinarily smooth and well-organized. We did La Monte's Piece for Henry Flynt – 566 slow crashes on the piano – and his fifths piece on the organ. We did the Knowles' "Proposition," and a wonderful thing happened. An impatient Dane came to snitch a carrot. I banged him on the head with a salad spoon. The bowl of the spoon flew off, hit a lady who had been making a lot of noise, and settled into the hands of a man who had dozed off. I laughed and the Dane ate his carrot. Another thing: there was an Ichiyanagi piece that was just form: things happened now, now and now, and they had to do with a piano, (it was called "Piano Piece No. 5"). Rather than play a now and then note, we thought of holding the pedal down and throwing things. Patterson suggested the darts for his "Sextet." The result was very beautiful: the upright piano was alone on the stage, pedal depressed, side to the audience From the wings darts flew in and struck the sounding board, producing a considerable variety of vibrations. Another beautiful thing: we did my second of Two Contributions for the Theater, in which you pick something to happen, wait for it to happen, and go away. A young man named Eric Andersen, then a refugee from Darmstadt and the International Stylists, now writing process pieces with a decidedly philosophical bent, this guy chose to wait till everyone else had left the stage. Emmett Williams sat down behind a lecturn and chose the same. Neither knew of the other's choice. For forty-five minutes they waited. Then someone told them that there would be an intermission in five minutes, assuming that they would stay there for the rest of the concert and perhaps beyond. But they understood that they were to leave in five minutes and did. So the only reason they left was because of a misunderstanding. But that was a marvelous fifty minutes, because what was happening was very interesting, the relationships between the two men waiting and the audience was always changing, it could be seen and figured out and even anticipated. Patterson did his Frog Pond, where you make one, two, or three syllable squeeking answers, questions, or exclamations when a mechanical frog, released by another system, hops into one of the three columns given each performer of eight in a square divided into thirty-six squares. Williams did his Litany for which I wrote a piano piece, Køpcke did "Music while you work," Williams did his Alphabet Symphony and the Ave Maria piece I described before, and so on. One performance was in a baroque theater. Alison Knowles did Patterson's "Solo for Dancer" – a rope was strung over the proscenium arch lighting bar. Knowles tied her foot up with the rope and pulled herself up the arch all the way to the top. She did Paik's "Serenade for Alison" and Patterson did his "Variations." I did a couple of walky pieces, Graphis 118 was designed for this stage. And we did some good Japanese pieces, alas, no Shiomi (isn't it interesting that Japan's best composer should be a girl, when Oriental girls have been given a raw deal for so many hundreds of years), but we did do Tone's Anagram, as sort of chronic Bartok glissando for double basses, Kosugi's Micro I and Anima I (where you rool up a rope on the floor till you mummify yourself in it), and some Ichiyanagi things. We did my Requiem for Wagner the Criminal Mayor which very much surprised the Danes and produced some interesting situations.

All in all, it was probably the most interesting Fluxus that we did.

It was followed by the Paris Fluxus, which was a very poetic fiasco. This began just a couple of days after the Copenhagen one, so most of us had to rush down from Copenhagen and we were very tired. /A dilletante poet who is the common bank roll for a large number of Paris poets and artists had been entrusted with the publicity and arrangements, although people whose basis of existence is challenged by a project should not be trusted at all. This dilletante was given 5,000 posters to mail and an evening of himself and his friends to arrange. Of course, he did a mailing of his own evening, and ignored the 5,000 posters. The hall was almost empty every night but his, when it was full. The result was that we had to cope with the problem of how to handle a nearly empty house. Emmett Williams' "Counting Piece," in which he counts the audience, came into its own and took on an extraordinary irony and majesty. We tried lots

POSTFACE 76

of long slow pieces. There was a very fine surrealist poet, not well-known in this country, by the name of Gherasim Luca, who said some of the most beautiful things we had ever heard about some pieces-mine, La Monte's, Maxfield's seemed to appeal to him particularly. In spite of our loathing of surrealists and their fascistic "ism" we were deeply moved by the old man's enthusiasm. I, for one, felt that the Paris Fluxus was worth all its financial catastrophe and its ridiculousness just because of this wonderful old man.

And so it came to pass that we lost most of what money Maciunas had left for Fluxus magazine in Paris, where many things have fallen before us, later to be accepted even there. But it was not all loss.

For one thing we got to know Daniel Spoerri, who is a real magician. He has never done a painting, yet he is a visual artist. He has glued things onto tables and hung the tables on the walls. He has devised any number of theatrical notions (alas, he feels that to devise a thing is enough, that it is not absolutely necessary to execute it in order to show what can be done. We most emphatically disagree, but each of his ideas is almost unbelievably relevant and concrete). These days he is particularly interested in the cullinary arts, although, unlike Edward Lear and myself, he is not at all hung up on the fantastic element in cookery.

Is there anything more glorious than a cool breeze on a hot day?

Too bad that we lost our shirts, but we made it up in experience. Alison had many times received marvelous Christmas cards, so we decided to spend Christmas in Germany. This resulted in midnight coffees and bad performances of the J.S. Bach Christmas Oratorio, with none of the Christmas trees and processions that we hoped for. If only we had had the good sense to spend Christmas in a muslim country!

So Alison and I were glad not to have to see too many of the wonderful people we love at Christmas, but Germany was just like I say it was in Germania Unveiled. So we fled to Turkey. Now Turkey is something else.

For two hundred years we smug westerners have laughed at the turks, because they were not as rich as we were. But today, only Turkey, Japan, and Malaya are industrial powers in the whole of Asia. Turkey, more than Isreal (which Turkey, I hear, was the first country in the world to recognize) belongs to the twentieth century.

So we went to Turkey, the land of a great people, who if they ever forget the wrongs that have been done them by the english, the greeks, and, before 1917, the russians, will be numbered among the few great peoples of the world. We travelled 1800 miles in Turkey, I grew to love those dour, sincere people, ungiven to witty or tactful wise-cracks. We went to big towns, to little sehirs, to wild mountains and to gentle hills. The greater part of Jefferson's Birthday, my present work, dates from this trip through Turkey. I loved Hami, Nevzat, Samil, Mehmet, Mr. Naki, Sayram, Suat, Ali, Kemal, Sinan, the twenty or so Turks that we got to know well. No matter what they do, Turks are honest, proud ecclectics. What goes on at Mersin is not their fault.

One village we visited was so small that the local school was let out to examine us honest-to-goodness flesh-and-blood yanks. We found it very inspiring that in little villages where, ten years ago, nobody could read, today everybody can, and does - they read at least two things, treatises on thermodynamics and Mickey Mouse.

I could go on for great length about our visits to wonderful little villages, and probably I will, one day. This is, after all, a people who did geometrical abstraction 1350 years ago, and who did

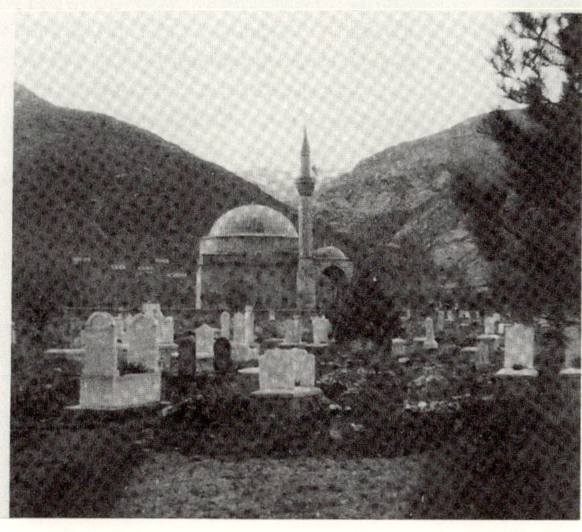

POSTFACE   78

Duchamp 700 years ago. However, having gone by devious routes via Ankara, Konya, Akşehir, Selifke, Mersin, Yenice, Ulukÿşla, Niğde, Kayseri, Ürgüp, the Goreme, Sultanhÿsar, Sivas, various towns in Paphlagonia, Samsun, Trabzon, along the Black Sea (whose sands really are black) to Istanbul.

Istanbul depressed us. It had no sense of breakneck progress, like Ankara and Sivas do. It was a seedy, European provincial capital. But all the other cities in Turkey - except Mersin, which was a little too wild - we loved. In Istanbul we received a telegram from Vostell, telling us to come at once to Germany, since the Düsseldorf Fluxus was about to happen. So we brought some turkish pastry and -

We went. There we found that the concerts consisted only of small pieces. What big pieces there were were collaged into simultaneities. This represented a step backwards, in that it was a concession to facile taste rather than a tactical progression, even though the Düsseldorf concerts were programatically the most successful we ever did.

After Dusseldorf we did a show in Cologne, Knowles, Køpcke, Vostell, and I. Knowles did an environment that included a quiet chair away from any fuss. I did three see-saws, called "troubles," in that their implications were troublesome - one was painful, one squeaked but had little else to distinguish it, and the third had enough flowers so that it could not be used as a see-saw. I also stuck a shoe in front of an easel on a wire with the caption, "The subject matter that an artist uses is always more interesting than what he does with it." I was much criticised (perhaps correctly?) for my poor display of technique and my disinterest in anything but what I was saying. Køpcke used whatever was in the place where we did the show, mostly glueing things down and spraying them a color he called "Silver - it's stupid." He did well. Vostell hung fish and suggestive items and toys in front of white canvasses, and lungs and chickens in front of two pieces. These last, naturally decollaged themselves, so that the gallery stank and could not allow the usual publicity activities, let alone any prolonged viewing and savoring of the show.

From Germany we fled, via Hamburg (with Køpcke) and Copenhagen to Stockholm. There we worked with Bengt af Klintberg, Stafan

                                    POSTFACE

Olzon, Lars Gunnar Bodin and Svante Bodin and Miecke Heybroek,
and others, on a preview of a hypothetical Fluxus festival, which
turned out to be not Fluxus concerts but two of the best concerts -
or was it four? - along those lines that I have ever seen. The language of the swedes made Emmett Williams's Tag come alive. It is
a very dancy language. And I did my Graphis 118 and Graphis 117

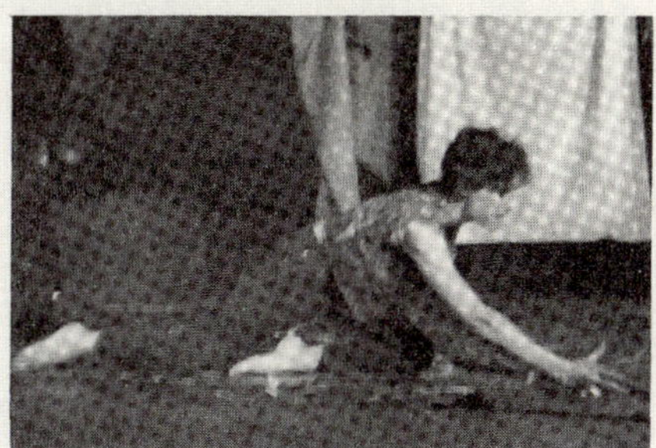

in a theater borrowed from Mr. Ingemar Bergman, which was a pretty
glamorous situation. Alison did Patterson's "Solo for Dancer" and
I wrote - and did - my "Gangsang," not realizing, as I think I mentioned before, how close it was to Patterson's "Stand Erect." But
one of the great things that happened was this. When we got to
Stockholm, the Baltic Sea was frozen over, even the river that flows
through Stockholm was frozen solid, so that the newspapers were
full of worries for the ducks that live in the river. But the day after
we arrived it began to thaw. It was the coldest winter in forty years,
but the spring came. And a few minutes before one of the concerts
we found the first balloon man of the year. In Sweden you know it
is Spring when there are men selling balloons. So we bought up
most of his balloons, and did Bob Watts'"Event 13" in which balls
are rolled down a ramp, and every time a ball hits the bottom, a
balloon is released. It was a wonderful way to welcome in the spring,
and every time one of the balloons flew up, the swedes cheered.

But one cannot remain out of one's country forever. So we came
back to the states from Sweden.

It was colder here than in Sweden. And we had to visit and see people. So the rate at which I made notes and filled in my notebook dropped
abruptly. In the month after our return we did only one concert, and in
the six months since then we have done only one. So there is a natural

separation between my activities included in Jefferson's Birthday and those which I will start into the works soon. We did some things at Douglass College in April, we did some things at the Yam Show, I did some things at Segal's Farm in May. Since then I have been working over the Jefferson's Birthday stuff, making some new pieces - including two movies, and being a good husband and hopefully a good printer. You can only be a good artist and a good worker too if you are as much a good worker as a good artist. Of this I am convinced.

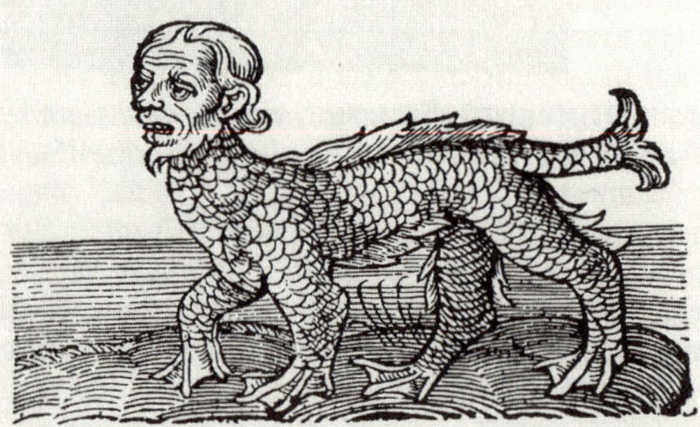

vi – all kinds of conclusions

Now I have described where many of us came from and where we are. We do not want the same things, that is clear.

The remaining thing for me to do is to try and extend my observations on my own activities.

Since the emphasis in my work is on simple things that happen or on moral and philosophical notions that catch my attention, there is no reason for me to emphasize one kind of work more than another. I am as much a composer as a poet or dramatist or, for that matter, printer.

Naturally when something takes one's attention, one ordinarily keeps
on thinking about it till one is through with it. Therefore, it seems
natural for me to make a whole string of works along the same lines.
There is a series of constellations, of concretions, of musical process, of contributions, of suspension plays, of danger musics, of
lectures, and so on. These are not necessarily forms – my forms
arise from my – or occasionally from my performer's – intentions.
My names for each series are of no importance whatsoever except to
signal that this piece probably has something to do with that. But
since something of my orientation might be clarified by explaining
them, I think I will. A constellation is simply my image of a group
of things happening simultaneously – whether or not they begin or
end together, at some point they overlap. A concretion is a physical
manifestation of an intellectual structure, concept, or point of view.
I used to just think about ways of things happening, in the abstract,
and so I did a lot of constellations and concretions. But I do not
think like that much any more, and so I do not call pieces "constellations" or "concretions" any more. I picked up the terms from common parlance, used them for my own purposes, and now they don't
seem relevant any more.

My notion of a "contribution" was of something that neither opposed
nor directly derived from the structure of and simultaneous events in
its vicinity. This relationship was precisely that of butter and bread.
I have digested this relationship pretty much, and no longer do pieces
that emphasize it exclusively.

A lecture, taken aesthetically, seemed to me to be any didactic
statement of a point or point of view in which there was a distinct
difference between the teacher, the person being taught, and the
material being taught. For me it was an unattractive situation, to
be used only if none other seemed capable of making one's point.
Therefore I have done very few lectures. Even an essay is too close
to lecturing, so I do very few essays. But there is no question that
it is an effective way of putting ideas into the air, so perhaps it is
best not to avoid it entirely.

A musical process is simply any way of putting events into time ab-
stractly – ie., with the narrative and/or causal structure concealed.
It is implicitly where I began, and is at the basis of so much of the
things that are going on. However when the emphasis is no longer

POSTFACE   82

on the system being used but on the particulars of what happens, then the musical process aspect of the activity may be assumed but it is less important to note it than something more specific.

A suspension play for me is one in which causation and sequence are suspended. I usually do this by setting the events which take place into correspondence with lighting or other environmental cues. A performer takes his cues not from something someone else says but from the change of light, from the fact of someone's asking him a question, from the warmth of the air, or from how well he likes something he smells. These events may take place over and over, and they take their context from proximity. The result is that rather obstruse intellectual points can be made very striking. The quality of the piece, as in any other sort of manufacture, artistic or otherwise, depends on the quality of the material used and on the workmanship with which it is used. In a didactic piece written this way, for example most of the longer pieces in Jefferson's Birthday, the method of working is to select fragments which, 1., seem to exemplify the points one wants to make, and 2., are capable of adding up cumulatively into an effective statement of one's point. I seriously question whether this is any different from the method used in writing any other kind of didactic piece. However the peculiar suitability of the suspension play for didactic use does not mean at all that it cannot be used for any other kind of theater piece. My first work in the form was Stacked Deck, a sort of procession out of a seventeenth century book of characters. My second, the Tiger Lady episode in the Ladder to the Moon is simply poetic and cumulative, without any particular end in goal - thus emphasizing the musical process aspect of the form. It is only with The Tart or Miss America that I began to develop the didactic potential of the form. There I first started to suggest people as presences, to insist that a man is as he does, that he has not the slightest existantial being. One thing I like best about The Tart is that the people we see change their being almost completely every time they are in a new situation or persona. They are more like the people that I know than the people in any sort of narrative drama. Since that time I have used the suspension play principle to make critiques of perversions of love (Vanity Fair or Yezhovchina), heroic interpretations of history and rugged individualism (Tamerlane I and II), various national characteristics, the cultural effect of war (Nicopolis 1396), urbanism (City of the Dead), and so on.

All the same, there exist, side by side with these didactic suspension plays in Jefferson's Birthday pieces such as Lavender Blue or
the middle section of Adam and Eve, equally based on my insistence
that if you add people up they become factions while if you take them
apart they become lies, and yet less anti-psychological than deliberately structured, cool, and autonomous, no more purposeful and no
less than a Bach fugue.

The nature of purposelessness interests me very much. It is a great
source of mental refreshment to do something for no particular reason, especially when it is not interesting or refreshing. One simply becomes very conscious of nothing in particular. That phenomenon is implicit in a lot of my work. I am not so interested in the
possibility of doing something gratuitous, like Paik, or in the "purpose -"that comes before the "-lessness" (without which the concept
is impossible, as I am in finding a fish somewhere.

Somewhere in his Magnalia Christi Cotton Mather complains that
when he preaches to his congregation about how they had come to
this continent to begin a land of righteousness and to found the kingdom of god on earth, someone in the back piped up, "Nonsense, we
came to catch fish."

That brings me to my danger musics. The first tells how I began
doing them. But of course, it was just the accident of my thinking about the kinds of danger in the arts and in our times at the point
when I was hoisted up that determined the entire series. The series
is mostly finished now. I am not so interested in doing more pieces
as I was.

But the danger musics are a sort of arbitrary group - a choice was
made, to think about danger, and it happened, the pieces became
thought up, and after a while they weren't thought up so much any
more. They are, then, a sort of extension of my older idea of concretions.

"Concrete" means: "Real, no ideal; Of or pertaining to immediate
experience; physical, not abstract or general." If one wants one's
work to be immediately striking and to avoid any of the dichotomy of
an extraordinary situation, such as going to an expensive concert, as
opposed to a daily sort of situation, such as walking around the house,

POSTFACE 84

if one wants this, one might well try to do the most concrete possible work.

Whether or not such work is or is not art is a purely academic question; it is surely something. Nor is it, as one sometimes hears, anti-art, since it is not an attack on art but a simple entity in its own right. It is, perhaps, non-art just as a baker is a non-welder or a shoe is a non-vegetable, but to call such work non-art is not particularly relevant. When I make a piece, such as "Danger Music Number Twenty-One (Comb Music)" which consists solely of the one word, "Colored," I am suggesting a great many associations and possibilities, even the possibility of provoking perhaps a beautiful vaudeville, so that we are back in the situation where beautiful art may be provoked by my non-art, which is the traditional relationship between a painter and his subject matter, to choose an obvious example.

Since the point of many other pieces is not aesthetic but intellectual, these might be described best as non-art producing more non-art using means conventionally associated with art. But more to the point is just not to pay much attention to the art-ness or non-art-ness of work. I think art is as art does, and that's that so far as I'm concerned. There is no relationship between the degree of concreteness of work and its quality or its effectiveness. On the one hand, one project I have going at the moment is a collection of games that are suggestive of social points of view - Tag, in Jefferson's Birthday, is one of these - I have as another project a large set of fugal textures for the theater called just that, Fugal Textures. I am not sufficiently interested in formal consistency to allow any technical consideration to keep me from doing whatever seems appropriate at a given time. I do not care deeply what I do so long it seems constructive, or, even more, suitable.

That is why I like to think of what I do as just sort of generally a folk-cultural activity, like the songs we all have sung and the games that we have played.

One very warm April day in 1959, I was sitting, scarcely even thinking. Over the rooftops the smoke came slowly up from the factory chimneys. There wasn't much sense to it, but it was very quiet and hot and nice. I was reflecting that not all axioms apply to art

85   POSTFACE

all the time. In art the whole does not have to be greater than any
of its parts or equal to their sum. I began to think about doing a
piece which, by its directions, was independent of the numbers of
people doing it, of its duration, even of its own quantities of material. It should be free to grow and to shrink and to use its own
life for its own suggestions. I did the piece very simply. I wrote
simple material on cards, and I wrote directions separately. If a
lot of performers want to do a long performance, they can look over
the cards on which the material is written, see what kind of things
are used, and do more of the same. Or the pack can be divided a-
mong a large number of people and repeated extensively. On the
other hand, one performer might like to do a very short performance.
So he can perform just one card. Either is equally a good way to do
the piece. I was thinking about all this, and my idea split. One
half later became the very boisterous theater piece, Clown's Way.
The other half, Some Quiet Chimneys, turned out to be a poem that
simply reflected the quiet of the day and the rooftops and the smoke.

I know what I want to do next – more movies. Movies are completely untapped as yet. The narrative movie begins to become increasingly hackneyed, no matter how fine the acting or how gorgeous the
color. The art movie is isolated from its society because it assumes
an ethic that is hostile to any socially productive activities. I have
in mind a whole slew of people from Jack Smith to Truffaut, from
Stan Brackhage to Resnais. The violence of universal sexuality,
of a life devoted to poetic activity, and of the severance of personal feelings is both the underlying tie between these people and the
reason why this work seems rather limited in its scope, more suitable to those who advocate a life of violence for its own sake –
leading perhaps to a march on Rome – than to any sort of devotion
to the end of giving all men meaningful lives through meaningful
and rewarding work. The art movie has come to wear a black shirt,
its philosophy is Nietsche. So standardized this is that any film
which does not insist on the sublime, the universal sexuality and
poetic violence is stigmatized as an anti-film. It is very easy to
run around waving a camera, shooting the dead, the destroyed, and
all kinds of exhibitions of emotionalism short-circuiting. The resulting kind of apocalypse seems more vital than it is because of its
nervous energy. But when the result is not charming or titillating or
raucously funny (fine qualities, I think, but rare) it is socially nau-
seating. There is nothing revolutionary in refusing to say no (or yes

either), in denying that the sky is blue because one claims to speak a different language. This is, in fact, precisely what the makers of the art films are doing, and it is precisely what the Goldwaters and Welches, like the Hitlers and Mussolinis before them, would like them to do. There is no challenge to the mind in boasting of one's social impotence. The Smiths and Brakhages I predict will wind up supported vigorously by the Fords and Rockefellers for a while, until the fashions change.

The result is that the film has yet to begin. The film, as an art, is not a mauled and scorched, chemically and physically altered raped object, so much as it is a means of documenting what can be seen by a single, objective-by-definition eye-lens. One shows the eye what one loves, what one hopes and dreams, what is terrible or beautiful, anything, anything at all. A camera is innocent. It just keeps on looking, so long as one winds it up or flicks its power switch, while the film maker just notices and thinks and considers.

Therefore I am going to do lots and lots of film work, among other things.

One hopes to draw the mud, somehow, from the water.

But a century which began with the end of the US Civil War and the supremacy of a kind of culture suitable to another age is fast ending. This is the time our fathers hoped for. We flowers thrive on compost heaps. And some of us may turn out to be trees. The more trees, the bigger the forest.

We have many lives to live, among us.

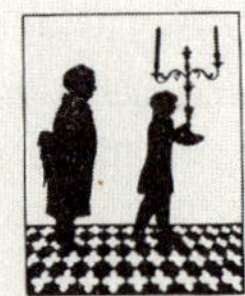

POSTFACE

FOOTNOTES

1. John Macolm Brinnin, The Third Rose (Boston: Little, Brown and Co., 1959), p.324.
2. Gertrude Stein, Narration (Chicago: The University of Chicago Press, 1935), p.19.
3. Filippo Tommaso Marinetti, "Doppo il Teatro Sinetico e il Teatro della Sopresa..." in Noi, Rivista d'Arte Futurista, Numero speciale (Rome, 1924).
4. Robert Creeley, "Air: 'Cat bird singing...'" in Black Mountain Review VI (Black Mountain, No. Carolina, 1956), p. 164.
5. Joel Oppenheimer, "The Rain," in Black Mountain Review V (Black Mountain, No. Carolina, 1955), p. 34.
6. Joel Oppenheimer, "Un Bel Di," in Evergreen Review, Vol. VII, No. 28 (New York, 1963), p. 86.
7. Robert Filliou, "PERE LACHAISE NO. 1," in phantomas 38 –40 (Brussels, 1963), p. 22.
8. Tristan Tzara, in "Inquiry among European Writers into the Spirit of America," in Transition XIII (Paris, 1928, p. 252.
9. Morton Feldman, "Dr. Schuller's History Lesson," in Kulcher 9, (New York, 1962), p. 88
10. Morton Feldman, "Sound, Noise, Varese, Boulez," in It Is. 2 (New York, 1958), p. 46.
11. Dick Higgins, 100 Plays (New York: Richard C. Higgins, 1961.
12. Dick Higgins, The Musical Wig (New York: Richard C. Higgins, 1961.

Postscript to *Postface*

Fifteen Years Later

Originally published in *The Word and Beyond: Four Literary Cosmologists* by Dick Higgins, Richard Morris, Donald Phelps, Harry Smith, Anne Conover Heller, editorial coordinator, New York: The Smith, 1982.

Time ain't waitin' for nobody. Some of my friends and colleagues, discussed in "Postface" have stopped making art processes. Køpcke and Maxfield are dead. Happenings got absorbed into a newer tradition—Art Performances. Fluxus, which wasn't a "group," has become one, somehow, as the people continued to know each other and to work with each other, and as common characteristics emerged among the group—the games and gags, the minimalist (more than impersonal) styles. Beat and Black Mountain poetry fused—I was, I find, quite right in discussing it as a single style, the "Going Thing" School—and converged into the St. Mark's in the Bouwerie style of the 1960s, best remembered now for Anne Waldman's and John Giorno's op-pop frame of reference. But the break that I detected then in what we (our people, whether they knew it or not) were doing after, roughly, 1958—as being qualitatively different in conception and teleology from the art and music and literature that had come before (and which still exists as an invalid entity, supported by transfusions of dollars and media-blessed prestige: the best poems of the 1950s are being written today by John Ashbery & Co.)—that break was more profound, even, than I could realize when I wrote "Postface." Analyzing its implications for art history and theory has been my main preoccupation, apart from my art work itself, during these years.

"Postface" itself has an interesting history. It was written as part of my feeling that an artist must not only create his work but also, if that work presents any difficulties, create a conceptual environment or paradigm in which its difficulties can be surmounted. Maciunas, the organizer of Fluxus, seemed to take a very emblematic view of our history: naturally my work, which belongs to many worlds at once, confused him. I felt it might, similarly, confuse other people. He had invited me to collect a full year's worth of my writing (to publish my complete works, which he had offered to do, would have been unfeasible, I felt)—so I chose April 13th, 1962 as my starting date, which turned out to be Thomas Jefferson's birthday: thus the title of my projected book, *Jefferson's Birthday*. As the collection evolved, I found myself explaining more and more history to Maciunas and others, and finally decided that I should make a full essay of it, which set down my commitments and views within a broader context. Thus it became a "Postface" to *Jefferson's Birthday*, to be published with it, back-to-back in one volume, so you would have theory on the one hand, practice on the other. Alas—Maciunas was ever just one step ahead of the creditors. And moving all the time kept him broke. He returned to America in 1963, and took a studio downstairs from my own, at 359 Canal Street, where he had a "Flux Shop," gave Fluxus festivals, and published Fluxus books, which were always tiny, since that was all that could be afforded.

I gave him my manuscript around June of 1963, but heard not a word until November, when the book might be expected to have been produced. Finally, I cornered him: "When!"

"A year from next spring."

Disaster. I went out and got drunk. Then I came back, took the manuscript upstairs to my desk and went out to get a little more drunk. In the wee small hours

I stumbled home to Alison Knowles, and announced that we had founded a press: I'd do the book myself.

"Really," she said. "What's it called?"

I didn't know. I said something feeble, like "Shirtsleeves Press."

"That's no good," she said. "Call it something else."

And so was founded the Something Else Press. The name was written down that night, and in the morning I nursed my hangover and struggled along—delighted by the new project and writing my "Something Else Manifesto." The name pleased me. Whatever the Going Thing types would do, I would do "Something Else." Automatic expulsion of the trendy and fashionable types from my publishing house.

And, in due course, *Jefferson's Birthday/Postface* appeared, a 384-page monster (in terms of trade publishing, anyway), which set the stage for the next development of Happenings and Fluxus into the ferment of the mid-sixties. The Press did rather well for itself; it introduced Concrete Poetry to America in the form of the first substantial anthology here, Emmett Williams's *An Anthology of Concrete Poetry*, which sold 18,000 copies. There was a series of inexpensive pamphlets, large works by John Cage, Marshall McLuhan and Claes Oldenburg, as well as fascinating books, which the public barely discovered, by George Brecht, Robert Filliou, Toby MacLennan and even myself (ah well). When I was told by those who should have known better that what I was doing (or, rather, what my Fluxus friends were doing) was "dada," I decided to show that we weren't by showing what dada was, minus the historicistic prattlings of Herr Doktors and Amurrican Art Historians, by reissuing the *Dada Almanach*. We also reissued all the works of Gertrude Stein that we could, to steal her back from the rarebook freaks and collectors who had appropriated her. It was a very heady time.

As for "Postface," I updated it to 1965 for a book that Vostell was doing in Germany: the whole thing was to be done by him. In fact, the book used only a whiff of the earlier essay, though they did use my update. The result was a very weird hybrid with weird proportions. *Jefferson's Birthday/Postface* went out of print in 1967 or 1968. I kept thinking I would like, if it ever were reissued, to do the whole text: but now that the time has come to do it, I see that a cow doesn't need two extra legs to walk—six legs are no better than four. The history of Fluxus after 1963 is closely tied up with the history of Something Else Press and running it two more years into the next beast serves no purpose at all. One day a fuller history will be needed: the life of that Press (which was so much like an art movement of its own) should be told. But not now. So I've scrapped my extra pages: they're to be found in the Wolf Vostell and Juergen Becker *Happenings* (Reinbeck bei Hamburg: Rowohlt Verlag, 1965), if one must find them. I think that this version of the text has its own integrity, and there's little point in dragging it out on a Procrustean Bed. Except for a few corrected spellings and facts, and a few sentences that had been scrambled, it is now the 1963 version once again.

So much has changed, and so little. Feldman is still grinding out the same music now as he did then, and my objections are still the same. Some of the Black

Mountain poets, notably Jonathan Williams (who, for instance, has done some outstanding concrete poetry), have stopped doing the Going Thing and have emerged with considerably greater stature.

Something Else Press is gone now. I left it in 1973 to concentrate on my own work, and the people who took it over had no instinct for fundraising and grantsmanship or for major sales. It went bankrupt in 1974. I started a new publishing operation, Unpublished Editions, which is completely a co-op. Each of the seven members does his or her own books, we have a joint catalogue and other such group efforts, and each is paid as books are sold. So each book is unique to its artist as an autograph is unique: no conservatising editor meddles. In a way this extends the old Something Else Press vision.

But Fluxus too continues. Old members have left and others join: the movement, if that is what it is, has never fractionated and ruptured à la dada or surrealism. Maciunas is not a pope. We work separately and we work apart; thus nobody gets claustrophobia. The program is broad enough to allow for a good deal of variety. It would have to be.

I heard a young writer say, the other day, "Oh, she's a *pure* poet," by which, I take it she (whoever she was) was not doing intermedia of any kind—sound poetry, visual poetry or whatever. Before Fluxus and the kinds of things that are discussed in "Postface," I don't think there would have been such a strong sense that one *could* be pure, as such—one wouldn't know what it meant. "You don't know what good health is until you're sick," as the saying goes. Well, not, of course, that Fluxus or Happenings are sick (or were). But their sensibility has spread far beyond the people who had firsthand experience of them: they have become points of reference. And the cultural shifts of which they are a part have continued. With that in mind, one can, I think, correctly read or re-read my "Postface." I was writing about a small world that has since grown.

New York, December 9, 1977

Fluxus: Theory and Reception

Originally published privately as a pamphlet, Barrytown, NY, 1987. Revised and republished in *Modernism Since Postmodernism: Essays on Intermedia*, San Diego: San Diego State University Press , 1997.

Fluxus is not: —a moment in history, or
                 —an art movement,

Fluxus is: —a way of doing things,
                 —a tradition, and
                 —a way of life and death.[1]

i. To begin with

To begin with, this is not an introductory text on Fluxus. To explain what Fluxus is and was and where it came from is not my primary purpose at this time, having already done so in my long essay *Postface* [1963] and my short one, "A Child's History of Fluxus," among other pieces as well. Others have done so, too, of course, each in his or her own way. My concern here is, rather, to try to deal with some aspects and questions in Fluxus: What do we experience when we experience a Fluxus work? Why is it what it is? Is there anything unique about it, and so on?

In other words, this is an essay intended for the thoughtful person who already knows some Fluxus materials, who has perhaps thought about Fluxus in relation to Dada and Surrealism and the other iconoclastic art movements of our century, who may have attended a Fluxus performance, who may have reservations about Fluxus works in one way or another, but who, at any rate, already has some ideas on the subject. For him or for her I want to frame some questions and suggest some answers. With any luck, the whole inquiry should have an erotic, that is, a pleasure principle, one of its own.

One must, here, bear in mind that Fluxus was something that happened more or less by accident. In the late 1950s we Fluxus artists began to coalesce, sometimes thinking of ourselves as a group, unnamed, doing the work that later became known as Fluxus. We did not consciously present ourselves *to the public* as a group until 1962 when George Maciunas organized his festival at Wiesbaden, intended originally as publicity for the series of publications he wanted to issue that were to be called *Fluxus*. The festival caused great notoriety, was on German television, and was repeated in various cities beside Wiesbaden, which is well documented elsewhere and need not concern us here. The point I am getting at is that in connection with these festivals, the newspapers and media began to refer to us as "die Fluxus Leute" ("the Fluxus people"), and so here we were, people from very different backgrounds. Knowles, Vostell, and Brecht were originally painters. Watts was primarily a sculptor. Patterson, myself,

[1] This is the text of a rubber stamp I made up around 1966 and used to stamp the endings of my letters.

and Paik were composers. Williams and Mac Low were writers (I was that, too), and so on. Here we were, being told we were The Fluxus People. What *should* that mean? If we were to be identified publicly as a group, should we become one? What did we have in common?

The concept arose of consciously constituting ourselves as some kind of "collective." Maciunas was particularly pleased by that idea, since he was very much a leftist and, instinctively, a goodly portion of his approach to organizing us and our festivals had at least a metaphorical relationship with leftist ideology and forms. The collective clearly needed a spokesman, to be what a commissar was supposed to be in the USSR but seldom was. Maciunas was not yet an artist but a graphic designer,[2] and, as editor of the *Fluxus* magazine or annual or whatever it was to be, he seemed the best suited of us to be the commissar of Fluxus, which role he assumed and held until his dying day. In this there was a parallel to the role of André Breton in Surrealism, though Maciunas was less monolithic and more ceremonial (or he was supposed to be).

[2] Maciunas was educated in architecture and industrial design, but he seems always to have had an interest in art which intensified over the years. His major works date from the later years of his life. For a fuller biography of Maciunas, see Jon Hendricks's *Fluxus Codex* (1988).

We never accepted Maciunas's right to read people out of the movement, as Breton did. Besides, it wasn't really a movement, but more of that later. Occasionally Maciunas tried to do this, but few others followed him on this point. We would continue to work with the artist who was banned by Maciunas until, eventually, Maciunas usually got over his own impulse to ban the person and accepted him or her back into the group. Surrealism without Breton is inconceivable, but, crucial though Maciunas's contributions were, Fluxus was less centralized on him. The degree of centralization is even today a matter of discussion.

As for us, looking back into history, we saw Futurism as important but as having no strong or direct relationship with us in any direct sense. Dada works we admired, but the negative side of it, its rejections and the social dynamic of its members, splitting and feuding, that we did not wish to emulate. Surrealism had, perhaps, minimal influence on us so far as form, style, and content were concerned, but aspects of its group dynamic seemed suitable for our use, subject only to the limitations on Maciunas's authority that lay in our nature as having already been a group with some aspects of our work in common *before* Maciunas ever arrived on the scene. More of this in a moment.

Fluxus was therefore:

a) a series of publications produced and designed by George Maciunas;

b) the name of our group of artists;

c) the kind of works associated with these publications, artists, and performances that we did (and do) together;

d) any other activities that were in the lineage or tradition that was built up, over a period of time, which is associated with the publications, artists, or performances (such as Fluxfeasts).

Whether or not Fluxus still exists and—if it does, then in what sense—depends on whether one is talking about history, works, forms, or some general spirit. Fluxus was not a movement in that it had no stated, consistent program or manifesto that the work *must* match, and it did not propose to move art or our awareness of art from point A to point B. The very name, "Fluxus," suggests change, being in a state of flux. The idea was that it would always reflect the most exciting avant-garde tendencies of a given time or moment (the Fluxattitude), and it would always be open for new people to "join." All they had to do was to produce works in some way similar to what other Fluxus artists were doing. Thus, the original core group expanded to include, in its second wave (after Wiesbaden), Ben Vautier, Eric Andersen, Tomas Schmit, and Willem de Ridder; in the third wave (by 1966) Geoffrey Hendricks and Ken Friedman; and, in the later waves (after 1969), Yoshimasa Wada, Jean Dupuy, Larry Miller, and others. It was thought of as something that would exist parallel to other developments, providing a rostrum for its members and a purist model for the most technically innovative and spiritually challenging work of its changing time(s). One received one's Fluxhood from Maciunas, but after that it was up to one to justify it.

An overview of how the Fluxus forms developed might be mapped out like this:

1) Once upon a time there was collage, a technique. Collage could be used in art, not just in visual art.

2) When collage began to project off the two-dimensional surface, it became the combine (Rauschenberg's term?).

3) When the combine began to envelop the spectator, it became the environment. I don't know who coined that term, but it is still a current one.

4) When the environment began to include live performance, it became the Happening (Allan Kaprow's term, usually capitalized in order to distinguish it from just *anything* that happens).

5) When Happenings were broken up into their minimal constituent parts, they became events. I first heard that term from Henry Cowell, a composer with whom both John Cage and, many years later, I myself studied. Any art work can be looked at as a collation of events, but for works that tend to fissure and split into atomized elements, this approach by event seems particularly appropriate.

6) When events were minimal, but had maximum implications, they became one of the key things Fluxus artists typically did (or do) in their performances.

That is, I think, the real lineage of Fluxus.

A digression into language seems in order here. In Fluxus one often speaks of Fluxfestivals, Fluxconcerts, Fluxpeople, Fluxartists, Fluxevents . . . I myself am to blame for that one. Maciunas was very much interested in the odd byways of baroque art. I told him about the work of the German baroque poet, Quirinus

Kühlmann (1644–88), a curious messianic figure who was eventually burnt at the stake in Moscow where he had gone in an effort to persuade the Tsar that he was a reincarnation of Christ. Kühlmann wrote various exciting books of poetry using "proteus" forms and other unconventional means, among which is the *Kühlpsalter*. This includes Kühlpsalms, evidently to be performed on Kühldays by Kühlpeople, and so on. Maciunas was delighted by this, and thenceforth made parallel constructions of his own that were based on it. There were "Fluxfests" or "Fluxfestivals," to be performed by "Fluxfriends" who were also "Fluxartists," wearing "Fluxclothes," and eating "Fluxfood," and so on. This dissociated such artists, festivals, and the like from regular ones. Its purpose was to get beyond accusations that this was "anti-music" as our aural works were sometimes accused of being, or even "non-music" (which would mean anything not music, from mushrooms to silverware). Our aural pieces were, simply, "Fluxmusic." Of course one was not an "artist" or even an "anti-artist" but a "Fluxartist," something presumably quite different.

I began this essay by observing that I was trying to write theory here, not to give a basic history or critical discussion. The difference, as I see it, is that criticism attempts to provide an understanding of individual works, to explain why and how they work, or why and how they fail to do so. Theory, on the other hand, attempts to provide the underlying assumptions and policies of those works and of the criticism of them, if such criticism is to be appropriate. If one were to undertake both criticism and theory, one would have to describe a great many works, and this essay would become hopelessly cumbersome and lengthy. Therefore, at the risk of frustrating the reader, I will concentrate on the theory and only bring up the individual works where it is necessary to provide examples. Thus, there is no need for such purposes to mention all the major Fluxartists. No slight is intended to those who are not discussed. Instead, the focus must be on works and artists who make good examples of the key points, who typify something or other, and let us hope that the reader has some familiarity with at least some of the works alluded to, or with some of the artists.

ii. Some antecedents of Fluxus

On one hand, Fluxus appears to be an iconoclastic art movement, somewhat in the lineage of the other such movements in our century—Futurism, Dada, Surrealism, and so on. Indeed, the relationship with these is a real and valid one. Now we are ready to go into more detail concerning these in relation to Fluxus.

Futurism was the earliest such movement. It was founded by Marinetti in the first decade of the century, was proclaimed on the front page of the *Figaro Litteraire* and elsewhere, and it developed a group character which was sustained from its early years until World War II. This means it lasted at least thirty-plus years. Marinetti was its leader, though not in a totally dictatorial sense. Its members were supposed to follow along pretty much with what he said, but he usually forgave them when they didn't. He proclaimed *parole in libertà* ("words at liberty," a form of visual poetry); *teatro sintético* ("synthetic theater," that is, performance pieces that were synthesized out of extremely raw-seeming materials, similar to the *musique concrète* of the post-World War II era); simultaneity, a time related form of Cubism; music of noises; and many such formal innovations or unconventional arts that are still fresh to consider. If, however, one hears the existing recordings of the music of Luigi Russolo, for example, one of the main futurist composers, one finds something far more conventional than what one might have expected from reading his famous *Arte de Rumori* ("Art of Noises") manifesto. One hears, to be sure, amazing noises being made over a loud speaker—roars, scraping sounds, and suchlike. But one hears these superimposed over rather crudely harmonized scales. If one goes into the content of Marinetti's writings, one finds him a very old-fashioned daddy type, rather hard on women, celebrating war as an expression of masculine virtue, and the like. Even the visual art, in the works of Balla and others, being the summit of Futurist fine art, is rather conventional with regard to its formal structures and implications. It is certainly rather conservative when compared to the innovative Cubism of France at the same time. In other words, Futurism is a goddess, nineteenth-century style, with one leg in the future and one in the conventional past and not too much in the present. Considering that the two legs are moving in opposite directions, it is no wonder that Futurism falls a little flat in the evolution of modern sensibility. Of course, it is of great technical and historical interest, as a starter and a precursor, but its works have only moderate intrinsic interest as works.

Dada, when one looks at it in isolation, seems more unique than it is. But most of the Dada artists and writers came out of Expressionism, and if one compares the Dada materials with those of their immediate antecedents, they are less unique than one might have imagined. Perhaps an anecdote is appropriate here. In the 1950s and 1960s, the journalistic image of Dada had become so extreme, so far from the reality of the work, that Dada was considered to be the limit of the extremely crazy in art—as wild as possible, as droll as possible, simply inexpressibly "far-out," to cite the slang of the time. Thus, early Happenings and Fluxus (like the works of Rauschenberg and Johns) were often dismissed as "neo-Dada."[3] This was, of course, extremely annoying and embarrassing to those of us who knew what Dada was or had been. For example, I knew several of the old dadaists, had been raised on their work, and there was no doubt in my mind that what we Happenings and Fluxus people were doing had rather little to do with Dada.

Skipping ahead to 1966 for a moment, when I was publisher of Something Else Press, in various ways a Fluxus enterprise, I knew that, before the split between the French and German dadaists, Richard Huelsenbeck had published

[3] The first public Fluxconcert in Europe, which took place a few months before the Wiesbaden festival in 1962, was not called "Fluxus" but it included only materials later classified as Fluxus, and was organized by Fluxartist Ben Patterson and Maciunas. It was called "Neo-Dada in der Musik" after a lecture Maciunas had given soon after his arrival in Europe, thus suggesting that Maciunas did not yet think of Fluxus as a body of work apart from his proposed publications. An account of the term "Neo-Dada" is in Susan Hapgood's *Neo-Dada Redefining Art (1958–62)* (1994: 11–12, 58 fn. 1).

an anthology of Dada materials, the *Dada Almanach*. I therefore got Huelsenbeck's permission to reissue it in facsimile. The response to it was very revealing: I was told that this was "not real Dada!" The material seemed too conservative, far too close to the Expressionism of the pre-World War I years to gibe with the image that my 1960s friends and colleagues had built up in their mind as to what Dada was. Yet Huelsenbeck, at the time he did the *Dada Almanach*, was not a conservative at all. He had published a wildly leftist booklet, *Deutschland Muß Untergehen!* ("Germany Must Perish!"), and he saw no difference between political and cultural innovative and revolutionary thinking. His poems were as experimental as those of the other dadaists, Raoul Hausmann, for example. In other words, the journalistic myth had come to replace the substance to such an extent that the substance was overwhelmed. It is for this reason that the very term "neo-Dada" seems naive and inadequate today, since we now know a great deal more about Dada than was the case in the 1950s and early 1960s.

Surrealism is, of course, an outgrowth of Dada, historically. It was, quite self-consciously, a movement, unlike Dada, which was more unruly, spontaneous perhaps, and undirected. Surrealism was presided over by the relatively benevolent Trotskyite *littérateur*, André Breton. Breton was much given to cafe politics, to reading people out of his movement or claiming them for it, proclaiming them and disowning them according to their conformity or non-conformity with the theoretical positions he built up analogously to Marxist theorizing in his various Surrealist manifestos. Ideology may have masked personal feeling in many cases, as if to say, "If you hate me, you must be ideologically incorrect." The commonplace about Surrealism is that it is of two sorts, historical and popular.

Historical Surrealism usually refers to what was going on in Breton's circle from the mid-1920s until the late 1930s in Paris (or in Europe as a whole), usually involving the transformation of social, aesthetic, scientific, and philosophical values by means of the liberation of the subconscious. This led, of course, to a kind of art in which fantastic visions were depicted extremely literally. A concern with the subconscious was typical of the time, and the story is told of that great liberator of the subconscious, Sigmund Freud, that someone asked him about surrealist art. His reply? Normally, he said, in art he looked to see the unconscious meaning of a work, but in surrealistic art he looked to see if there was a conscious one. Well, to return to my main concerns, with the passage of time and of the entry of Surrealism into popular awareness, "surrealist" came to be more or less synonymous with "fantastic" or "dreamy" in art. Popular Surrealism, then, has little to do with historical Surrealism, although careless critics tend to equate the two. However, historical Surrealism has a far fuller history than our usual image of it. Breton lived on into the 1960s, and as long as he lived, "Surrealism" as a self-conscious, self-defined movement continued, with new people joining and old members being obliged to withdraw. During the years of World War II and immediately after, Breton and many of the surrealists lived in the United States, and their impact is not sufficiently understood either in Europe or America. They became the most interesting presence in the American art world. Magazines such as *VVV* and *View* were the most exciting art magazines of the time. The surrealists constituted the nucleus of the New York avant-garde. Some of us who later did Fluxus works were very conscious of this. I, for example, attended school with Breton's daughter Aubée ("Obie," to us) and, being curious what her father wrote, acquired a couple of his books. That was my *entrée* into Surrealism as a place to visit. Furthermore, from time to time there would be surrealist "manifestations," and some of these were similar to the "environments" out of which Happenings developed. These were, in any case, locked into our sensibility, as points of reference in considering our earlier art experiences, and for Americans at the time Surrealism was absolutely the prototypical art movement as such. We shall return to this, but I would like to consider a few points along the way.

1) Fluxus *seems* to be a series of separate and discrete formal experiments, with rather little to tie them together. In this way it seems to resemble Futurism. This is a point I will answer when presently addressing the actual ontology of Fluxus.

2) Fluxus *seems* to be like Dada, at least like the popular image of Dada, in being, well, crazy, iconoclastic, essentially a negative tendency rejecting all its precedents, and so on. In fact, there is some truth to this, but it is oblique. Fluxus was never as undirected as Dada, never as close to its historical precedents. Dada was, in fact, a point of discussion on those long nights at Ehlhalten-am-Taunus, during the first Fluxus Festival at Wiesbaden in 1962, when George Maciunas, myself, Alison Knowles, and, occasionally, others would talk into the wee hours of the morning, trying to determine what would be the theoretical nature of this tendency to which we were giving birth, which we found ourselves participating in. Maciunas was intensely aware of the rivalry between the French and German dadaists; we wanted to keep our group together and avoid such splits as best we could. What could we do to prevent this fissioning? The answer was to avoid having too tight an ideological line. Maciunas proposed a manifesto during the 1962 festival at Wiesbaden that is usually printed as "The Fluxus Manifesto." But only a few of us were willing to sign it. Some did not want to confine tomorrow's possibilities by what they thought today. Others did not like its tone. I myself felt it was a poor job since it was so unclear, and I urged Maciunas to rewrite it. That manifesto as it stands is perhaps Maciunas's own manifesto, not a full-fledged and programmatic manifesto of Fluxus. Interspersed with cut-up images from a dictionary definition of "flux," the manifesto says that one must "Purge the world of . . . bourgeois sickness, 'intellectual,' professional & commercialized culture . . . of Europanism [sic] . . . PROMOTE A REVOLUTIONARY FLOOD AND TIDE IN ART . . . promote NON ART REALITY." It says little about how one is to do this; it is too general. It says nothing about *why* one should do this. It says nothing about who will carry it out, nor does Maciunas say what "non art reality" is or should be. At the time when Maciunas put together this manifesto, I hoped it would be rewritten in a more persuasive and less strident way with more concrete points. Today I believe it would have been a mistake to do anything of the kind, since the

group would have split apart, just as the dadaists did, if our program seemed too confining.

3) Surrealism lasted more or less forty years as a viable tendency and, among other things, spun off a popular version, as I have said, lower-case surrealism. This seemed like a fine model for the Fluxus people. But how could we make Surrealism a model for Fluxus?

Before we leave this matter of antecedents and basic definition, it would be well to mention some individual artists who are sometimes reckoned among the forefathers of Fluxus, and a few of those who are thought of as Fluxus but who are not.

When Ben Vautier speaks of Fluxus, he usually evokes the names of John Cage and Marcel Duchamp so repeatedly that one might well wonder if he had ever heard of any other artists at all (he has), nor is he the only person of whom this is true. In fact, an editor from a newspaper once became quite indignant at me for suggesting that Cage was not the actual founder of Fluxus (and Happenings as well).

The fact is, both Cage and Duchamp *are* much admired by the Fluxartists. Duchamp is admired largely for the interpenetration in his work of art and life, the "art/life dichotomy," as we used to call it in the early 1960s. In 1919, as is well known, Duchamp exhibited a men's urinal as an art work, a simple, white, and pristine object, classical in form, when one separates it from its traditional function. Since many Fluxus pieces, most notably the performance ones, are often characterized by their taking of a very ordinary event from daily life, and by then framing these as art by presenting them on a stage in a performance situation, there is a clear connection between such Fluxus pieces and Duchamp's urinal.

For example, one often-performed Fluxus piece is Mieko (formerly "Chieko") Shiomi's "Music for Face," in which the performers come on stage and smile, gradually relaxing their faces until the smile disappears.[4] This is something that happens often in daily life, and it is somehow refreshing to think of an art performance that is both daily, uninsulated from one's diurnal, non-art existence, unlike most art works. Nevertheless, apart from a couple of musical experiments, Duchamp never did a performance work, nor did he have any great interest in them. At Allan Kaprow's seminal *18 Happenings in 6 Parts*, the first Happening presented in New York (in which I performed, and which has some oblique relationship with Fluxus), Duchamp was in the audience and I watched him; he seemed quite uninterested in what he was seeing, and I do not recall that he even stayed through the entire performance. It seems doubtful that he saw any particular connection between the performance he was watching and his own work. Nor, later, when he knew some of us and our work, did he see such a connection then, either. It seemed to be his effort to make life visually elegant, while we, on the other hand, chose to leave life alone, to observe it as a biological phenomenon, to watch it come and recede again, and to comment on it and enrich it in or with our

[4] Another Fluxus tradition is making pieces which answer other pieces. For instance, I have a piece in my "Metadramas" cycle of the 1980s in which one "looks for the vanishing smile." This refers to Shiomi's much earlier piece, but one need not know this to enjoy it.

works. We focused on different aspects of his work from those that had concerned him. When one sees a Duchamp work, one knows whether it is sculpture or painting or whatever; with a Fluxus work, there is a conceptual fusion; "intermedia" is the term I chose for such fusions, picking it up from Samuel Taylor Coleridge, who had used it in 1812.[5] Virtually all Fluxus works are intermedial by their very nature: visual poetry, poetic visions, action music and musical actions, Happenings and events that are bounded, conceptually, by music, literature, and visual art, and whose heart lies in the midground among these. Duchamp was an extreme purist; we were not, are not. He, therefore, makes an awkward ancestor for us, much as we may admire his integrity and his *geste*.

[5] This subject is discussed in greater detail elsewhere and in two others of my books, *Horizons* (1983) and *A Dialectic of Centuries* (1979).

Cage was rather a different matter. Some of us (myself, Brecht, Maxfield, Hansen, and others) studied with Cage. But in his case, like Duchamp, he strove towards "nobility." This, for him, meant the impersonal or the transpersonal, often obtained by means of systems employing chance, in order to transcend his own taste. For us the greatest contribution he made was in his way of noticing a piece in external reality, rather—dragging it out of himself as most artists had done.[6] Mac Low, Brecht, Maxfield, and myself used chance systems, "aleatoric structures," but few other Fluxus artists did, at least with any frequency. As for Cage, he seemed to find Fluxus works simplistic, at least when he first saw them. They did (and do) often employ some extreme minimalism that was not one of his concerns. Too, Fluxus pieces can be quite personal, and this would place them beyond Cage's pale. For most of his life his own work was seldom intermedial. Though he wrote poems and composed music, one tended to know and be conscious of which was which. Of course, Cage's work changed throughout his life, and in later years he wrote a great deal of visual poetry. But at the time when Fluxus appeared this still lay in the future. Cage and Duchamp should, therefore, be thought of more as uncles of Fluxus rather than as direct progenitors or father figures. Fluxus, it seems, is a mongrel art, with no distinct parentage or pedigree. There is a relationship to Cage and to Duchamp, but it is mostly by affinity and the example of integrity, rather than that Fluxus developed out of their work in any specific way.

[6] He perceived his pieces rather than conceived them, as I have put it elsewhere.

To summarize the discussion so far, the better one knows the Fluxworks, the less they resemble Futurism, Dadaism, Surrealism, Duchamp, or Cage.

iii. Is there a Fluxus Program (or Was There)?

Is there a Fluxus program?

I have already argued that Fluxus is not a movement, and this is, I feel, the case. Maciunas called it a "tendency," as we shall see. Nonetheless, if Fluxus is to be a useful category for considering work, it must have more of a meaning than simply as the name of Maciunas's proposed publications or the artists associated with it. That is to say, there must be certain points in common among the works in a body of works; they must hang together by more than mere *Zeitgeist*. This means that the works will have some aspects of a movement, though not all of them.

Usually a movement in the arts begins with a group of artists coming together with some common feeling that something needs doing, that, as I put it awhile ago, the arts have to be moved from point A to point B. A kind of imagery has been neglected and needs to be introduced: Pop Art. Art has become too cold, and it must be warmed up with an appeal to the transrational: Romanticism. In other words, there is a program, whether or not that program is ever actually written out in a prescriptive manifesto, describing what is to be done and by whom and how, or whether or not the discovery is made by a critic that certain artists have something in common and constitute a group of some sort. Naturally, the world is full of pseudo-movements—works with something or other in common, which some ambitious critic then claims as a movement or tendency in the hopes of earning professional credit—"Brownie points," one might say—for having "discovered" the movement. But if these points are too artificial, if there is no natural grouping that enforces the feeling that these works belong together, it will soon be forgotten as a grouping.

But with a real movement, the life of the movement continues to take place until the program has been achieved; at that point the movement dies a natural death, and the artists, if they are still active, go on to do something else. Fluxus had (or perhaps has) no concrete prescriptive program. Maciunas's "Fluxus Manifesto" is, as noted, very general and intellectual (for all its strident anti-intellectualism). Few Fluxworks were intended to destroy or even change the world of cultural artifacts that surrounded them, though they might affect how these were to be seen.

Nevertheless, there are some points in common among most Fluxworks:
1) internationalism,
2) experimentalism and iconoclasm,
3) intermedia,
4) minimalism or concentration,
5) an attempted resolution of the art/life dichotomy,
6) implicativeness,
7) play or gags,
8) ephemerality,
9) specificity,
10) presence in time, and
11) musicality.

These eleven points (really, they are almost criteria) can be taken up one by one.[7]

Fluxus arose more or less spontaneously in various countries. In Europe there were, in the beginning (others joined shortly afterwards), Wolf Vostell, Nam

June Paik, Emmett Williams, and Ben Patterson, among others. In the United States there were, besides myself, Alison Knowles, George Brecht, Robert Watts, and the others I have already named, also La Monte Young, Philip Corner, Ay-O, and still others. In Japan there were Takehisa Kosugi, Mieko Shiomi, and more. Probably there were about two dozen of us in six countries, with little besides our intentions in common (for one thing, not all of us had studied with Cage). Thus, Fluxus was not, for example, the creature of the New York art scene, the West German art scene, the Parisian one, or anything else of that sort. It was, from its outset, *international*. At one point Maciunas tried, in structuring his proposed Fluxus collections, to renationalize them, but it simply did not work. One might also note here that Fluxus, aiming to be inclusive, consciously sought to include people from backgrounds as diverse as possible, notably women and blacks. In the latter it was less successful, including only Ben Patterson and the elusive Stanley "This Way" Bro[u]wn. But there were a number of women: Alison Knowles, Mieko Shiomi, Shigeko Kubota, Yoko Ono, Carla Liss, and (later) Alice Hutchins. In this respect, Fluxus was like Berlin and Zürich Dada but unlike Futurism, French Dada, or Surrealism.[8]

It was a coming together of *experimental* artists, that is, or artists who were not interested in doing what all the other artists were doing at the time; they mostly took an iconoclastic attitude towards the conventions of the art establishments of their various countries, and many have since paid the price of doing so, which is obscurity and poverty. No matter: they have their integrity intact. This experimentalism took the form, in all cases, however, of formal experimentalism rather than of content as such. There was the assumption that new content requires new forms, that new forms enable works to have new content and to lead to new experiences.

In many cases this experimentalism led the artists into *intermedia*, to visual poetry, some varieties of Happenings, sound poetry, and so on. At the time, we called these "hybrid artforms," but that term disappeared in favor of "intermedia."

In order to state such forms in a very *concentrated* way, a great measure of purification and distillation was necessary, so that the nature of the form would be clear. One could not have too many extraneous or diverse elements in a work. This led, inevitably, to a stress on brevity, since, by keeping a work short or small, there would be less time for extraneous elements to enter in and to interfere. This brevity constituted a specific sort of *mini-realism*, with as much concentration in a work as possible. As noted, La Monte Young wrote a musical piece that could last forever, using just two pitches. Wolf Vostell composed a Fluxus opera using just three words from the Bible for his libretto. George Brecht wrote many Fluxus events in his *Water Yam* series, using just a very few words, three in one event, twenty in another, two in a third, and so on.

[7] In 1990, Ken Friedman expanded on my original nine criteria which were in the early versions of this essay, adding the last two which are specifically relevant to performance pieces. His articles were published as "The Twelve Criteria of Fluxus" in Friedman's catalogue essay "Fluxus and Company" for Emily Harvey Gallery and in *Lund Art Press* (vol. 1, no. 4). I am indebted to him on this point and others.

[8] Though Surrealism included a huge number of participants, the only women who come to mind are Leonora Carrington and Meret Oppenheim.

Working so close to the minimum possible made the Fluxus artists intensely conscious of the possibility that what they did would not be art at all in any acceptable sense. Yet, there was also the sense that most art work was unsatisfying anyway, that life was far more interesting. Thus, a great deal of attention was given to the resolutions of the *art/life* dichotomy, which has already been mentioned.

A sense existed that working with these materials implied an avoidance of the personal expression so characteristic of the arts in the period just before Fluxus began, in the early and middle 1950s. But the personal, as a mode, was by no means rejected out of hand in Fluxus if it could be presented in a way that was not overly subjective, which would be limited in relevance. Thus, Alison Knowles performed with her infant daughter, for example.

There was also the danger that working with such minimal material would lead to facile meanderings, to Fluxartists grinding out endless mountains of minimalist pieces that had no real *raison d'être*. Thus, a very important criterion for avoiding this danger came to be the notion that a Fluxpiece, whether an object or a performance, should be as implicative as possible, that it should imply a maximum of intellectual, sensuous, or emotional content within its minimum of material.

In the period just before Fluxus began, the dominant style in visual art had been abstract expressionism and in music post-Webernite serialism. Both of these were apt to be extremely solemn and tendentious affairs indeed, and, in fact, seriousness tended to be equated with solemnity. Fluxus tended often to react against this by moving in the direction of humor and gags, introducing a much-needed *spirit of play* into the arts. This also fitted well with the iconoclastic side of Fluxus.

"Play" covers, of course, a good deal of territory. One plays for fun, but there is also the play of a cat with a mouse, of water in a fountain, the play of championship sports or bridge. All have their place in Fluxus, especially the humor. The private lives of the Fluxpeople were frustrating; most were poor, and spirits had to be kept up. Maciunas especially was oriented towards comedy and even farce. Further, it was startling and even shocking to many viewers that grown people would *play* their art. There was often, then, something defiant about the playful Fluxpieces, a lost quality now that Fluxus is better known and is even presented as mostly fun and games. This is, of course, a misprision and an unseemly one at that. The other sorts of games are also part of the picture, and the high seriousness of Fluxus cannot be understood without recognizing this.

There was also the sense that, if Fluxus were to incorporate some element of ongoing change, which is what "flux" implies, then the individual works should themselves change. Many of the Fluxus objects, therefore, were made of rather *ephemeral* materials, such as paper or light plastic, so that as time went by the work would either disappear or would physically alter itself. A masterpiece in this context was a work that made a strong statement rather than a work that would last throughout the ages in some treasure vault. Also, most of the Fluxartists were (and are) very poor, and so they could not afford to work with fine and costly materials. Many of Robert Filliou's works eventually disappeared into the air, for example, though other Fluxworks are, in fact, made of standard materials and will perhaps last (for example, works by Vostell or myself).

Maciunas's background, as I already mentioned, was in graphic and industrial design. The design approach is usually to design *specific* solutions to specific problems. Designers characteristically distrust universals and vague generalities. Generalizations are used in Fluxus works only when they are handled with all the precision of specific categories and necessities. They must not be vague. This was Maciunas's approach, and it remains typical for us now that he is gone.

Presence in time is an inadequate way of describing the quality that the longer Fluxperformance works have of incorporating time as a sort of equivalent of a large canvas with the events revealing themselves gradually. This presence in time becomes, in effect, the form of the piece in such works as La Monte Young's "Composition 1960 #7" (already noted) in which a B and an F-sharp are "to be held for a long time," hours or days or longer. The sound becomes not just an environment but a frame of reference for whatever is around it. Also, some patterns (or horizons of experience) simply cannot be absorbed in a minimalist statement. They require time to reveal themselves effectively. The pieces are, necessarily, harder to understand for an audience; the past experience of the members of the audience usually has led them to expect more entertainment values than they are likely to get. One hears it said, "I liked the little pieces, but the big ones went on too long." What one hopes is that the boredom, if any, will be temporary, while the receiver tries, hopefully, to fit his or her horizon to that of the piece. Boredom is, of course, not the aim of the piece, but it may be a necessary stage on the path to liking it. Therefore, with such pieces the characteristic length is apt to have to be sufficiently long to allow the receiver to get through the boring phase and into the spirit of the event afterwards. This is why Fluxus pieces are apt either to be very short (two minutes perhaps) or very long (twenty minutes or more).

Musicality here describes the quality of many Fluxperformance works of behaving like lyrical music rather than the theater or vaudeville. They are without climax or dramatic structure and are, in one way or another, sensuous or intellectual investigations of the nature of reality. In ancient times, in Boethius's *De Musica*, for instance, the term for this kind of piece is *musica speculativa*.[9] In a sense John Cage revived the concept in composing pieces that reflected the reality around them, and many Fluxpieces, such as my "Constellations" series, took off from this point. Audiences and participants alike seem to sense this and, for this reason, evenings of Fluxus performances seem better described as Fluxconcerts than as Fluxtheater.

[9] A "speculum" is a mirror. Two other ancient classifications are *musica mundana* ("music of the worlds"), which we call by the medieval term "music of the spheres," and *musica humana* ("human music"), which describes the normative "playable" music, whether art music or popular music.

Clearly not every work is likely to reflect all eleven of these characteristics or formal points, but the more of them a work reflects, the more typically and characteristically Fluxus it is. So, supposing one sees a work and wants to decide if it is Fluxus or not (whether or not it happens to be by a Fluxartist is not the issue here), all one need do is match it against the eleven formal points. The more it matches, the more Fluxus it is, logically enough. Perhaps there are other such formal points, but these eleven are sufficient.

Similarly, not every work by a Fluxartist is best described as a Fluxwork; typically Fluxartists do other sorts of work as well, just as a collagist might also print, or a composer of piano music might try his hand at writing something for an orchestra. In this way, also, Fluxus differs from music. *All* the work of a surrealist was expected to be surrealistic. An abstract expressionist would be unlikely to produce a hard-edged geometrical abstraction. But Vostell would do such a performance piece as "Kleenex" (1962), which he performed at many of the early festivals, while at the same time he was also making his "dé-coll/age" paintings and Happenings, having nothing to do with his Fluxus work except for their frequently intermedial nature. Maciunas used to like to call Fluxus not a movement but a *tendency*; the term is apt here, when one is relating a kind of work to its historical matrix.

Returning to intermedia, not all intermedial works are Fluxus, of course. For instance, the large-scale Happenings of Kaprow and Vostell are not Fluxworks in that their centers of gravity lie in areas outside those of Fluxus.[10] Nor are most sound or concrete poems. These usually have their intermedial nature in common with Fluxworks, but Fluxus was certainly not the beginning of intermedia. For instance, the concrete poetry intermedium of the 1950s and 1960s was an immediate predecessor of Fluxus. The visual impulse in poetry is usually present, even if only subtly. After all, one customarily experiences it first with one's eyes. Nevertheless, visual poems (that is, poems so visually oriented that they are both visual *and* literary art) have been made at least since the second millennium before Christ, and they are found in most literary languages, European and non-European.[11] These pieces existed well before 1912 when Apollinaire made his *calligrammes* and so focused the eyes of the Western poetry world on the potentials of this intermedium. But, with concentration enough and with the other formal points I have mentioned, a visual poem could indeed be a Fluxwork.

Many intermedial performance works existed before Fluxus. For example, in his anthology, *Technicians of the Sacred*, Jerome Rothenberg presented an enormous number of rituals and "performance poems" from the so-called primitive people which, when taken out of their usually sacred context, are so close to Fluxus pieces as to be nearly indistinguishable from them. Even had there been no immediate precedent of futurist performance pieces, no Dada or Surrealism, Fluxus might still have developed out of the materials of folklore. This point was

[10] Maciunas, unlike the rest of us, had a stormy relationship with Kaprow, many of whose works of the late sixties seem appropriate to Fluxus and distant from his earlier Happenings. As for Vostell, with whom Maciunas's relationship was also stormy, some of his Happenings, such works as the *T.O.T.* (1973), seem like collections of small and concise Fluxus events.

[11] My *Pattern Poetry: Guide to an Unknown Literature* (1987) documents some 1800 visual poems from before 1900 C.E. in Greek, Latin, Hebrew, Hungarian, Italian, French, German, Scandinavian, Dutch and Flemish, British and English-language, Spanish, Portuguese, Catalan, Polish, Russian, Ukrainian, Croatian, Chinese, Japanese, Sanskrit and the Prakrits, Gujarati, Hindi, Marathi, Tamil, Burmese, Persian, Turkish, Arabic, and Ancient Egyptian literatures. No doubt there are more. Nor are these works necessarily by obscure poets, as is sometimes charged, but that is another story.

not lost on Rothenberg, who included several examples of Fluxus performance pieces in his book.

Also, in the nineteenth century there was a tradition of parlor games that are sometimes very close to Fluxus. My Something Else Press, already mentioned as a publishing project that was in various ways a Fluxus enterprise, published a collection of such games by one William Brisbane Dick, *Dick's One Hundred Amusements*.[12] Fluxus might well have developed out of this popular-culture tradition as well. In fact, a few of the pieces from both the Rothenberg and Dick collections have been included in Fluxperformances with no noticeable incongruity.[13]

There are two other points worth mentioning in this part of the discussion. These are more in the way of Flux-traditions. Usually Fluxus performances have been done in costume. Either one wears all white, or one wears a tail suit, tuxedo, or formal evening dress. The former reflects the desire for visual homogeneity, which Maciunas, as a designer, tended to prize. The latter reflects his fondness for the deliberately archaic, formal, and obsolescent being presented in a new way. One sees a similar current in his use in his publications of extremely ornamental type faces, such as Romantique, for the headings, box covers, or titles.[14] These contrast with the very austere type he used in most of his setting of the body texts in Fluxus publications, IBM News Gothic, this last the version of the sans serif News Gothic on the IBM typesetter he used most of the time in the early days of Fluxus. There is no reason in particular why either of these traditions should be preserved; they are not integral to Fluxus. Perhaps this is one of the few areas in Fluxus in which there is room for sentimentality; both traditions have been carried on in Maciunas's absence.

Another tradition of Fluxus that is not a criterion as such is the emphasis on events that center around food. Many art works and groups of artists have dealt with food, but in Fluxus it becomes one of the main areas of involvement, perhaps because of its closeness to the art/life dichotomy. There were not only pieces themselves using apples, glasses of water on pianos, beans, salads, messes made of butter and eggs, eggs alone, loaves of bread, and jars of jam or honey, to name just a few that come immediately to mind, but also there were innumerable Fluxfeasts of various sorts, concerts or events that used the feast as matrix. No doubt these will continue as long as many of the original Fluxpeople are alive. One might speculate that the reason for this is the typical concern with food on the part of poor or hungry artists. But that seems secondary to the art/life element, and for me the fact that for works that are so much on the border of art and life, art and non-art, as Flux-pieces, the convention of a concert is not always suitable. For casual occasions with small audiences, feasts using food art are the equivalent of chamber music concerts. Feasts have included such non-delicacies as totally flavorless gelatin "Jell-O,"

[12] Please note that it is the author's surname that is referred to in the book's title, not my first name.

[13] The Swedish Fluxus artist Bengt af Klintberg is a professional folklorist. Many of his works have a direct relationship to folklore.

[14] In a later essay ["Two Sides of a Coin: Fluxus and the Something Else Press"], Maciunas's design style is discussed more fully.

side by side with delicious loaves of bread in the form of genitals, chocolate bars cast in equally startling shapes, blue soups, and so on. Whether or not such foods are totally satisfying from an esthetic point of view is not the question. The point is, rather, that there are non-determinative but nevertheless typical involvements in Fluxus side by side with the characteristic formal points.

iv. Evaluating Fluxpieces

But what of quality? How do we judge these works? Clearly, with Fluxus the normal theoretical positions will not apply. Fluxus works are simply not *intended* to do the same things as a Sophoclean tragedy, a Chopin mazurka, or a Jackson Pollock painting, and it is absolutely pointless to make the effort to fit Fluxus into a system to do this. Fluxus may have its thrills, but it is qualitatively different from most other art at least with respect to its teleology, its purposes, its ends.

First of all, what is it *not*?

1) It is not mimetic. It does not imitate nature in any narrative way, though it may be "natural" in the sense of "imitating nature in its *manner* of operation" (Coomaraswami's phrase)—its craziness, the kinds of patterns that it evokes, and that sort of thing. This is only to say that Fluxus could, in its own way, be realistic, very much so. There could be a genre of the Fluxus story, but it would have to be extremely generalized, stripped down to a bare minimum. A kiss—that might be a Fluxstory. But we don't usually think of that as mimesis.

2) Neither does it fit into the normative Romantic/Classic or Apollonian/Dionysian dichotomies. Perhaps it has something in common with the work of Novalis and the Schlegel brothers in German Romanticism, but it does not attempt what either romantic or classical art attempts, a world transformed by the imagination or by feeling; it is not visionary; quite the opposite, in fact. In terms of its assumed effects, it does not attempt to move the listener or viewer or reader emotionally or in any other way. Neither does it attempt to express the artist emotionally or intellectually. Thus, one would not call it expressive in the normal meaning of the term. The Fluxartist does not even *begin* to reveal himself or herself through the work. Perhaps the viewer or listener is to reveal himself or herself by experiencing it, at least to himself or herself, but that is a different matter, and we shall return to it later. The important thing here is that the artist is as far away from the assumed eye or ear of the viewer or listener as is possible in an art work. Any expression is objectivized and de-personalized to the point of becoming transpersonal. One does not, as in experiencing so many works of art, see through the work to the artist. There may be an individual style (most Fluxartists have those), but that, too, is a different matter, more akin to having one's own idiolect than to presenting a subjective vision of something.

3) Neither are Fluxworks, in the main, pragmatic. That is, they teach nothing except, perhaps, by example. They do not convey moral principles, nor do they

present "correct" political or social views. They may be political, but this is apt to be in a symbolic way. For example, all the elements of a performance behave democratically; none dominates the others. But this is more apt to be the sort of thing that the artist thinks about than anything a viewer is concerned with.

4) Nor could they be called "objective" in the T. S. Eliot sense. They are not simply objects to contemplate; they are too minimal for that and, often, too active as well. They imply too much. Actually, some few Fluxworks do belong in this vein, but atypically.

5) Neither is the Freudian or symbolic analysis of a Fluxpiece apt to be very rewarding or extensive. One does not have enough materials to work on. Ninety-eight percent of Fluxus pieces have no symbolic content. Their psychological processes are too far and few between. Since the artist is not making a statement of any personal, psychological nature, an analysis of this sort would make very little sense.

6) A political analysis, Marxian or otherwise, might be interesting, but it would more likely satisfy the critic than the reader of the criticism, since Fluxus is only metaphorically political.

7) Since meaning is not the point and the conveyors of the meaning are so incidental that rather few patterns can be detected, the semiotics of a Fluxpiece are minimal enough to be problematic or even irrelevant. Of course, there *are* some such conveyors, but these require only the simplest of identifications. No patterns of communication would be likely.

8) The same holds true of structuralist analysis. The linguistics of Fluxus would be a mentalistic exercise, not that Fluxus lacks its overall grammar, but the typical is only sixty percent of the corpus, with the rest being exceptions of one kind or another. The whole analysis, rather than developing a meaningful critique or picture, would devolve into hairsplitting distinctions of *langue* and *parole*. Few patterns would be revealed. One might analyze a concert as a whole, but the concert *as a work* is a fairly arbitrary unit, and each concert tends to be quite different from each other concert (within certain limits), so that a structuralist analysis of recurring patterns would be rather pointless.

Yet, a person who attends a Fluxconcert, after the first shock, typically gets caught up in the spirit of it and begins to enjoy it, without consciously knowing why. Perhaps, there isn't even any shock. What is happening? To get to the answer to this will take a moment.

There is one critical approach that usually works, hermeneutics, the methodology of interpretation, both with regard to the artist and the recipient (the viewer, hearer, or reader). This approach, pioneered in recent times (it has an earlier history, too) by Heidegger, Betti, Gadamer, Jauss, and others in philosophy, can be used to theorize the workings of Fluxpieces fairly well. Usually the relationship between the recipient and the work is described in terms of a hermeneutic-circle idea of a work, leading to manifestation of work, leading to recipient, leading to recipient's own thought processes, leading to new idea of work, leading to further thought processes, leading to modified perception of work being manifested, leading back to altered perception of the idea of work. In other words, what the recipient sees is colored by his or her perception of it. This is an implied part of the piece, even though it may be quite different from what the artist thought of it or as the performer manifested it.

In practice, going through the whole hermeneutic circle is a terribly cumbersome process to consider. My own preference is to streamline it by borrowing the horizon metaphor from Gadamer. Let's take performance as the standard, for the moment. The performer performs the work. He or she establishes a horizon of experience; what is done, its implications, and whatever style the performer uses are all aspects of this horizon.

The viewer has his or her own horizon of experience. He or she watches the performance, and the horizons are matched up together. To some extent there is a fusion of these horizons (*Horizontsverschmelzung*). When the horizons fuse, wholly or in part, they are bent, warped, displaced, altered. The performance ends, and the horizons are no longer actively fused. The viewer examines his or her horizon. It is changed, for the worse or for the better. The best piece is the one that permanently affects the recipient's horizon, and the worst is the piece that the recipient, acting in good faith, cannot accept at all.

The key processes here are being conscious of the two horizons, completing the fusion process (by paying close attention to the performance), and then the discovery of the alterations in one's own horizon, as one notices that, for example, the performance has affected how one has been thinking about beans, butter, smiles, or eggs. Such criticism focuses a great deal, of course, on the viewer. In performance work it more or less ignores the original Fluxcomposer, who may or may not be the same as the performer.

But this is only true as far as the viewer is concerned because there is a similar fusion of horizons taking place between the composer and the performer. The composer makes the piece. The performer looks at the performance area and available materials, and only then decides just how to do the piece under the specific conditions of the performance. The performer next matches the horizon he or she has built up with the horizon of the original piece as he or she sees it. Even if the performer is performing his own work, there will still be something of such a fusion of horizons between X-as-composer and X-as-performer, because X adapts his or her own piece, takes the responsibility to make slight changes. If a piece is performed many years after it was written, perhaps X has changed it, and the interaction with the piece suggests different significances. The piece is viewed from many different angles, with different aspects revealed by each.

Now we can see why the viewer can enjoy the concert without knowing why, instinctively, he or she is matching horizons, comparing expectations, participating in the process; the more actively he or she does so, the more likely he or she will be able to enjoy the experience.

Nonetheless, for the viewer of Shiomi's "Music for Face," already mentioned, the composer is more or less an object of speculation. One wonders who might this

"Mieko Shiomi" be. It is surely a Japanese name, but more one cannot tell. All one sees is the work being done. One does not really have any way of knowing if the performance is staying close to the Fluxcomposer's work or if the performer is taking liberties with it. What the recipient sees is the performance, no more, no less. But in the case of works as minimalist as Fluxus ones are apt to be, the more actively the performance is observed, the more likely one is to enjoy it, as noted above.

A question may well occur at this point, a natural question in viewing any unfamiliar art work: "Of what is this thing that I am seeing an example?" That is part of discovering one's meaning for a work. We love to classify. We involve ourselves in the naming of things, frame the work in its context, investigate its taxonomy. Of course, while I am talking about performance work, *any* Fluxwork—literary or fine art—would have analogical processes. But if one goes to a concert of familiar music, this question is minimized, because one knows, before one sets a foot in the door, that if Chopin is on the program, the concert is likely to include at least some Romantic music with a certain kind of sound to it. Thus, the taxonomy is not so important here. On the other hand, if one turns on a radio and finds oneself enjoying some unknown piece, part of the key to enjoying the piece is recognizing the question "Of what is this an example?" One tries to figure out what it is to match it with similar experiences in one's memory bank and so enjoy the work even more.

The fusion of horizons takes place in any hermeneutic art process. It is inherent in the discovery of the horizons. But in watching a Fluxperformance, examples are all the more important since they involve discovering the pattern of the performance, the what-is-being-done. Quite often this discovery, detecting the example aspect of the horizon, comes to the viewer with a striking impact; it is like "getting" the point of a joke. In fact, the similarity between even non-humorous Fluxpieces and jokes is striking.

Even when the piece is serious, one tends to react as if the piece were a joke, since a joke is the nearest thing on one's horizon to many Fluxpieces. For example, one is in an audience watching the stage. A balloon appears. A second balloon comes along. A third balloon comes along. One notices that the name of the piece is "Eight." Suddenly the pattern is clear. One laughs. Why? There is nothing inherently funny in the pattern, but it has enough in common with jokes so that each balloon, as it appears and confirms one's anticipation that there will in fact be eight balloons, feels like a stage along the way. Perhaps the metaphor of "joke" is implied by the piece. But what would happen if, in the piece, only seven balloons appeared? One would be annoyed, probably feel cheated. It would seem as if the Fluxcomposer were being overly clever. That would not be interesting. It would be like a tricky joke that dissolves into excesses of cleverness and amuses only the teller.

Some assemblages of Fluxpieces have been presented as other things besides concerts and feasts: rituals have a certain place in Fluxus, too. A ritual is, basically, a ceremonial act or series of such acts, symbolically recognizing a transition from one life stage or situation to another. Three notable Fluxrituals have been a Fluxmass, a Fluxdivorce, and the Fluxwedding of George Maciunas himself. In this last, Maciunas and his bride cross-dressed, as did the bridesmaids and best man (Alison Knowles). The wedding ceremony was based on a traditional Anglican one, but was altered with deliberate stumbling and falterings, the substitution of "Fluxus" for various of the critical words in prayers, and so on. Instead of anthems and special music, there were various special Fluxus pieces that were, in one way or another, suitable for a wedding. Afterwards there was an erotic feast, which included the special bread already mentioned above. According to classical theory one might expect such a reversal of the normative, with the solemn made light of and the religious made profane, to seem like a satire upon marriages in general. But no, the dominant feeling was one of joy. It was not a travesty but an incorporation of the horizon of Fluxus into that of marriage. The result was certainly serious: Maciunas and his bride Billie did, in fact, actually marry, though they also had a civil ceremony at another time. One felt that the participants were sharing the joy of the basic ritual with their Fluxfriends including one fifteen-year-old girl, a friend of one of my daughters, who came to the Fluxwedding without ever having seen a Fluxconcert or any other such event before. This young woman, whose horizons were thoroughly conventional, might have been expected to be shocked or offended or at least startled by the erotic feast. But as a whole the situation was so far from the normative that normative standards did not apply; she did not reject the fusion of horizons but entered into the situation and enjoyed herself as thoroughly as one might at any other kind of wedding.

Ultimately, of course, the purpose of achieving such a fusion of horizons is to allow the possibility of their alteration. I have not gone into Fluxobjects, Fluxboxes, and Fluxbooks, but the situation is the same as with the performances; one sees the work, considers its implied horizons, matches them with one's own, and these last, if the piece works well, are altered and enriched.[15]

In one of the "pages" (works) in George Brecht's series "The Book of the Tumbler on Fire," one sees the words "notice green" in cork letters on a large wooden tablet. The tablet and words are painted red. There is a displacement: should the piece be green? One matches what one is seeing with what one might expect to see.[16] Should the piece have been green? The word says something different from what one would expect from the color. One thinks about labels, green and life, craft and its absence, simplicity and complexity. Perhaps one turns one's head away from the piece and looks at a white wall. After staring at red, one will see its complement, green. Perhaps one imagines a whole rainbow of "green" on tablets ranging from red through violet and brown, perhaps even including black and white. Any of such pieces would work reasonably well, though arguably the red-green juxtaposition is the most vivid. Still, had the piece been painted black or white, other meanings would appear from the color/non-color dichotomy. The horizons would

[15] This approach will work with many other works outside of Fluxus, of course, works which one's gut feeling tells one are "good" but which one finds hard to explain. It is through horizons that, for instance, I found myself enjoying such a Joseph Kosuth construct as his Wittgenstein show in Vienna; though not particularly a friend of Fluxus, Kosuth seems somehow very relevant to it.

[16] This is the Jaussian *Erwartungshorizont* ("horizon of expectations"), to which we will return later.

work, and the implications, while different, would follow somewhat along the same pattern: see, identify what it is, compare it with what it might be, consider, digest, anticipate the next possibility, observe the transformation of one's own horizons, and enjoy the process. Each of such pieces is an example of the possibilities. When one sees such a piece, one imagines its alternatives. The alternatives are implied in the piece. The work is, in this sense, exemplative: it does not exist, as most art does, in its most definitive and perfect form possible. It exists in a form that suggests alternatives. This is true of many recent works, not just Fluxworks. They encourage the creativity of the viewer, listener, or reader, that is, of the receiver.

Such implications are a key criterion for evaluating the quality of a Flux-work. If it has them, if one is conscious of them on the intuitive and imaginative level (rather than forcing them through an act of will), the work is good. That is, it is achieving its potential. The extent to which it lacks implications, conversely, is the extent to which it is not good, the extent that it fails. One can, for metaphysical reasons, reject such value judgements on the conscious level, of course, but one experiences them nonetheless and performs an act of criticism and, hopefully, of self-enrichment when one allows one's horizons to be changed.

The best Fluxworks imply a whole set of other possible Fluxworks; they are exemplary. In terms of performance style (or style of execution as Fluxart, Flux-boxes, and Fluxbooks), the best performances are, therefore, those that are most direct, so that one can perceive at least some of the alternative possibilities to the form in which a given work appears. This avoids what would be a problem in these works of becoming involved with noticing craftsmanship and the definitiveness of the statement they may contain. The best performance style for Fluxpieces is, thus, that which allows the piece to be experienced with a minimum of consciousness of the performer intervening between piece and receiver.

The same is also true of some kinds of non-Fluxus performances, of comedy, for instance. A comedian who intrudes on his joke by laughing, by expressing himself in a subjective way, by commenting "This is a great joke," by reducing the joke's effect by calling attention to himself, is likely to wind up as the only person laughing at his joke. In such cases the horizons of "joke" and "audience anticipation" fail to fuse. Buster Keaton, whom Maciunas claims in the lineage of Fluxus on his chart histories, always presents the humor in his films in an altogether deadpan way, while a twelfth-rate jokester in a hotel bar does much of the laughing and expressing himself—and bores the audience. So it is with Fluxus. The proper style for Fluxus is the most low-key and efficient one. One does not mystify the audience (that is not the point), but one lets it have exactly enough information to discover the horizon, and then one lets the piece do the rest. It is never necessary to joke about the Fluxpiece or to comment about it in an evaluative way—"Next we will have a great piece from 1963 by Ben Vautier . . ." That would constitute an intrusion, and, far from making the piece more likable, would detract from it.

What a pity it is that the public, including the professional public of organizers as well as performers, likes to lay emphasis upon the Fluxus artist him- or herself, and to encourage the production of what one might call "signature performances," those that derive their authority from their association with the originator of the work. Yet, I know I am not the best performer of my work, and most of us in any case can only present one perspective. We need more. It is always exciting to see what a new performer can contribute to an old piece. Of course, there is a certain numismatic thrill, not unlike collecting coins, in saying, "Oh, I saw Tschaikowsky on his last tour of America in 1898," or it might be Paderewski ca. 1938 or Nureyev or Julian Beck just a few years ago. Dear me, just what was it that he *did*?

Thereby hangs the problem: the personality and presence of the performer in such a signature performance tend to dominate the performance, to blind the spectator to what is being seen or heard or done, to break, putting it technically, the hermeneutic circle with an extraneous element that establishes new and perhaps irrelevant ones. Too, such performances are not good for the signer, since they convince him or her that *only* he or she can do the work. This would establish a silver umbilical cord to the work that may be nurturing but is not healthy after a certain point.

What is to be done? Of course, one must not avoid signature performances entirely or, for the Fluxartist, avoid doing them; it may be the only occasion when one will see some work one wants to see, or one can do whatever one wants to and not some (by now) familiar old work. But one must take the signature performance with a grain of salt, must note it as only one of the possibilities. That way the works will live as they should, and so will we, as artists, spectators, and thinkers. Pieces grow and change, just as people do, according to their changed contexts.

There is a slight difference between European Fluxus and American Fluxus. The Europeans have tended to perform their Fluxus works in the context of festivals, while the Americans have tended to let the life situations predominate more often. Almost all the Fluxperformances in Europe have been in such concert situations, except for a few in the street: in America both of these have happened, but the feasts and the Fluxrituals have virtually all happened in America. The reason for this is not a difference in attitude, but rather, the European Fluxartists are more scattered so it takes a well-financed festival to bring them together. On the other hand, in spite of the worse financial situation in America, there are more Fluxartists or Fluxpeople there, and they form one or several communities. For instance, in New York City alone there are perhaps thirty Fluxpeople in residence, so to bring them together is not hard.

Also, the European Fluxworks, more typically than the American ones, come out of an expressive tradition. Since, to build up an emotional impact, one usually needs to work on a scale that is beyond the minimal, the collation sort of work is more typically European, while the minimalist one is more typically American or Japanese. Besides, even if an American wanted to work on the larger scale, funding and obtaining rehearsal time would be problematic, so that the economics militate against doing such pieces in America in contrast to Europe.

To return to the question of judging the work, then, it is my opinion that the most appropriate method, one that viewers or experiencers of Fluxworks often do intuitively, is to match their own horizons with those implied by the work. If their own horizons are thereby made more vivid or are expanded, emotionally or intellectually or however else, then the work is doing its job. If not, the work has failed.

v. Horizons of Reception and Expectation

What about other aspects of reception—artists, public, and institutions?[17] The reception of Fluxus—its popularity, influence and, in general, its acceptance—varies considerably, according to who is seeing the work. The least problematic area is that of the general public. If even a relatively unsophisticated person attends a Fluxperformance or an exhibition of Fluxus works, such a person is apt to have an interesting and pleasurable experience. Even at the very beginning of Fluxus this was true. At Wiesbaden in 1962 the *Hausmeister* (janitor) of the museum was so delighted by the performances that he brought his family and friends to the concerts as well. Not a formally cultured man, he nevertheless was sufficiently enthusiastic about the concert to exert himself and bring those with whom he wanted to share it. Furthermore, some of the more successful Fluxus performances have been done in the street or on boardwalks and in other public spaces. One performance by Benjamin Patterson comes to mind. It took place in New York's Times Square, on the edge of a red-light district. He stood on street corners, waiting till the lights turned green, and then simply followed the light to the next corner. Several young women (they appeared to be prostitutes) watched him do this for a while, and then they joined in. This situation was not as exceptional as one might imagine. Thus, it cannot be argued that, simply because it is formally unconventional, Fluxus is lacking in potential popularity. Because of the comparative simplicity of most Fluxus pieces, this is less true of Fluxus than of other avant-garde tendencies.

For most avant-garde art, one needs to know quite a considerable amount of art history and even of technical procedure in order to get one's bearings enough to be able to fuse one's horizons and experience pleasure. The difficulty of doing this is apt to become more pronounced, in fact, with the progressive intellectualism of the audience, since it has more expectations of what will or should happen. An audience with the baggage of ideas to which it feels some commitment has more to overcome than an audience without them, and it must overcome the false horizons in order to be able to fuse them and experience pleasure. An audience with a strong commitment to one or another alternative set of ideas—intellectual or derived from precedent and fashion—has to learn that these ideas are not under attack in Fluxus situations, that they are simply irrelevant to the work at hand, and this takes time.

As I have said, Fluxus performances and situations are popular with the

[17] The most thorough account of the reception of Fluxus by the public and of different interpretations of what it is is Hannah Higgins's "Fluxelephant: A Reception History of Fluxus" (Ph.D. Dissertation, University of Chicago, Chicago, IL, 1994).

[18] In 1979, a Fluxconcert was presented by The Kitchen in New York. Originally scheduled for three evenings, the staff reduced it to one. Several hundred people were crowded in over house capacity, and over a thousand people were turned away. In Paris in 1989, for a Fluxus evening at l'Ecole des Beaux Arts, more than three thousand viewers were unable to fit into the hall. Special Fluxus issues of magazines have all done well, some going out of print within a few days of publication.

public once the public is confronted by them. Many, many times "professionals" in charge of the programs of institutions have grossly underestimated the appeal of Fluxpieces; they devote an evening to Fluxperformances when they might have devoted several, and then they are surprised at the frustration among those who have to be turned away. They program an exhibition, print 500 catalogues, then find that the exhibition breaks attendance records and that they must print another thousand or so catalogues. The public, therefore, is not the problem.[18]

As for artists, few who do performance works can attend a Fluxus performance without, subsequently, including Fluxus-type elements in their own next performance. Naturally, these are usually not acknowledged, but a sensitive viewer can detect them. For example, in the 1960s, the famous Living Theater picked up fragments of Fluxworks, especially from Jackson Mac Low and myself (we had both worked with the Living Theater at various points), and included them in their program, "Shorter Pieces."

An interesting instance of the absorption of Fluxus into a larger context happened during the 1970s, when "performance art" or "art performances" became common. Typically, performance art was different from Fluxus, in that it included much more narrative and subjectively personal content, usually focusing on generating a public persona for the artist. Works by Laurie Anderson are a good example of this, stressing the bright young ingenue in the high-tech world of New York City (not always justifiable, but usually fairly convincing in performance). The persona may be quite different from the private personality of the artist. However, the minimalist structure within which the performance takes place, the untraditional narrative matrix, the absence of most theatrical techniques, suggest a debt to Fluxus (and perhaps to Happenings). The performances of "performance artists" match many of the Fluxus formal points given above, and, but for their knowledge of Fluxus, it is unlikely that their work would assume the form it did. Since the artists who did this work were, for the most part, younger than the Fluxus people, they naturally did not wish to present themselves as traveling in the wake of Fluxus or Happenings. They describe themselves as qualitatively new and different, although there are at least three overlaps, artists who have done major Fluxwork but who are accepted as performance artists as well. These are Alison Knowles (one of the original Fluxpeople), Geoffrey Hendricks, and Jean Dupuy. This legacy area can and should be explored more fully at some point.

Fluxus has had a complex relationship with museums and galleries. Maciunas himself pretty much despised them as playthings of the rich and purveyors of corrupt views, presenting dead art as the only possibility. Many Fluxartists, however, have seen them as the best means of breaking beyond the charmed circle of *cognoscenti* into a larger, more real world, and whatever it would take, short of a complete misprision, to make this break seemed (and seems) desirable. In recent years there have been at least a dozen major museum exhibitions of Fluxus works, sometimes accompanied by performance evenings. These have expanded the public enormously, but at the same time they have led to the propagation of simplistic views, an over-stress on the fun-and-games side of Fluxus, best explained as a horizon of expectation: 1) Fluxus's main participant was Maciunas; 2) Maciunas's most unique contribution was his playful designs for the covers of the Fluxboxes, his games; 3) therefore such games are the heart of Fluxus.

The would-be curator or collector constructs a horizon of expectations built on that notion and is then confronted by works by most of the other Fluxus artists or works made since Maciunas's death in 1978 by almost any of the Fluxartists. These present a horizon of some other sort. Rather than abandoning his or her horizon, the curator or collector concludes that this other work is not really Fluxus.[19] This can be a real problem, since it leads to misprisions and a false image of what Fluxus includes. But how does one expand the horizon of how Fluxus is perceived? Does one call work done since 1978 "post-Fluxus?" Is it meaningful to speak of an artist today (1994) as a Fluxartist? Can one do so without downgrading Maciunas's importance to the group as a whole? For all his occasional deviousness, Maciunas remained loyal to his group; he would probably say to downgrade him and survive. But most of us are reluctant to survive by attacking him. Anyway, that is a problem more for the artist than for the larger public. Time will surely resolve the problem one way or another. It always does. Many Fluxartists have produced their best work since 1978. This simple fact is sure to be discovered sooner or later, whether the collector or curator wants to call it "Fluxus" or by some other name. When the horizon of expectations viewers have, whether looking at the objects or the performances made by the Fluxartists, no longer matches what we are told "Fluxus" covers, then a new name will appear. It is not something the Fluxartists can control, because theirs is the horizon of poesis, which is quite different. Their focus is on the nature of what they intend, and this is only partly what the viewer sees and experiences.

To reiterate what I have said, before closing off, Fluxus differs from most art in being more conceptual or formal, less craft-oriented. It is of course a group of people and a historic tendency, but one of its main contributions is to show that one can make works with the eleven typifying characteristics I already mentioned (internationalism, experimentalism and iconoclasm, intermedia, minimalism, an attempted resolution of the art/life dichotomy, implicativeness, the spirit of play, ephemerality, specificity, presence in time, and musicality).

The best ingress into the work, since it does not usually offer the same

[19] Many Fluxartists, including myself, have experienced this problem in their professional lives as well. The scenario goes like this: artist takes his or her work to good gallery. Gallery owner says artist is a Fluxus artist and they are not a Fluxus gallery: "Try so-and-so" (which has shown Fluxus). Artist goes to so-and-so. Work is shown. Collector comes along with his or her horizon of expectations built up into a fun-and-games focus. Collector says, of the new works, "This is not Fluxus." Thus, be it ever so fine a work, the work goes unsold. Artist is thus placed into a survival bind: "Should I conceal my Fluxus past (of which he or she is proud)? What should I do to downplay it?" Naturally, no new gallery wants to show the Fluxus artists, be they ever so famous, because they know almost all would-be Fluxus collectors have the old horizon of expectations. They also know there are very few surviving works from the early days of Fluxus which are not, by now, in museums or in collections which are likely to go there, certainly not enough to base a business on.

experience or have to match our normative expectation for art, is via hermeneutics, via the horizon concept. Historically, Fluxus had an influence on art performance but also on artists' books (bookworks), which I have not discussed. Its real impact, however, will probably be when new artists can take up the Fluxus format without being self-conscious about it, to make into their own whatever they themselves need from the area.

II

The Something Else Press

"In 1963, when Happenings were about five years old and Fluxus was about one year old, I had a loft on Canal Street in New York where I used to make up mimeo scripts of my work, usually wearing a loin cloth and playing 'The Ride of the Valkyries'."

Thus begins a fascinating video lecture by Dick Higgins, entitled "Something Else Press & Since" (Western Front Productions, 1981). Higgins's plan was to publish a series of "Variations on a Theme of Book" and to "publish source materials in a format which could encourage their distribution through traditional channels, however untraditional their contents or implications . . . to have a balance between European/American, famous, infamous and unfamous, past and present."

Something Else Press was founded by Dick Higgins in 1963, published its first book in 1964, and incorporated in the state of New York on March 4, 1965. After moves from New York to California to Vermont, Higgins withdrew editorial and financial support from the Press in mid-1973, and the Press declared bankruptcy in late 1974. Within the period of one decade, the Press issued approximately 116 books, pamphlets, newsletters, cards, catalogues, graphics, deluxe editions, posters, and flyers, described and pictured in the checklist that follows.

The checklist builds on *Something Else Press: An Annotated Bibliography* by Peter Frank (McPherson & Company, 1983). A distinct feature of the checklist is the descriptions of the publications in the words of Dick Higgins. In addition to the standard succinct ad copy, Higgins often wrote extensive prefaces, introductions, and jacket notes that provide an ongoing critical history of the press and represent an important—though overlooked and otherwise unpublished—aspect of his body of theoretical writing. Together with publication notes, mentions, and ads in the newsletters, catalogues, prospectuses, and other ephemera, a far-reaching body of information about the Press is accumulated here and provides clues for sorting out a range of bibliographical questions.

One fascinating detail of the checklist for me personally is the list of books at the end that were intended but never published. Some of these were formally announced and some were only an idea. Taken together they form a shadow list with their own near-publication history, sometimes bearing ISBN numbers, page and illustration count, price, date of publication, and occasionally, as in the case of *Abraham Lincoln Gillespie: The Collected Poems*, edited by Hugh Fox, Higgins's 550-word jacket copy essay presented here in full.

—SC

A Something Else Manifesto*

Originally published on the inside of the dust jacket of *Jefferson's Birthday/Postface* in 1964, then reprinted in Great Bear Pamphlet #8 Manifestos in 1966. The additional notes here were published with the Manifesto in *A Dialectic of Centuries: Notes Towards a Theory of the New Arts*, New York: Printed Editions, 1978.

W hen asked what one is doing, one can only explain it as "something else." Now one does something big, now one does something small, now another big thing, now another little thing. Always it is something else.

We can talk about a thing, but we cannot talk a thing. It is always something else.

One might well emphasize this. It happens, doesn't it? Actually, everybody might be in on this Something Else thing, whether he wants it or not. Everyman is.

For what is one confined in one's activity? Commitment on a personal level can be plural. One can be committed to both salads and fish, political action and photographic engineering, art and non-art. One does, we hope, what seems necessary, or, at least, not extraneous, not simply that to which one has committed oneself. One doesn't want to be like the little German who hated the little Menshevik because the little German always did his things in a roll format, and when the little Menshevik did that kind of thing too, the little German got into a tizzy. If one is consistent and inconsistent often enough nothing that one does is one's own, certainly not a form, which is only a part of speech in one's language. One must take special care not to influence oneself. Tomorrow one will write Schubert's *Fifth Symphony*, cook some kohlrabi, develop a non-toxic epoxy, and invent still another kind of theater; or perhaps one will just sit and scream; or perhaps . . .

When you touch a fact it is a fact. No idea is clear to us until a little soup has been spilled on it.

So when we are asked for bread, let's give not stones, not stale bread. Maybe we have no bread at all, anyway. But why not give a little chicken?

Let's chase down an art that clucks and fills our guts.

New York City, Summer, 1963

*The manifesto was used to define the editorial position of the Something Else Press—itself not just an avant-garde publishing house but, cumulatively, a critical statement.

When you influence yourself in order to match your self-image, what becomes of your freedom? Which is more crucial to your inner life?

What to Look for in a Book—Physically & Catalogue 1965–66

Originally published by Something Else Press, 1965.

What to Look for

in a Book

— Physically

&

Catalogue 1965-66

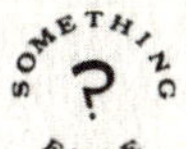

The Something Else Press, Inc.

New York   Paris   Cologne

What to Look for in a Book —Physically

The Problem

At the same time as the book publisher has available to him a greater variety of binding materials and type faces than ever before, the business of conventional design has led to an extreme deterioration in the quality of hardcover editions. First, when confronted with a manuscript, the designer is told what size the book can be, how long, and what the book is to sell for. This price is divided by 4½—standardly—and the result is the maximum cost which can be allotted to each copy in the physical production of the book. Some type faces need more room than others; naturally, larger sizes need more room too. So, if a given manuscript is to be a given length, it has to be set in either of three or four sizes or faces. This much is basic economics. On the other hand, the publisher assumes that the reader is interested only in large type, not in the durability or quality of his binding, and not in actual legibility. Therefore he binds his books badly and compensates a little for this by using large type sizes, although the lines are so close together that they are difficult to read.

However, a fallacy is involved here. This is that, if one is buying the hardcover edition of any book, one is anxious to have the text in a more permanent and more enjoyable form than if one buys the paperback edition of the same book. In a paperback, one looks above all else for economy. For most purposes this is sufficient. A paperback can go places that a hardcover edition can never get to, simply by its inexpensive and unpretentious format. On the other hand, paperbacks are not particularly useful to people who want to save their texts and come back to them again some day, let alone to libraries.

But in evaluating hardcover editions of books, very few people know what to look for. We are therefore going to outline a few points.

— 3 —

Paper and Page Design

A book is no better than the paper it is printed on. What is the use of the best binding in the world, if the paper dries up and flakes away in a few years? Evaluating good paper comes fairly easily. First: ignore the color. Good papers exist in any color—yellowish, blue-white, ivory, grey. That's the least problem. Second: feel the surface. A sort of fibrous feel often means low-grade paper, or it can be characteristic of paper which is made too bulky. Bulk in paper means thickness, and it is measured in the number of pages per inch. A book that is four hundred pages long should be about one inch thick, if it is printed on a good, normal-weight sheet. If you have a book which is about three hundred pages long, unless it *weighs* the same as the four hundred page book (which means it has sufficient fibers per cubic centimeter to justify its bulk), it is probably on an unusually bulky piece of paper and will not wear well. Third: squeeze such a book near the back of the binding. If it gives, if it seems spongy rather than crisp, the paper is probably too bulky and the book may come to pieces in time, in spite of the binding. Naturally, publishers like you to feel you are getting a nice, thick book for your money, but often the thinner book is the better one. Fourth: look to see how much you can see through the paper to the back of the next page. On a good piece of paper you should see almost nothing. Fifth: fold part of the page repeatedly. The ability to retain strength in spite of repeated folding is characteristic of good paper.

The page design is a subjective matter. On the right-hand page, a designer often draws a line from upper left to lower right and builds his print along this line. This is good. But if he builds his page from a point to the left of this line, it can become hard to read. If he builds it from a point to the right, facing pages tend to look a little as if they were floating out from the spine of the book, but they are easier and less distracting to read.

— 4 —

Paper and Page Design

In a hard-bound book this is desirable, since the words do not seem crowded into the spine. In a paper-bound book the binding opens flatter and so there is less of a problem. This inside margin, called the "gutter", is a main factor in legibility (which in this case does not coincide aesthetically with the visual unity of facing pages).

Binding Design

The first and most important thing in a binding is the quality of the cloth. This is where the strength of a book binding comes from. If a hardcover book is bound all in paper, one might as well buy the paperback edition, if there is one available. It simply will not last, period. On the other hand, the most crucial place to have cloth rather than paper is over the hinges, since this is where most wear-and-tear occurs. Some books have reasonably good cloth on the spines and hinges, but have paper sides. This can be very decorative, but the bindings will tend to become dirty with time, and the dirt will show more than with cloth. Also, if the book is removed from a shelf and replaced with any frequency, the paper will tend to pull off. If one is really looking for quality, one should not buy a hardcover book which has any paper at all on the outside of the binding, when there is a paperback edition available. An exception would be if the paper were just for design and were protected by a permanent jacket in heavy acetate or similar solid material. Further, even in a book which is bound all in cloth, the quality of the cloth is a big factor. The weakest cloths are hardly stronger than paper. The

— 5 —

Binding Design

heaviest and most solid cloths cost so little more per copy—perhaps nine cents manufacturing cost on a normal size book with 10,000 copies—that it is only to be attributed to public lack of knowledge that these are not used more widely. Here are ways of evaluating cloth: taste it. If it is sticky or sweet, it is overly stiffened with starch and lacks rigidity. Buy the paper edition; the difference in quality will not justify the difference in price. On relatively smooth or matte-finished cloths, notice the fineness of stitches and weight of the fibers. The fewer fibers per square quarter inch, the less substantial the cloth. Notice the thickness of the cloth, which you can see on the inside of each binding, at the corner of the paper. The thicker the more solid.

The grey boards that are inside most bindings are also an important factor in the ruggedness of a book, particularly of a rather large book. Cheap novels are bound with what is called "pasted board." No matter how thick, it tends to bend and buckle with changes in humidity or temperature. Recognize it by its comparative flexibility, compared with "binders board," which is required by law, for example, for most textbooks, and which any quality binding should have. Large size books need thicker boards, which, on smaller size books, seem clumsy. But both materials exist in most thicknesses, and one should be on the lookout for the quality of the board.

The overhang of the boards over the trimmed pages is called the "square." Certain publishers always specify that their squares should be small—about three thirty-seconds of an inch—on the theory that this is aesthetically neater. However, this is questionable, particularly on thicker books. The purpose of the squares is to protect the pages and keep them clean. As a book becomes older and the binding loosens slightly, the pages tend to sink down a little. If the square is not large enough to protect them—an eighth of an inch or even five thirty-seconds—they can be severely battered, in which case, again, the purpose of buying a hardcover edition is defeated.

— 6 —

Binding Design

Exceptional books have other criteria, and other factors should therefore be noted. In buying a book of eight hundred or so pages, over an inch and a quarter thick, one should open the front cover and feel the thickness of the cloth that parallels the spine on the very inside. On normal books this is a light, thin, gauzy material called "crash." On a really heavy book it should be reinforced by a heavier material, such as muslin. Since the book will have an abnormal amount of weight being pulled around every time it is opened, it must have an abnormally heavy reinforcement material to take the strain. The same applies to very large format books. Another point to notice is the trimmed top of a book. Occasionally this is colored or "stained." This stain is not merely a question of display. It means that the book will not show the dust as badly as one which has no stain, particularly when the stain is of a relatively dull color. Books which are intended to be kept indefinitely, for many, many years or generations or for reference, should really be stained. It is less a point against a book that it is not stained than one in favor of it if it is. At the spine end of the top and bottom of the sheets of a book there often appear colored bits of cloth called "headbands." These do not serve any structural purpose, though they are often very elegant. However, the commonest manufacturing problem in the making of books is that a little extra glue seeps out at this end of the sheets and shows as an ugly blotch. The headbands conceal this.

The stamping on a book is a very important form of display. There are shiny gold and metallic foils, duller foils and off colors, made with ink or with pigmented leaf. Generally speaking, the shiny metallics, except for gold and silver, will rub off fairly quickly, and the book cannot be identified on the shelf easily. Publishers often use these colors because they are very striking, but we would be better off if they didn't. A second generalization is that the duller metallic foils tend to be more permanent than the shiny ones, but technology will surely alter this in the next few years.

— 7 —

Quality and
The Something Else Press

We publish the sort of avant-garde work which offers a real alternative to the conventional art forms and which normal publishers do not know how to handle. Because of our specialization, our prices have to be relatively high. It costs only slightly more to do two thousand than one thousand of a given title, but divide any figure by one thousand, then by two thousand, and you will see our problem. We try to offset this as much as we can by doing as much of the work ourselves as we can—all the camera work on our new titles, for example—and by offering the best manufacturing quality possible. We believe we are the only publisher in America with this emphasis—certainly the only one with such adventurousness.

We are not interested in built-in obsolescence. We want our books to be as fresh ten years from now as they are today, and as much of a joy to behold.

Filliou handing out questionnaires

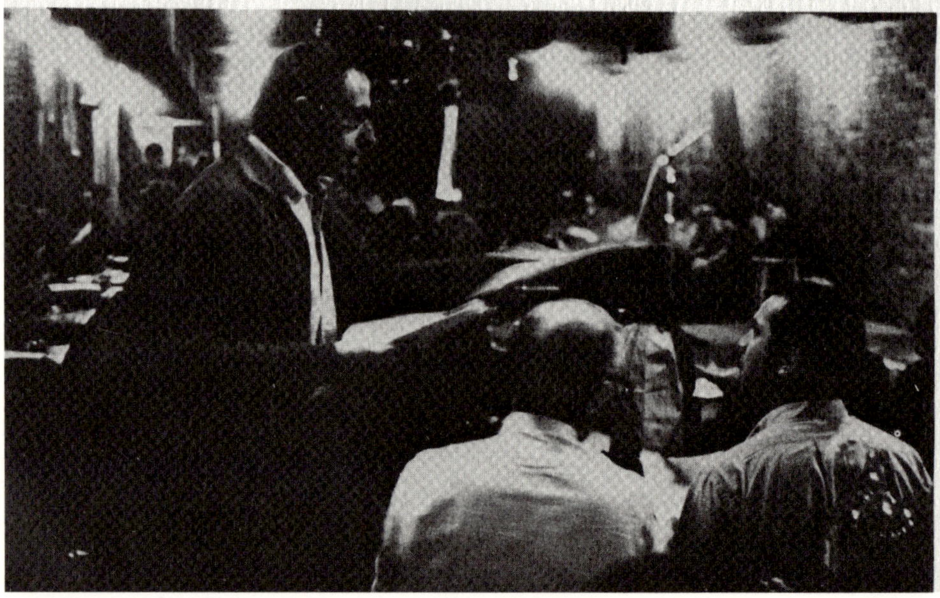

Catalogue 1965-66

Ample Food for Stupid Thought
by Robert Filliou

Filliou is a well-known French artist and poet, one of the very, very few with any degree of experimentalism. This book consists of apparently pointless questions which lead in fact to highly poetic speculations.

Originally this book was conceived as a set of postcards, with one question per card. Each card could seem appropriate for any number of friends of the reader and could be sent off. So we made up a card edition. But once the cards are sent away, the book is incomplete. So we made a normal book edition, too.

The excellent jacket notes are by Jackson Mac Low, and there is also introductory material by Arman, Kichka Baticheff, George Brecht, William Burroughs, Christo, Diane di Prima, Brion Gysin, Dick Higgins, Ray Johnson, Joe Jones, Allan Kaprow, Alison Knowles, John Herbert McDowell, Jackson Mac Low, Nam June Paik, Benjamin Patterson, Diter Rot, Daniel Spoerri and James Waring. 96 pp.

Book Edition (bound in cloth), $5.00

Card Edition (in wooden box) $9.00

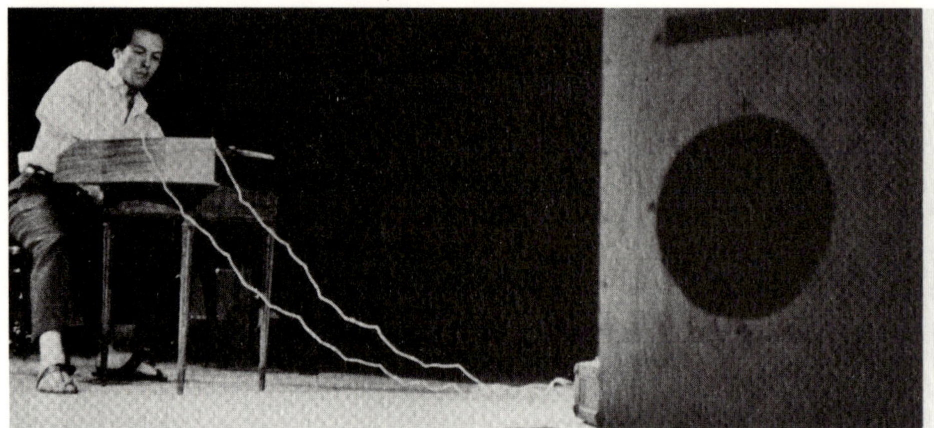

Corner playing Corner

The Four Suits

by Philip Corner, Alison Knowles, Benjamin Patterson and Tomas Schmit

The Four Suits is a collection of very different directions, intended to show the variety of work being done in the general field of happenings and happening-related work. Corner is represented by a collection of his musical events; Knowles has written a dictionary of the letter "T" which is mostly unperformable; Patterson's performance pieces are psychological experiments along the lines of Zen koans; Schmit has contributed utterly classical, private pieces which are done for the benefit of the performer and are best-off without any audience at all.

The importance of this book is dual: it places the current situation of happenings in the foreground, and de-emphasizes the earlier, painting-derived phase. And it provides texts and methods for those who want to study what is being done today in the way of artistic experiments. 208 pp. Illus.

Regular Cloth Edition, $5.00

Special Edition (10 copies only), $30.00

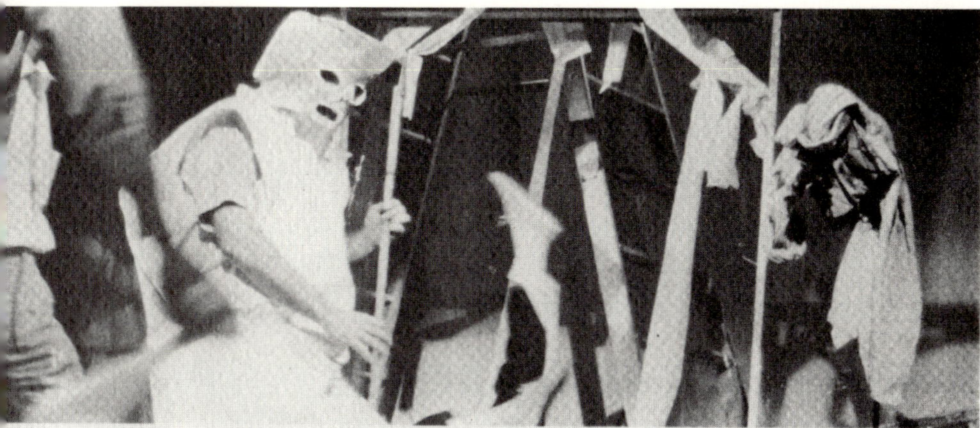

Scene from Al Hansen's *Parisol 4 Marisol*

A Primer of Happenings & Time/Space Art

by Al Hansen

Intended primarily for use by young people as an introduction to the general field of happenings and their artistic cousins, this is easily the most basic book on its subject. Hansen is best known for his Hershey Bar wrapper collages. Yet he has been the most prolific of all the happening makers. There is fascination and authority when Hansen says, "Back in the summer of 1958, in Cage's class at The New School. . . ." 160 pp. Over 100 illus.

Regular Cloth Edition, $4.50

Special Edition (with an original Hansen), $59.95

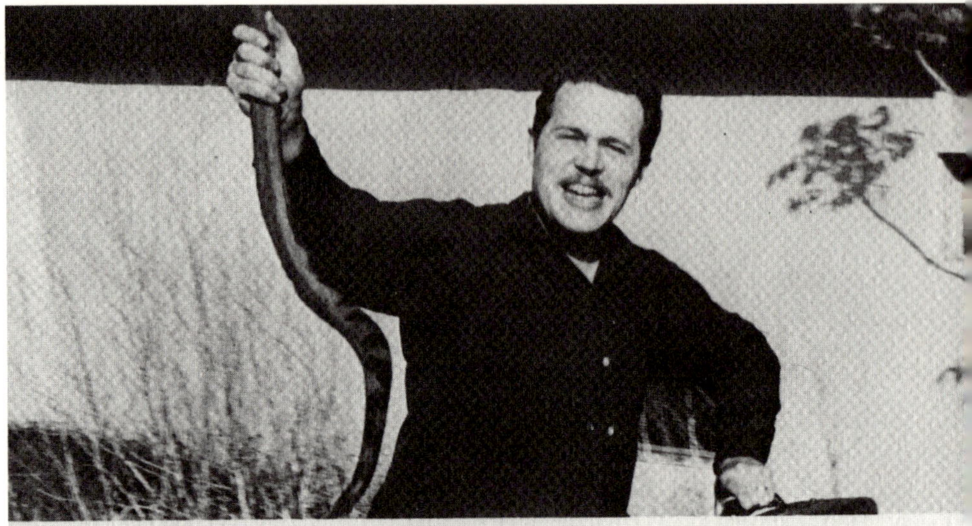

Dick Higgins and a friend performing *Snake in the Grass*

Postface/Jefferson's Birthday
by Dick Higgins

These two separate works are bound back-to-back in one volume. *Postface* is a reminiscence about how happenings began by one who was there. It goes on to explain the necessity for happenings, where they went to and what is being done now. The description of Fluxus, the curious explosion of happenings which enormously expanded the audience and numbers of participants in the movement, primarily in Europe, is virtually the only material on the subject in print.

Jefferson's Birthday contains all the work Higgins wrote between April 13th, Thomas Jefferson's birthday, 1962 and April 13th, 1963. As such, it is an excellent cross section of the works, primarily theatrical, of this quite unique writer. 384 pp. Illus.

Regular Cloth Edition only, $5.95

The Paper Snake
by Ray Johnson

Ray Johnson is not only the finest of American collagists, well represented in the Museum of Modern Art (New York), the De Cordova Museum (Lincoln, Mass.), etc. He is also the author of innumerable whimsical fantasies and reminiscences, often pointed, which masquerade as playlets, poems, letters. These are mailed to friends, to friends of friends, to anybody to whom it seems appropriate to mail something, and have been described as The New York Correspondence School of Art. A cross section of his work, received by Dick Higgins over the years, has been assembled into this, one of our most beautiful books. 50 pp. Illus.

Regular Cloth Edition, $3.47

Special Edition (with an original Johnson), $12.00

Ray Johnson among his collages

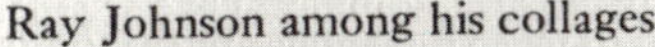
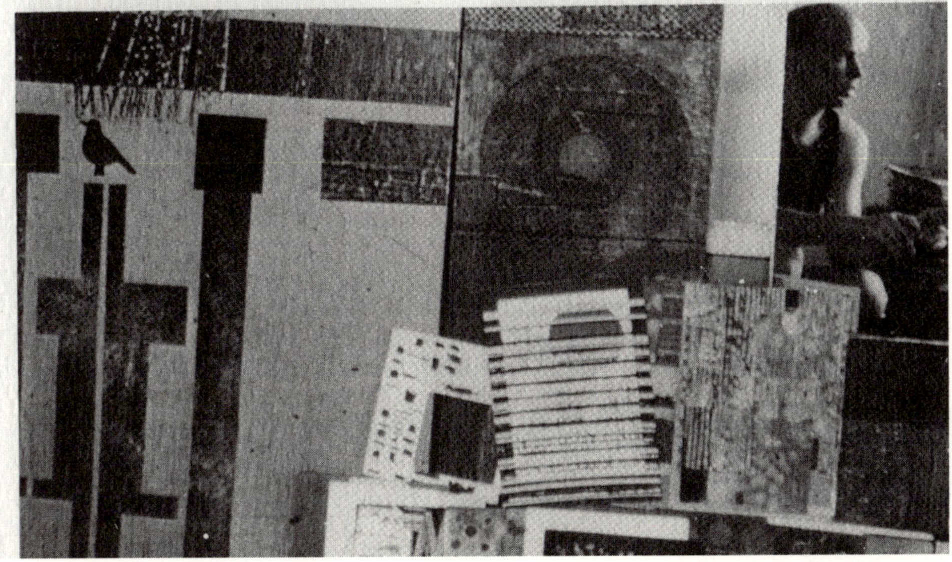

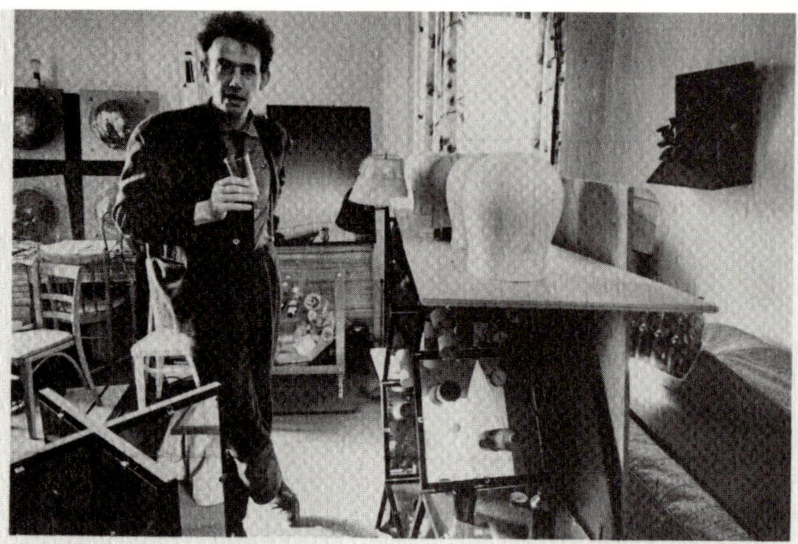

Spoerri in one of his environments

An Anecdoted Topography of Chance
by Daniel Spoerri, ed. Emmett Williams

This is the only complete edition of Spoerri's nouveau realiste classic, *Topographie Anécdotée du Hasard*, translated and supplemented by Spoerri's close friend, the poet Emmett Williams, and further expanded by Spoerri himself. On the surface the book is a history of all the objects on a table in Spoerri's room in Paris. In fact, however, it is a cosmology of Spoerri's existence, with the objects suggesting friendships and relationships among people he knows. Williams' expansions further deepen the associations of these objects, and Spoerri's expansions on Williams suggest ever-widening circles of experience. 240 pp. Illus.

Regular Cloth Edition, $5.00
Special Edition (10 copies only), $60.00

Coming in 1966—

Stanzas for Iris Lezak and other works, by Jackson Mac
Low (designed by Wolf Vostell)

Store Days, by Claes Oldenburg

The Golden Armadillo, by Camille Gordon

A décollage book by Wolf Vostell

All photos in this catalog except that of Ray Johnson are by Peter
Moore.

If you are interested in our activities, please fill in the coupon below and send to: Something Else Press, Inc., 160 Fifth Ave., New York, N.Y. 10010.

Please send me the following:

______ *Postface/Jefferson's Birthday*, by Dick Higgins ($5.95)
______ *The Paper Snake, regular edition*, by Ray Johnson ($3.47)
______ *The Paper Snake, special edition*, by Ray Johnson ($12.00)
______ *Ample Food for Stupid Thought*, book, by Robert Filliou ($5.00)
______ *Ample Food for Stupid Thought*, cards, by Robert Filliou ($9.00)
______ *The Four Suits*, regular ed., by Corner, Knowles, Patterson, Schmit ($5.00)
______ *Primer of Happenings & Time/Space Art*, regular ed., by Al Hansen ($4.50)
______ *An Anecdoted Topography of Chance*, regular ed., by Daniel Spoerri ($5.00)
______ More Information on the Press and Its Activities (free)

Name ____

Street Address ____________________________________

City ________________ State __________ Zip __________

Our books are available at The 8th Street Bookshop, The Gotham Book Mart and Wittenborn's in New York, and at good bookstores everywhere.

Two Sides of a Coin
Fluxus and the Something Else Press

Originally published in *Visible Language,* vol. 26, nos. 1/2, special issue *Fluxus: A Conceptual Country*, edited by Estera Milman, 1992.

i.

In the late 1950s, when Happenings and events began to be performed in New York and elsewhere, while there was some consensus that the works that visual artists performed in spaces of their own devising (usually constructed in art galleries or sponsored by these) constituted "Happenings," there was no name for the works made by people who were not primarily visual artists. These were spoken of, simply, as "events" because that was a convenient term for them used by myself and my fellow students in John Cage's class in "Experimental Composition," taught at the New School for Social Research.[1] At first, the artists who were doing the latter had no agreed-on name for what they were doing, but the performances of this kind of work at Yoko Ono's loft on Chambers Street in New York (1960–61) and at George Maciunas's AG Gallery on Madison Avenue (1961), also in New York, made it obvious that a name was needed. Maciunas gave up his art gallery in 1961 and undertook the design and production of La Monte Young and Jackson Mac Low's *An Anthology*.[2] When his work was done, he found that he still had a large amount of intriguing material he wanted to publish, so he proposed a magazine and publication series, to be called "Fluxus." Maciunas went to Europe at the beginning of 1962 and, to promote Fluxus, organized a series of performances, called "Festum Fluxorum" ("Feast of Fluxusses"), the first of which was to take place at the art museum in Wiesbaden, Germany. Alison Knowles, Emmett Williams, and I were among the participants in those "Fluxus Concerts," which would later be described as "Fluxconcerts." These concerts caused a great scandal. The press began to call the work "Fluxus," and the participants they named *die Fluxus Leute*, that is, "the Fluxus people."

After performances we stayed at Maciunas's house outside Wiesbaden, at Ehlhalten-am-Taunus, staying up most of the night, trying to figure out the implications of what we were doing, discussing Turkish music and Heideggerian hermeneutics,[3] which I saw as an appropriate theoretical underpinning to our work. Along the way we planned the tactics of our next steps, mapped out new pieces, dined on such delicacies as pink or green mashed potatoes (we put food coloring into the dish), and imbibed Unterberg, a bitter liqueur. If we were "the Fluxus people," what was this Fluxus we had unleashed, and what was it for?[4]

At Ehlhalten we had lots of time to talk about the history of what we were doing. Maciunas was well aware of Greek visual poetry that paralleled our

[1] The term "event," used in this way, is of uncertain origin; the composer Henry Cowell, with whom both Cage and myself studied, used it, but Cowell may have picked it up from Cage as well.

[2] La Monte Young, ed. *An Anthology* (New York: Jackson Mac Low, 1962). The book was reprinted by the Heiner Friedrich Gallery in New York in 1970.

[3] While Maciunas viewed Heidegger as a lifelong fascist whose work was a justification for fascism, I didn't. If I wanted to persuade Maciunas of Heideggerian ideas, I had to phrase them so he would not recognize them.

[4] It was already several years too late to write a proper manifesto setting out our program, as most movements have. Maciunas drafted one, but only a few people signed; we were too far along in our work and too diverse for that. He never had the authority within our group that, say, André Breton did among the surrealists. Maciunas might try to read people in or out of Fluxus, but as a group we operated . . . *(con't)*

[4] *(con't)* more by consensus, regarding Maciunas as a member of the group who had great gifts for publicity and energy for correspondence, but ultimately as just one among equals. Though tempted to be dictatorial at times (who isn't?), Maciunas was glad to accept that Fluxus was a collective and, usually, to function within that context.

[5] Actually the seven principal Greek visual poems are much older, and the few Byzantine pieces are derivative of earlier works. On all this I subsequently expanded in *Pattern Poetry*.

colleagues' concrete poetry, though he mistakenly ascribed it to the Byzantines.[5] I told Maciunas about Quirinus Kühlmann (1644–88), a German visionary poet who made visual poems called "Kühlpsalms" that were printed in his Kühlpsalter and recited on "Kühldays." Eventually, Kühlmann was burnt as a heretic by the Tsar of Russia in Moscow, whither he had gone to see if the Tsar would like to found a new church with him. Maciunas was delighted by the story. From Kühlmann we picked up the habit of using terms like "Fluxconcerts," "Fluxartists," "Fluxfriends," "Fluxreasons," and "Fluxanythings." These terms were useful to us since we were not happy with the connotations of "art" with its liminality and perhaps overly elitist associations. We preferred to think of the art-life dichotomy lying at the basis of Fluxus, of "Fluxart" as being somehow closer to life than other art forms.

ii.

[6] Zaccar Offset became the main printer for Maciunas and Fluxus. The 1977 feast in honor of Maciunas took place on the premises of Zaccar Offset, though by then they had moved to a different space from the one described in my *Postface* (1964).

[7] The general story of Something Else Press has been described elsewhere, most fully by Peter Frank in his monograph *Something Else Press* ("Documen-Text." New Paltz: McPherson and Company, 1983). I will therefore not repeat the anecdote of how "the Press" was named, how it ran its course, and, in 1974, died and was replaced by "Unpublished Editions," a cooperative whose name was changed in 1978 to "Printed Editions" and which lasted until 1986. Instead we will focus on how Something Else Press related to Fluxus.

[8] Since those days Ms. Moore has written memorably about Fluxus.

Before Maciunas returned to America in 1963 to present Fluxus formally in the USA, he had asked me to prepare for publication the large manuscript of what became *Jefferson's Birthday*, a cross section of my work from 1962 to 1963. Since I had been trained as a printer, was working at Zaccar Offset,[6] and was used to copy-editing, design, and all the technical side of printing and publishing, it was a natural thing for me to be involved in the production of my book. However, when my book did not materialize in what seemed to me a reasonable amount of time, and when Maciunas could not promise when he could get to it, I founded Something Else Press,[7] incorporated on February 2, 1964, as "Something Else Press, Inc." *Jefferson's Birthday /Postface* was bound in August, 1964. *Postface* was an account of the background and beginning of Fluxus, and the two books were bound together so that theory would not be divorced from practice. I called myself the "President" (and, for a time, sported a necktie in "presidential blue"), while the first editor of Something Else Press was Barbara Moore.[8] When she left in 1966, Emmett Williams moved from Europe to New York and became the next editor. The Board of Directors varied slightly, but it usually consisted of myself, Alison Knowles, and Emmett Williams. While the Press never had more than five employees at one time—as many people as one could stuff into a taxi cab—we did have some interesting people aboard over the years who went on to distinguished careers elsewhere. At the shipping and order desk alone we had dancers Meredith Monk and Judy Padow, composer-violinist Malcolm Goldstein, artist Susan Hartung, poets Denis Dunn and Lawrence Freifeld, writer Mary Flanagan, and others, not to mention the artists and writers who worked for the Press in other capacities, Fluxartists Al Hansen, Ken Friedman, and Ann Noel Stevenson.

Between 1966 and 1973, when I finally left "the Press," we produced ninety-five books. After my departure, two others were produced: Manfred L. Eaton's *Bio-Music* and a facsimile edition of Gertrude Stein's *A Book Concluding with As a Wife Has a Cow*, which was printed but not distributed. My successor at the Press was Jan Herman, a good editor who wanted to run the operation, but it turned out he had no gift for fundraising or for diplomacy. While he would wrap packages and do chores, he would not do what the president of an organization should do: write grant proposals, visit with possible patrons, handle major sales, and so on. By the autumn of 1974, the debts of Something Else Press had accumulated to about $240,000, and, though its assets were worth much more than that, I was in no position to return to the Press and work this out. As co-owner (with Emmett) of the Press, I filed for bankruptcy for it.[9]

The problems we faced at Something Else Press were typical of those of any small, independent publisher. Even though the prices of the books were high for the times, we lost so much money through distribution that our best-selling titles[10] were a threat to our very existence. Furthermore, although I was interested in publishing, I was above all an artist. My art work had been suffering because of my extensive responsibilities at Something Else Press. I could not simply go away and work somewhere: who would pay my co-workers? My secretary, Nelleke Rosenthal, saw these things clearly, as did I, but it was she whose advice it was to discontinue the Press, to self-publish for a while, and to start a new small press when another opportunity arose.

I followed the first part of her advice in 1972 and started a program of publishing very small, model editions of my works using the name "Unpublished Editions." In 1976 Alison Knowles joined me in the project, and in 1978 so did John Cage, Philip Corner, Geoffrey Hendricks, Jackson Mac Low, and, soon thereafter, Pauline Oliveros and Jerome Rothenberg.[11] In 1978 we also changed the name of this new small press to "Printed Editions," as witness to our new identity (as our catalogue put it). Structurally, the

[9] Jan opposed the bankruptcy, as did Emmett, though he had no idea where new capital might be found. In the aftermath of the bankruptcy the two of them attacked me roundly, accusing me, in an interview published in *West Coast Poetry Review* (Winter 1976–7), of, such things as, when "things got rough," taking a pleasure jaunt to Frankfurt, Germany, with my secretary, Nelleke Rosenthal, and implicitly wasting the Press's resources. Well, I did have a part-time secretary, Nelleke, who was Dutch and who had a brother in Frankfurt. In September 1973, although I had left the Press in July, I decided to attend the Frankfurt Book Fair, and Nelleke came along to visit her brother and to help staff our booth at the Fair. We worked hard and sold more books in one week there than Jan Herman had sold during the entire year. While Emmett came to understand this, Jan Herman never did figure out just what had gone wrong.

[10] We produced a total of 18,000 copies of Emmett Williams's *An Anthology of Concrete Poetry* (1968) and 17,000 copies of Claes Oldenburg's *Store Days* (1969), respectable numbers by any accounting.

[11] All but Oliveros had been Something Else Press authors, and an Oliveros book had been proposed.

new press was an unincorporated syndicate. The books were produced by each artist-member and sold through the network that had been built up for Something Else Press. All promotions were done on a cooperative basis (mainly a catalogue), and the moneys received were credited to the artist-author and paid out. There was only a minimal overhead to deal with. The system worked well until the end of 1986, at which time so many other publishers wanted to produce our main titles that we had no major books for Printed Editions. So we agreed to disband. Mission accomplished. That was the end of my formal involvement in book publishing.

As for Maciunas, his own first publications appeared in 1962 and 1963. *Fluxus*, intended as a magazine, never appeared except as an annual, while the reproduction proofs that we had carefully corrected at Ehlhalten were never printed and were eventually destroyed in a flood in Maciunas's car. But it was also the imprint on the yearbooks, books, and "Fluxboxes" that did appear, starting in 1963. Maciunas set up shop on Canal Street among the surplus stores, and there he bought plastic boxes, collected the makings of kits, and pasted Fluxlabels onto the covers. At the time of his death, in 1978, Maciunas was still producing Fluxus publications of one sort or another,[12] mostly Fluxboxes. A few were even produced to his specifications posthumously by Barbara Moore's Reflux Editions.

[12] Good documentation of these is in Jon Hendricks's *Fluxus Codex*.

iii.

This is the matrix, then, of the Fluxus publications and of the Something Else Press. The stories that surround the various books and the people who worked on them—authors, artists, editors, and so on—are worth telling, too, but that must await another time. Every book has two stories, the story it tells and the story that surrounds it. I like to think that the stories surrounding the Something Else books are more a part of them than those of most other publications and have begun the "anecdotalization," if there be such a word, of the Press in a videotape lecture,[13] but that is a major project. What we can note now is the relation between Fluxus and Something Else Press, how they fit into their context at the time, and the relation between their legacies and traces today.

[13] *The Something Else Press & Since* (Vancouver, BC: Western Front, 1981).

Maciunas's way of publishing stressed the original design, the unusual materials, and the handmade. Objects in boxes and printed sheets held together by nuts and bolts—that was his orientation. But making these is, of course, hand work. The advantage of object books is that it costs little to prepare in advance to make a work; there are minimal editorial costs, no binders' dies and sample cases to worry about, and the like. However, the unit cost (the cost of making each copy) is relatively high. Their disadvantages are that the results cannot be sold universally and that the production of large numbers of them takes too much time. For example, Maciunas set us up with piles of papers to crumple and then unfold for

Mieko (formerly "Chieko") Shiomi's page in the *Fluxus Yearbox* (1963). It took three people an evening to produce the papers for her one page. There were to be forty or so pages. How on earth could we produce all those? This is why so few copies of the *Fluxus Yearbox* were produced. In fact, Maciunas sometimes only produced each copy of the publication to order, waiting a few weeks until the orders had built up and then assembling whatever was needed.

Maciunas's politics were crypto-Communist; while never a party member, he loved to affect a conspiratorial manner, and his adoration of the USSR was not precisely rational. However, he had very little of the popular touch. Most of our circle, Fluxartists and Fluxfriends, were liberal in our politics, or leftist, but we had a strong populist streak that made us concerned about whether the Fluxboxes and publications were too elitist. Our productions were "collectibles," and perhaps we were simply producing as much "for the collector" as traditional artists. With this on my mind, around 1964 I began to have a vision of our publications being sold in supermarkets. How could this be brought about?

Nobody seems to know how Maciunas first learned graphic design. But throughout the 1960s he made his living doing design, paste-ups, and mechanicals, what was known in the trade as "finished art," often for the Jack Marchard Studio.[14] But Marchard's main business was brochures, labels, logotypes, posters, and pamphlets. The normative style of the time was the "Helvetica look;" set everything in Helvetica typeface, give it lots of room, and let it go. Maciunas favored a tight, energetic look, which he achieved by using sans serif types, especially News Gothic, which he then juxtaposed with old-fashioned and florid display faces, such as the old wood type faces in the Romantique family. The layouts themselves were those appropriate to Marchard's business. Usually they were based on grids, into which or over which the types were laid out so as to suggest a cellular form. For the Fluxus publications, for which Maciunas was not limited by the needs of Marchard's clients, Maciunas frequently placed his types upside down or at least on their sides; this, too, had the effect of emphasizing the grid, as well as having a humorous effect.

By contrast, though I, too, rejected the "Helvetica look," after a brief time making bank checks (which taught me type face recognition, if nothing else). I worked mostly for offset printers and, eventually, book publishers and manufacturers. I, therefore, became familiar with the available materials and suppliers, with cost-accounting practices, and so on. As for design, my design style became whatever was appropriate to book formats. Grids were, for the most part, useless for such large-scale work. So I laid out my pages rectilinearly but lined up the elements along the diagonals of the pages, setting my type to form triangles and trapezoids wherever possible, and, also, where feasible, I set poems and short chapters flush bottom on the type pages (usually they are set in the middle). I used larger and bolder running heads at the tops of pages than is customary in order to tie the page together and because I liked the legibility it gave to a sometimes rather scattered or

[14] Marchard's studio had the advantage of being a place where nobody smoked, important to Maciunas since he had terrible asthma.

15 To do this, I would make a list of up to thirty-six faces, assign a number to each, then use dice to select a number between one and thirty-six, and then start from whatever face I had selected. This resulted in some of the Something Else books being set in unusual faces or faces which are normally only used for display.

unorthodox page. Since I did not wish to develop favoritism among type faces, I used what ever faces a particular supplier had, often making my selections by means of chance operations, using dice.[15] In this way, I became familiar with many seldom-used or old-fashioned fonts that later gave the Something Else Press books their look of old-but-new. I liked Maciunas's designs, but he never commented on mine, so I assume he didn't reciprocate. But what Maciunas really did not like was the withdrawal of my energy from the production of Fluxus publications.

Yet, the move had been all but inevitable all along. I wanted to offer Fluxus to everybody, to have Fluxus and Fluxus-type work (similar works by other artists who were outside our circle) available in airport book shops and grocery stores. Maciunas focused on the work being cheap but gave little attention to making them accessible to ordinary people, to promotion and distribution beyond the order forms that were printed in his *CCV TRE* newspapers, which, of course, had to circulate among the right people to function at all, people who already had some idea what they were looking at. Concern about this made my withdrawal from the production of the publications more or less just a matter of time.

I had protested strongly to Maciunas over his threat to withdraw his legal sponsorship of Ay-O and other foreign Fluxartists (whose status required letters of support) if they participated in Allan Kaprow's production of Karlheinz Stockhausen's *Originale*, which was being produced as part of Charlotte Moorman's Festival of the Avant-Garde for 1966. Both Moorman and Stockhausen were anathema to Maciunas, the former as an exponent of European cultural chauvinism (was American cultural chauvinism any better? I asked) and the latter as an unprincipled opportunist. This was in line with the Marcyism of the *Workers' World* politics of Henry Flynt, a marginal Fluxperson who took an interesting but, I felt, unproductive anti-art position that saw art as bourgeois, a view even Lenin had once denounced as "typically Trotskyite." In fact, this is why, by way of contrast, Emmett Williams and I, the next year, invited the W.E.B. DuBois Clubs, a Communist youth group, to contribute a manifesto to the *Manifestos* pamphlet published by the Something Else Press in our inexpensive Great Bear Pamphlets series in 1967. All the other manifestos in that booklet were either by Fluxus artists or were somehow in the same spirit as these. I was adamantly opposed to our potential marginalization for the sake of ideological purity; we were already marginalized enough in the cultural world without adding to the problem. Most of the Fluxartists were, in any case, quite apolitical in spite of the typical political militancy of the times.

Maciunas chose to view my protest and involvement in the production of *Originale* as a withdrawal from Fluxus. He denounced me in the chart histories he constantly revised as histories of and statements about Fluxus. He said in two of the versions of the chart that I had withdrawn from the group to found a rival organization. However, I kept describing myself as a Fluxperson, and my Fluxfriends kept including me in their projects. So I was not really excluded from Fluxus. Then in the summer of 1966, Maciunas and I sat down in the city park that was outside the Something Else Press office and which served me as a private conference room, and we talked over our objectives. Maciunas and I might not have agreed about the relation of our activities to society as a whole, but we did agree on the objectives of our publishing activities. While the Fluxus publications should serve as paradigmatic models or prototypes of various sorts, the best role for Something Else Press was as an outreach series, useful for getting our ideas beyond the charmed circle of *cognoscenti* to which, reluctantly, we belonged, one which could present to the larger public all kinds of alternative and intermedial work. Maciunas would do his boxes, while I would be the one to do books. The Press tried always to be "something else" than what commercially oriented trade publications were doing or, since there was The Something Else Gallery in the front room of Alison's and my home, what commercial galleries were showing. This was a position Maciunas heartily approved, and thus the schism ended. I was again included by Maciunas in Fluxus, and so it continued until his death, which occurred in 1978. There also developed another kind of reciprocity. For example, when Ken Friedman appeared on the scene in 1966, I felt he belonged in Fluxus as much as in Something Else Press, and so I brought him to Maciunas, with whom he worked from then on as well serving as the Director of Something Else Press in 1970–71 while it was located in California for a year.

Fluxus was, then, to be thought of as having four aspects: a series of publications, a group of artists, the forms associated with the publications and their performances, and the theoretical positions inherent in these. This made it not so much a movement, with a clearly defined group of artists setting out to achieve a particular program, as a "tendency," organized on a collective basis, something more pluralistic and less exclusive than the other iconoclastic movements of our century that it resembled in one way or another—Dada, Futurism, Surrealism, and Russian Constructivism. Fluxus was also pluralistic and in any case more suited to the cultural climate of the 1960s and 1970s, usually (and inadequately) defined as "postmodern."

By contrast, Something Else Press was to be a parallel expression, covering much the same ground but with historical and other related materials added, through which we could develop the context of Fluxus and intermedial art forms by bringing the work to the largest possible public in an undiluted form. But whatever we did, it would have to follow with our name, to be "something else" from what the commercial publishers were doing. Already in the 1950s the Fluxartist Robert Filliou had issued his *Manifesto d'Autrisme*, declaring the need always to be doing something other than the normative routine. This was very close to the Something Else Manifesto, which I had written in 1963 when I decided to start Something Else Press and before any of the books had, as yet, appeared.[16] But if the purpose of the Press always would be to publish the valuable work that differs from the

[16] Both manifestos are included in the *Manifestos* pamphlet, already mentioned. I have been unable to find out where Filliou's manifesto first appeared, and was unaware of its existence when I wrote my own manifesto; mine was first printed inside the dust jacket of the first Something Else Press book, *Jefferson's Birthday/ Postface* (1964), also already mentioned.

[17] Such works include Emmett Williams, *An Anthology of Concrete Poetry* (1968), Eugen Gomringer, *The Book of Constellations* (1970), and the various books of Williams's own poetry that we produced.

[18] Daniel Spoerri's *An Anecdoted Topography of Chance* (1966), my *A Book About Love & War & Death* (1972), Kostelanetz, ed., *Breakthrough Fictioneers* (1972), and Toby MacLennan's *1 Walked Out of 2 and Forgot It* (1973) are of this sort.

[19] For example, such works would include Richard Huelsenbeck's *Dada Almanach* (1966) or Gertrude Stein's *The Making of Americans* (1969) and the four other Stein works we reissued. These last began the current popularity of Stein today, since, at the time we were doing our reissues, Stein was sometimes discussed but, since her works were so hard to obtain, she was very seldom read.

[20] This book, already mentioned, documents some 1800 visual poems from before 1900 C.E. from all over the world (not just from the West) and also presents a gathering of related phenomena, such as old graphic musical notations.

fashionable or the conventions of the times, then to fulfill its role, however, the Press would have to include other kinds of intermedia than simply Fluxus. Otherwise, we would not be creating an appropriate context for our reception. The editorial board—Emmett Williams (and, earlier, Barbara Moore), Alison Knowles, myself, and, at the end, Jan Herman—focused on other possibilities, printing such intermedial areas as concrete poetry (which Emmett Williams had pioneered),[17] new forms of fiction or proto-novel,[18] and works of past avant-gardes we felt were important and either misunderstood or under-appreciated.[19] This was in keeping with Maciunas's and my view that cultural innovation is cumulative, that each innovation adds to the store of possibilities and does not simply replace some earlier mode forever as, by contrast, is often true in science. The assumption that replacement applies to culture and art as much as science, that the introduction of a new form does not simply add to the available possibilities but makes the older ones obsolete, is what I call the "neoteric fallacy" ("neoteric" is a rare word but it is not my coinage; it denotes a taste for or interest in the new). Opposed to this fallacy would be Maciunas's and my view that brothers and sisters in artistic innovation have always been active, that the avant-garde is eternal, but that many of the most worthwhile innovations have been lost over the centuries or have been repressed. This would be true of secular drama in the Middle Ages, of unusual styles of music in the late fourteenth and early fifteenth centuries, or in some non-Western classical music traditions (notably Central Asian, Turkish, and Mongol styles), as well as of such forms of intermedia as visual poetry and graphic musical notation. Maciunas announced several issues of his *Fluxus* magazine that would be devoted to this kind of material. However, they never appeared, and, in fact, he barely had a chance to scratch the surface, gathering together the actual materials. I was more fortunate, because when I left Something Else Press I had the leisure to gather materials of this sort together, resulting in my book *Pattern Poetry: Guide to an Unknown Literature* (1987).[20] I also worked out the start of a hermeneutic theory for intermedia art in general and Fluxus in particular,[21] thus completing some of the objectives that had been set out during our late-night discussions at Ehlhalten in 1962, namely, clarifying the historical context and roots of Fluxus and beginning the task of establishing its theoretical matrix, without which it is hard to evaluate individual works or to develop a critical vocabulary for Fluxus or, indeed, for many other art currents of recent years—conceptual art, art performance, or, arguably, of Language poetry.[22]

iv.

So Fluxus and the Something Else Press had related objectives, but they were different, too; the Press largely grew out of Fluxus and Unpublished/Printed Editions out of the Press. The Press could not have performed its outreach if it had used the kind of experimental formats that were appropriate to Maciunas's Fluxus publications, nor could he have provided the experimental prototypes if he had confined himself to books. Of course, there are exceptions to this, as well as overlaps. Maciunas did, in fact, do several traditional format books early on in Fluxus, as already mentioned, and Something Else Press issued several books in boxes or on cards or portfolio books.[23] But these are just that, exceptions. Most of the Something Else books were only experimental as regards the printed page, not in format, trim size, or binding. We also published twenty pamphlets on handsome colored papers, the Great Bear Pamphlets. These cost up to $2 and were thus rather inexpensive, even for the time. They were in fact our vehicle for achieving my dream of having our works available in at least one grocery store, the Berkeley Co-op in Berkeley, California, where they were available for some time on a display case beside the vegetable counter.[24] We also became the object of a satirical wisecrack in an article in *Harper's Magazine*, which mocked the "poetry readings at the Something Else Gallery." The only reading we ever had there was a nonstop marathon reading of James Joyce's *Finnegans Wake*. Maybe Joyce was too modern for them. Anyway, the appearance of such a mention in an establishment magazine, or the reviews of the Williams *Anthology of Concrete Poetry* in *Vogue* and *Newsweek*, indicated that we were getting to places the new arts seldom penetrate, and this too was appropriate to our program.

Not only did Fluxus and Something Else Press include many of the same participants, but our objectives were closely parallel. They were twin sides of the same coin. Although it included fewer people, Printed Editions had similar objectives to those of Something Else Press, objectives more suited to the role of Printed Editions as a

[21] These theories originally appeared, for the most part, in the *Something Else Newsletter*, starting in February 1966 with "Intermedia," which revived that term from S. T. Coleridge. The early texts went through various revisions, as they began to compose parts of a whole, until they reached their final versions in two books, *A Dialectic of Centuries: Notes towards a Theory of the New Arts* (1st ed., West Glover, VT: Printed Editions, 1978 and [revised] 2nd ed., West Glover, VT: Printed Editions, 1979) and *Horizons: The Poetics and Theory of the Intermedia* (Carbondale, IL: Southern Illinois University Press, 1983).

[22] Most of what passes for criticism in those areas offers potential vocabulary but little insight, since the relationship among the words is not clear and no contextualization is offered for the work in terms of its diachronic or current relationships. This point I expand on in an article, "Five Myths of Postmodernism" in *Art Papers* 13:1 (1989).

[23] Robert Filliou's *Ample Food for Stupid Thought* (1965) came in two editions, a traditional book one and a postcard set in a box. Wolf Vostell's *dé-coll/age Happenings* (1966) came in a box which included a set of black and white reproductions of his Happenings notations, a book with their texts, an Alka Seltzer® packet glued to a piece of aluminum foil, and a trimmed matzo cracker. Allan Kaprow's *Calling* (1967) was arranged as a visual poem on vinyl sheets with plywood covers. My *foew&ombwhnw* (1969) was bound as a prayer book. There were also others. Somehow these publications can also be viewed as early artists' books.

[24] I used to have a photograph of the rack of Great Bear Pamphlets beside the green peppers.

smaller small press, a term that covers too many independent publishers, but our needs and purposes were appropriate to a cooperative, and our entire program was devoted to aspects of our *members'* work and its contexts rather than to the larger problem of promoting broader art forms—as did the program of Fluxus performances and Fluxboxes and as did Something Else Press with its purview and programs in Fluxus and concrete poetry, new fictions, avant-garde theory, and so on. The relationship between Fluxus and Something Else Press was, therefore, a symbiotic one, while Printed Edition was a focusing in on a portion of Something Else Press. All three form an overall story.

The Something Else Press

Notes for a History to Be Written Some Day

Originally published in two parts in *New Lazarus Review,* vol. 2, vo. 1, 1979 and vol. 2, nos. 3/4, 1980.

Part 1

In the early days of Fluxus, say, in 1962 and 1963, George Maciunas and I agreed that we were happy with our work in the art and non-art area, but that the key problem in Fluxus—as in society as a whole—was how to get the goods to the people. His solution was the inexpensive, almost-ephemeral, hand-made art multiple. Mine was to compose a series of Variations on a Theme of Book—to publish source materials in a format which could encourage their distribution through traditional channels, however untraditional their contents or implications. In 1962 Maciunas proposed to me to publish my complete works. I said that would be impossible—I did too much in too many diverse areas, why didn't he instead publish a year's cross section of my work, everything done for a year following April 13th, 1962 (which was a date when I had written one of my favorites of my "Danger Music" series). The date turned out to be the birthday of Thomas Jefferson, whom I admire. So the book was to be called "Jefferson's Birthday."

When the manuscript was complete, I felt it needed some critical remarks to set the material into context. So I wrote a postface to it, *Postface*, and proposed to publish the two texts back-to-back, theory and practice in one book. Maciunas liked the idea. But the manuscript was over four hundred pages and, thus, expensive to produce. After waiting for many months I asked him when he would have it ready. He said, "A year from next spring." So I said that was no good, I needed the scripts now. Too bad. He couldn't do it. So I went out and had a few drinks, went by his studio, picked up the manuscript and took it upstairs to my studio,

Went out and had a few more drinks and went reeling home to Alison Knowles, with whom I was living at the time. I said we'd founded a press, and she said, "Really? What's it called?"

"Shirtsleeves Press."

"That's no good. Why don't you call it something else?"

I did. Her almost-serendipity name suited my editorial purposes perfectly. I liked the double entendre colloquialism of the name—as when a teenager says of his favorite record, "That's something else!" And more seriously, I liked the implication that whatever the commercial publishers chose to publish, we would always publish something else. In fact, the next day from when this exchange took place, I wrote my "Something Else Manifesto," since reprinted a good many times. But it took me from then, summer, 1963 [likely October, ed.] until October, 1964, to cause the *Jefferson's Birthday/Postface* book physically to exist—pasting, planning, proofreading, editing, and so on. Lettie Eisenhauer—long vanished from our world into that of art history, but then a fabulous performer in my happenings and those of Allan Kaprow and others—did most of the typing, on an old IBM Executive machine with the same "News Gothic" typeface that Maciunas used in the Fluxus publications.

But I meant from the outset to realize my plan of a press specializing in the avant-garde but working through the "book trade" format rather than that of small presses as such. I was frustrated by the provincialism of mod, pop-art New

York, where cosmopolitanism was one millimeter deep, and beyond that lay chauvinism ("If it ain't been done in New York, it ain't been done") and naiveté (the myth of American uniqueness, the notion that innovative thinking was peculiar to our time). So I planned to introduce European materials and always to have a balance between European/American, famous, infamous and unfamous, past and present.

So our second book was Ray Johnson's *The Paper Snake*, a collection of his correspondence art sendings to me from 1959 to 1964. And the fourth and fifth were Al Hansen's pop and very American *A Primer of Happenings & Time/Space Art* and the very elegant, very international *The Four Suits*, featuring post-Happenings works—Philip Corner (composer), Tomas Schmit (artist and sometime Fluxist), Alison Knowles (Fluxartist), and Benjamin Patterson (Fluxus composer turned educator). In January, 1965, I rented a little office at 160 Fifth Avenue in New York, and Barbara Moore came to work with me as the editor, since I have always been better at planning than execution, paragraph-construction than spelling, visualizing than reading—and so on. I tend to see through a manuscript to its potential as a book, where a fine editor sees the manuscript itself and polishes it to its best shine. Barbara Moore was a master editor, the best we ever had. She edited all the books through 1965 and into 1966, while I planned, designed, produced and publicized them.

This included our translation of Daniel Spoerri's *Topographie anécdotée du hazard*, which was our third book. Daniel Spoerri was a key figure in the Paris scene of the early 1960's, a member of the *nouveaux réalistes* group and though aloof from Fluxus (which he saw as unprofessional), friendly to many of its members. Maciunas published a book of his. Anyway, he was best known for his *tableaux pièges*, "snare pictures." These were table tops "frozen" by having whatever objects happened to be upon them at a moment glued down, so that the moment of finding them to be art was fixed or "snared." One day in 1962, after a quarrel with his mistress Kichka, he found himself considering the objects on his blue breakfast table, where he had gotten this, on what occasion he used that. It occurred to him that he could "snare" the table in a literary way by documenting the objects and those people with whom they were associated. And he did, in a delightful little book published by the Galerie Lawrence in Paris. I enjoyed the book enormously, and as soon as I started my press one of my top priority projects was to do a translation of it, with "expansions to keep it up to date," as Spoerri and I discussed it.

One of the early Fluxus people, Emmett Williams, was an old friend of Spoerri's from the late fifties when they had both been involved in the Darmstadt group of concrete poets. Lately he had moved to Paris, so Daniel Spoerri and I agreed that Emmett should translate and expand the work to novel length, anecdoting anecdotes, annotating annotations, and so on. This Emmett did masterfully, with (as the title page says) "the help of his very dear friend, Robert Filliou." "His" was Spoerri's but also Emmett Williams's—and also mine. The resulting project was one of the early Press books that pleased me most.

Another was Filliou's *Ample Food for Stupid Thought*, a series of questions conceived by Filliou and written by himself with a few suggestions from friends, printed on postcards, in one edition, and in another printed as a book, so as to provide a permanent record of the questions, which were mostly rather flippant things which could provoke not-so-flippant responses—*especially* when taken out of context. That 1965 postcard book was much imitated over the next years by the "pudgies," our name for the one-track professional establishment who tended to follow in the tracks of us and Fluxus, then as now.

One hot day in the summer of 1965 I went to get a cup of cold water from our office water cooler, which we got from the Great Bear Company, named (I presume) for my favorite constellation. On my desk was a folder of Alison Knowles' performance pieces, too few for a book but enough to make an attractive unit of some kind. "Why not," I thought, "make a series of 16-page pamphlets, miniatures in a sense of our books, and (hopefully) as refreshing as this water I'm drinking?" Thus began our Great Bear Pamphlet series. Sometimes the books were too expensive for our friends to buy, but the pamphlets? Not really, though to hear our friends talk one wouldn't believe that. The first ten pamphlets paralleled the books we were doing, for the most part—small works by Alison Knowles, myself, George Brecht, Claes Oldenburg, Allan Kaprow, Wolf Vostell, Jackson Mac Low and a collection of manifestos by all kinds of interesting people having in common only their innovative thinking—Öyvind Fahlström, Bob Watts, the W.E.B. DuBois Clubs (a communist youth group, though we were scarcely communists), Nam June Paik, Ay-O, John Giorno, Diter Rot (as Dieter Roth then spelled his name), and others. Later, in 1968–69, a generous friend made possible a second series too, works by Filliou, David Antin, Bengt af Klintberg, Luigi Russolo, Diter Rot and others. The pamphlets, all twenty of them, were able to get places that the larger books couldn't. For example, in the late 1960's they were sold from a rack beside the produce stand at the Berkeley Co-op in Berkeley, California; we were always delighted by the notion of a shopping basket containing ice cream, the makings of a good salad—and our pamphlets! A paying proposition they were not, and bookstores *hated* them, damned them as nuisances and ephemera. But they did reduce the danger of our being dismissed as snobbish avant-gardists ("SPECIAL—NOT FOR US") which is ever-present when one doesn't affect the normative li'l-ol'-me pose that American mind-workers are supposed to have. Ah well.

Alas, it couldn't last forever. One sad day in the fall of 1965 [early 1966, ed.] Barbara Moore told me she was going to have a baby and would have to leave the Press eventually, except (hopefully) for some freelance work. I congratulated her, then set about the grim business of finding her replacement. It turned out not to be so grim at all—Emmett Williams was available and willing, and in February, 1966, he arrived from Europe where he had been living for the previous seventeen years.

The first project he was given was Claes Oldenburg's *Store Days*; notes, works, drawings, happenings, scenarios from *The Store*, a real store with art things and performances which Oldenburg had done in 1961–1962. Oldenburg was brilliant in executing his ideas, but he had no master plan, no sense of what he wanted to do. Furthermore, he had an older brother, Richard "Dick" Oldenburg who had been a trade editor at Macmillan and who later presided over the decline of New York's Museum of Modern Art—an archetypal pudgy if there ever was one. Anything that anyone said to Claes Oldenburg convinced him—and any disagreement was taken personally. So every evening, while Emmett and Claes were working on "the book," I would be phoned at 11:30 PM (I usually worked late) by Emmett—"We've put the book to bed, and it's terrific. Stay there at the office, I'll take a taxi up and show it to you." Then, while Emmett was riding uptown would come a second call, this one from Claes—"Don't open the package that Emmett is bringing you. I've got doubts. The book's in trouble. Maybe I should show it to Dick." And in this way passed the spring, summer and fall of 1966—highlighted by melancholy conversations with Claes who did not see at all what a good writer he was when he followed his own nose, and whose brother (judging from what I heard indirectly) seemed bent on turning *Store Days* into the usual, boring Macmillan art book.

I remember one marvelous New Year's party at Claes's loft—Patty Oldenburg's fine roast ham with her own glaze, magnificent "soft" Oldenburg sculptures sewn by Patty, and Dick Oldenburg, studiedly natural, telling me, "This book should not be published during Claes's lifetime." The strongest version of it, inevitably, was not the one which Claes and Emmett came up with in the end, but was the one which Emmett worked up mostly from Claes's notebooks. It contained very sharp remarks about other artists, but these were not offensive: rather they were the kind of attacks that an artist always makes on others as part of the process of whittling down the possibilities into a definition of one's own point of view. There were some very harsh comments about me. Claes seemed to think I should be offended. I had to tell him there was no reason why I should be; in context they were just "stages along the way," and they were interesting for what they revealed about Claes more, perhaps, than what they said about my own work. However these, like most of the other similar and fascinating materials, were not included in the final book. A few sets of galley proofs are all that remain of the best version of the book. It would have been a masterpiece, if Emmett had put his foot down. After all, if I had wanted a pudgy editor, I could have found a dozen Dick Oldenburgs to choose among. My hope was that Emmett would be true to his convictions.

Publicity was always a crucial problem. Major media have responsibilities not only to their readers but to their advertisers, and oftentimes it seemed that they were more interested in the latter than the former. One way to call attention to our books was to show them and the work of the artists we were publishing. So, since I was living in a renovated brownstone house behind the Chelsea Hotel (at that time the hotel where our European artist friends usually stayed when they were in New York), and since there was a palatial living room on the first floor in which I always felt ill at ease and never used, I turned it into The Something Else Gallery, 238 West 22nd Street, New York, NY 10011. Al Hansen, Happener Extraordinary, became our gallery director. And there we showed a program, through the spring of 1966, of "object poems," concrete poetry (the first New York exhibition of these works), works by Wolf Vostell (we also sponsored his major happening, *Dogs and Chinese Not Allowed*—the title came from the grim slogan of the Belgravia Club in pre-World War II Shanghai) and Alison Knowles and others. Knowles' main work at the Gallery was *The Big Book*, a one-of-a-kind book object that was ten feet tall, sixteen pages long, with a tunnel, a portable bathroom facility, hot plate and telephone—one could virtually live in that book. It was later reconstructed and shown in Europe.

The Gallery was not supposed to last forever, and it didn't. Its program was limited—four shows. But it was revived from time to time as long as I lived in that house, for concerts—memorable ones of Satie and of piano ragtime music—a marathon reading (nonstop) of James Joyce's *Finnegans Wake*, organized by James Tenney, and even two more art shows over the years. But our shows had the honor of being insulted in *Atlantic Monthly* and other pudgy media, and of being reviewed seriously in the *Village Voice* and even the *New York Times*. We never did quite make being attacked in *The Partisan Review*, but ah well, you can't have everything.

Also in 1966 I decided to get my past/present dialectic going, to reprint neglected masterpieces from the past and use them to pay for our present productions. Our Happenings and Fluxus works were constantly being attacked in the name of Dada, inevitably by people who did not know what the Dadaists had done. Well, my stepmother was a Weimar-period German intellectual, I was raised on Dada and Expressionism, and it is part of my childhood. Fluxus is, like Dada, an iconoclastic tendency and there is a certain spiritual continuity between them, but it is in no sense a revival of Dada nor is it haunted or intimidated by it. There was only one irrefutable way to clarify the relationship with Dada: do a Dada classic. And we did. We reissued the *Dada Almanach* with Richard Huelsenbeck's blessing (he wanted and received 10% of the edition)—in facsimile from the 1920 edition. That book is actually an anthology produced just before the violent split between the Paris and Berlin Dada groups, so it is as authentic a statement of what Dada consists of, actually and not theoretically, as one can imagine. So we did our book, clarified that point (and, by the way, it sold even in bookstores which did not have foreign-language books normally—showing that the American public would read German books if they were interesting enough)—and even so, I recall Bernard Karpel telling me, at the Museum of Modern Art where he was the librarian, that the *Dada Almanach* wasn't truly Dada, which was ephemeral. Ah well. Also, our German friends were very startled to receive copies of a German-language classic from the USA. It led to a whole rash of reprints of Dada and related facsimiles there, which was fine for all concerned. We always dreamed of doing an English language translation, and Benjamin Patterson began one, but every time we went to see Huelsenbeck he used the occasion for some kind of family or social gathering, so the work never got completed. As I keep saying, ah well. And now he's dead, like the Press.

I never meant to live my life in New York City; cities, even the best of cities, give me claustrophobia. I find myself confusing myself with other people. Even worse—I get visited. By that I mean that I am contacted by people who do not want to speak with *me* but with my name. This came to be a problem already by 1967. So I bought a small farmhouse in Northern Vermont—more of what that meant later—and tried to run away to there, at least for the summer. But my work ran after me. Emmett Williams was supposed to be in charge, in my absence. But he was less an editor than a technician. The economics of publishing did not enter into his thinking, and yet an art without economics is apt to become a disaster. At one point he proposed that we spend half our annual production budget on a full page advertisement in the *New York Times*—as if we had the sales organization which could follow-up an advertisement like that (we didn't—we had one lone but quite enterprising commission salesman—Russell Chaskin). At another point he wanted to do a four-color book by an unknown artist about salt shakers: a delightful book it was, but he would have had to forego his salary and we would have had to cancel all other books for the year to do the thing, on top of which such an elaborate book by an unknown would have been terribly hard to publicize. And if the book cost anything near its unit cost, who could afford it? Evidently this did not concern him. In fact it did not concern him with a vengeance. And so it came about that some basic editorial decisions had to be made without him—or even in spite of him. And that created distance, distance between the two of us; and it meant that my work had to follow me. Very well, then why couldn't the Press follow me too? Why not move to Vermont? Wouldn't overhead be less there? Couldn't we concentrate on our work there and not get visited? Those were my questions from 1967 to 1969.

I was unhappy that we had no dance book in our program. Very well, why not start at the top? I called Merce Cunningham, whom I knew slightly but who was a dear friend of many friends, and whom I admired enormously. Why not do something like our Oldenburg *Store Days* with his notebooks? He was delighted by a book on the dance rather than on the dancers. He came right over to the house and we talked about it, that Autumn day in 1966, Merce, Emmett and myself. Emmett said he was not qualified to do the editing, so we thought through a chain with my secretary (who was a dancer) doing part of the work, Emmett doing the rewriting and technical part of the work, and myself doing the overall planning with Merce. Two years later the troika arrangement was replaced by one person, Frances Starr (who also edited George Brecht and Robert Filliou's *Games at the Cedilla*) and in due course the book appeared as Merce Cunningham's *Changes*, of which Lincoln Kirstein—surely the pudgiest, most negative figure in the American dance these days—said that as long as *he* had anything to do with Lincoln Center (or was it the Museum of Modern Art?) *that book* would never be sold in their bookstore. So you know it's a great book. It is too—full of ideas, which one watches as one watches choreography, rather than reading in a purely linear way. Ah well.

Anyway, Merce Cunningham said that he was about to go on tour, and I observed that we badly needed a manuscript for a spring book, could Emmett put together a quickie anthology of concrete poetry? He allowed as how he could, "in his sleep." And Emmett set to work to do the book, not in his sleep either. We agreed that

I would not be in the book except as designer; a precedent was needed for exclusions, since we agreed that the focus should be on those who had done the strongest work in the area, from whatever country, and not on what it was most political to include or which of the then ten million New York poets who were absentmindedly churning out armfuls of visually-structured typewriter poems to include and which not. Alas—a few fine people got left out in the process—Richard Kostelanetz, Tom Ockerse, others too. But then we could point to myself, who had done concrete poetry since late 1958 and was certainly involved at the Press, and could say—"Well, he isn't in it either."

That way nobody got hurt feelings and, in fact, the book was a howling success. *Harper's Bazaar* printed a few pages of concrete poetry culled from Emmett's anthology in their November, 1967 issue. *Newsweek* reviewed the book favorably. Emmett became, overnight, a pundit and much sought-after by the lion-hunters. This delighted me, because now he could represent the Press at official functions leaving me to my work or even to Vermont. And he was far more suitable for being "visited" than I. Our anthology sparked others (in most of which I was included). Ours had the author's touch about it—selections were made by the poets in most cases, and so were the captions. Others had a better pedagogic quality; Mary Ellen Solt's *Concrete Poetry: A World View* (1968) had her brilliant introduction, some color plates, and some excellent theoretical materials. Eugene Wildman's *Anthology of Concretism* was another outstanding volume. But the Emmett Williams *Anthology of Concrete Poetry* was one of the outstanding books that the Press produced.

Many people looking at my own writings saw a relationship to Gertrude Stein. There is a relationship between myself and Stein, but it is a digested and allusive influence, not an overt, technical one. To see this one must know the Stein originals, and to know the Stein originals in the middle and late 1960's was impossible for all but billionaires. She was collected more than she was read. What to do? Do Stein. *The Making of Americans*, one of her early masterpieces (1906–1908), was in the public domain, thanks to a requirement of American copyright law that all books by American authors published in English be manufactured in the United States or that an American edition must, within a few years, follow an edition manufactured abroad. Otherwise copyright is lost forever. Stein was an expatriate, living most of her life in Paris and being published there more than anywhere else. Thus her works that appeared in her early career were almost all in the public domain. At first I wanted our editions to be authorized ones, but I found that the Stein estate was not, at that time, realistic about the value of the works. This is no longer the case, I hear. So I went ahead and published *The Making of Americans* in 1966, and we continued the Stein program up until the Press was discontinued, doing *Geography and Plays*, *How to Write*, her most lyrical novel *Lucy Church Amiably, Matisse, Picasso and Gertrude Stein* and *A Book Concluding With As A Wife Has A Cow*. Wolf Vostell made some lovely illustrations for *Before the Flowers of Friendship Faded Friendship Faded*, and halftones were made but the book was never printed. I wonder if the printer still has the halftones and the type that was set?

And so it went. Reprints, newsletters—all that kind of thing was handled by myself. Sometimes, when it was embarrassing to use my own name in letters from the Press, I used the name Camille Gordon. After a while Camille developed a very vivid personality of her own—a critic, married to an ethnomusicologist who specialized in Turkish and Afghan music (which I love), a bookkeeper, a source of general information—Camille was many things. Many people at the Press, over the years, became "Camille Gordon." At different times both Judith Padow and Meredith Monk, fine dancers both of them, worked for the Press to pay the rent. For them it was a great convenience to be able to be "Camille Gordon" and not their professional names (which were their own names). When Judy Padow went with me to an art opening, she was Camille Gordon, which was quite interesting to those who doubt that Camille existed. I liked it that Camille's initials in her name were "C.G." which I took to suggest the French "Ci Git" or "Here Lies." The sardonic tone pleased me. Once in a while Camille was involved in a tactless embroglio, and on such occasions she was replaced by "Charles Gagnon" (for the source of which, see Dickens' *A Tale of Two Cities*)—which is also a "C.G." name. In fact, since that time, I have for years done commercial work and writing under all sorts of "C.G." names. Camille had her own newsletter for a while, "Camille Reports." She became quite the gossip. At one point she mentioned her silver shoe buckles in a newsletter, and Ray Johnson promptly printed a poster with a picture of Camille's shoe buckles. When Camille "left us," once again, she was picked up by the *New York Review of Sex* which I found a little embarrassing. But, shortly after I wrote to its editor, Sam Edwards, she left that job—as did Mr. Edwards. Ah well.

The newsletters grew out of "Camille Reports" postcards, which were purely gossip. As part of my effort to "let people in" on the mysteries of Fluxus, concrete poetry and others of our activities, I felt it was crucially important to write some theoretical articles in colloquial language. The first and by far the most important newsletter that I wrote was a short article, "Intermedia," named for a term from Coleridge which he used in 1812 in exactly the sense in which I used it (my first use of the term, actually, had been several years earlier, in a lecture in 1963). The idea of an intermedium was simply the concept that some works fall between traditional media. Concrete poetry is an intermedium between poetry and the visual arts. Happenings are a three-way intermedium between drama, visual art and sound art. Sound poetry lies between poetry and music. And so on. And, of course, intermedia can become media, and are no guarantee of the relevance of a particular work—only an aspect of it. Thus there can be no "movement" based on intermedia (this was an attack on the Brazilian concrete poets, who saw concrete poetry as a movement).

Then the term was picked up, used and abused. Every so often some pudgy would come along and say, "You didn't invent the term," and I was delighted to be able to say that I had *found* it in Coleridge. The pudgies kept trying to see me as a mindless neoteric, carrying on some war with the past. They could present me as that—but it didn't fit. Anyway, for that kind of argument I had no time. If I were one of them I would have made a career out of having found the term "intermedia," the way some of my happenings friends did. That was not my style. But I was pleased to see the term become widespread. Theoretical articles like those we published in our newsletter had no commercial outlet; even more than other media, art magazines served their galleries and other advertisers more than their readership. Most were idea-free. Their critics had ideologies but not ideas, correctnesses and purities without any discernible art involvements. Fluxus people had no time for that: our ideology had to be concrete, and it was often inseparable from the paradigms of Fluxus work. All in all, over the years, the Press did fifteen newsletters [twenty-two, ed.]. They were our chief promotion, mailed out free to our mailing list of 5000 people—they were read, abused and bought from. I like them. For anyone who is interested in them, a few of my theoretical articles are in my book *foew&ombwhnw* (New York: Something Else Press, 1969) and all are in *A Dialectic of Centuries* (New York: Printed Editions, 1978).

By 1969 my problems at the Press had become harder and harder, and I was finding it virtually impossible to keep my private life alive. My success as a publisher was making my success as an artist unlikely. I was desperate to move to Vermont and come to New York only for long visits. Alison Knowles was equally desperate to stay in New York. We compromised and moved to California, where we were both miserable, though for different reasons. Mostly she missed New York. Mostly I missed my Fluxus friends and the Vermont-New York circuit that I had become used to. In California both Alison and I were teaching at the California Institute of the Arts which, because of its association with the Disney family (and money) was known to its victims as "Mickey Mouse University." It was a total chaos, where department heads were fired in front of the assembled faculty, skilled professors who had been lured there partly by the promise of sufficient secretarial help to get books typed had to load packages at the local supermarket in order to pay for that typing to be done, more than half the student body left after the first year, and so on. I had turned in my New York brownstone for a canyon house near Newhall, just north of the San Fernando Valley. There I taught, since I could not take the madness of our campus at Burbank. My time was divided among three departments, and while I found that this did mean that I didn't have to go to as many departmental emergency meetings as many of my colleagues, it also meant that no department was willing to admit me as one of theirs. My marriage ended, in September a chaparral fire came to within half a mile of my home (I spent the night hosing down the roof), a December snowfall ruined half my fine old live oak trees—and oh, California drivers in the snow! They would drive at sixty to a ravine that was filled with slush, would screech to a stop, hop out and peer, and

then

hop

back into their cars and drive through the ravine at sixty. I, being used to snow driving, poked along at twenty-five. It drove the Californians crazy. And then one morning, I awoke to a total silence at 6:00 AM. This was eerily extraordinary. Usually animals in the canyon would be waking up, roosters crowing, burros braying

159

and so on. But animals have instincts that we don't. Suddenly I heard a noise like a subway train. The earth heaved, and a huge bookcase fell onto my bed, right where I would have been sleeping if I had not sat up when I sensed something was wrong. In a flash I was into my twin daughters' room. One was hanging for dear life onto the post of her bunk bed. "Get up, kids," I yelled, "It's an earthquake!" "What's an earthquake, Pa?" asked my Hannah. Jessie just cowered. I grabbed a twin under each arm, kicked a door open, and ran out by our swimming pool. The sound enveloped me—it came from all space, the most multiphonic sound experience I have ever had. The earth had waves in it, with the trees bobbing to and fro as if they were afloat. Half the water flew out of my swimming pool. It would have been beautiful if it were not so terrifying. I've heard the same said of migraines and of war, and hope never to experience either. After the quake the neighborhood children organized themselves into a sort of militia, to see that everyone was all right, to find out what the damage was, to advise us strangers to the area what to do ("Pour water because the town water will probably not be safe in a few hours, when seepage begins—and turn off all gas utilities in case of explosion.") I asked if this happened often. "Oh no," they said, "It's been several years since the last time this happened." I decided then and there that whatever the problems I would face, not earning an income from teaching or whatever, that this was no environment to write or publish in. That maybe even "someone" was trying to tell me just that. I'd rather be broke in Vermont than affluent but shell-shocked in California. Later in the day my phone rang, which was odd because we had been told not to make any phone calls except for dire emergencies, to send telegrams instead to friends and relatives assuring them that we were all right. It was a paper salesman in New York who had simply dialed me in California and, by fluke, had gotten through. I asked him to tell my mother we were all okay. In fact, she heard we were okay before she heard there had been an earthquake near Los Angeles—and the epicenter was a scant four miles from my house, almost at the Oak of the Golden Dream where gold was first found in 1837 in California (ten years before the larger and later gold rush). Ironic. I also asked this salesman to tell our distributor that I was moving back east—which he had been after me to do for all that year.

The success of *An Anthology of Concrete Poetry* and of our Stein books had obliged us to pool resources with a distributor, Michael Hoffman who, first with the "Small Publishers' Association" and later with "The Book Organization," tried to out-professional the professionals—or, as I would put it, to out-pudgy the pudgies—and ended by becoming one. He had a fine little photography magazine, *Aperture*, excellent contacts and business know-how—but also had delusions of grandeur that led him to build empires of seventy salesmen north of the Arctic circle (figuratively) while neglecting such silly things as actually filling orders. As long as I was there and could keep an eye on things this was no problem. The orders got filled. In fact I think I watched his orders more closely than he did. But I did not like to keep an eye on orders. This led to problems, especially after our move to California. I saw our arrangement as temporary, but kept this view to myself since I saw no immediate alternative. Instead it lasted five years, almost.

Our success also caused problems with Emmett Williams. I was constantly annoyed by his erratic working habits—one day he would come into the office at 8:00 AM and the next day at noon, and he would spend as much time polishing one simple Great Bear Pamphlet as working on a whole book. I also was frustrated by his unwillingness to make suggestions about projects we should do, or to show me how a project was shaping up until it was virtually complete. Our relationship was apt to be tempestuous, then—warm today and cold tomorrow. At one point he puffed off to Iceland with Diter Rot to do one book, sent me an entirely different one to publish, and seemed outraged that I was confused by this (and misinterpreted my questions as a rejection). The Press had never paid him much of a salary, though he was paid as well as I could manage. I myself was never paid anything. We did have a parallel foundation to the Press, and it could be used to get money for productions, but overhead was always hard to finance. Most of it was done by rolling over our debts constantly, by borrowing money from Bank A on the east side, then going to Bank B on the west side to borrow money to pay back Bank A and to pocket a little besides to pay salaries. I was constantly gambling in one way or another, investing in scrap copper in Venezuela and in all kinds of strange speculations. This paid the salaries, but it was horrible for my nerves. I constantly quarrelled with Emmett, and when his success meant he could get teaching invitations, he switched his main line of work from art and editing to teaching.

His skill as a copy editor remained fabulous. When, in 1969, I decided that a book of my own short pieces should be worked up, it was he who did all the hard editorial work. And so my book *foew&ombwhnw* appeared, bound as a prayer book (since it was the nucleus of my canon). Emmett's workmanship is evident on every page, although in this case he preferred to be anonymous and nowhere is he credited to the extent that he deserves. He also undertook the proofreading of an incredibly complex book we did, Jackson Mac Low's *Stanzas for Iris Lezak*. He was part owner of the Press, and even after he was no longer working with us daily, he worked very hard indeed on some specific projects.

Part 2

During the California time Emmett and his wife, Ann Stevenson Williams (who had briefly been my assistant at the Press, who had in fact come to the United States to work with me, had been introduced to Emmett one day in November, 1968, had almost at once found him to be her gentleman of destiny and had, ultimately, married him) during that time they had living with them off Laurel Canyon Emmett's son by a previous marriage, Eugene. Since they were both working, they were in no immediate need of money. Also at that time I had a chance to buy some incredibly beautiful land with half a pond back in Vermont, which I did. And I paid Emmett in land instead of money for the work he did for the Press. The idea was that he and Eugene would make a father and son project of building a log cabin on the land. When the school year ended at the California Institute of the Arts, I looked for someone to share the driving with me. The logical person was Eugene. So we packed and went. My last glimpse of "Cal Arts" was of its new building, standing at one end of a kilometer-long corridor down which, slowly coming towards me, drifted a melancholy student in drag—not just drag, but in a bizarre gown with camel bells and green lipstick on his face. Ah well.

And on the way I fell in love with Eugene. The tale is told in my *amigo* poems and their sequels. Those days are passed, now. He is married to a lovely wife, Jutta, and they have an equally lovely daughter, Sarah. As I write this they are staying in my old studio, across the road, having moved to Vermont this spring. We are very close friends. But this is 1978, and that was 1971. I was nearly hysterical, looking for peace, drinking far more than I could handle. He had been in the California drug scene and was looking, in his own way, for a family and stability. Was I it? I tried to be. We drove from Los Angeles to Vermont by way of San Francisco, where I renewed my friendship with Jan Herman, then the editor of Nova Broadcast publications, and via Alaska—which I had always wanted to see. I fell in love, and though he was not gay, he was very kind to me. To outsiders it seemed as if this wild young man was sponging off me. Many told me so. Actually he was a very good friend and on numerous occasions helped me get my act together.

And in 1971 to 1973 I *did* get my act together. I saw the Press differently now. I wanted to do books which reflected the new life styles. Mushroom books for instance, since gathering wild mushrooms had always been my hobby—since before I studied with John Cage (another mushroom-loving artist, and my friend and former teacher), since my childhood when my stepmother taught me the mushrooms' names in German because she did not know them in English. I decided to do a reissue of the unavailable classic, MacIlvaine's *One Thousand American Fungi*. And we did it, with a cover picture of a chanterelle mushroom by Alison Knowles, with whom I remained close. I also contracted to do an index, cross-referencing Latin nomenclature which, in the mushrooms, is in a terrible state of flux—a boon to any mushroom hunter. After I left the Press, this project was abandoned but Orson K. Miller, whose project it was, eventually published it in Germany, a strange fate for a book on North American fungi. It is admired but is horribly expensive and unknown to most mushroom collectors. I wish we could have done it.

I also withdrew from Michael Hoffman's distribution network. He owed us a great deal of money, and it took the harshest efforts of my stepfather, Nicholas Doman, a lawyer, to get him to pay us. He had gotten numerous grants from organizations who wanted to help the Press, and who thought that by supporting The Book Organization, they were supporting us. Hoffman's plans remained grand as ever—huge warehouses, bookmobiles that had no drivers—that was his style. But it was a style to which we could not afford to become accustomed. "We" was now myself, my secretary Nelleke Rosenthal (who, with her husband Michael, had become friendly with me in California and had come to wonder what was this Vermont I always pined away for—she lives here still), occasionally Emmett—and now we were joined by John Kimm, my uncle's stepson, a delightful ex-bass guitar player from Indiana (which he missed), and by Jan Herman. John had no editorial gift, but he had a great deal of business experience and acumen. He was able to get loans for us from the banks, credit from the printers, to rebuild our own distribution system with some dozen salesmen, even to set up a New York local distribution arrangement for efficient local service (which can be crucially important, especially at Christmas). He hired Ann Brazeau as his secretary, rented a warehouse in Barton, Vermont, hired Perry Fraenkel, Ann's sometime lover, as the warehouse man, and all seemed set, organizationally. He was loyal and gifted. But his style was straight.

Jan Herman was religious, but his god was William Burroughs and all that Burroughs stands for. His only gift was editorial. Outside of editorial work his motto was "Think small," and I don't mean in the sense of miniaturization. He could write in a dozen styles—but seldom did so. But once he decided to write a catalog for the Press—it is dated 1973–1974, and it is the last we did—and he was simply brilliant at copying my style, with all my mannerisms and expressions to the point where the catalog made me simply roar with laughter. Jan's style was not straight.

And now that a new organization had been built, perhaps I could spare a moment for my own work, and to organize my private life? I did not want to lose the Press. But I was sick with alchoholism, and I needed to recover. I made certain good editorial decisions, lined up more books by Stein, by the *transition* writer of experimental texts from the 1930s, Abraham Lincoln Gillespie, salable texts on the new life styles—if the organization was solid, it now had the chance of moving into the black, of becoming a viable economic entity. But trouble was a brewing.

Organizationally the Press was too closely identified with a particular kind of book. We had done a delightful letter by the artist/stockbroker Walter Gutman: it did not sell. We did a magnificent book on gardening in northern Vermont, the best book on northern gardening ever, written by my neighbor Cary Scher and edited by Jan Herman, *The Ten Week Garden*. It too did not sell. I had written my *amigo* poems, at the end of a long dry spell from 1969 (*foew&ombwhnw*) through my California time, when I wrote almost nothing except a light radio play, *City With All the Angles*. I've been told they are my best work. But Jan Herman did not like them. Emmett Williams seemed embarrassed by them. Eugene was embarrassed by them. So I decided that I would Unpublish them—they were too good to bury—and print them in a small edition, which I would give away the same day the books arrived at my house. I did it. Those who read them were delighted. And Nelleke suggested that I do more Un-publishing, as Unpublished Editions— editions of small, ephemeral things, but handsomely produced. I agreed this would be a good idea. And in this way I got back into the small press world and away from the Something Else Press, which was such a sap on my energy. Every year I did one or two small books—and though my books eventually became larger, after this year [1978] they will revert to small size again. The imprint changed from

Unpublished Editions to Printed Editions—but that is getting ahead of my story.

But it meant that my time for art was divided between my publishing and my creative work. On top of that my publishing energies were divided between Unpublished Editions and Something Else Press—and on top of this were the usual problems of supporting a complex household as a single parent, my illness, and my love involvement. I loved Eugene. Eugene loved Ann Brazeau. As did John Kimm. Ann loved Perry. And Jan Herman and Emmett Williams (when he was there) were simply cynical and amused by it all. It was a mess. Ah well.

On the surface things looked idyllic. Jan Herman took the editorial chores well in hand. We worked on a John Giorno book of poems, very much in the Burroughs world—*Cancer in My Left Ball*. Giorno wanted a cover by Les Levine. It would have been too expensive, so I whipped up a simpler design and sent it off to the printers. The printers bungled my instructions, the result looked horrible, and instead of giving me a chance to revamp the situation, John Giorno and Jan transformed my design into the ugliest jacket that the Press ever did. I decided that this would be the right time to withdraw from the Press, rather than risk an ulcer. Maybe if I stopped publishing, I could stop drinking.

In the meantime Eugene had come and gone several times in my life. Often he hung around in Vermont, waiting for Emmett to come and build that cabin. But Emmett never came. He dropped out of school, got onto drugs (which I helped him get off of). But Emmett never came. He had a contractor dig a cellar hole on Emmett's land, waiting for Emmett to order the logs, if logs must be ordered from a prefabricated "log home" company. Emmett tried to get a bank loan, using art works as security—art works by Diter Rot, who is hardly known in America. Naturally he was turned down. So once again, Emmett never came. But somehow I had gotten involved in the contract to get the logs—and *they came*. I had a pretty lot at the top of my field, one which would make a natural unit. So I offered it to Eugene with a balloon mortgage, which he accepted. I dreamed of him and his living up on that hill, and of I and mine (whoever that might be) living back across the road, working with Eugene and, perhaps just occasionally . . . Oh, well, it wasn't really very realistic. The cellar was built up on the hill, most of the "log home" was erected—and then poor Eugene's ménage à trois situation became too much for him (I didn't help either, with the demands I was making on him)—and he left. But oh what a summer that summer of 1973 was. Warm and sunny, and none of us in this strange situation were willing to admit what problems there were. I was "free" of the Press—and free to do my work with Eugene as my technical assistant (by now I had trained him into a fairly good technical worker in graphics, especially in graphic arts camera and silk-screen work). I embarked upon a wildly ambitious series of one-of-a-kind silk-screen graphics, *7.7.73*, which, when completed at the beginning of 1975, had over 800 different prints and screened objects, requiring nearly 500 different screens! Oh Vanity, thy name is Higgins! But they were swell prints. In the fall of 1973 I had my first one-man show—mostly of *7.7.73* prints—in Berlin, Germany. And Nelleke took her vacation in Europe and helped me to staff a booth at the Frankfurt Book

Fair. It was my next-to-last official act at Something Else Press. We also sold a lot of books, at least enough to pay for the stand—and who knows how much "good will" and publicity we lined up? We even sold the Norwegian rights to Cary Scher's gardening book. This was the trip which, in one of his later attacks on me, Jan Herman described as "taking off to Europe" with my secretary just when things were getting thick at the Press. In fact, I was so disgusted by the way things were going at that Press (even to me it was obvious that I was in no position mentally to become active there again). My job was to regroup my finances, not to fight for a Press in which I felt like an alien. Sometime that summer or fall I even resigned, not just from the management of the Press, but from the Board of Directors as well.

I've said that John was in love with Ann. Well, I haven't seen John in years, so I cannot check it out. But he seemed to be in love with her and she thought he was in love with her. But she, like Jan, was wild—and his straightness turned her off. Every day we would go off to skinny dip in a beautiful lake nearby. Every day John would want to come along (I'm told)—and every day he would not be there—and Jan and Ann would laugh about him behind his back. I was disgusted.

Finally, one day just after my resignation, John came to me and said that if I didn't fire Jan, he would have to quit. And he went away. Ten minutes later Jan came to me and said that if I did not fire John, then *he* would quit. I pointed out to each of them that I no longer worked for the Press, that they should work it out since I could fire nobody. It seemed then that *both* would quit. So I decided that Jan understood at least a little more about the objectives of the Press than John, so it should be John that went. And I accepted John's resignation (which, technically, I had no right to do). It was a mistake. John left, and with him went, basically, the support organization that I had worked two years to build up. I had left John and Jan with a list of important cigars to light if money was needed. John understood the importance of lighting such cigars. Jan did not. He went nowhere, lit no cigars. His way of doing business was to go down to the warehouse and wrap books—which is fine for a helpful editor, but death to a senior executive whose job is to keep the books and money flowing like blood in the veins of an organism. When I asked about this, he said he couldn't afford to travel. John would not have said that; he would have hitch-hiked across the country, if need be, to see a gentlemanly foundation director who might help us with a grant to do a book. Jan neglected the roll-over at the bank—it made him nervous—and so debts came due at the bank and at the printers. Jan blamed me. (Incidentally, when the Press finally went bankrupt, it owed well over $325,000!!!)

Everywhere and to everybody he blamed me. He said I'd left him with an empty larder. I said the larder had always been empty, that the trick was to make it look full so that someone would come along who would, in fact, fill it up. He did not believe me. In the midst of it all, he arranged to publish the complete notebooks of William Burroughs (as if Burroughs couldn't, easily enough, find his own publisher). He produced a very strange yearbook—a project which he had inherited from me, but which he took into a curious and personal direction. And finally he did a book by one Manfred L. Eaton, *Bio-Music*—a reissue of an article from *Source* magazine, not even a very authoritative article. It was the last Something Else Press book, and it appeared sometime in 1974. After I saw that yearbook, surely the worst-assembled of all Something Else Press books, I felt no identification with the Press any more. Ah well.

But stranger things were afoot. After Eugene panicked about the house, I had two options—sell it to some friend or finish it and sell it on the open market. It had been planned that it would be a Williams house. I offered it to Emmett but asked him to get a mortgage from the bank. Several days later I saw a banker friend in town. "Your friend passed in a pretty weird mortgage application," he said. "We'll have to turn him down." Emmett had applied for a mortgage—and goodness knows what he had said. But I really wanted him there. And he told me he was earning over $20,000 a year—this to get the mortgage. In fact the mortgage payments to me came to nearly $500 a month, or $6000 a year. And Emmett was earning something like $10,000 a year. On such an income, surely to accept a mortgage of that size would be utter folly. But Emmett wanted that house, and he began his occupancy there sometime in early 1974.

Somewhere at that point Eugene realized that this situation with Ann and with me was a disaster. And he left for Nova Scotia, where Emmett was teaching, telling us that he was heading south, and that he would *not* suicide (as he had been threatening all fall) for at least six months. So Ann and I went out and got drunk. It was my last drink. I had reached the point where I could not sleep through the night without a big glass of wine by my side to enjoy at 2:00 in the morning, so I could go back to sleep. They tell me I stayed gentlemanly, that I seemed sober even when I really was not. I do not recall. What I do know is that I had had enough. And after I drove home from Ann's house, having miraculously *not* driven off the road, I set my full bottle of Pernod on the seat of her car (which was non-functional and sitting in my driveway) and I drank no more. In the morning I hallucinated—I saw the face of Meredith Monk in the clouds (though we are not particularly close, I have always admired her and her art enormously). By the time the hallucinations cleared up, I was on the phone to my sister in Connecticut, who lived down the road from a fine sanitorium, Silver Hill, in which my grandmother had been interested and where I had gone when I got into difficulty as a teenager. She got me Silver Hill's number. I called and committed myself. When one has gone to such a place one gets newsletters and requests for funds for years afterwards, so I knew that alcoholism was a disease which Silver Hill had been very effective in combatting. I knew that alcoholism was our major national public health problem, and that only some 10% of its victims ever bring it under control (it can never be cured). And I knew I wanted to be one of that 10%. I also called the poet Michael Cooper to come run my house, which, basically, he did for the four months that I was away. My last drink was on January 13th, 1974—now, over four years later, I am still one drink away from madness, and am enjoying that distance one day at a time.

I was supposed to stay at Silver Hill for five months. But I stayed just under four. I came home thinking that now that I was not drinking, the world would be a big cheese just waiting for me to slice off a big piece. I was dry, but I was not sober. I thought I would write some huge work, finish *7.7.73* (I had a new technician, Jennifer Carlson, to work with in my studio), and perhaps that fall see if it made sense to go back to the Press and try mending it again—or perhaps try and sell it (there were still all those books on hand). Jan Herman was still snarling around in a desultory way, talking about Burroughs' notebooks. Why have dealings with him? Emmett Williams and Ann and their child Garry were all in the log house on the hill. They had a mortgage holiday until September, per our agreement, but the mortgage had not yet begun to pinch Emmett. Eugene came back. We spent a lovely summer together. I was working on *Modular Poems* as a large Unpublished Editions book, and working with Jennifer on *7.7.73*. But it was clear that this could not continue. It was a fool's paradise. I went with my daughters to do a show in South America. While I was away, the IRS got into my affairs and claimed that Something Else Press had never been a serious business, that the business losses which I had deducted all those years were invalid, and I was not an artist at all (in a business sense), but a tax dodger—and then everything began to collapse. In my pinkish haze I had decided to gamble on my future and build an indoor swimming pool. I couldn't afford it, did it anyway—and found that between taxes on that, the IRS lien on my thin-as-paper finances, and, next, the inevitable default of Emmett on his mortgage—I now went to pieces and had a serious nervous breakdown. But I was not so shot that, one day in December, 1974, I couldn't be driven home to Vermont by my mother, meet a lawyer at the house in Barton, and, in my capacity as majority stockholder of the Press (and against Emmett's and Jan Herman's wishes), sign the petition to put the Press into bankruptcy.

The time passed. I recovered, though it took me many months—and now, four years later, I am still under medication. The IRS is still after me, harassing me. Emmett defaulted in the summer of 1975, and I had to take possession of the log house. He thought I should pay him back his equity in the place—but in no way could I do so, even had I wanted to. Besides, his default literally drove me out of my home; I gave it up—it has been on the market for the past few years—pool, offices, studio, house, a remarkable white elephant of a place and all that is left of the physical plant which housed the Something Else Press. Many of the Press records disappeared during the bankruptcy in the course of moving. The IRS claimed that the Press had never kept good business records—though Jan Herman's wife Janet was a Certified Public Accountant, kept the books, and was extraordinarily good as a bookkeeper. The agent perhaps thought it was a way to get me. But the records turned up in the cellar of the Vermont Tomato Company, which belongs to the brother of the bankruptcy trustee. In this matter, I am still embattled. And that is not good for the digestion. But the books went out. They were not pulped, as I had feared they would be. They were remaindered, distributed, sold to libraries, sold on bargain tables to people like us at Great Bear Pamphlet prices. The legend has grown, but the books are far more durable than the legend. Their ideas last.

After the bankruptcy, Jan Herman and Emmett Williams acted cordially to me, perhaps while they thought there was something to be gained. But Jan had written and had accepted several articles, post mortems of the Press, which were harsh attacks on me. I was portrayed as an erratic slave driver, an exploiter in these and in an interview with Emmett, which typifies that class of attack, in *West Coast Poetry Review* 17 (Autumn 1977). But I never made a penny on that Press; not that I would apologize if I had—I always meant to—but part of my problem was that I was a very bad judge of character. Emmett, for instance, is not a bad man, but he is of a type that is familiar to anyone who has read Matthew Arnold's *Essays in Criticism* or *Culture and Anarchy*—a total "Hellene" with none of the necessary "Hebraic" leavening, an aesthete without any mollifying moral fervor. He is the ideal companion to toss a glass with and to sit in front of a fire roasting chestnuts—but a dangerous man to have confidence in where he thinks his interests might be crossed. Thus he claims to have brought his *Anthology* in a suitcase from Europe, where the idea for it was actually worked out that spring day of 1967 (of course he *may* have conceived of such a book earlier, but it was not in his suitcase—much of it was on my bookshelves, in the collection I was making for our Something Else Gallery show, and so on). Thus he let Eugene down with those logs. Thus he misled me about his income to get a mortgage from me, and thus he told Jan Herman that he had "rescued" me from having to sell the log house. Ah well. I can live with the books he's done, while I no longer have to live with the man. He is now a Harvard Professor, and I haven't heard of his publishing any books of new writing lately.

Ironically, it is now I who live in the house on the hill. It's much smaller, but it's enough for my needs.

What went wrong with the Press? In a way, nothing; in another way, every thing. The Press lived out its natural life, given the interests of the people involved. We meant to publish and to do so profitably; but only as part of a way of deepening our cultural and literary lives. Given that, the Press should have been terminated when Jan and John both wanted to have the other one sacked. Or it should have been given to John to build using freelance editors.

But it was also structurally weak. While I was wrong to trust either Jan or Emmett and perhaps myself, it was also a mistake on a far more profound level to try and do such unconventional books with unconventional and heavy-cultural implications, while using a thoroughly conventional organizational structure. I will explain what I mean.

The Press was a normal, subchapter S corporation, with the usual power flow structure—President, Vice President, Secretary, Board of Directors, Manager or Publisher, Editor, Publications Director, Production Manager, Publicity Director, Rights and Permissions department, and so on. Of course most of us who worked for the Press over the years wore two or even more hats. But basically it was all compartmentalized. It provided jobs, people depended upon it to provide those jobs, and this means that *at no time was it ever conceived that the overhead could be cut by eliminating the jobs once and for all.* It is easy to get money to do books. It is hard to get money to pay for organizational support. But who would work for an organization which provided no jobs? Who doesn't care a good cigar in Hades how the organization is set up? Well, somebody does—namely, the authors. So why not eliminate everybody but the authors? This brings me to some of the ideas of another Something Else Press author whom I have not yet discussed in detail, John Cage.

John Cage travels light. He owns no house, bothers with no institutions (though he is friendly with many), and concentrates on what he does best—or tries to, when the phone doesn't ring too much. And what he does best is music, poetry, visual art, philosophy—and all the intermedia in between. We did a text of his—part three of the "Diary" series—as one of our Great Bear Pamphlet series; graphically it is one of the most striking things we ever did. His art spills over into life at every turn—and fuses with it, reflecting it. Life has chaos on many levels, some more interesting than others; Cage rolls with all of them instead of fighting them. He made a collection, for fundraising purposes, of sample manuscripts of as many composers of the twentieth century as he could. We did the catalog. Catalog? It's a page per composer, with a chance-structured text that is a mosaic of quotations from the composers included—hundreds of them. That book, the catalog, *Notations* is another of our most striking books. He pasted it up slowly and carefully with Alison Knowles, who did all the camera work. At first it looks confusing, coarse. Slowly the materials assume unique identities. One follows each text through graphic metamorphoses. Could any organizational system have supported it? No. A conservative editor would have intervened—would have said: "The salesmen won't like that." It would have been pudgified to death. But has such a book no right to exist? The book wasn't edited, in fact, except through its actual execution by Alison and John, perhaps with a quick checkover for typos by Emmett (I don't recall). There was no intervention. It is the happy result of the fact that each of us from the Press who were involved in the project wore all the hats.

So what happened *after* Something Else Press to which this experience with *Notations* refers? Well, I returned to New York, hopefully to get a degree, a PhD in English. I like to say that I don't like my name, that I want to change "Dick" to "Dock." But that's not really it. Coming out of my breakdown I needed to remind myself of the whole panoply of literature and the other arts of which English-language literature is a microcosm. Reading systematically through our language was one approach. It could as well have been Comparative Literature—I enjoy reading in other languages and am especially fascinated by the new forms of criticism which have arisen in the last few years: structuralism, hermeneutics, deconstructionism, phenomenological criticism, and so on. These have been the property of academics to date. But it need not be so. They are studied more in Comparative Literature than in English. But ah well. I chose English. And I chose to study at New York University, where the nineteenth-century area is very, very strong. I did not want to know just the moderns, in the formal sense, but to know a period deeply outside of our own. Being in New York—and having my daughters with me—I was shortly close again with Alison. We had tried for a reconciliation before, in 1972–1973, but then it was all too soon, too strange, and too wild. Now in 1975 it worked. We found ourselves together.

So I opened up Unpublished Editions to her, and we arranged to be distributed by a distributor, Christopher P. Stephens. When he phased out his business in 1977, we went to a group in California, and, when they did not work out, we went to Truck Distributing (now called Bookslinge) in St. Paul, Minnesota. They are one of several organizations specializing in the problems of small press distribution. At the time I did Something Else Press there were, as such, no such organizations. Hoffman's group was almost a prototype, but it assumed huge production plans and required gargantuan budgets to function at all. Truck assumes only editorial quality, sells hard, and carries on in a businesslike way, but is small and prefers to keep it that way, good for pocket publishing and not just mega-publishing.

Now we are seven—Alison and myself, joined by John Cage, Philip Corner, Geoffrey Hendricks, Jackson Mac Low, and Pauline Oliveros. Sound familiar? Only Pauline Oliveros never did a Something Else Press book—and that was *not* because I didn't try to encourage her to do so, but because it simply never happened that she and I could zig or zag together. When one zigs while the other zags, it's hard to reach a meeting of minds. Each person tries to do a thing or so each year. If each person did one project each year, that would be seven per year, or seventy items in ten years—and that would make a *big* little publisher of us. In fact we are doing things even faster than that. And where is the organization? There isn't any. Each person produces sher own books (his or hers) at sher own expense, and as the books are sold, each is paid back. There is no overhead to support, no secretary's salary to afford. This year Alison and Geoffrey Hendricks are doing the catalog, Philip Corner is treasurer, and I am handling publicity and relations with the distributor. Perhaps next year Philip will have my job, I will have his, and Alison and Jackson will do the catalog. We got a grant for Mac Low to do his next book—which will be a large one. There is no waste, no administrative cost. Part buys his time (he is a professional editor and otherwise could not afford to do his own work), and part buys the printing. Very simple. What expenses there are we split, on catalogs, mailings and suchlike. All we are is a name. We are a group because we say we are a group. The books must be kept *meticulously* since sooner or later we are sure to be audited, and it must be clear that this is not a hobby-publishing situation (which would not be tax deductible). But otherwise our structure is as unorthodox as our books, and it is suited to them. There is no waste; we lose no time reading manuscripts that are submitted—we have agreed that we do not want to grow by taking on more members, so we simply return them unread.

It works for us because we are who we are; it is the only way that any of us would have time to involve ourselves in publishing at this stage in our careers. We are dead serious about it; in June 1978 we changed our name to "Printed Editions" because "Unpublished Editions" no longer seemed accurate as a means of describing us, and "Printed Editions" seemed both commercial and sufficiently broad-based to cover most of what we would want to do.

But any group of artists, or writers, or even composers could form a group (or a non-group like ours), and could publish as we do. All that is needed is a common identity and purpose; something that goes beyond the idea that "Well, we all need to get into print." Otherwise, why not simply self-publish, as I did at first, both before the Something Else Press and with Unpublished Editions. Possibly a tighter organization would be needed in some cases—something which was technically nonprofit in order to be usable for grant-writing purposes. But even there, there is flexibility in smallness. I think the future of publishing will include many, many small groups like ours. "Trade publishing"—the publishing industry which produces books by the thousands while we do only hundreds—has the key role, of course. We cannot replace it; volume means economy, economy means low prices, and low prices mean more readers and, ultimately, more sales. That is simply arithmetic. But publishing with trade publishers is for *after* the audience for an artist has been built. Groups like ours are for before that has happened, or for situations (like Cage's) where the particular project is simply not salable on a large basis. In a sense, groups like ours can become the research and development part of the literary portion of the publishing industry. Perhaps the trade publishers should support us on this basis and for this reason. We can provide them with paradigms and models to imitate. Ah well.

And that is just what Something Else Press has now become. The organization is gone; because of the lessons to be drawn from this I have gone into more rehashing of the old disasters than was really congenial to me. Most of the books are not gone, but they are no longer generally for sale. They are in libraries, etc. Perhaps some will now become collectibles and valuables. Perhaps others will be more or less lost. Surely some will be reprinted, hopefully by trade publishers at low prices.

The organization is gone, but the model remains. The Press exists as a standard for those who are attracted to its work to imitate. In that way it continues to propagate its influence. Knowing that it was once there makes the image we have of the late sixties and early seventies seem, maybe, more cultural than it was. One forgets what a dry time it really was, culturally, with everything so severely and narrowly politicized. The struggle is really not so interesting to remember, except for its lessons. The model of the Press—crazy collage *that* it was—that is as important, perhaps, as the books.

I saw this in its clearest lineage when, just over a week ago, I walked down Spring Street in Soho. Outside the New Morning Book Store I saw three serious-looking young people. I overheard a few words that they were saying and they were talking about the Something Else Press. I walked slowly, so as to hear more. One was saying to the others, "There's nothing like that Press around these days." I felt like going over to him and saying, "Isn't that a challenge? Do it—and do it better." I didn't. I was wrong. I should have.

West Glover, Vermont, June 20, 1978

Letter to Ray Johnson

Originally published in the *Journal of Black Mountain College Studies*, vol. 8: *Celebrating 50 Years of Ray Johnson's* [The] Paper Snake, guest edited by Michael von Uchtrup, 2017.

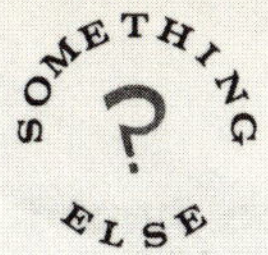

SOMETHING ELSE PRESS
New York Nice Cologne

November 17th, 1964

Ray Johnson
176 Suffolk Street
New York, New York

Dear Ray:

Could you please write out the following in black crayon on
the enclosed sheet of paper and send it back to me post haste?

T H E   P A P E R   S N A K E   b y   r a y   j o h n s o n

A few years ago you sent me a blue and white collage, very neatly
cut into three pieces, submerged in a huge carton of ripped up
collages. I rescued them, and now I figure maybe the right thing to
do is to use them for the cover of the book, with Ray Johnson
lettering running down the two slots. Okay?

Since you cut the collage very neatly and straight, the lettering
would run unless it's straight too— sort of, anyway.

423 Broadway, New York, N.Y. 10013

The way everything's shaping up, the books will be bound by around
January 21st. But the official publication date will be Valentine's
Day- that's when the book goes to the stores, when reviews and
all that happen, and, well, you can imagine. I am going to need
another thing: I'd like to borrow your mailing list, if you have
one. I'll get my mailing house to send announcements to your list,
and then all the people you'll want to know about the book will.
I want to send out the mailing just after New Year's.

On Valentine's Day we'll rent a fine old Irish bar downtown that
has a beautiful pie-shaped room that looks like it's on a Mississippi
river boat, we'll get a chinese or a roumanian caterer, and have
a celebrate-Ray's-book party. Okay? Or maybe not? What do you
think? We can send out a second mailing, invite about 900 people
(most of whom just might show), charge 25¢ to get in (or 50¢)-
which would cover food costs- distribute paper snakes, and so on.
That could be interesting.

It turned out that to do about 700 books cost very nearly the same
as to do 1700, so I figure on doing about 1700, selling them at $3.47
(mostly by mail), and so on. Each book will cost about $1.65 to
make, so, counting shipping, if I sell half the books I'll break
even. Based on that, I figure on giving you 45% net profit (after
store discounts, which are pretty bad- 35% and 40%, which is why
I'd rather sell by mail). You should also get the copyright, so
that when I get sick and tired of the Something Else Press, as you
can bet your ass I will, all rights will automatically go to you.
That means, if people anthologize from the book in 15 years, you
get the price of a good dinner. What I should now ask you for (or,
rather, reserve for The Something Else Press) is the exclusive
publishing and selling rights- plus all residuals- in the english
language on all the works included, throughout the world, throughout
the life of the copyright. This is more of a jawbreaker than
anything else. What it means is that if Typographia Magazine in
London decides to reprint a page, it should be my responsibility
to collect some sort of royalty from them and split it as I described
with you.

To copyright in your name, I need your legal name. How do you
sign your income tax forms?

Well, so much for all that. Really, I do expect to sell about ¾ of
the books over two years or so, and I plan to plan accordingly. Not
exactly interesting considerations, but once considered, eliminated,
or anyway aside. Say, what's the word on schmalz herring? Can we
dig up a barrell by Valentines' Day?

       Love to the Amu Darya,

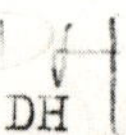

DH

A Something Else Press Checklist

Compiled by Steve Clay

This checklist is a work in progress. It includes regular and deluxe editions of books, the Great Bear Pamphlets, the *Something Else Newsletter*, newscards, Camille's Reports, prints, posters, graphics, and other publications and ephemera. The descriptions are primarily derived from the Press's catalogues, dust jacket copy and newsletters, and are written by Dick Higgins unless otherwise credited. Edition sizes were provided by Dick Higgins to Peter Frank for his 1983 bibliography and are copied here as a point of reference. —SC

SOURCES KEY:

ANM = *The Arts of the New Mentality: Catalogue 1967–1968* by Dick Higgins. Something Else Press, 1967.

CAP = *[Untitled Catalogue as Poster]* by Dick Higgins. Something Else Press, 1968.

CAT 69–70 = *Catalog 1969–1970 Something Else Press* by Dick Higgins. Something Else Press, 1969.

CAT 73–74 = *Catalogue Fall/Winter 1973–1974* by Dick Higgins and Jan Herman. Something Else Press, 1973.

CC = Cover copy.

Frank = *Something Else Press: An Annotated Bibliography* by Peter Frank. [New Paltz, NY]: A Documentext Publication, McPherson & Company, 1983.

JC = Jacket copy.

MIP = *Mail-Interview Project–Part 1* by Ruud Janssen. Breda, the Netherlands: TAM-Publications, 2008.

SEN = *Something Else Newsletter* edited by Dick Higgins. Volumes and numbers, as noted.

SEP&S = *Something Else Press & Since: A Lecture* by Dick Higgins. Vancouver, BC: Western Front Productions, 1981. Two-part 1:14:37 video featuring Dick Higgins discussing the history of SEP and selected books as well as projects from the subsequent imprints, Unpublished Editions and Printed Editions. The video can be viewed online at Vimeo.com using the above-noted title.

TAGT = *Tomorrow's Avant Garde Today . . . Catalogue 1970* by Dick Higgins. Something Else Press, 1970.

WTLF = *What to Look for in a Book—Physically & Catalogue 1965–66* by Dick Higgins. Something Else Press, 1965.

BOOKS

1964

Dick Higgins. *Jefferson's Birthday/Postface*. New York, 1964.

Cover photograph by Wolf Vostell. Cloth over boards with dust jacket printed on both sides, the inside of the jacket prints "A Something Else Manifesto," 1200 copies.

These two separate works are bound back-to-back in one volume. *Postface* is a reminiscence about how happenings began by one who was there. It goes on to explain the necessity for happenings, where they went to and what is being done now. The description of Fluxus, the curious explosion of happenings, which enormously expanded the audience and numbers of participants in the movement, primarily in Europe, is virtually the only material on the subject in print.

Jefferson's Birthday contains all of the work Higgins wrote between April 13th, Thomas Jefferson's birthday, 1962 and April 13th, 1963. As such it is an excellent cross section of the works, primarily theatrical, of this quite unique writer. (WTLF)

1965

Ray Johnson. *The Paper Snake*. New York, 1965.

Cloth over boards with dust jacket, 1840 copies; 197 copies comprise a special edition and include original collage or ephemera by Johnson.

Ray Johnson is not only the finest of American collagists, well represented in the Museum of Modern Art (New York), the De Cordova Museum (Lincoln, Mass.), etc. He is also the author of innumerable whimsical fantasies and reminiscences, often pointed, which masquerade as playets, poems, letters. These are mailed to friends, to friends of friends, to anybody to whom it seems appropriate to mail something, and have been described as The New York

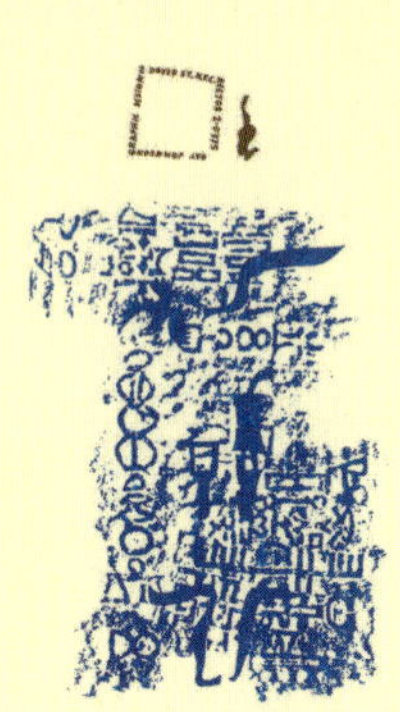

Dear Dick,

I enclose some fur.

I enclose my signature.

I enclose a novel of suspense.

I enclose a three-legged animal.

I enclose a Lucky Strike.

I enclose a Y (a fragment of RAY).

I do not enclose a man with his left hand in his jacket pocket

with a black shoe on his left shoulder.

I do not enclose Jesus Christ.

I do not enclose Lucky Str

I enclose hands stirring and hands mixing.

I enclose a highly magnified view of potato rot.

I enclose a white-silver circle fragment.

I do not enclose a small kitten in a muff.

I enclose a small animal stencil.

I do not enclose three hummingbirds.

I do not enclose Irv Rosenthal's Christmas shoes.

I do not enclose a red apple.

Ray J.

January, 1960

Dorothy Podber is going to put 183 agents in your apartment.

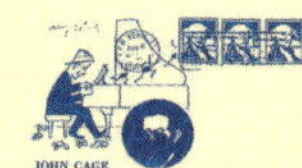

Dear Dick,
Merce
Cunningham
is my only
fan.

P.S. I want to live and die like an egg.

For Dick Higgins

A baby, a man's shoe and a spider are
in a bottle.
Federal law for-
bids sale or re-use
of this bottle
Wing Lee Wai Hong Kong

Wouldn't you cry if *your* drum sticks
were taken away?

February 27, 1962

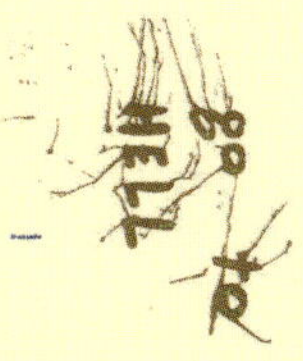

Dear Dick,
P.S.
I enclose four booms.
Boom, boom, boom, boom.
They can be re-arranged, thus:
boom, boom, Boom, boom.
Today I sent George Brecht his
grandfather's clock.
Broom, broom, broom, broom.
They have a saying in Arizona among
the folks out there. They say "in
god we trust".
Today I only like the folks of Arizona
and I enclose a maid.

Ray

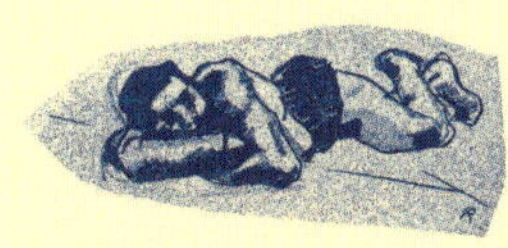

Pages above from *The Paper Snake* by Ray Johnson.

Correspondence School of Art. A cross section of his work, received by Dick Higgins over the years, has been assembled into this, one of our most beautiful books. (WTLF)

The meaning in Ray Johnson's work is not logical, like an Aristotelian syllogism, but counterlogical, like a psalm. All art represents reality, there is no non-representational art. The first principle of Ray Johnson's art is that anything isolated is beautiful, albeit opaque. The second principle is that meaning awakens in that isolated beautiful thing when it is juxtaposed to something like it (counterparts, like rhymes, for the romantic; counterpoints, like puns, for the ironic) . . . To Dick Higgins he has written, "I want to live and die like an egg." Ray Johnson's art is always *see and say, show and tell*; it is also imaginary, inarticulate, and eggshaped. —William S. Wilson (JC)

Something Else Press was founded on the spur of the moment. First I did my book *Jefferson's Birthday/Postface* (1964). But before the thing was even printed, I decided the next book should be a cross section of the things Ray had sent me over the previous six years. So, having little room at my own place, I packed them all into two suitcases, visited my mother and spread everything out on her dining table. I sorted the book into piles—performance pieces, poems, collages, things to be typeset, thing to be reproduced in Ray's writing—taking care to include at least some of each category. I knew the book would be hard to sell, so I didn't want to make it a Big Important Book; I chose the format of a children's book, set the texts in a smallish size of Cloister Bold (an old-fashioned Venetian face), decided on using two colors to simulate four (which I could not have afforded), and then laid out the pages in a way which I felt would invite the reader to experience Ray's pieces as I did on receiving them. Ray, who had at first been displeased by the project, perhaps feeling it would lock him into a format too much, became very enthusiastic as the project developed. Where at first he had refused to title the book, later he called it "The Paper Snake" after a collage and print he had made. He also wanted the price to be "$3.47," for reasons I have never known (prices of that sort were always $3.48 or $3.98). And when, one winter day in 1966, the book was being bound by a New York City binder, I took Ray over to the bindery to see it being cased in (when the covers are attached to the book). By then he was delighted and wrote me one of the few formal letters I ever received from him thanking me for doing it. (MIP)

Al Hansen. *A Primer of Happenings & Time/Space Art*. New York, 1965.

Cover and interior photographs by Peter Moore, with additional photographs by Terry Schutte, Martha Holmes, and Harvey Gross. Cloth over boards with dust jacket, first printing, 1072 copies. According to Frank, second and third printings were issued in paper wrappers, 2013 and 1800 copies respectively. We find evidence to suggest there were instead two clothbound printings and one in wrappers. One hardcover state is bound in yellow cloth with blue lettering on the jacket, another in red cloth with silver lettering on the jacket. Both jackets bear the price $4.50. Priority is unknown. There was also a special edition (quantity unknown) "with an original Hansen. $59.95." (WTLF)

The happening is the most delightful and exciting challenge to theatrical deadweight in many a year. Increasingly the young people put them on, while the theater institution wonders where everybody is and whatever became of Broadway.

This book is the first book that attempts to deal in a concise way with all the aspects of the happening and its related forms and analogues. Al Hansen, one of America's leading pop artists and a pioneer in the development of the happening, here presents his delightful account of what this very lively medium is all about. No work of scholarship, the intent of this book is to inform, to provoke original thought on the part of the reader, and perhaps to suggest that he try his own experiment. (JC)

Intended primarily for use by young people as an introduction to the general field of happenings and their artistic cousins, this is easily the most basic book on the subject. Hansen is best known for his Hershey Bar wrapper collages. Yet he has been the most prolific of all of the happening makers. There is fascination and authority when Hansen says, "Back in the summer of 1958, in Cage's class at The New School . . ." (WTLF)

Alison Knowles, Tomas Schmit, Benjamin Patterson, and Philip Corner. *The Four Suits*. New York, 1965.

Cloth over boards with mylar jacket, two printings (each 1000 copies); the second printing has colored endpapers. There was also a special edition of ten copies. (WTLF)

The Four Suits is a collection of very different directions, intended to show the variety of work being done in the general field of happenings and happening-related work. Corner is represented by a collection of his musical events; Knowles has written a dictionary of the letter "T" which is mostly unperformable; Patterson's performance pieces are psychological experiments along the lines of Zen koans; Schmit has contributed utterly classical, private pieces which are done for the benefit of the performer and are best-off without any audience at all.

The importance of this book is dual: it places the current situation of happenings in the foreground, and de-emphasizes the earlier, painting-derived phase. And it provides texts and methods for those who want to study what is being done today in the way of artistic experiments. (WTLF)

Robert Filliou. *Ample Food for Stupid Thought*. New York, 1965.

Cover photograph by Peter Moore. Introductions by Arman, Kicha Baticheff, George Brecht, William Burroughs, Christo, Diane di Prima, Brion Gysin, Dick Higgins, Allan Kaprow, Ray Johnson, Joe Jones, Alison Knowles, John Herbert McDowell, Jackson Mac Low, Nam June Paik, Benjamin Patterson, Diter Rot, Daniel Spoerri, and James Waring. Cloth over boards with dust jacket, 992 copies plus 500 postcard sets, 104 of which are in a wooden box.

The last carnival is being pulled down buildings and stars laid flat for storage last of the old showmen there selling an empty suitcase to an empty house. Remember when we beat the hotel in East St. Louis? (Train whistles cross a distant sky.) They can keep my suitcase. It's full of rocks. —William Burroughs (from the Introduction)

Filliou is a well-known French artist and poet, one of the very, very few with any degree of experimentalism. This book consists of apparently pointless questions which lead in fact to highly poetic speculations.

Originally the book was conceived as a set of postcards, with one question per card. Each card could seem appropriate for any number of friends of the reader and could be sent off. So we made up a card edition. But once the cards are sent away, the book is incomplete. So we made a normal book edition too.

The excellent jacket notes are by Jackson Mac Low. (WTLF)

1966

Daniel Spoerri. *An Anecdoted Topography of Chance (Re-Anecdoted Version)*. New York, 1966.

Translated and annotated by Emmett Williams. Illustrated by [Roland] Topor. Cover photograph by Vera Spoerri. Cloth over boards with dust jacket printed on both sides, 2020 copies; second printing in paper wrappers, 5586 copies. There was also a special edition of ten copies. (WTLF)

Some Unsystematic Reflections for Filliou & Others (23 Feb. & 21–4 March 1965)
by Jackson Mac Low

Robert Filliou's **AMPLE FOOD FOR STUPID THOUGHT** can be read or performed. On 8 Feb. 1965 I [Mac Low] performed it, with an audience at the Cafe Au Go Go in Greenwich Village, by addressing the questions, one at a time, to individuals in the audience. If one person didn't answer, I continued asking the question until someone else answered.

Constantly during the performance I restrained myself from arguing too much with answerers with whom I disagreed, and from expanding, more than minimally, some answers with which I strongly agreed. Possibly I shdnt have restrained myself. Maybe we shd have let ourselves go altogether on some questions & answers. Right then I thought this might not be consonant with Filliou's intentions &—perhaps more pressing—might prolong unduly this opening work of the program.

Performing with **AMPLE FOOD FOR STUPID THOUGHT** was partly like teaching a class, partly like chairing a meeting & partly like leading a discussion. I found myself automatically sabotaging each of these attitudes whenever it seemed predominating too strongly. Often I slapped down all these public rôles—to ask a question as personally as then possible. This fluctuation between public and private "stances," & their kinds, pervades my remembered experience of the performance. Usually I tried to be dry and serious, & to drain possibilities of "cuteness" from certain questions by asking them with undue seriousness or postponing them till times when they might operate as wit rather than cute humor (what a goddamned tightrope *that* is!)—or as unexpected seriousness.

I liked the last piece on that program best: Filliou silently sitting crosslegged, rear stage left, & Phil Corner, right center stage, occasionally pulling a rope hung with gongs, bells & cymbals & tied to a chair. For long periods no one on stage was doing anything, but some of Filliou's oafish friends "enlivened things" by throwing sugar cubes onto the stage.

"Anything to make a mess!" I think I thought.

Much too messy myself, I often deplore "nonessential messiness" in artworks & audiences, tho no devotee of neatness as such. A partisan of the "carefully painterly," for tho I enjoy many "linear" works (peace, Wölfflin!), I'm alarmed at the present rage for what, I'm sorry to say, they call "hard-edge." "Not more messy than necessary, but not compulsively neat!"—a consistent esthetic for this anarchist, Mac Low, who's also an Aristotelian (not a Thomist) & a Buddhist (among other things): devotee of easy self-governance according to the Mean & the Middle Way.

But what's that got to do with *Filliou*?

His works, if not his audiences, are neither too messy nor too neat—but what I'd like to ask him is, Why do you wish to provide **AMPLE FOOD FOR STUPID THOUGHT?** There are plenty of questions that might provide **AMPLE FOOD FOR INTELLIGENT THOUGHT** (his title might be ironical—but is it); why not ask some of them? (Is the answer merely, "That's not the *piece!*"?) The fact that many of Filliou's questions can be construed very seriously indeed does not necessarily prove the title ironical, since much stupid thought is expended every day on terribly serious questions. (When Filliou read this he said, "Of course, irony. Because whenever I ask questions—no matter how serious—I usually get stupid answers. It's like hitting my head against a stone wall.")

Even such presently pressing questions as "What's the quickest way to get the US Armed Services out of Vietnam?"—"Why are the supposedly kind-hearted Americans allowing their government's soldiers openly to torture Vietnamese men, women & children, & to burn them & their homes & crops with jellied gasoline?"—& "My God, what can a man do to stop this horrible war against the Vietnamese?" have given rise to as much stupid thought as any of Filliou's "stupider" questions.

Nevertheless, write your congressman, write your senator & write President Johnson to stop that goddamned war *now*—by getting all US troops out of Vietnam, South & North.

If you don't care that people are dying & suffering torture, reflect on the money-cost of the Vietnamese War to the USA: a conservatively estimated 6 to 7 billion dollars so far.

Money talks, I hear.

Does it talk to you? (JC)

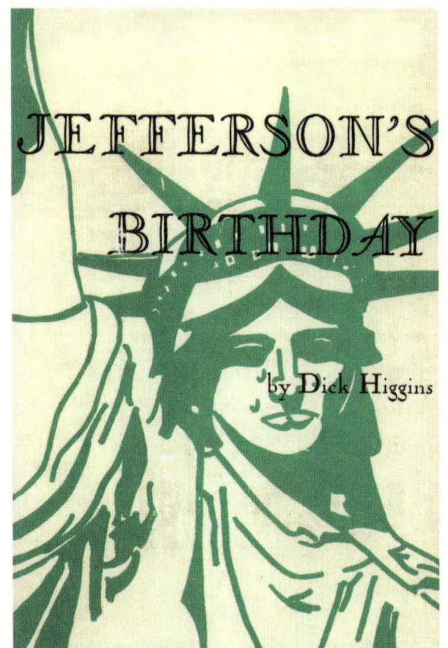
JEFFERSON'S
BIRTHDAY
by Dick Higgins

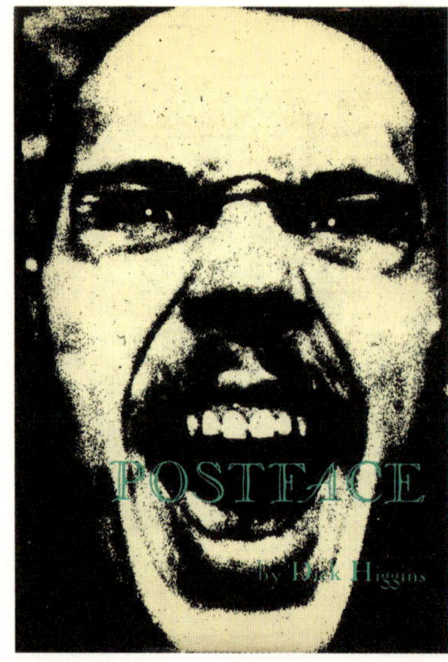
POSTFACE
by Dick Higgins

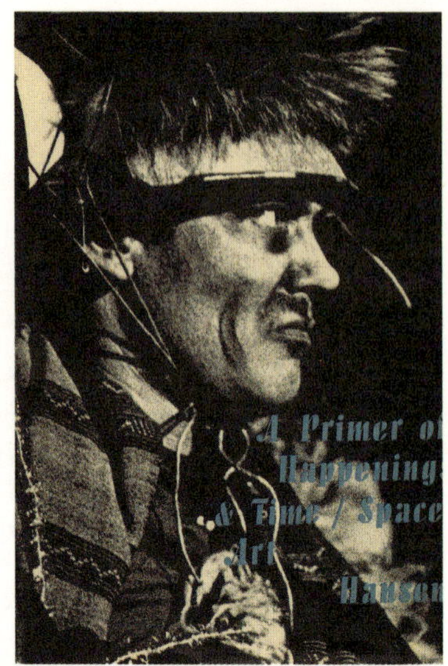
A Primer of
Happenings
& Time / Space
Art
Hansen

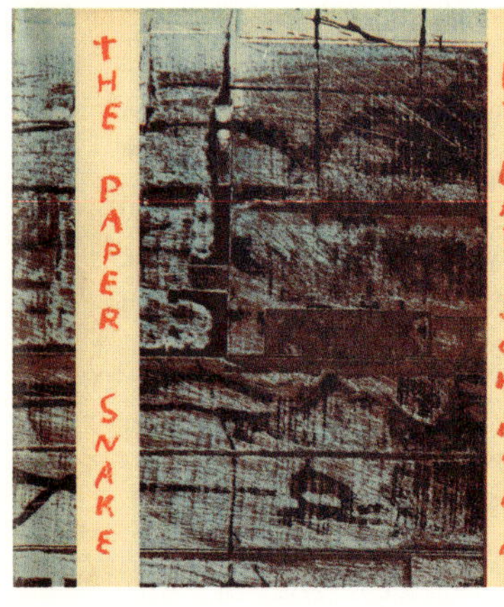
THE PAPER SNAKE
BY RAY JOHNSON

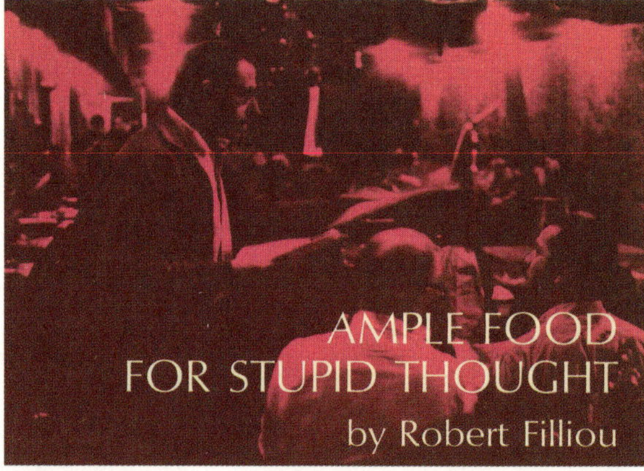
AMPLE FOOD
FOR STUPID THOUGHT
by Robert Filliou

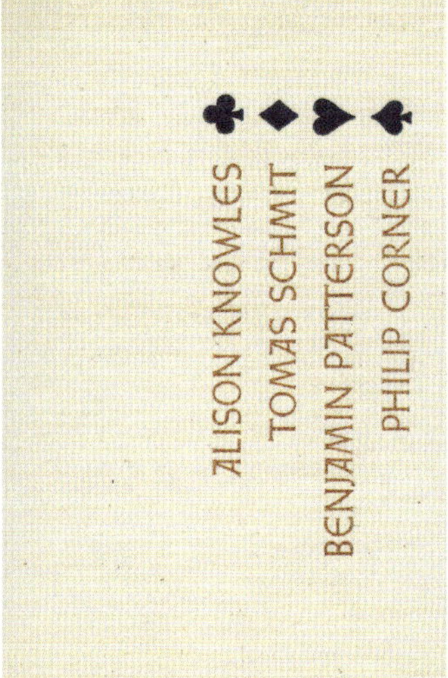
ALISON KNOWLES
TOMAS SCHMIT
BENJAMIN PATTERSON
PHILIP CORNER

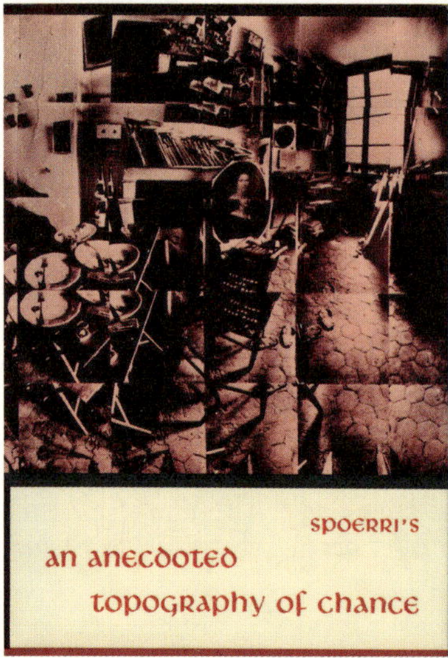
spoerri's
an anecdoted
topography of chance

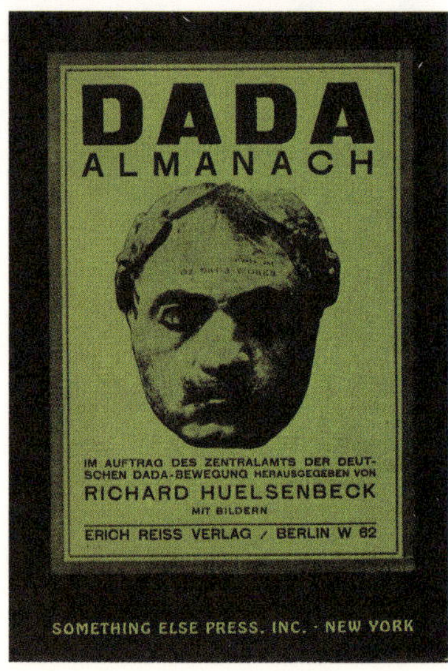
DADA
ALMANACH
IM AUFTRAG DES ZENTRALAMTS DER DEUT-
SCHEN DADA-BEWEGUNG HERAUSGEGEBEN VON
RICHARD HUELSENBECK
MIT BILDERN
ERICH REISS VERLAG / BERLIN W 62
SOMETHING ELSE PRESS, INC. · NEW YORK

The wisdom of scholars seems to be the process of concentrating on the small detail until the universal in it is discovered. The universal of what? Electrocardiograms? The eagle's speech in Chaucer's *House of Fame*? Such universals are perhaps valuable, but they're not entirely delightful.

Daniel Spoerri, on the other hand, has applied critical and scholarly methods to the arbitrary debris left over from his process of living, namely, the objects on a table. Each is analyzed and recollected, with precision and humor, by Spoerri and by his equally delightful translator and annotator, Emmett Williams. The universals are established this time in terms of Spoerri's life as one of today's best-known artists. And these are fascinating and meaningful to us all.

Is his private life for sale, as one critic has suggested? Well, what could be more fun than invading it, we ask. And isn't the sharing of the private order for us to see what we do, too? Spoerri defines art as what artists do. This is no solipsism, but an insistence that art be connected directly to life. It is new realism at its best. (JC)

This is the only complete edition of Spoerri's nouveau réaliste classic, *Topographie Anécdotée du Hasard*, translated and supplemented by Spoerri's close friend, the poet Emmett Williams, and further expanded by Spoerri himself. On the surface the book is a history of all the objects on a table in Spoerri's room in Paris. In fact, however, it is a cosmology of Spoerri's existence, with the objects suggesting friendships and relationships among people he knows. Williams' expansions further deepen the associations of these objects, and Spoerri's expansions on Williams suggest ever-widening circles of experience. (WTLF)

Richard Huelsenbeck, editor. *Dada Almanach*. New York, 1966.

Typography by John Heartfield. Facsimile of the Erich Reiss Verlag 1920 edition. Cloth over boards with dust jacket, 2060 copies.

Dada is like the weather. Everybody talks about it, but nobody does anything about it. Even worse, in fact, because while two people might well agree on what a thunderstorm is, they could probably not agree on what dada is. The main reason for this is obvious. The more that is written about dada the more far-fetched one must become in order to be original, and the more obfuscated scholarship in the field in its turn, becomes, until we reach the present situation, where literally nobody knows what he has been talking about all these years . . . the *Dada Almanach* is, then, the statement of the various dada positions on the basis of which our present misconceptions must be reformed. The dada attitude, it will be seen herein, is profoundly contemporary. Without understanding it, it is simply not possible to evaluate accurately a great deal of the art and philosophy which is most current today. (JC)

The Dada Almanach, edited by Richard Huelsenbeck, is the most important primary source for the entire movement, since it antedates the great feuds that sapped the vitality of the movement and submerged the actual materials in a mire of legal problems for half a century. Since what we know about dada is based on a vague image of iconoclastic behavior, charming anecdotes and manifestos unbacked up by work, it comes as a shock to find how modern and pertinent the actual materials are. The facsimile edition (German with French) we have now completed (hardcover only, $4.50), and we will do the Benjamin and Pyla Patterson translation into English some time next year. (SEN, vol. 1, no. 4.)

Gertrude Stein. *The Making of Americans: Being a History of a Family's Progress, 1906–1908*. New York, 1966.

This is a facsimile of the original 1925 edition. Cloth over boards with dust jacket, 2084 copies; second printing (c. 1973), paper wrappers, approximately 2000 copies.

An avant-garde classic, this dynastic novel begins as a thinly disguised three-generation history of Stein's family and ends trying to encompass "all who ever were or are or could be living." Stein's belief that the essence of an individual is revealed in movement rather than content of word and thought becomes the method of this revolutionary and influential work, generally unavailable for over 40 years. (ANM)

Wolf Vostell. *dé-coll/age-happenings*. New York, 1966.

Translated by Laura P. Williams. Printed wooden box with plexiglass lid containing a paperback book, fifteen folded posters, one numbered and signed photo silk-screen, one packet of Bromo Seltzer mounted on a sheet of mirror-paper, and one matzoh, 500 copies.

Wolf Vostell is Germany's leading Happener—"D]é-Coll/age: unpaste, tear off, the take-off of an airplane" term is applied to Vostell's erasures, demonstrations, events, happenings and the international avant-garde anthologies he's edited since 1962. This is a collection of all Vostell's scenarios to date, large black and white reproductions of 15 gorgeous Happenings notations, objects chosen by Vostell and a signed numbered colored silk-screen print, all in a wooden box. (ANM)

1967

William Brisbane Dick. *Dick's 100 Amusements*. New York, 1967.

This is a reprint of the 1879 edition and issued as a Joyous Harper Book. Cloth over boards with dust jacket, 488 copies; paper wrappers, 2500 copies.

One of the more delightful, if neglected, fields of the 19th Century Americana is the work of William Brisbane Dick (1827–1901) and, to a somewhat lesser extent, that of his son, Harris B. Dick, the former Philadelphia writer and publisher who produced innumerable collections of playlets, games, proverbs, wisdom, stock letters, etc., from *The American Hoyle; or, Gentleman's Handbook of Games* to *Brudder Bones' Book of Stump Speeches and Burlesque* (featuring such specialties as "Vegetable Poetry. For 2 Males" or "The Echo. Act for Two Negroes" or "Lecture on Cats") or *Dick's Book of Toasts, Speeches and Responses*. An idea of the variety of the Dicks' interests may be found in the advertisements printed at the end of the present book, William Brisbane Dick's masterpiece, which the publisher, alas, regrets he cannot yet supply. None appear to be available.

How much of the actual writing was done by the Dicks will probably never be known. Certainly many of the treasures must have been commissioned from others. However, the senior Dick appears to have been a particularly brilliant editor, at the very least, in that all his collections fascinate and show a consistent taste for the light and for the surprising.

Dick's One Hundred Amusements is a collection of do-it-yourself theater and humor. Because of the basic simplicity of the pieces, they seem startlingly contemporary, ancestors of such modern avant-garde theater forms as the Happening or the Event Piece; and at least, when they are less directly related to our times, they reflect a period charm, as well as exemplifying an interesting social function later played by the theater and by the movies. (JC)

This is a facsimile of the 1879 edition concocted by Dick, long gone (died 1901) Philadelphia editor-publisher. Douglas Blazek reviews in *Olé*: ". . . a rundown of all sorts of weird & diverse parlor games—some weird enuf to allure you into doing the thing, a great bk for someone else to own & you to read while they're taking a bath . . . a bk to thumb thru like the Sears Catalog." (ANM)

Marshall McLuhan. *Verbi-Voco-Visual Explorations*. New York, 1967.

Cloth over boards with dust jacket, 2000 copies; paper wrappers, second and third printings, 3695 and 3500 copies respectively. The second printing has a printed price of $2.75 with brown ink used on the front cover and with a printed yellow bellyband; the third printing has a printed price of $2.95 with green ink used on the front cover.

Once upon a time I spent my first summer in New York, and one hot day, with a thirst for such things, I went to take a Pierian sip at the Gotham Book Mart, where one never knew what marvelous little magazine might turn up. That day, in August 1958, I found *Explorations*, a small (one dare not say "little") magazine edited by Marshall McLuhan and Edmund Carpenter. McLuhan I knew of at the time as a Joyce scholar and an expert on Wyndham Lewis, who was a hero of mine. So I bought it.

Great was my surprise when I got home and discovered that it was not a magazine at all but a superb essay documenting, analyzing and detailing the implications of the arts through their sensual impact on the intellect and, especially, through their cumulative effect. This last insight is perhaps McLuhan's major contribution to criticism. So much of the criticism of the past is purely qualitative; the McLuhan essay that forms the bulk of this book is quantitative. In dealing with its subjects it examines the typical and ignores the exception, except in the sense of an alternative, just as an anthropologist prepares his field studies. The approach is utterly objective. One had the feeling that McLuhan knew all about what he was describing, yet was, possibly, annoyed by it. With all the insight of hindsight we could, perhaps, draw a parallel with Ibsen, who was accused of being a nasty fellow because he documented in his dramas the weakness of his time, and was therefore identified in the non-participating mind with the very problems he was anxious to eradicate. But this is not a symmetrically opposite parallel. Another temptation would be to say that McLuhan, in his more recent work, is denouncing the media that he seems to be highlighting and praising, and that his public among the media-oriented Advertising Creativity personnel are mistaking his subject for his objectives. But this is not entirely true either, in my opinion. (JC)

This early fusillade (1957) is trained comprehensively and comprehensibly on the word: taps for the written culture, a victory salvo for the oral revolution. (ANM)

"The swing to the oral mode, individually and socially, is inevitable as soon as there is a serious challenge to the monopoly of print as a means of social communication."
—Marshall McLuhan (ANM)

Emmett Williams, editor. *An Anthology of Concrete Poetry*. New York, 1967.

Cloth over boards with dust jacket, 2000 copies; paper wrappers, 3000 copies; paper wrappers, second and third printings, 3000 and 3945 copies respectively, with the back cover different in each printing. 1000 sheets from the first paper wrappers printing were for the Hansjörg Mayer edition.

Concrete Poetry is not one style but a cluster of possibilities, all falling in the intermedium between semantic poetry, calligraphic and typographic poetry, and sound poetry. It first crystalized out of these earlier modes in the early 1950's in the works of such people as Eugen Gomringer (Switzerland), Carlo Belloli (Italy), Diter Rot (Iceland), Öyvind Fahlström (Sweden),

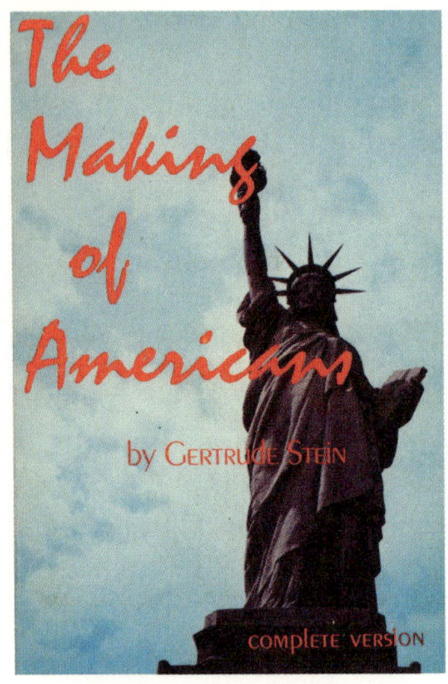

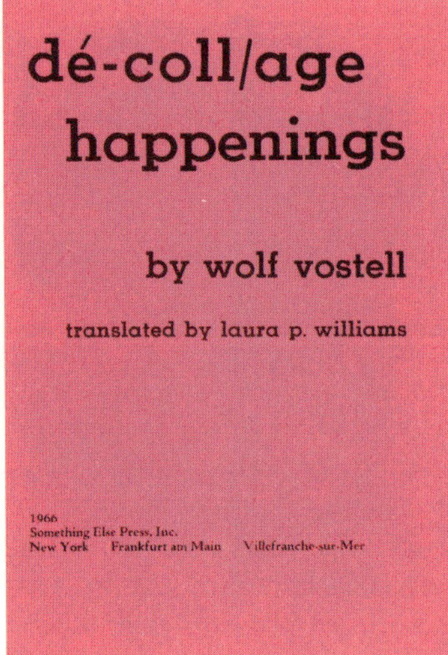

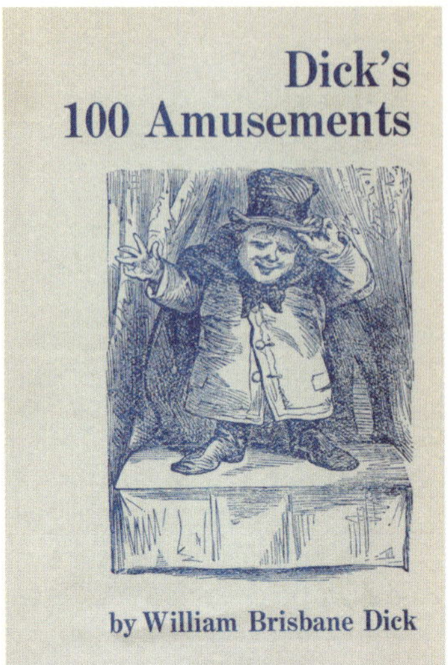

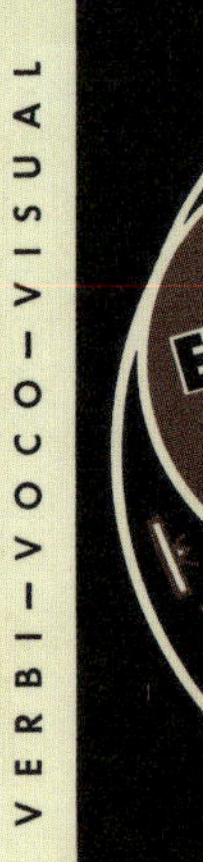

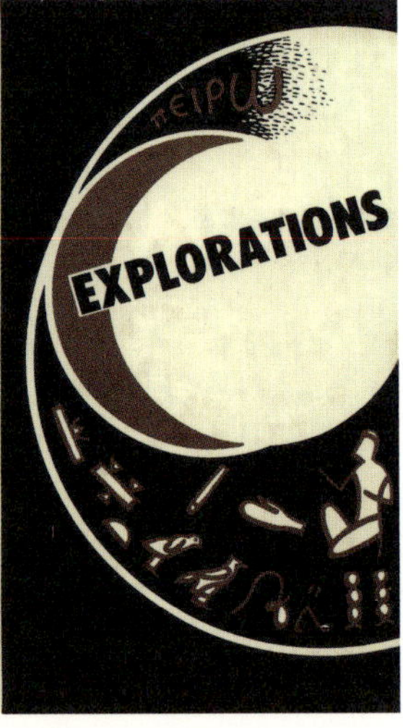

The book you are looking at is the largest **Anthology of Concrete Poetry** to appear to date, and the first major one to be published in the United States. **Edited by Emmett Williams,** one of the founders of the movement, and with the over-300 selections translated wherever possible from their original languages and glossed where translation would not be feasible, all supplemented by detailed biographies of the poets, the publishers of **Something Else Press, Inc.,** take great pride in presenting a cross-section of this most active of modern poetry movements and in introducing so many major writers from so many countries between these covers for the first time to the American reading public.

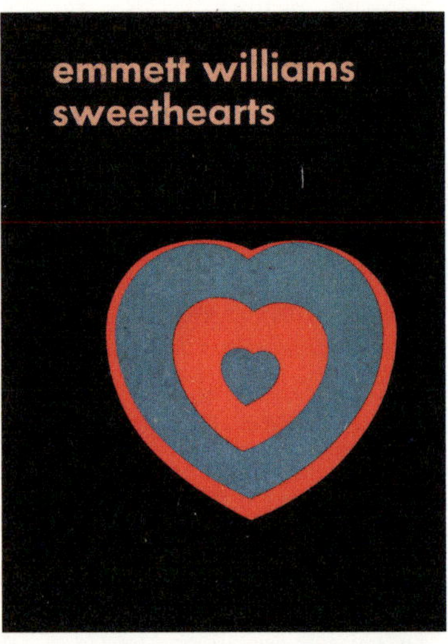

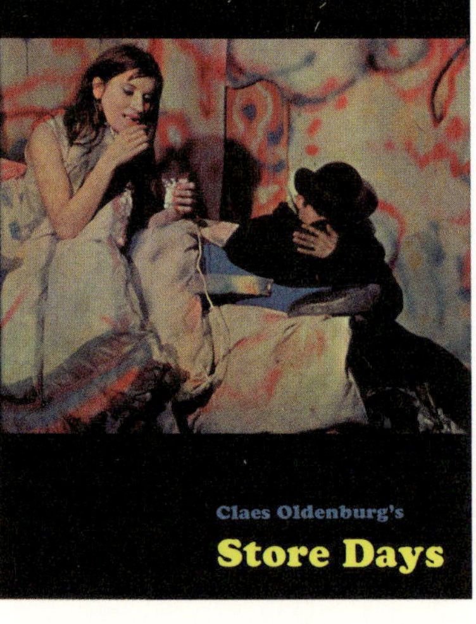

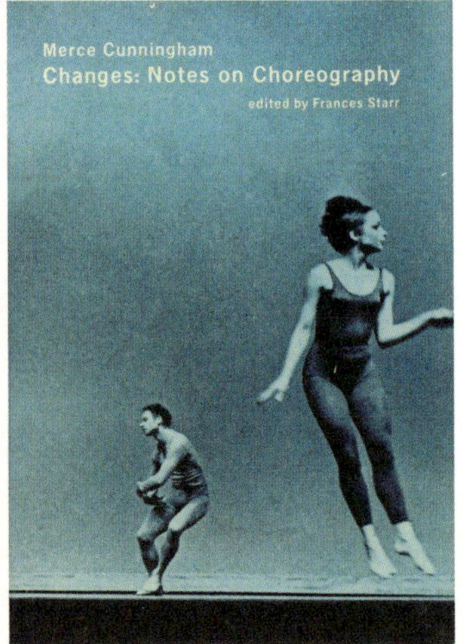

Games
at
the
Cedilla,
or
the
Cedilla
Takes
Off

by
George
Brecht
and
Robert
Filliou

the Noigandres Group (Haroldo and Augusto de Campos, Decio Pignatari and others, all from Brazil), Carlfriedrich Claus (German Democratic Republic), Gerhard Rühm, Friedrich Achleitner and H.C. Artmann (Austria), Daniel Spoerri and Claus Bremer (West Germany), and Emmett Williams (United States, then living in West Germany). In recent years a second generation of major figures have added to the movement, including such people as Hansjörg Mayer (West Germany), Ladislav Novak and Jirí Kolár (Czechoslovakia), Edwin Morgan and Ian Hamilton Finlay (Scotland), Bob Cobbing (England), bpNichol (Canada), Mary Ellen Solt and Jonathan Williams (United States), Pierre and Ilse Garnier (France), Seiichi Niikuni and Kitasono Katue (Japan) and many others. The very fact of the appearance of parallel work more or less independently in so many nations and languages indicated one of the unique aspects of the movement, namely its source being in the development of a new mentality in which values become fused and interrelationships established on a more complex plain than was the case in the purer, earlier modes of poetry.

Emmett Williams, as one of the original practitioners of concrete poetry, has been in a unique position to observe the development of the movement since its beginnings, and the selection in this volume therefore reflects a view of this evolution from within the movement rather than from a distance. However it is far too soon to regard any anthology of Concrete Poetry as being definitive, since the movement is extremely active and major new works have yet to appear in this most interesting of current poetry movements. (JC)

Emmett Williams. *Sweethearts*. New York, 1967.

Front cover illustration *Coeurs Volants [Fluttering Hearts]* (1936) by Marcel Duchamp. Cloth over boards with dust jacket, 609 copies; paper wrappers, 1692 copies.

"Emmett Williams' *Sweethearts* is a breakthrough. It is to concrete poetry as *Wuthering Heights* is to the English novel; as *Guernica* is to modern art. *Sweethearts* is the first large-scale lyric masterpiece among the concrete texts, compelling in its emotional scope, readable, a sweetly heartfelt, jokey, crying laughing, tender expression of love." —Richard Hamilton (JC)

A poetry cycle derived from the letters of the word s-w-e-e-t-h-e-a-r-t-s, like no other book you have ever seen, read, or heard of. It can be cinematic (if you like movies), poematic (if you like word play), erotic (if you like foreplay), or just plain flippable (if you merely like to flip). *Sweethearts* also happens to be an engrossing, engaging, and marriageable long poem. It's a book you wouldn't want to be divorced from, for sure. —Jan Herman (CAT 73–74)

George Brecht and Robert Filliou. *Games at the Cedilla, or the Cedilla Takes Off*. New York, 1967.

Released in January 1968 according to ANM Errata and Addenda. Cloth over boards with dust jacket, 1945 copies.

Some things are hard to verbalize, others to verbalize about. The last is true about *Games at the Cedilla*, because the concepts in the book are inherently not verbal, in the primary analysis, and are, in fact, anti-conceptualizations. In fact this point is precisely what the book is—an assemblage of aesthetic researches, done very much as a scientist might document his experiments, and in the same spirit. Since he is researching a very large number of quite different subjects, no overall conclusions are possible, on the one hand (in fact they would violate the spirit of the work). On another hand (there are more than two), it is inevitable that the different fields of research should be presented in a sort of parallel chronological order, as they would be in a scientist's notebook in which he happened to tend two quite different bodies of investigation, perhaps towards quite different ends, rather than broken down into sections—all the "one minute scenarios" here, the poems there, the visual materials in another place, etc., as would happen in a normal collection.

What we have is actually not so anarchic as it sounds. This book is a selective distillate of the notebooks kept by George Brecht and Robert Filliou, the one an American artist and scientist (in whose name there are a number of industrial patents at Washington, D.C.) and the second a southern French sceptic, Robert Filliou, among whose other credits are working on the United Nations white paper on the post-Korean War economic recovery for South Korea and also other economic theses, as well as various uniquely reputed poems, plays, art exhibitions and revolutionary exploits. The Cedilla itself is LA CÉDILLE QUI SOURIT, a shop they operate at Villefranche-sur-mer on the Côte d'Azure where small works of avant-garde art are sold along with postcards, jewelry (by Donna Jo Brewer/Jones) and all kinds of things which do or do not have a cedilla in their (French) name. And at the Cedilla the notebooks are kept, as the researches are developed, in the manner appropriate to the investigations, with a bottle of either the cheapest pleasant wine or the pleasantest cheap wine, depending upon the occasion. In this way that dread disease to all artists, humorlessitis, is prevented from appearing, and the artists involved (and the others too) remain in good aesthetic health. (JC)

Claes Oldenburg. *Store Days: Documents from The Store (1961) and Ray Gun Theater (1962).* **New York, 1967.**

Edited by Emmett Williams. Photographs by Robert R. McElroy. Attached to the front free endpaper of both editions is a small glassine envelope that contains a business card for "The Store." Cloth over boards with dust jacket, 5000 copies; a second printing was also issued in cloth over boards with dust jacket, 3000 copies. Dust jacket price on first edition was $10.00, on second edition, $12.95.

The source of nearly all of the ideas in Pop Art was Claes Oldenburg's store, which functioned from 1961 to 1963. After all, didn't Andy Warhol buy the first of Oldenburg's big blue shirts? But what's missing from the literature is not the history of the movement, but a direct confrontation with the ideas posed by it. For example, here is an extract from one of Oldenburg's notebooks of the time: "The fact that the store represents American popular art is only an accident, an accident of my surroundings, my landscape, of the objects which in my daily coming and going my consciousness attaches itself to. An art of ideas is a bore and a sentimentality, whether witty or serious or what. I may have things to say about US and many other matters, but in my art I am concerned with perception of reality and composition. Which is the only way that art can really be useful—by setting an example of how to use the senses." These notes, scenarios for happenings (some of which were extremely socially conscious), sketches and projects have been collected together and a selection made by Emmett Williams and Claes Oldenburg. The resulting work is called *Store Days*, which costs $10 and will be ready by April 15. Most of the ideas that this kind of art is about will have to be revised once this book is ready. (SEN, vol. 1, no. 5.)

It's ready!!! Claes Oldenburg's *Store Days*! After nearly two and a half years of planning and making. Claes Oldenburg and Emmett Williams went over thousands and thousands of notes, scenarios, photographs, drawings, etc., and came up with a distillate of the first real masterpiece, The Store, in the Pop Art format. It is presented in a lyrical manner, rather than a documentary one, since we wanted to represent the ideas (and the sources of more recent ideas) rather than the network of precedents involved in the book. We wanted to make a primary source, which The Store was, rather than a secondary one, which it wasn't. (SEN, vol. 1, no. 6)

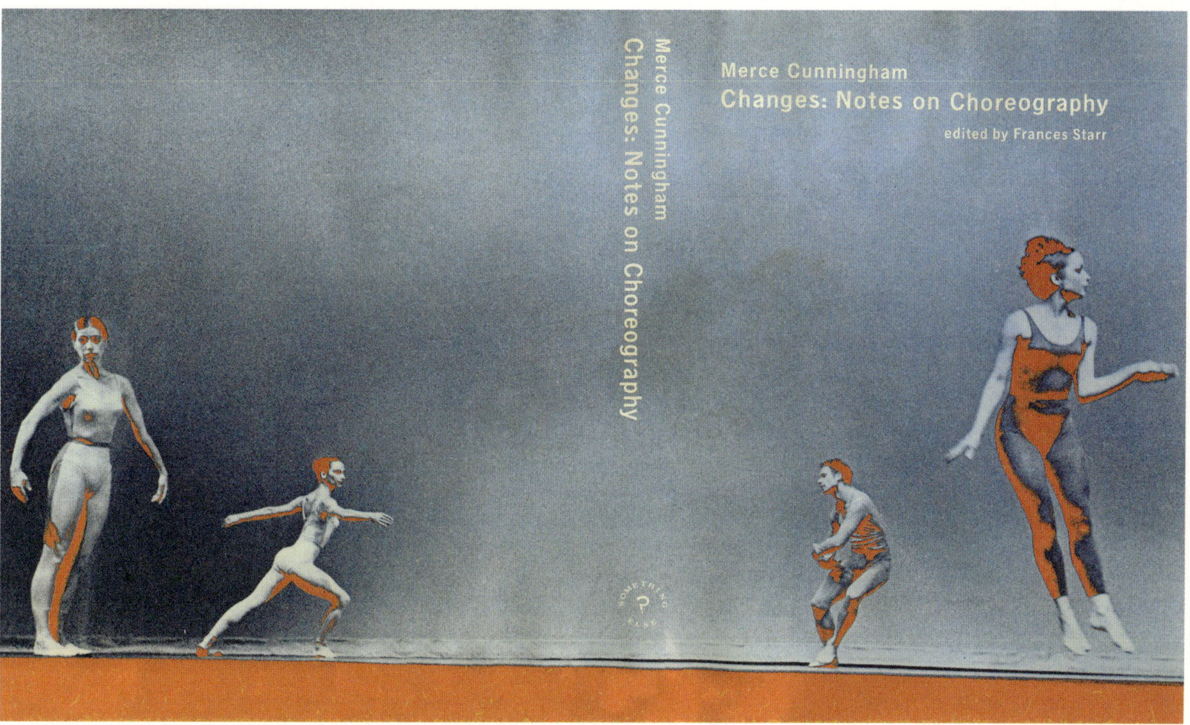

I wanted to do a dance book which would not simply be documentation of a dancer's career but which instead would have the actual ideas and working materials and notes on choreography which a dancer would use, so we did Merce Cunningham's *Changes: Notes on Choreography* ...

The cover that you are looking at here is the way I wanted it. Broken down into orange and blue. However, when I showed this to Jasper Johns, who was Merce Cunningham's closest advisor for visual art and the visual director for the Cunningham Dance Company, Jasper accused me of having made one of the women [far left] into a monster ... and he told me I should start the cover all over again. Now this conversation took place in the dressing room in the Brooklyn Academy where Merce Cunningham was giving a recital. So instead of designing the thing all over again I simply took Merce Cunningham's make-up crayon and I crayoned in all the things that you see here as orange ... That's the form [see cover on page 186 -ed.] in which the book was finally issued, far less exciting from a certain point of view than if had been done in orange and blue but that's the way it goes. (SEP&S)

1968

Merce Cunningham. *Changes: Notes on Choreography*. New York, 1968.

[Cover photographs by Marvin Silver.] Edited by Frances Starr. Cloth over boards with dust jacket, 3761 copies.

Changes, a look into the working notebooks of Merce Cunningham, is the most comprehensive book on choreography to emerge from the new dance. Cunningham's reflections on his art engage the reader in an awareness of both his own sensibility and the potential of the medium.

Its pages are reproductions of the in-progress notes for the individual dances—to indicate the method—superimposed with speculation—to define the problem—and complemented with visual and other material relevant to the performing arts.

Cunningham approaches the dance in terms of its primary elements—movement in space and time—and the source from which they spring—stillness. He examines the theater in terms of the presence—or absence—of movement, sound, light, décor and costume. He explores these elements separately, then superimposes them upon each other, and sometimes back upon themselves. He further opens his work to the possibilities inherent in each element through chance, a means of introducing variety into the compositional procedure.

"Although the notes began," he writes, "as necessary, if inadequate, ways to further choreographic ideas, the use of chance methods demanded some form of visual notation to allow for possibilities. A crude computer in hieroglyphics."

Cunningham's ceaseless explorations give his work, as evidenced in this book, a continuing vitality. (JC)

Ruth Krauss. *There's a Little Ambiguity Over There Among the Bluebells*. New York, 1968.

Drawings by Marilyn Harris. Cloth over boards with dust jacket, 3401 copies.

One of the zaniest imaginations operating on the off-off-off-Broadway scene belongs to Ruth Krauss. This is a delightful selection of her short theater-poems: plays, shows, monologues, horse-opera-with-wings and the like. (ANM)

Welcome to Frances Starr, to our editorial department. Her first projects are a collection of Ruth Krauss' poem-plays, familiar to lovers of the Judson Poets' Theater, Actor's Studio, etc. . . . It'll feature delightful drawings by Marilyn Harris (officially our business manager, but actually . . . ?) and should be ready late in the Winter [1968]. Frances' other immediate biggy is Merce Cunningham's *Notes on the Dance* (tentative title), a very very special and explosive kind of dance book, due in the Spring [1968]. (SEN, vol. 1, no. 7)

Eugen Gomringer. *The Book of Hours and Constellations*. New York, 1968.

Translated and edited by Jerome Rothenberg. Cover photograph by Dick Higgins. Cloth over boards with dust jacket, 1477 copies; paper wrappers, 1570 copies.

Eugen Gomringer is best known as a founder of concrete poetry, which is usually equated, indiscriminately, with all visual poetry and therefore expected to be highly visual. But Gomringer concentrates the visual element of his poems in what I have called elsewhere "geometrical structures" of the underlying logic; and the work is therefore not apt to be visually obvious, which is why he has not yet shared in the recent plethora of concrete poetry exhibitions and in its general vogue.

This book is an attempt to make it clear what he has accomplished, what his work really entails. Jerome Rothenberg (one of the best known young poets and the editor (with David Antin) of *some/thing* as well as of Hawk's Well Press poetry books), translated this book of his (Rothenberg's) selections to set the record straight. He chose to concentrate on Gomringer's *Book of Hours*, as one of the most lyrical masterpieces of recent years, as well as on a selection from Gomringer's enormous series called "constellations," the complete version of which would probably have had to await many years, until that far-off moment when Gomringer no longer is mining this vein, still a very rich lode.

Gomringer considers, more profoundly perhaps than most poets working today, what he does and how he does it. He is, like Anton Webern in the music of the recent past, unwilling to produce the many many works needed to satisfy the demand. In fact, the bulk of his work has, in recent years, been his letters and essays. This combination of un-prolific output and unfashionable willingness to provide his own critical observations no doubt explains why, over all these years since the early 1950's, he has remained unknown to the English-speaking world.

But Gomringer is part of the new Revolution of Meaning which is sweeping the world of poetry, and which implies the new search to provide the most appropriate forms for the new meanings and intentions. So it is with the greatest pride that we present to the English-speaking world, the first book of magnificences by a very great writer in a very exciting movement, concrete poetry. (JC)

Diter Rot. *246 Little Clouds*. New York, 1968.

Cloth over boards with dust jacket, 1890 copies.

A very grey book from a grey December voyage on a tramp steamer where the not-so-grey Icelandic poet/designer drew many grey conclusions and produced this, his first and not-at-all grey text in English. With an introduction by Emmett Williams, an explanatory appendix, and almost 200 drawings by Diter Rot. (SEN, vol.1, no. 9)

As soon as we start looking into the European avant-garde we keep coming up against the name, unknown till now in this country except to a few connoisseurs, of Diter Rot. Some artists are one-man movements: but Rot is a multi-movement man. Very little of what is being done in purist design, minimal art, concrete poetry, object books, the new realism, pop art, the new pornography, etc., has escaped his influence, as originator, co-originator, etc. The present work is a sort of lyrical diary, simple and personal. If it is, perhaps, less overwhelming than the huge *Mundunculum*, less "far-out" than the concrete poems, it is also perhaps more accessible and a more suitable introduction to the work of the fascinating Icelandic Swiss chimera. In its own right, however, the *Clouds* show Rot as writer, Rot as visual artist, and Rot as book designer, and is therefore an appropriate indication of the scope of the man's work. (JC)

Gertrude Stein. *Geography and Plays*. New York, 1968.

This is a facsimile of the original 1928 edition. Cloth over boards, 1530 copies; paper wrappers, 1732 copies.

With a forward by Sherwood Anderson, this is easily accessible Stein and in her most characteristic style. Undoubtedly one of her major works, it was originally published in 1922 and was long unavailable until we re-issued it in typographic facsimile. Anybody who would like to sink their teeth into Stein for the first time could hardly do better. And for those already into her work, well, this one shows her wonderful Cezanne-like language in all its shining opacity. (CAT 73–74)

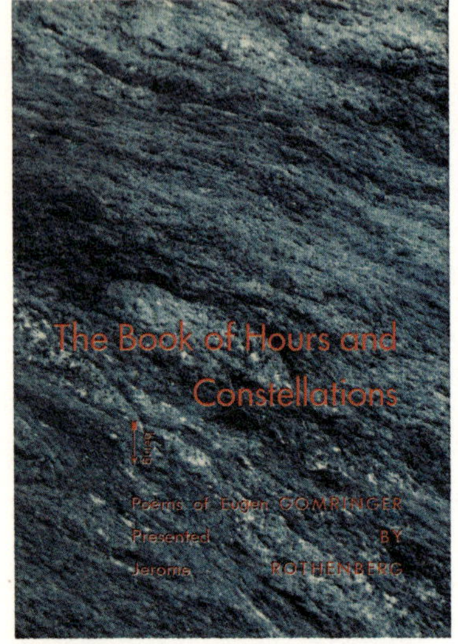
The Book of Hours and
Constellations
Poems of Eugen GOMRINGER
Presented BY
Jerome ROTHENBERG

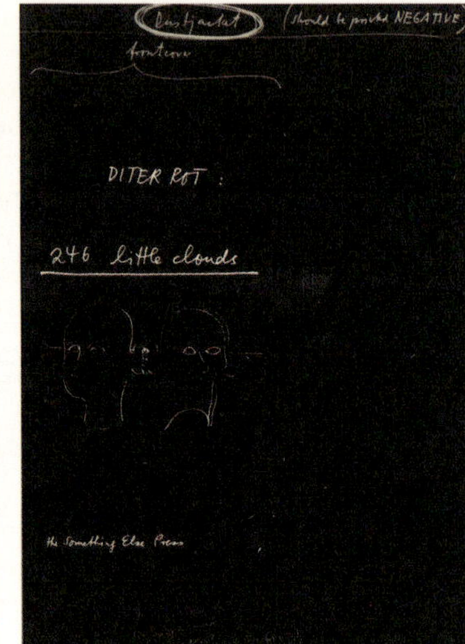
(should be printed NEGATIVE)
DITER ROT :
246 little clouds
the Something Else Press

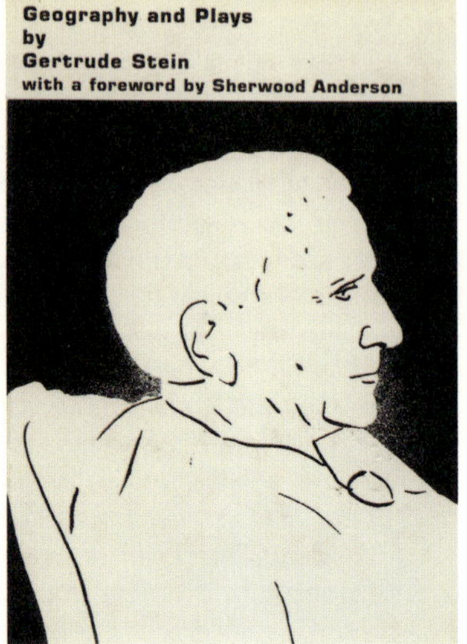
Geography and Plays
by
Gertrude Stein
with a foreword by Sherwood Anderson

foew&ombwhnw

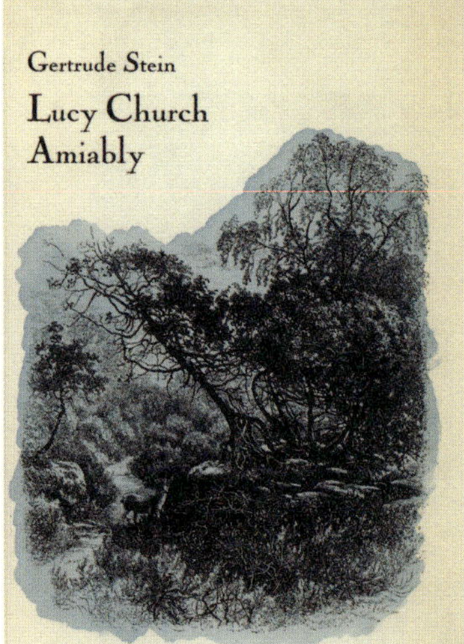
Gertrude Stein
Lucy Church
Amiably

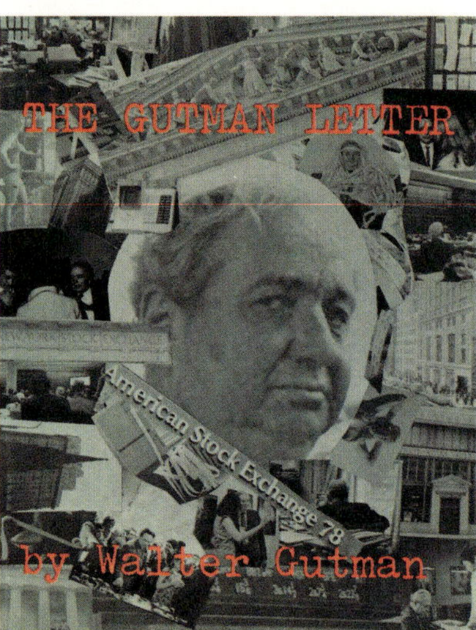
THE GUTMAN LETTER
American Stock Exchange 78
by Walter Gutman

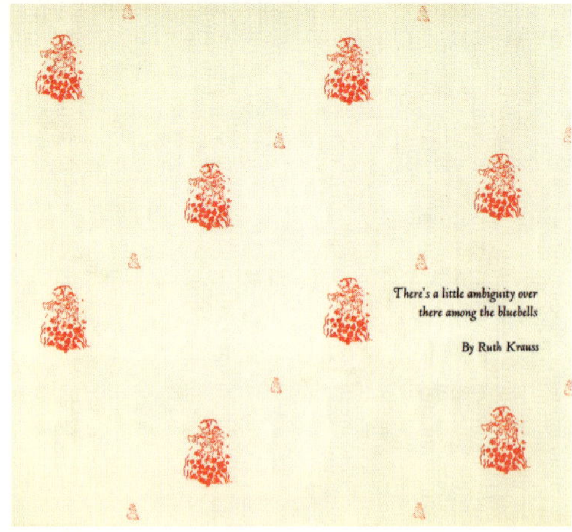
There's a little ambiguity over
there among the bluebells
By Ruth Krauss

NOTATIONS
John Cage

1969

John Cage. *Notations*. New York, 1969.

Preface by John Cage, edited with Alison Knowles. Cloth over boards with dust jacket, 3034 copies; paper wrappers, 4318 copies; second edition in wrappers, 3000 copies. The first edition in wrappers does not print the title on the spine; the second edition does.

This book illustrates a collection of music manuscripts which was made in recent years to benefit the Foundation for Contemporary Performance Arts. The collection was determined by circumstances rather than any process of selection. Thus it shows the many directions in which music notation is now going. The manuscripts are not arranged according to kind of music, but alphabetically according to the composer's name. No explanatory information is given.

The text for the book is the result of a process employing I Ching chance operations. These determined how many words regarding his work were to be written by or about which of two hundred and sixty-nine composers. Where these passages (never more than sixty-four words, sometimes only one) have been especially written for this book, they are preceded by a paragraph sign and followed by the author's name. Other remarks were chosen or written by the editors John Cage and Alison Knowles. Not only the number of words and the author, but the typography to letter size, intensity, and typeface were all determined by chance operations. This process was followed in order to lessen the difference between text and illustrations. The composition of the pages is the work of Alison Knowles.

A precedent for the text is the questionnaire. (The composers were asked to write about notation or something relevant to it.) A precedent for the absence of information which characterizes this book is the contemporary aquarium (no longer a dark hallway with each species in its own illuminated tank separated from the others and named in Latin): a large glass house with all the fish in it swimming as in an ocean.

The collection of manuscripts constitutes an archive, the contents of which are listed at the end of this book.

The editors are grateful to the many composers and music publishers who have made this presentation of mid-twentieth century music notation possible. —John Cage, May, 1968 (Preface)

Dick Higgins. *foew&ombwhnw*. New York, 1969.

The subtitle reads: *a grammar of the mind and a phenomenology of love and a science of the arts as seen by a stalker of the wild mushroom.* Bound like a prayer book with cloth over thin flexible boards, 4000 copies.

The first multi-track sensibility book. In four columns, the farthest left with big theater experiments, reflecting the author's background as a founder of happenings. The next column with works in an indefinable format, natural enough for the author who coined the term "Intermedia." The next column mostly with experiments in poetry and linguistics, which is a major part of Higgins's corpus. And on the far right, the little essays originally published in the *Something Else Newsletter*, the clearest and simplest statements of the theory underlying today's avant-garde, all bound together in prayer book format in this book with the incredible acrostic title (what it might stand for is given on page 8*)[*Freaked Out Electronic Wizards and Other Marvelous Bartenders Who Have No Wings]. (SEN, vol. 1, no. 12)

In five essays Higgins trains both a microscope and telescope on the avant-garde scene and makes good sense and good news out of the intermedia phenomenon, perceptual continuity, aleotropic means and blank forms and generally turns his back on the fixed-finished work to confront art with life in a constantly regenerative relationship. (ANM)

Stacked Deck

26. Once, at a point of his own choosing, during the piece he pulls a mirror from his pocket, looks at his reflection, and sings: "Oh Saturn. You cheat!" He bursts into mimed tears, drops the mirror, picks it or its pieces up and puts them in his pocket, singing: "How very much tobacco." This supersedes other cues.

27. If a woman gets in his way during a green light, or if she comes within six feet of him, he sings: "Kronos was nice, and same with Atreus. Will you come and see my stamp collection?" Here he grins stupidly or smirks. If she comes closer to him, he yells "Oh Saturn!" and runs away. If she follows him, he runs out into the audience, around in back of it, back onstage, and off into the wings. But he must be careful to do this with completely exaggerated grace and fairly slowly. The running is not so important as the movements of running. It might be convenient to think of a slow-motion film, and to imitate it, but not to run quite as slowly as most slow motion films actually are.

IV—The Man With a Brief Case

He is an urban suburban, complete to grey flannels. He carries an attache case. He is thoroughly suave.

28. He enters on any purple or brown light. For his first, third, fifth, etc. entrances he rushes onstage singing: "Tsut tsut tsut tsut . . ." in a falsetto voice as many times as necessary. He bangs any man on the head with his case and goes

138

Some Symmetric Magic . . .

$s = 4$. If $m = 9$, then $n = 45$, which wo have been easy enough to find out way. If $m - (w + y) = 3$, in o words, if $(m - w) - y = 3$, and know already that $m - w = 7$, then 4. Similarly we find that $m + y = (x +$ or $(m + y) + x = 11$. If $m + y = 13$, t $x = -2$. If $m - z = 9$, then $z = 0$. all checks through, because $2x + y$ $= 0$. Similarly, it is possible to const a magic square of the fifth degree g any three members of that square.

New Y April

Meaning It Is a Poem

April

Spread above from *foew&ombwhnw* by Dick Higgins.

Structural Researches

appropriate impressions and recollections of the places and people and items involved for future editions. The end result is an extremely open-ended structure which cannot ever be complete so long as Spoerri is living to select from the things that grab our attention and which we suggest to him as contributions—and perhaps not even then. And through this flux the people march—not characters but people, with names, with aspects seen by other people rather than selective opinions developed for narrative purposes, seen now doing this or that, but somehow independent and unexploited. It is as if we came to a marvelous party where we knew nobody—only one or another real thing was revealed about each person in the course of a conversation, something that might or might not be believed—and we hoped the party would go on forever, because we might never meet those people again. Well, this is the kind of party that can. That's part of its impact. Most serious novels, once finished, are placed on one's lap as part of the digestive process, while we try to figure out what we've read. Here we knew all along what we were reading, and, on completion, simply start the book again. And although it reads easily, like a novel, its meaning remains as different as its impact: the more it accumulates, the

139

Second New York Grass Rally

THE
SECOND NEW YORK GRASS RALLY

the Amalgamated Association for Grass and Air presents

a series of spectaculars, May 1st till May 26th,
praising something (for a change)
the world's leading event:

THE ARRIVAL OF SPRING

May 1, 2, 3, 4: Staying home, watching the first blade of grass.

Grass Concert #1, May 5, 6, and 7: Reading books, making love, observing tragic things, trying to consider other peoples' things, cooking brownies, and so on.

May 8, 9, and 10: Staying home, considering children and small furry mammals; once in this time finding an old friend.

Grass Concert #2, May 11, 12, and 13: Those people who cannot afford Bail Bond are looking for us, those people who want to sing are waiting for our songs.

May 14, 15, and 16: Staying home, looking forward to the sunrise and to next noticing a kitten: being very gentle.

May 22 and 23: Considering what one has said, been, and done; going swimming where it is neither profitable nor allowed.

Grass Concert #3, May 24, 25, and 26: Staying home, allowing what we are to say what we will be instead of what the bright ones say; giving both a damn and a hand; considering why we are hated.

This festival has neither subscriptions, capacities, nor information: it is ours to determine. Send no envelopes, no inquiries, because we all know it, all of us, already.

April 1965

A collection of pieces dating from 1958 by an artist who describes himself as "an amateur, that is, a lover of the actions," which in his case can be any form of cultural expression. The book includes the critical articles first printed in the *Something Else Newsletter*, such as "Intermedia," which gave a new word to the language, side by side with the huge abstract drama, *Saint Joan and the Beaurevoir*, the tiny playlets from Fluxus days in the *Act* series, long and short events and happening scenarios, long and short poems. These run side by side with one another, simultaneously, in four columns, and the whole book is bound, ironically, like a prayer book, which is precisely the spirit the work least invokes.

"A melee of avant-garde concepts that make clear Higgins's incredibly inventive, not to say obsessive, mind . . . Higgins is not an obscurantist, he cajoles the mind." —**John Gruen**, *Vogue*

"I give it my book of the month award, all kinds of good and intelligent things in it, mostly on intermedia." —**Jonas Mekas**, *Village Voice*

"In a time of often ludicrous literary pretense and band-wagon intellects, Higgins comes on as something refreshing." —**Martin Las**, *WBAI* (TAGT)

Gertrude Stein. *Lucy Church Amiably*. New York, 1969.

Cloth over boards, 2000 copies; paper wrappers, 2000 copies.

Of all Gertrude Stein's major novels *Lucy Church Amiably* remains one of the least known, in spite of being more accessible than others and more lyrical in tone, because of the mechanical facts of never having been published or widely distributed in an English-speaking country.

In keeping with the policy of the Something Else Press of gradually bringing about a situation in which all of the major works of Gertrude Stein are again available, we have reissued the 1930 Paris edition of this book, which Miss Stein described as "A Novel of Romantic beauty and nature and which Looks Like an Engraving."

"Gertrude Stein is often quoted, and her influence lurks in the prose style of most important American writers." —**Rosalyn Regelson**, *New York Times*

"The analytic manner serves at once the function of description and the function of song—to make awareness be experienced impersonally, and to make it come alive . . . 'Listen to a bird singing,' Stein suggested. 'It is always the same and yet it is always different each time.'" —**Stephen Koch**, *The Nation* (TAGT)

Walter Gutman. *The Gutman Letter*. New York, 1969.

Front cover collage by Suki Gallagher. Edited by Michael Benedikt. Cloth over boards with dust jacket, 4000 copies.

The life, loves, and stock market reports of "The Proust of Wall Street." Gutman is *on* the street, not *of* the street according to Emmett Williams, and if you open this book you'll see why. There is Gutman painting in his Provincetown studio and there is Gutman in the bathtub with Lucinda Love's legs around his neck, and there he is again reading the tickertape in his Wall Street Office, and then there's Jack Kerouac and Allen Ginsberg and G-String Enterprises, and Gregory Corso and David Amram, George Segal and Charlotte Moorman. And let's not forget the lady wrestlers. The book is a veritable treasure trove of anecdotes and enticements which ". . . do not constitute an offer to sell or the solicitation of an offer to buy." Take it from there. (CAT 73-74)

"A weekly market letter from a brokerage house is not a place one would expect to find a witty, speculative and off-beat writer who has a canny eye for what unites art and industry, the ways of a man with a maid, and a maid with a dollar. But that is where you will find Walter Gutman, an art critic, painter, admirer of strong women (circus performers, wrestlers, etc.), maker of underground movies, friend of the beats and artists of the avant-garde. He is also an advisor to the affluent . . . The book is generously illustrated with pictures showing the non-commercial side of the author: at parties, art shows, with his favorite models or sharing a bubble bath with a lady friend. Whether his weekly exhortations made money for his clients I am, alas, in no position to say, but if he has as sharp an eye for a winning stock as for feminine pulchritude, his clients ought to be in clover." —Thomas Lask, *New York Times*, June 17, 1969 (CAT 69–70)

Henry Cowell. *New Musical Resources*. New York, 1969.

With preface and notes by Joscelyn Godwin. Facsimile of the Alfred A. Knopf, Inc. edition, 1930. The edition was largely suppressed due to copyright problems. Cloth over boards with dust jacket, 4031 copies.

Since its original publication in 1930, Henry Cowell's *New Musical Resources* has become recognized, with Arnold Schoenberg's *Structural Functions of Harmony* and Paul Hindemith's *The Craft of Musical Composition*, as one of the three seminal technical studies by major twentieth century composers. While all three have gone out of print, the Cowell work has been, until now, the most difficult to obtain, owing to the small size of the original edition and the short time it was kept in print.

When it first appeared, *New Musical Resources* must have seemed incredibly visionary. Both the Schoenberg and the Hindemith works are backward-looking, into the history of harmony, with the proposed developments simply an extension of the past. While the Cowell work is not without its references to history, essentially it looks hardest at the phenomenon of music itself, and explains music in terms of what it is, not in terms of whatever conventions had been dominant in the preceding period. This has been an important characteristic of the American musical tradition, from Charles Ives and Carl Ruggles through to John Cage, Earle Brown and Philip Corner. (CAT 69-70)

"Even today [it] is still one of the few documents to treat concretely and shrewdly the ideas about musical theory developed during the first half of the twentieth century." —Mauricio Kagel, *Die Reihe*, vol. V, 1959 (CAT 69–70)

Wolf Vostell and Dick Higgins, editors. *Fantastic Architecture*. [New York, 1969.]

The English language edition was produced at the same time as the German edition (*Pop Architektur*, Droste Verlag, 1969) though released somewhat later, probably 1971. Dick Higgins cites 1971 as the date of publication in *Dick Higgins: A Bio/Bibliography* (Threadneedle Editions, 1979) and in the "Selective Bibliography of Dick Higgins's Work" which accompanies his February 14, 1973 interview with Eric Mottram (*Spanner*, no. 9. January 1977). Jacket illustration is *Guggenheim Collage* by Richard Hamilton, 1967. Book design and preface by Wolf Vostell. Introduction by Dick Higgins. The texts by Joseph Beuys, Raoul Hausmann, Franz Mon, Gerhard Rühm, Wolf Vostell, and Stefan Wewerka were translated from the German by Joachim Neugroschel. Cloth over boards with dust jacket, 2000 copies.

Many of our best creative minds have been attracted by the relationship of living people to architectural works, to the possibility of living in, around or through these works. This is a collection of possible and impossible ideas, projects, fantasies, dreams by artists, poets, musicians, philosophers and others working actively in the cultural fields. (ANM)

This documentation of ideas and concepts of a new polymorphous reality is offered as evidence of the new methods and processes that were introduced by Fluxus, Happenings and Pop. A demand for new patterns of behavior—new unconsumed environments. The accent in all the works in this book lies on change—i.e. expansion of physical surroundings, sensibilities, media, through disturbance of the familiar. Action is architecture! Everything is architecture! —Wolf Vostell (from Preface)

An artist is a researcher into the potential impacts of media, taking meaning, for the moment, simply as another medium, in order not to rule out the value of abstract, pure art. He structures his perceptions as he finds them, and bases his work less on the categorical imperative than on a general sense of "Here this is, what is it? What can we do with it, if anything?" His milieu may be social, political, formal, perceptual, any combination of these and of other similar values as well. It is the lack of this element of art as aesthetic research which makes architecture so tedious today, with its endless cubes, conchoid curves, volumes and static relationships.
—Dick Higgins (from Introduction)

For years architecture has been stagnant, in the sense that it has been influenced by other arts while at the same time having no influence whatever on them in return. Very little of modern architecture, so-called, has had any salutary effect on our daily lives, and very few of its potentials have been realized.

Here the German radical artist and the American dramatist-critic have assembled a collection of projects of artists of a number of disciplines—musicians, painters, poets, Happeners, even one or two architects—intended to confront the architecture of our time and to provoke and initiate new and better responses. Some of the projects have been realized, some could be, some most definitely could not. But all are relevant. Contributors include such diverse figures as Claes Oldenburg, Alison Knowles, Carolee Scheemann, Stefan Wewerka, Diter Rot, Dennis Oppenheim, Ben Vautier, Richard Hamilton, Raoul Hausmann, Gerhard Rühm, Joseph Beuys, Franz Mon, Robert Filliou and many more. (TAGT)

1970

R[ichard] Meltzer. *The Aesthetics of Rock*. New York, 1970.

Cover photograph by Ken Greenberg. Cloth over boards with dust jacket, 1494 copies; paper wrappers, 4133 copies.

The Aesthetics of Rock is the summation, *summa cum laude*, of "mere" (one of Meltzer's key words) philosophical inquiry as applied to rock 'n' roll. It is a masterpiece of the academic language of category and definition; applied to the antithesis of that language, rock. It is *not* explanation. It is phenomenological. It is n-dimensional: rock as the only complete expression of body and soul and mind of our time — — — — rock slipping through the guises of art and non-art and anti-art — — rock as the contemporary free and endlessly self-creating thing, resisting all attempts to identify it, plagiarizing itself and innovating with equal un-self-consciousness. (JC)

Over the past few thousand years, philosophical inquiry developed its systems, its schools and its terms upward, outward, onward, downward, inward and backward—far from their humble Hellenic or early Chou beginnings.

And then along came rock.

And along came R. Meltzer (he doesn't use the "Richard" very often), self-confessed "former scholar who doesn't give much of a crap for any of that stuff," composer of songs for the Soft White Underbelly, producer of 3-hour films about boxing, writer of articles on rock for *Crawdaddy* and author of *The Aesthetics of Rock*. (CAT 69–70)

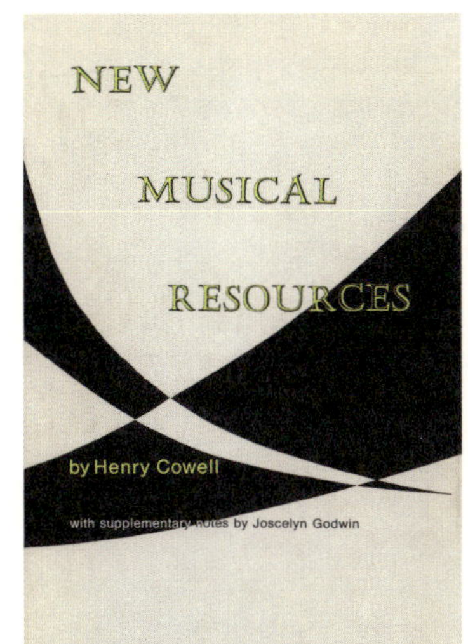
NEW
MUSICAL
RESOURCES
by Henry Cowell
with supplementary notes by Joscelyn Godwin

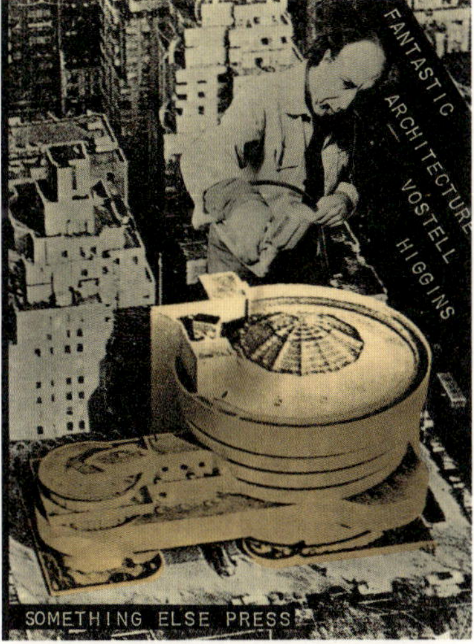
FANTASTIC
ARCHITECTURE
VOSTELL
HIGGINS
SOMETHING ELSE PRESS

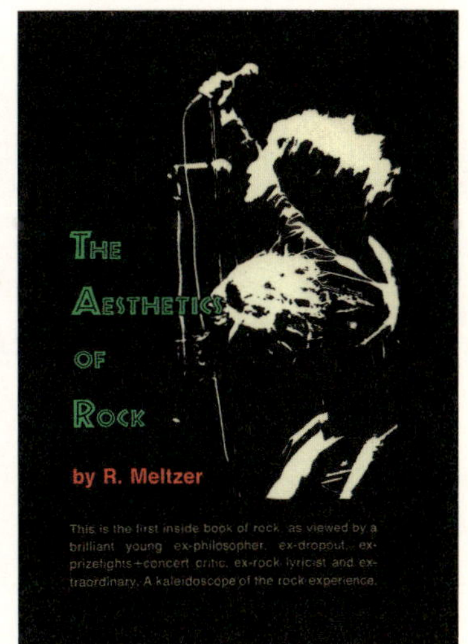
THE
AESTHETIC
OF
ROCK
by R. Meltzer
This is the first inside book of rock, as viewed by a brilliant young ex-philosopher, ex-dropout, ex-prizefights+concert critic, ex-rock lyricist and extraordinary. A kaleidoscope of the rock experience.

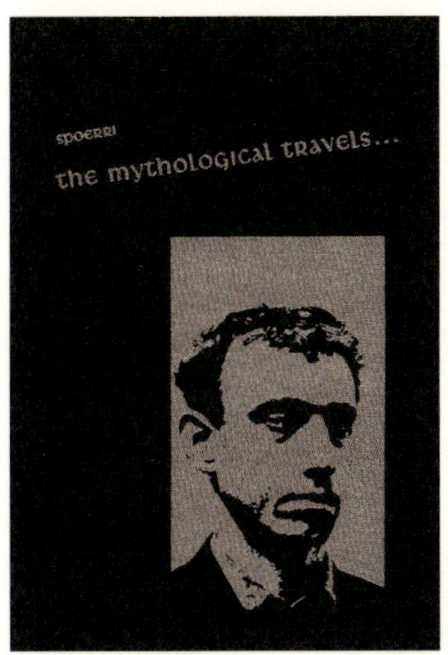
SPOERRI
the mythological travels...

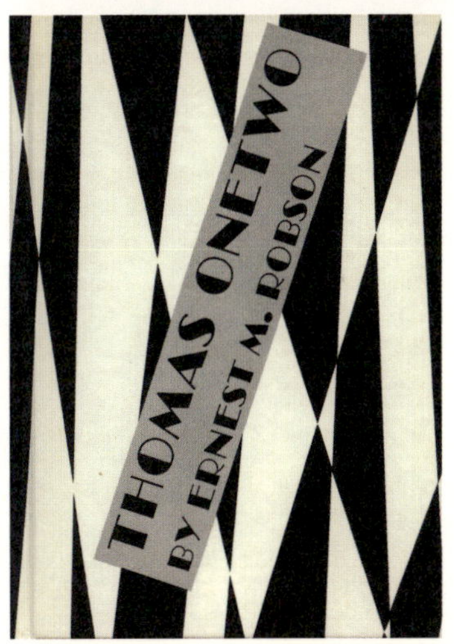
THOMAS ONETWO
BY ERNEST M. ROBSON

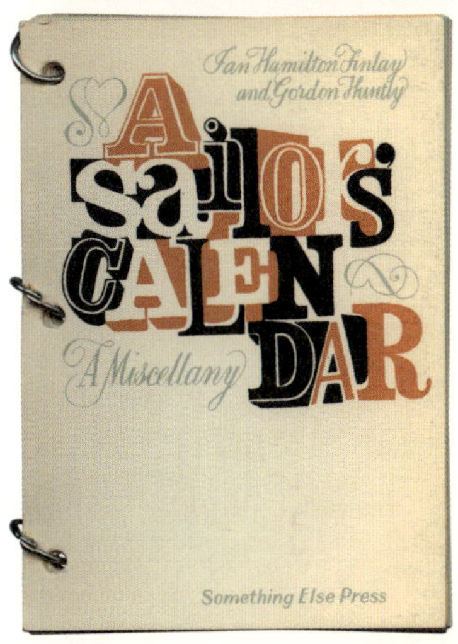
Ian Hamilton Finlay
and Gordon Huntly
A
sailor's
CALEN
DAR
A Miscellany
Something Else Press

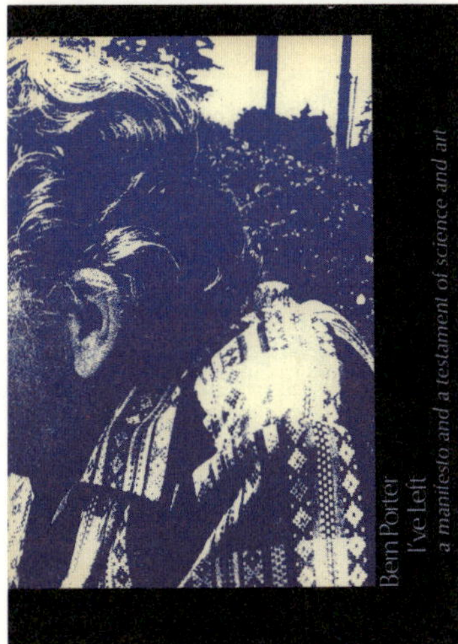
Bern Porter I've left
a manifesto and a testament of science and art

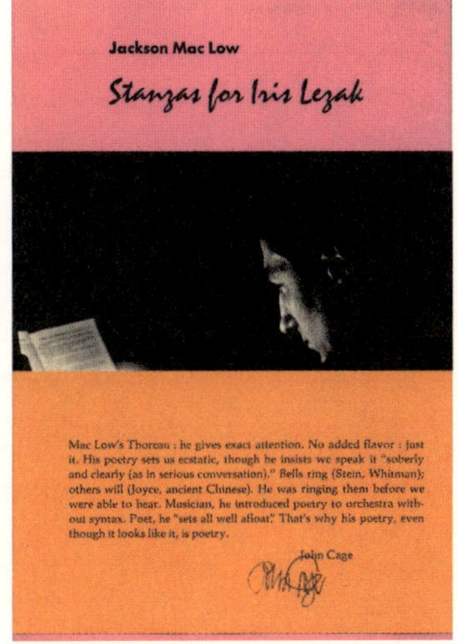
Jackson Mac Low
Stanzas for Iris Lezak
Mac Low's Thoreau : he gives exact attention. No added flavor : just it. His poetry sets us ecstatic, though he insists we speak it "soberly and clearly (as in serious conversation)." Bells ring (Stein, Whitman); others will (Joyce, ancient Chinese). He was ringing them before we were able to hear. Musician, he introduced poetry to orchestra without syntax. Poet, he "sets all well afloat." That's why his poetry, even though it looks like it, is poetry.
John Cage

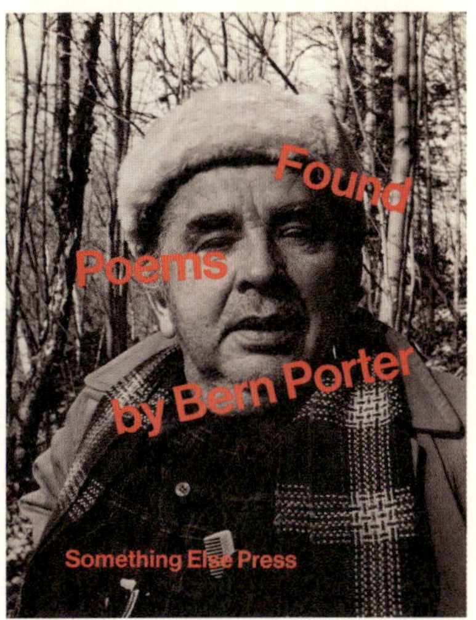
Found
Poems
by Bern Porter
Something Else Press

Daniel Spoerri. *The Mythological Travels of a Modern Sir John Mandeville, Being an Account of the Magic, Meatballs, and Other Monkey Business Peculiar to the Sojourn of Daniel Spoerri Upon the Isle of Symi, Together with Divers Speculations Thereon.* **New York, 1970.**

Translated and annotated by Emmett Williams. Cover photograph by Vera Spoerri. Cloth over boards with printed mylar dust jacket, 2985 copies.

Daniel Spoerri once opened his room in New York's Chelsea Hotel to the public as an art gallery, "a hotel room where he (the artist) slept, made love, cooked marvelous meals, and defecated. His constructions crowd the space, mingling with the bed, the clothes, the odor of lasagna," was how Allan Kaprow described it. And critic Nicolas Calas boasted of this show, "To avoid offensive smells . . . I spare myself the pleasure of seeing Spoerri's creations." (*Village Voice*, April 1, 1965)

But here's where it's April Fools on Mr. Calas, because Spoerri's art is far from ephemeral even though it is so closely intertwined with his life. Out of the phenomena of his experience, Spoerri makes poetic images and situations that seem surrealistic because of their extreme richness. If this work is simply a journal of objects found and meals consumed on a small Greek island called Symi, then *Gulliver's Travels* is surely just a highly improbable travelog. Somewhere along the line meaning and style enter the picture and transform both works.

Spoerri's other book, *An Anecdoted Topography of Chance* (see the back list section) received, among others, the following praise: "Daniel Spoerri's book . . . is a fascinating and absolutely delightful nouveau roman." —David Bourdon, *Village Voice*

"This is a delightful spoof (complete with some of the most unrelenting, unabashed punning I have ever seen) in the full spirit of today's most significant art form. Here is a genuine 'pop' book, for pop collections." —George Adelman, *Library Journal* (TAGT)

1971

Ernest M. Robson. *Thomas Onetwo.* **New York, 1971.**

Preface by Dick Higgins. Illustrations by Ken Friedman. Printed paper over boards with glassine jacket, 3393 copies.

Those who think are often relevant outside their so-called field of competence. This is true of Robson, who is one of the main popularizers of astronomy among semi-amateurs, who has worked as a chemist and invented rug shampoo, who has been a trapper, and who is presently a lecturer and writer on linguistics, structural aspects of poetry, orthography, and the technology of using sound in literature. *Thomas Onetwo* bears a relation to Robson's works similar to that of *The Hunting of the Snark* to Lewis Carroll's. The book is pleasantly illustrated by Ken Friedman. (CAT 73–74)

Ian Hamilton Finlay and Gordon Huntley. *A Sailor's Calendar.* **New York, 1971.**

Drawings and lettering by Gordon Huntley. Silk-screened card covers, ring bound, 1000 copies.

This gem of a book by Scotland's well-loved poet consists of a miscellany of poems. But they sound so wonderful to the ear that it's difficult to say whether they fall more properly into the tradition of sound poetry or into the visual, concrete vein for which the author is generally known. The drawings are by Gordon Huntley, hand silk-screened in color. The book comes bound in a three-ring binding designed by the author. (CAT 73–74)

Bern Porter. *I've Left: A Manifesto and a Testament of SCIence and ART (SCIART).*
New York, 1971.

Introduction by Dick Higgins. Cloth over boards with dust jacket, 895 copies; paper wrappers, 1855.

Bern Porter is, like Charles Ives (whom he resembles in the inventiveness and originality of his work, which is produced in isolation but is thoroughly cosmopolitan), a one-man movement. Science and Art, Sciart.

When one speaks of Porter, one has to ask which Porter one is speaking of: the atomic physicist, the poet, the surrealist, the first U.S. publisher of Henry Miller and of a number of the best poets of his generation, the sculptor, the early practitioner of "found poetry," the graphic illustrator, etc. Most of what is most lively, technically, in the cultural environment today has been touched on by Porter at some time over the pasty 30 years. He seems here to hold a position for the 1970's analogous to that of Marcel Duchamp for the 1960's. And, as with Duchamp, most of the work has appeared in miniscule editions, privately produced, if at all. A large part of his corpus is, in fact, produced in "an edition of one," and is on deposit in the special collections of the library of the University of California at Los Angeles, waiting a more favorable time for its launching.

But there is also the person behind the mask, the man who was born on Valentine's Day, 1911 (which perhaps explains his many loves), and, as with others of his generation such as John Cage and Kenneth L. Beaudoin, Porter has no difficulty with his role. He can be artist and scientist. It is as both that he wrote the Sciart manifesto, originally published in the 1950's in Tasmania, Australia, and *I've Left*, originally published (with the manifesto included) in 1962. Porter has said that he wanted to summarize everything he knew in *I've Left*, and it's in this spirit that the work should be taken. Epochal it is, and it should serve as a preface to Porter's uncommonly terse and blank-filled works, whose meaning is provided primarily by the reader, but whose humor, style and general aesthetic quality are implicit in Porter's constructions. As an example of these, we have included a small bouquet of the *Found Poems* (1928–), deliberately undated, at the end of the present edition.

Modern culture consists of many voices in lots of rooms. One of the larger of these, to which we hope the present volume provides the key, is that of Bern Porter. (JC)

1972

Jackson Mac Low. *Stanzas for Iris Lezak*. Barton, VT, 1972.

Title pages reads 1971; copyright page reads 1972. Cover photograph by Peter Moore. Cloth over boards with dust jacket and orange bellyband printing a comment by John Cage, approximately 2000 copies.

Jackson Mac Low's poems, plays, simultaneities and articles have been widely published since 1940. This volume is a collection of stanzaic-acrostic chance poems written for his wife in 1960. The separated stanzas, with words and phrases drawn from such widely different sources as newspapers and scientific treatises, have been used as texts for simultaneous performances comprising musical sounds and noises. (JC)

Mac Low's Thoreau: he gives exact attention. No added flavor: just it. His poetry sets us ecstatic, though he insists we speak it "soberly and clearly (as in serious conversation)." Bells ring (Stein, Whitman); others will (Joyce, ancient Chinese). He was ringing them before we were able to hear. Musician, he introduced poetry to orchestra without syntax. Poet, he "sets all well afloat." That's why his poetry, even though it looks like it, is poetry. —**John Cage** (Bellyband copy)

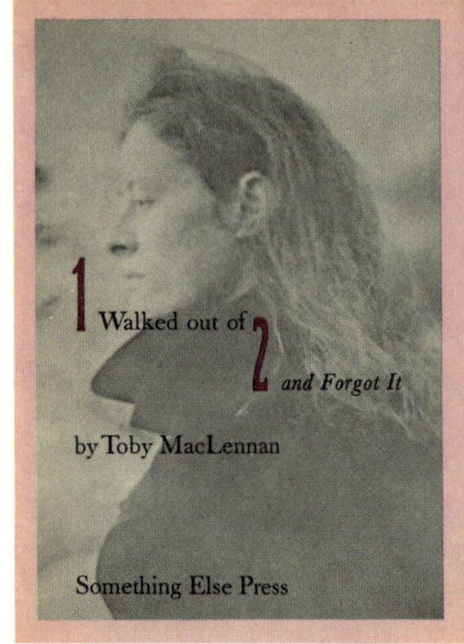

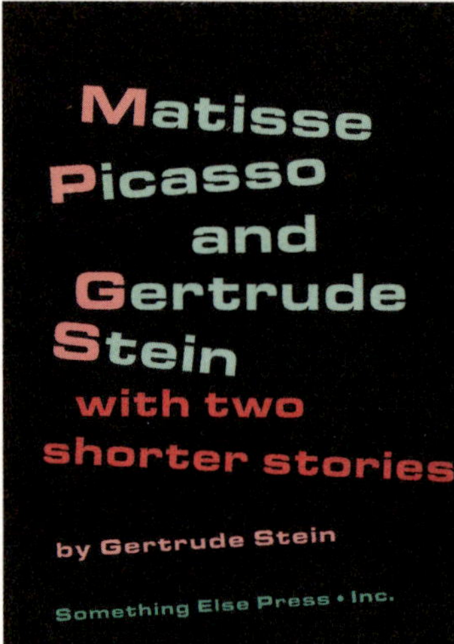

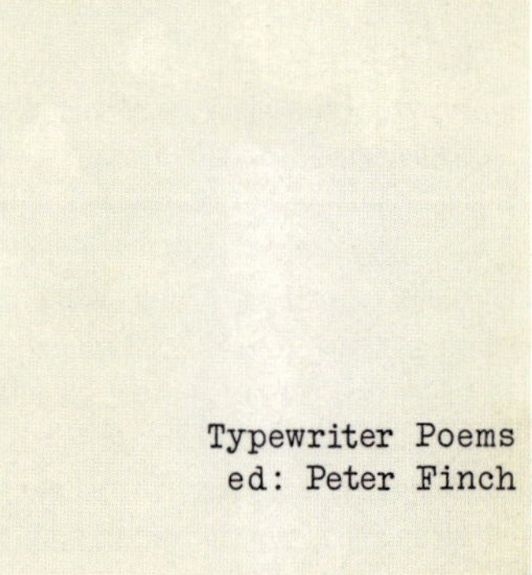

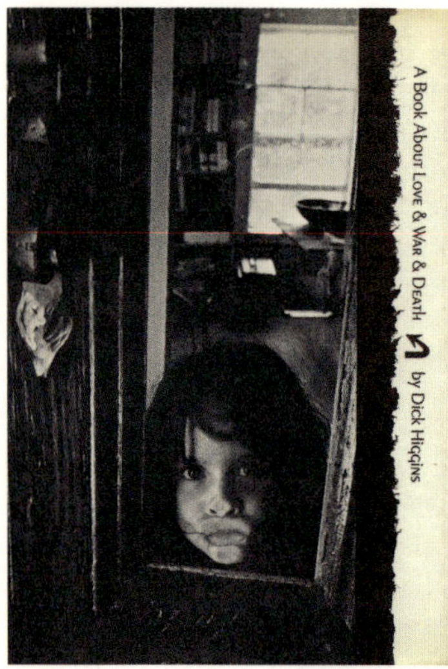

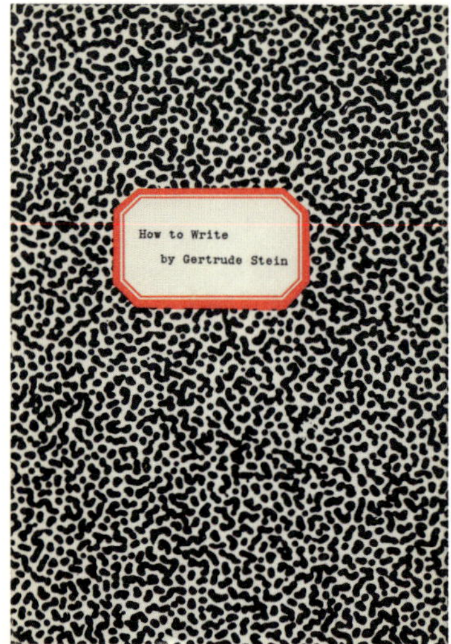

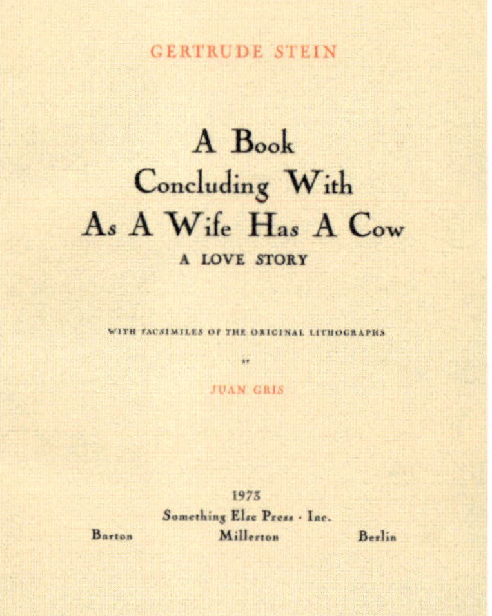

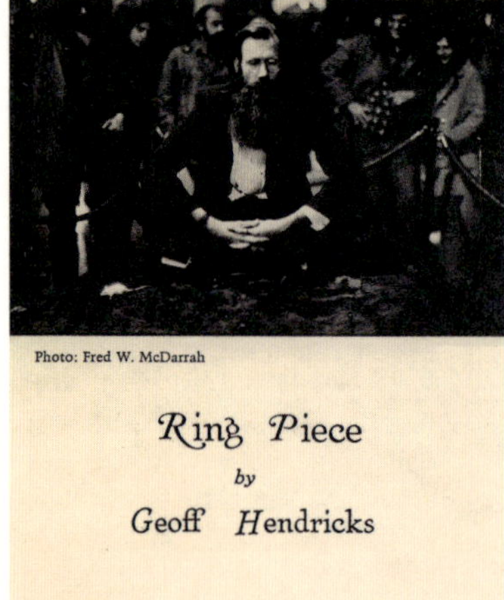

For years there has been both idle chatter and serious discussion of the expansion of the possibilities in fiction of the broadest sort—the art of narrative, of time applied to language. And so, the writer and **editor, Richard Kostelanetz,** has prepared the international anthology you are holding of the **Breakthrough Fictioneers.** Included are visual works, schematic legends, linguistic sequences and even a few almost-traditional yarns, but all of them are in some sense stories. The intention was to be inclusive rather than exclusive, informative rather than hermetic (hence the biographies at the end), to present a rare text by Gertrude Stein side by side with works by the most recent figures and to treat it all as contemporary. We of the **Something Else Press** hope that prose will never again be the same.

Bern Porter. *Found Poems*. **Millerton, NY, 1972.**

[Cover photograph by Dick Higgins.] Cloth over boards with dust jacket, 976 copies; paper wrappers, 2043 copies.

Porter the ideologist (author of *I've Left*) and Porter the atomic scientist, Porter the social planning expert (whose 1969 plan for Knox County, Maine is a widely-acclaimed classic) and Porter the artist all come together in Porter the Poet. Porter's *Found Poems* have the same seminal position as Duchamp's *objets trouvés*. Does this reflect Porter's own 1930's surrealist past? Only time can answer that. (JC)

Toby MacLennan. *1 Walked Out of 2 and Forgot It*. **Millerton, NY, 1972.**

Cloth over boards with dust jacket, 1000 copies.

This first novel—by an expatriate American living in Canada—looks like precious little surrealistic stories: but it feels like a hurricane.

The nameless protagonist (unless "he" is the only name he has) is not merely faceless, he is defaced and raped. Violence, cruelty and callousness are implicit in almost every one of the episodes. The style is brutal in its cleanness, a sort of ice-tract expressionism.

Toby MacLennan is the first really tough novelist of her Vietnam-and-since generation: yet most of her work is purely visual. A Detroiter, by birth, she holds an MFA in painting from the Art Institute in Chicago, and has taught painting and drawing in Mexico, the USA and Canada (Halifax). Presently she's working on a photographic book under a Canada Council grant. But the writing keeps happening. It's hard to stop writing when you think so much and do it so well. —Camille Gordon (JC)

Gertrude Stein. *Matisse, Picasso and Gertrude Stein* [also known as G.M.P.]. **Barton, VT, 1972.**

This is a facsimile of the 1932 edition. Cloth over boards with dust jacket, 1000 copies; paper wrappers, 2000 copies.

This is the unmentionable book in the Stein canon. For one thing there seems to be some serious disagreement among the Stein experts as to whether or not it's about her sexuality, and for another thing it's written in her most beautiful but difficult "cubist" style. For both reasons it has baffled her (mostly male) critics. Nobody would call this an easy book, but it's a heck of a human one. It needs reading more than talking about. (CAT 73–74)

Peter Finch, editor. *Typewriter Poems*. **Cardiff, Wales and Millerton, NY, 1972.**

Released in 1973. Co-published with Second Aeon Press. According to Frank, the edition was largely suppressed due to Higgins's dissatisfaction with the editing of the book. Paper wrappers, 1000 copies.

From its beginnings, concrete poetry has had a special relationship with the typewriter, due to the simple fact that all typewriter characters on a given machine (certain electric models excepted) are of equal width, which opens up vast graphic possibilities . . . Some of the most interesting work in this typewriter genre within the general medium of concrete poetry was and is being produced in the United Kingdom. And since one of the most interesting of serious magazine editors is *Second Aeon*'s Peter Finch, he was in a position to make up one of the most exciting collections. The ultimate universal collection it is not—it makes no pretense at internationalism. But a constellation from an epicenter of the whole concrete earthquake it is. And it's in that spirit that we are proud to present it. (Preface to the U.S. edition)

Dick Higgins. *A Book About Love & War & Death*. Barton, VT, 1972.

According to Frank, released in 1973. Cover photograph of Hannah Higgins by Dick Higgins. Cloth over boards with dust jacket, approximately 1000 copies; paper wrappers, approx. 2000 copies.

Poets, writers, artists, composers—they all like to pretend that they knew all along just what would happen when they began their newest work. Experiment is a dirty word, like avant-garde or even art. After all, in a sense, no art work can match the impact of the bullet that goes through your head, the poverty that ruined your childhood or the prejudices that made your life a hell for a time.

Dick Higgins is a different kind of artist. In his essays (many of the theoretical ones collected in *foew&ombwhnw*, published by Something Else Press) he anticipated many reactions to the new arts and new art intermedia, and tried to place them in a realistic sociocultural context. But in his art work, he seems always to be testing new media, means of communication, and hoping through this somehow to find the right and unique voice for the emotion that hasn't yet been sounded. Experiment is implicit.

A Book About Love & War & Death is one of the three major literary works he is irresponsible for, the others being the unpublished *Legends and Fishnets* and the unfinished *1000 Essays*, irresponsible being the attitude he takes towards the details of subject matter, and his work being the defining of the matrix in which the details happen. He seems to feel if the matrix is right—and for that he takes full responsibility—the work will somehow feel right and encompass a tremendous expressional gamut. Plan the society right and within it people experience tremendous freedom of choice: structure the art work right, and the audience will find their minds extraordinarily exhilarated and joyful. To him that's the real use of art. (JC)

1973

Gertrude Stein. *How to Write*. West Glover, VT, 1973.

This is a facsimile of the 1931 edition. Cloth over boards with dust jacket, approximately 1000 copies; paper wrappers, approx. 2000 copies.

How to Write is the "difficult" Stein at her best—and often the most difficult pieces are the most delightful.

Stein was not difficult for its own sake. Her work was as it was because her intentions could not be realized in normal prose. She was no hermetic. But in her best-known self-explanations—*Narration*, "Composition as Explanation," "An Elucidation," *An Acquaintance with Description* and *Lectures in America*—she gives in to the temptation, to work within the confines of "straight," traditional prose, and to repudiate her own most characteristic style. Not that all the above books are not extremely valuable insights—they are, into her work, into literature and into philosophy. But somehow they seem *about* literature rather than *being* literature, as a good essay should be. They also seem self-defeating—if her style is necessary for the points she wants to make, why not discuss her art in her own style? Of course one can make apologies and explain that most of Stein's other critical writings are based on the transcriptions of lectures, and this is partly true.

But fortunately *How to Write* exists, is now available for the first time since the early 1930's, and allows us to see her discussing her art by example rather than by mere explication

Furthermore, the essays in this book, while undated, stem from her richest period when she did her most unique artistic innovation, roughly 1910 to 1929, while in the other critical works, she writes of herself in the past tense and creates a sense that her mission has basically been achieved.

These essays are, then, from the thick of the battle against old baggage. As such, they have a trimness and resilience which the others lack. (JC)

Gertrude Stein. *A Book Concluding with As a Wife Has a Cow*. Barton, VT, 1973.

With illustrations by Juan Gris. Reprinted from the 1926 edition. In his Something Else Press & Since lecture, Dick Higgins said this book was "almost never distributed because it came along just about two months before Something Else Press finally petitioned for bankruptcy." Paper wrappers, approximately 1000 copies.

Long unavailable, with illustrations by Juan Gris, this is a facsimile edition of the original, which was printed in 1926 for André Simon and Company. It includes the well-known story whose title was taken for the book, as well as short invaluable texts. (CAT 73–74)

Geoff Hendricks. *Ring Piece: The Journal of a Twelve Hour Silent Meditation*. West Glover, VT, 1973.

Cover photograph by Fred W. McDarrah. 100 numbered and signed copies in cloth over boards with an original drawing; 2000 in paper wrappers.

Geoff Hendricks is a cloudsmith, specializing in cumulus and altocumulus formations, for aesthetic purposes, not only to canvas but also to shirts, clotheslines, packages, stairs, windows, porches, VW buses, and all kind of other appropriate surfaces.

When not forming clouds, Hendricks is apt to: a) teach at Douglass College in New Jersey, b) smile, c) dream, d) keep journals, e) seriously consider his children, Tyche and Bracken, f) be in love, g) travel to England, the Netherlands, Japan or Germany to perform and to present his work, h) enjoy a fine Sushi dinner, i) ask a serious question, j) wish he were at his Cape Breton (Nova Scotia) summer home, k) show you some of the chanterelle mushrooms he has gathered, l) wear his leathers, m) water the plants in his Church Street (New York City) loft, or n) walk someplace marvelous and find something. You can take this as a multiple choice question, but it doesn't matter which you choose, because they're all true. And somehow this work suggests his experiential world.

The book, *Ring Piece*, is, apart from the introduction, a small red journal—mentioned in #d above—such as Hendricks has been keeping since the early 1960's. Little red books. This one was written during the 1971 performance from which it gets its name.

Watch out. Hendricks is alive and to be considered dangerous. (JC)

It's the notes he wrote in his "little red book," a journal, during the New York Avant-Garde Festival in 1971. He was meditating for twelve hours, sitting on a pile of dirt in which was buried a box containing his wedding ring, from a marriage he had just terminated after ten or so years. White mice, released during a neighboring event, invaded his mound. Result: good words from the cloudsmith. (SEN, vol. 2, no. 6.)

Richard Kostelanetz, ed. *Breakthrough Fictioneers: An Anthology*. Barton, VT, 1973.

Cloth over boards with dust jacket, 500 copies; paper wrappers, 3000 copies.

For years there has been both idle chatter and serious discussion of the expansion of the possibilities in fiction of the broadest sort—the art of the narrative, of time applied to language. This international anthology includes visual works, schematic legends, linguistic sequences and even a few almost-traditional yarns, but all of them are in some sense stories. We hope this book does for prose what Emmett Williams' *An Anthology of Concrete Poetry* did for poetry. The collection is inclusive rather than exclusive, informative rather than hermetic (hence the biographies at the end). (CAT 73–74)

Emmett Williams. *A Valentine for Noel: Four Variations on a Scheme*. Barton, VT and London, 1973.

Co-published with Edition Hansjörg Mayer. 2000 copies in paper wrappers of which 100 of the Hansjörg Mayer edition are numbered and signed by the poet.

Recent long works which we are co-publishing with Edition Hansjörg Mayer of London and Stuttgart. The poet calls the book "four variations on a scheme" which is a humorous indication of his punning ways and his technical methods. There is the incomparable "IBM" poem with its sweet, jazzy flavor. Just listen to the opening lines: "red up going/perilous like sex/ yes hotdogs/evil jesus red black evil." There are also the suspense poem "Ego Hego Shego," the two-color tragic poem "Soldier," and the concluding, graphic poem "Fête Duchampêtre." Only 1000 copies are available for American distribution. —Jan Herman (CAT 73–74)

Leon Katz. *The Making of Americans: An Opera and a Play*. Barton, VT, 1973.

Cover photograph by Edward Burns. According to Frank, released in 1974. Cloth over boards with dust jacket, paper wrappers, press run unknown.

And while we're still on Stein, for goodness sakes don't miss Leon Katz's adaptation of *The Making of Americans*, with Al Carmine's music and Larry Kornfield's directing. If you can sneak away to NYC while it's still on—at the Judson Memorial Church's Judson Poets' Theater—you'll never feel badly for doing it. And nobody who cares about Stein can possibly forgive themselves if they miss it. All the Stein mayhem with families comes through crystal clear, as does the sweetness and richness of her language. You know we did the complete version of *The Making* years ago (it's four times as long as the abridged one), and it's still to be had for $10.95 in cloth. But now we're doing a giant paperback of it, for $6.45. (SEN, vol. 2, no. 6.)

Charles McIlvaine and Robert K. MacAdam. *One Thousand American Fungi*. Barton, VT, 1973.

Reprinted from the second edition of 1902. [Cover drawing by Alison Knowles.] Cloth over boards with dust jacket, 1500 copies; paper wrappers, 2500 copies.

This book, as long as it was available, was the mushroom collector's bible and, in fact, even today there is no exact replacement. We have reproduced the 1902 edition in facsimile (but larger than other editions and easier to read) except that we have chosen to do the plates in black and white since the old colors in the original did not match modern mycological

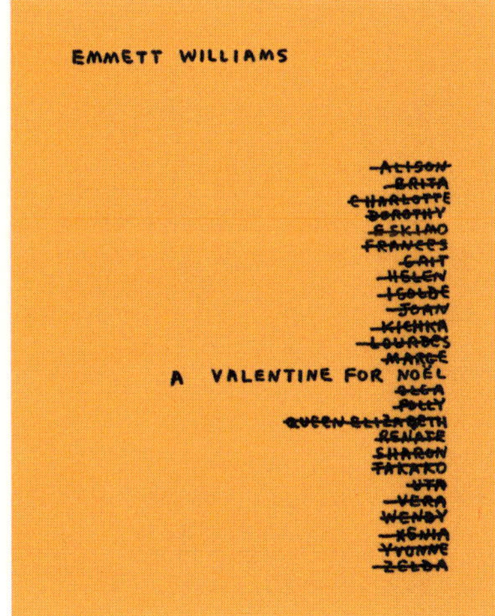
EMMETT WILLIAMS
A VALENTINE FOR NOEL

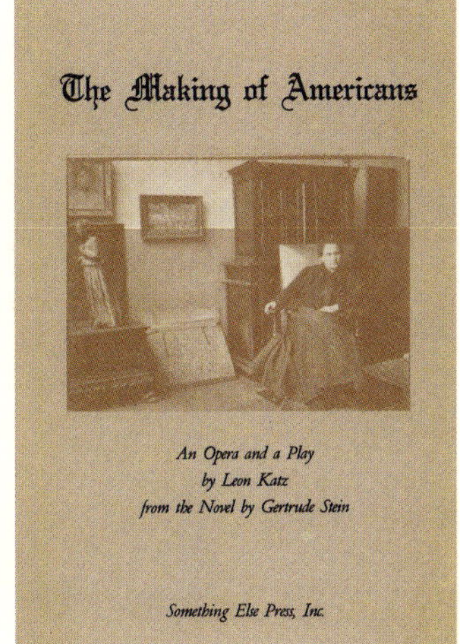
The Making of Americans
An Opera and a Play
by Leon Katz
from the Novel by Gertrude Stein
Something Else Press, Inc.

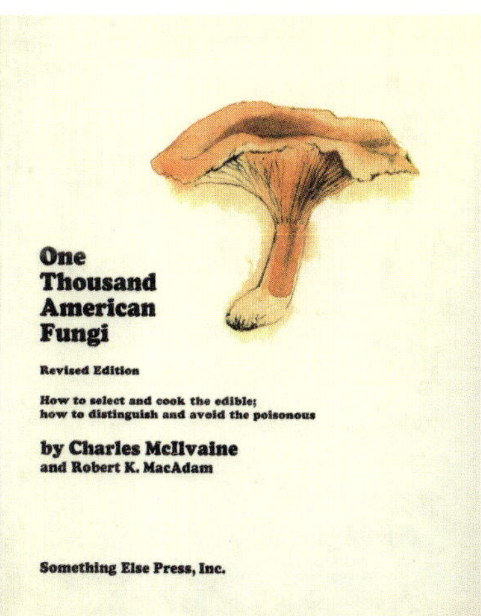
One Thousand American Fungi
Revised Edition
How to select and cook the edible;
how to distinguish and avoid the poisonous
by Charles McIlvaine
and Robert K. MacAdam
Something Else Press, Inc.

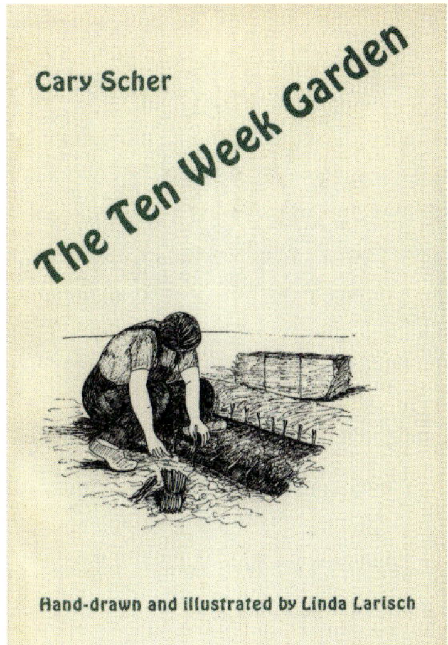
Cary Scher
The Ten Week Garden
Hand-drawn and illustrated by Linda Larisch

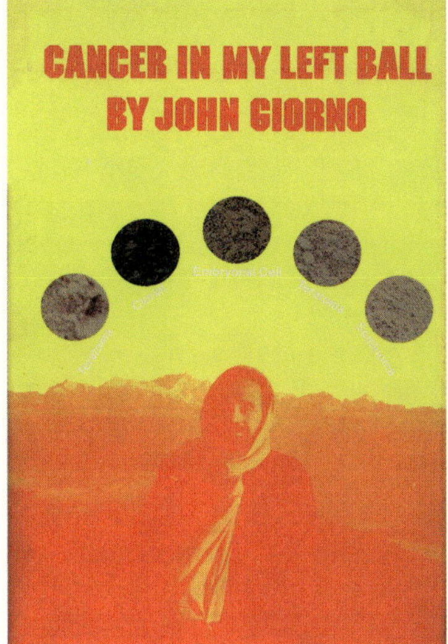
CANCER IN MY LEFT BALL
BY JOHN GIORNO

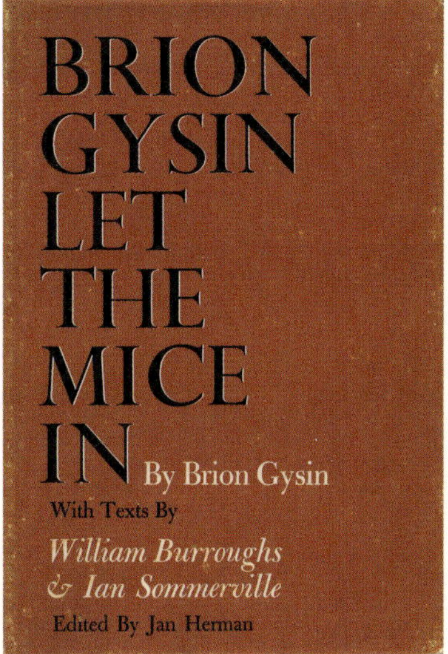
BRION GYSIN LET THE MICE IN
By Brion Gysin
With Texts By
William Burroughs
& Ian Sommerville
Edited By Jan Herman

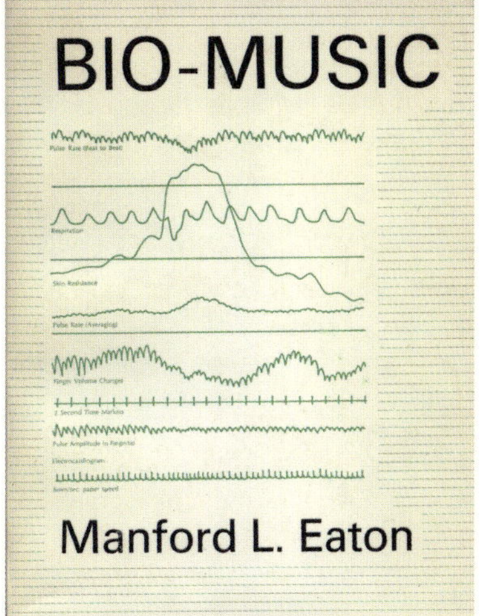
Something Else Yearbook
1974
sound art
things seen
poetry
nature
proposals
documentation
laughter
prose
commerce
occurrences
unspeakables
notations
reflections
interviews
SOMETHING ELSE PRESS, INC.
P.O. BOX H, BARTON, VT 05822

BIO-MUSIC
Manford L. Eaton

standards in any way and have virtually no taxonomic value. While the nomenclature has changed a great deal since McIlvaine's time, the accuracy of his macroscopic descriptions has not been surpassed. (CAT 73–74)

Cary Scher. *The Ten Week Garden*. Barton, VT, 1973.

Hand-drawn and illustrated by Linda Larisch. Cloth over boards with dust jacket, 1000 copies; paper wrappers, 2000 copies.

At last a charming and informative gardening book which uses the "organic method" pioneered by the late J.I. Rodale. The book is for homesteaders who live too far north for a normal growing season, or for those, like teachers and other professionals, who have limited gardening time in summer. No matter whether you are an adult or an 8th grader, the pace of the book is made to order for following instructions. —Jan Herman (CAT 73–74)

John Giorno. *Cancer in My Left Ball*. Barton, VT, 1973.

Cover by Les Levine. Cloth over boards with dust jacket, 3000–5000 copies; paper wrappers, 7000–10,000 copies. Exact press run numbers are unknown.

John Giorno dissects the American consciousness. With his scalpel he cuts through the layers that collectively make up America, and his poems expose all of the vileness and beauty.

His metaphors are the hells of heroin, the hungry ghosts of trashy pornography, the animals of hamburger cattle, the titans of B-52 bombers, the Gods of the cheap thrills of consummate bliss, and the human voice trying to figure out its own suffering.

He is a spiritual poet and his images are visualizations in his meditation. He is a Buddhist in the Tibetan tantric lineage of the Nyingmapa (Red Hat) Sect.

His use of repetition creates mantric rhythms, making the poems into heavy flowing chants singing the essence of poetry. —Jan Herman (JC)

Brion Gysin, William Burroughs, and Ian Sommerville. *Brion Gysin Let the Mice In*. West Glover, VT, 1973.

Edited by Jan Herman. Book and cover design by Graham Mackintosh. Cloth over boards with dust jacket, 500 copies; paper wrappers, 1000 copies.

I talk a new language. You will understand.

I talk about the springes and traps of inspiration.

IN SPIRATION—what you breathe in. You breathe in words. Words breathe you IN. I demonstrate Thee, the Out-Word in action both visual and aural, racing away in one direction to sounds more concrete than music and, in the other, to paintings like television screens in your own head. I am better than Transducer for I show your own Interior Space.

In the beginning was the Word—been in You for a toolong time. I rub out the word. You in the Word and the Word in You is a wordlock like the combination of a vault or a valise. If you love your vaults, listen no further. I spin the lock on your Interior Space Kit. Prison: Come Out!
—Brion Gysin (JC/Excerpt from book)

With texts by William Burroughs and Ian Sommerville, here is the story behind the experimental discoveries which Gysin made as applied to writing, primarily the early "cut/up" techniques (so successfully employed by Burroughs). It also includes a history of The Dream Machine, and the permutated poems. —Jan Herman

Gysin's friendship with Burroughs dates back to the early fifties . . . and it is the organizing principle behind the various pieces which make up (the book) . . . (he) has injected intoxicating doses of music and magic into the mainstream of modern writing. —Robert Palmer (CAT 73–74)

1974

Jan Herman, editor. *Something Else Yearbook 1974*. Barton, VT, 1974.

Paper wrappers, 2000 copies.

After all, it does get boring to see the same old writers and artists appearing together in book after book. So we refused to be anthologists in this one. Most anthologies are artificial reprints anyway, pure literary hocus-pocus, unless they've exhaustively mapped out a new terrain. We like to think of this Yearbook as more in the spirit of a workbook, something to record a year's worth from lots of people. —Jan Herman (CAT 73–74)

Manford L. Eaton. *Bio-Music*. Barton, VT, 1974.

Paper wrappers, approximately 500 copies.

Every large city now has alpha rhythm brain wave studios, it's become a fad, and we've all heard of bio-feedback. But you probably haven't heard of bio-music which describes "a class of electronic systems that use biological potentials in feedback loops to induce powerful, predictable, repeatable physiological/psychological states that can be elegantly controlled in real time." Eaton is a composer and communications researcher whose philosophy of non-chemical alteration of consciousness is based upon years of bio-music experiments. The purpose of this handbook is to provide guidelines for other researchers and to prevue the types of systems that are now or soon will be within the capabilities of the electronic art. It is engrossing reading both for the layman and the technician. —Jan Herman (CAT 73–74)

GREAT BEAR PAMPHLETS

All of the Great Bear Pamphlets were saddle-stitched in wrappers, 5½ x 8½ inches; sixteen pages with the exception of no. 8, *Manifestos*, which was thirty-two pages. There were two series each with ten pamphlets. Pamphlets in the first series (1965–1966) were assigned numbers 1–10 by the publisher. The second series (1967) was unnumbered. First printing sizes ranged from 500 to 3000. Most of the pamphlets were reprinted.

Upon completion of the first series of ten pamphlets, Dick wrote in the *Something Else Newsletter* (vol. 1, no. 4): "Next year the Great Bear will reappear as something else. The concept of the first series was that it should present short but important works, without regard to medium, by the major artists of our time, in an inexpensive form which could go places our more elaborate books could not, and thus serve the educational function of helping to create an informed mass audience of cultural flexibility, which is, after all, the purpose of the press." —SC

1. Alison Knowles. *By Alison Knowles*. 1965.

[This is the only pamphlet without the Great Bear logo (though the logo is present on the reprint) -ed.]

All the early performance pieces and events by the pioneering printer/artist of *Four Suits* fame.

2. Dick Higgins. *A Book About Love & War & Death, Canto One*. 1965.

The earliest (1960–1962) section of Higgins's largest work, designed to be read only aloud.

3. George Brecht. *Chance-Imagery*. 1966.

This 1957 article remains the basic one for the techniques and philosophy of chance in the arts.

4. Claes Oldenburg. *Injun & Other Histories*. 1966.

Two very early scenarios (1958) from before pop-art. With two drawings.

5. Al Hansen. *Incomplete Requiem for W.C. Fields*. 1966.

The gorgeous poem read by the artist in an early (1958) Happening while Fields's movies were projected on his bare chest.

6. Jerome Rothenberg. *Ritual: A Book of Primitive Rites and Events*. 1966.

A delightful anthology of Polynesian, Melanesian and American Indian events and performance pieces selected and adapted by the well-known poet, translator and editor.

7. Allan Kaprow. *Some Recent Happenings*. 1966.

Typical scenarios by the father of the Happening.

8. Dick Higgins and Emmett Williams, editors. *Manifestos*. 1966.

Calls-to-arms by Ay-O, Philip Corner, the W.E.B. DuBois Clubs, Öyvind Fahlström, Robert Filliou, John Giorno, Al Hansen, Dick Higgins, Allan Kaprow, Alison Knowles, Nam June Paik, Diter Rot, Jerome Rothenberg, Wolf Vostell, Robert Watts and Emmett Williams. A double pamphlet.

9. Wolf Vostell. *Berlin and Phenomena*. 1966.

Two characteristic Dé-coll/age-Happening scenarios by Europe's best-known Happener.

10. Jackson Mac Low. *The Twin Plays: Port-au-Prince & Adams County Illinois*. 1966.

Two of this most inventive poet's most exciting experimental dramas, using identical linguistic formal structures but in different versions of English.

[11.] John Cage. *Diary: How to Improve the World (You Will Only Make Matters Worse) Continued, Part Three*. 1967.

The latest in a series of essays in which Cage reflects lyrically on social questions. Printed in two colors structured by chance by the author.

[12.] Bengt af Klintberg. *The Cursive Scandinavian Salve*. 1967.

Short, lyric Happenings by the brilliant Swedish anthropologist/poet.

[13.] David Antin. *Autobiography*. 1967.

As the title suggests, these are informal recollections and collages by the well-known Brooklyn poet.

[14.] Philip Corner. *Popular Entertainments*. 1967.

The largest collage composition by the brilliant young composer.

[15.] Robert Filliou. *A Filliou Sampler*. 1967.

Typical short works by the only poet among France's nouveaux réalistes.

[16.] Allan Kaprow. *Untitled Essay and Other Works*. 1967.

The historic statement which accompanied the text of the first published Happening (1958) with a sampling of characteristic scenarios.

[17.] Di(e)ter Rot(h). *A Look into the Blue Tide, Part 2*. 1967.

die blaue flut ("the blue tide") is this Icelandic innovator's hugest work, and part 1 is a book in itself. These are selected pages from part 2. Heavily illustrated.

[18.] Luigi Russolo. *The Art of Noise*. 1967.

This Futurist is generally credited with being the father of noise music, and his classic 1913 manifesto, *L'Arte dei Rumori*, has till now been difficult to obtain.

[19.] Emmett Williams. *The Last French Fried Potato and Other Poems*. 1967.

A small bouquet of typical recent works by one of the founders of Concrete Poetry.

[20.] Peter Besas, editor and translator. *A Zaj Sampler*. 1967.

Examples of the highly original and inventive concept performances and non-performances by Spain's first avant-garde group of international importance since the Spanish Civil War. Works by José-Luis Castillejo, Ramiro Cortes, Javier Martines Cuadrado, Juan Hidalgo, Walter Marchetti, Tomas Marco and Eugenio de Vicente.

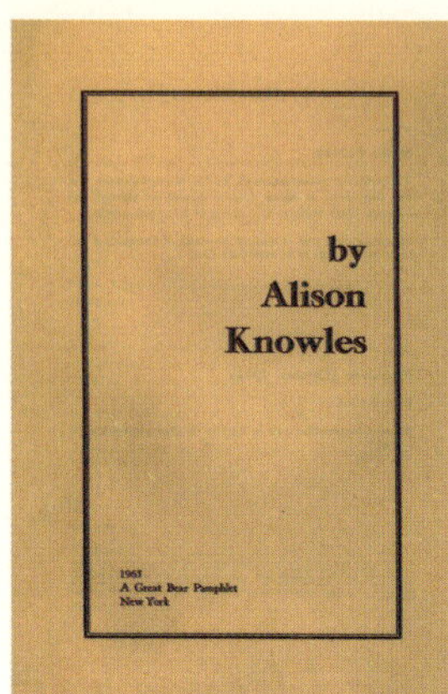

by
Alison
Knowles
1965
A Great Bear Pamphlet
New York

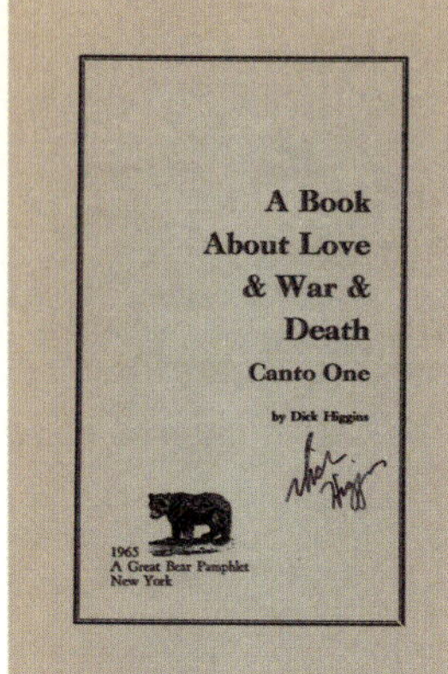

A Book
About Love
& War &
Death
Canto One
by Dick Higgins
1965
A Great Bear Pamphlet
New York

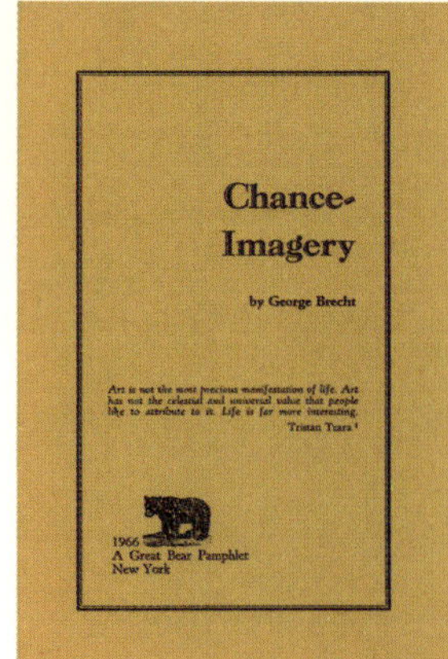

Chance-
Imagery
by George Brecht
Art is not the most precious manifestation of life. Art
has not the celestial and universal value that people
like to attribute to it. Life is far more interesting.
Tristan Tzara
1966
A Great Bear Pamphlet
New York

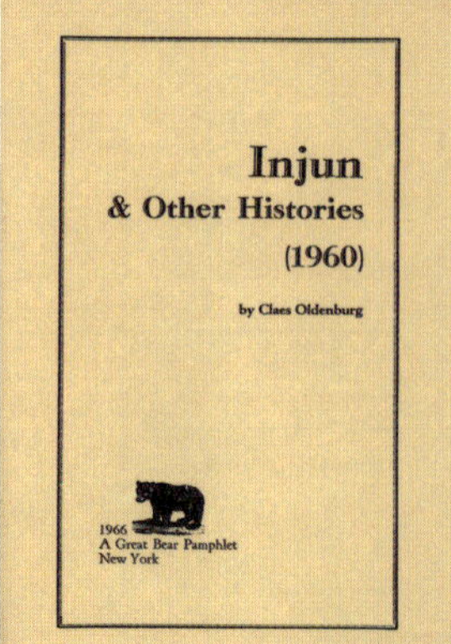

Injun
& Other Histories
(1960)
by Claes Oldenburg
1966
A Great Bear Pamphlet
New York

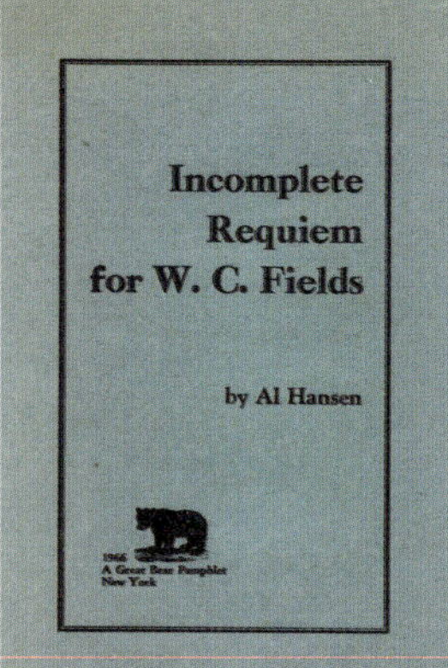

Incomplete
Requiem
for W. C. Fields
by Al Hansen
1966
A Great Bear Pamphlet
New York

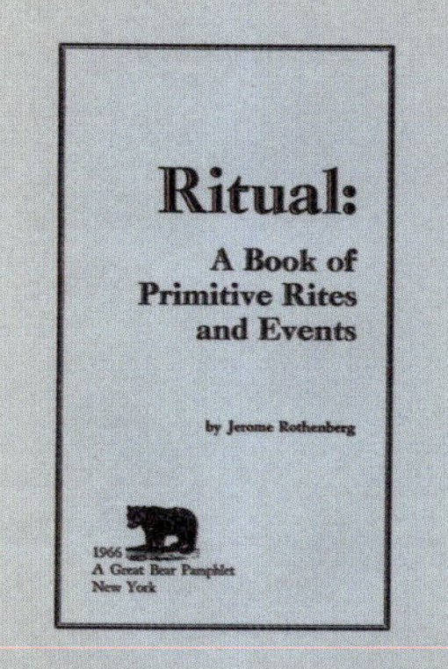

Ritual:
A Book of
Primitive Rites
and Events
by Jerome Rothenberg
1966
A Great Bear Pamphlet
New York

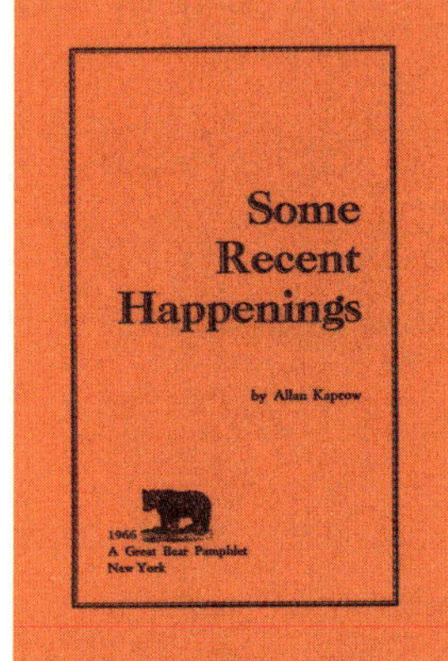

Some
Recent
Happenings
by Allan Kaprow
1966
A Great Bear Pamphlet
New York

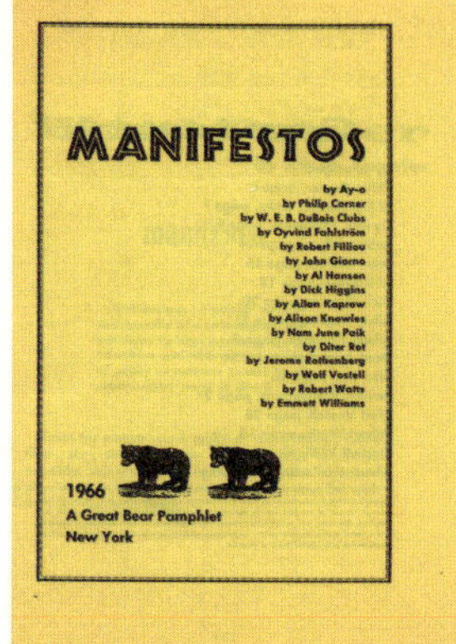

MANIFESTOS
by Ay-o
by Philip Corner
by W. E. B. DuBois Clobs
by Oyvind Fahlström
by Robert Filliou
by John Giorno
by Al Hansen
by Dick Higgins
by Allan Kaprow
by Alison Knowles
by Nam June Paik
by Diter Rot
by Jerome Rothenberg
by Wolf Vostell
by Robert Watts
by Emmett Williams
1966
A Great Bear Pamphlet
New York

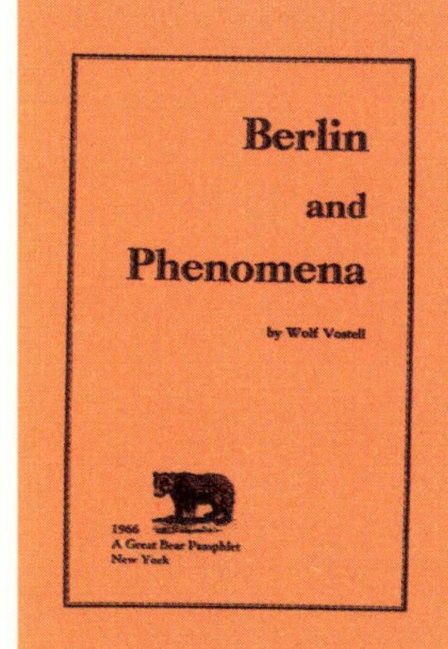

Berlin
and
Phenomena
by Wolf Vostell
1966
A Great Bear Pamphlet
New York

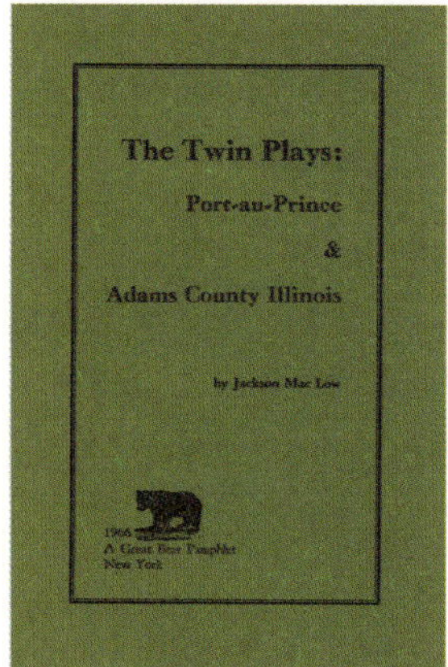

The Twin Plays:
Port-au-Prince
&
Adams County Illinois
by Jackson Mac Low
1966
A Great Bear Pamphlet
New York

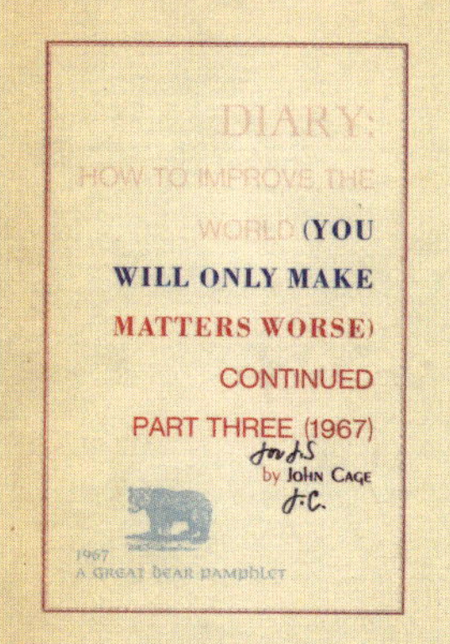

DIARY:
HOW TO IMPROVE THE
WORLD (YOU
WILL ONLY MAKE
MATTERS WORSE)
CONTINUED
PART THREE (1967)
by John Cage
1967
A Great Bear Pamphlet

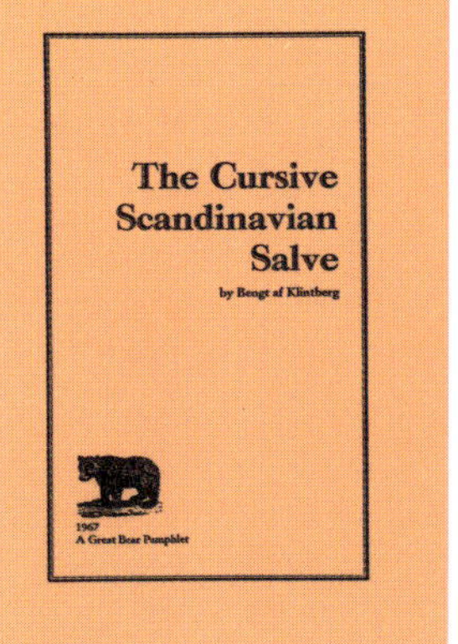

The Cursive
Scandinavian
Salve
by Bengt af Klintberg
1967
A Great Bear Pamphlet

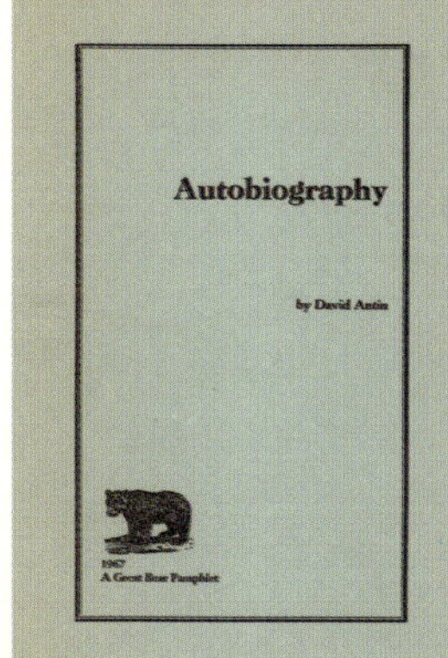

Autobiography
by David Antin
1967
A Great Bear Pamphlet

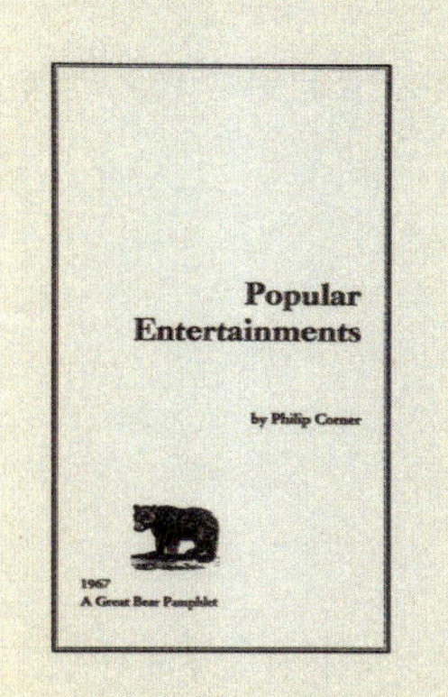

Popular
Entertainments
by Philip Corner
1967
A Great Bear Pamphlet

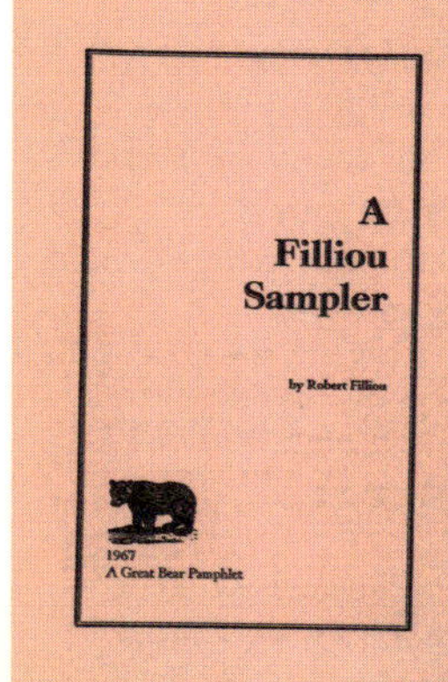

A
Filliou
Sampler
by Robert Filliou
1967
A Great Bear Pamphlet

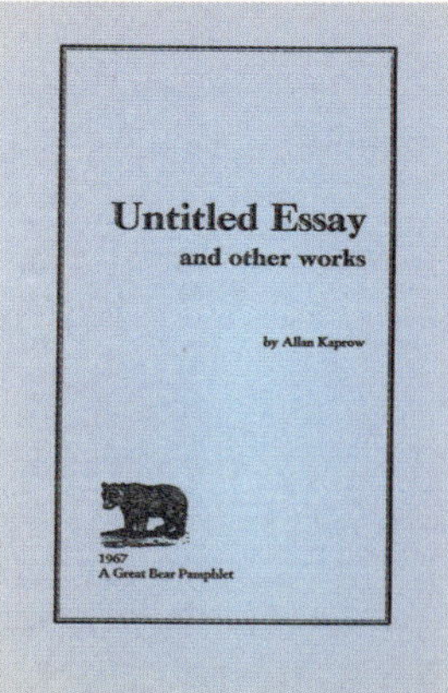

Untitled Essay
and other works
by Allan Kaprow
1967
A Great Bear Pamphlet

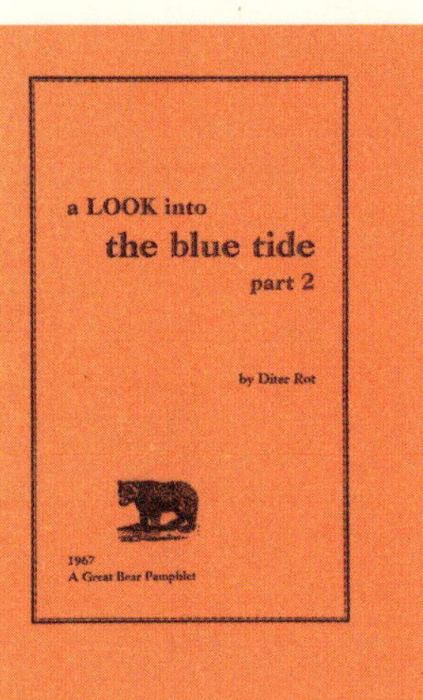

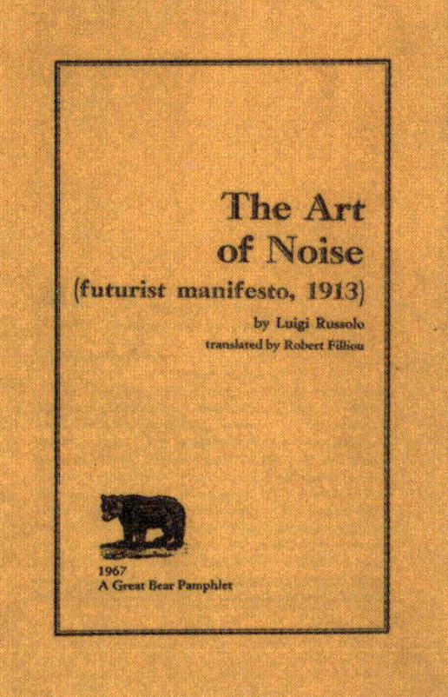

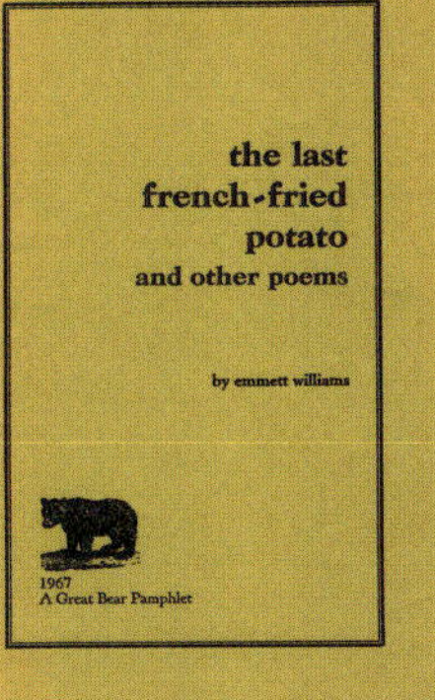

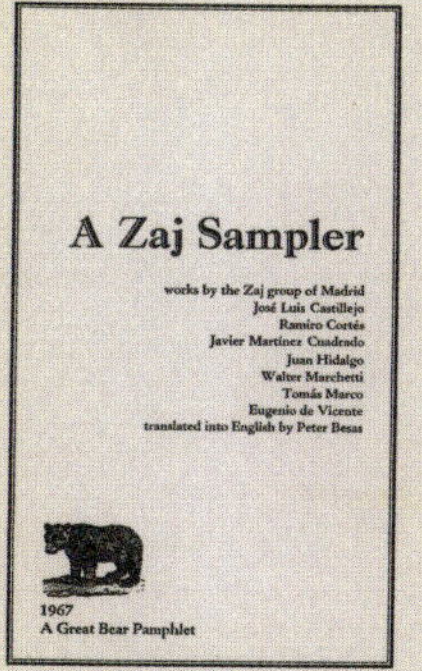

Camille's Reports #1

I'm back from Afghanistan in my new hat—sort of a Puritan gentleman's affair with one of the silver buckles on it that used to be on my shoes. Off and on I'll be doing the cards again—except now it's a newsletter. Usually.

I must be getting old, because I can remember way back to the early 1960's when, at the Judson Poets' Theatre, Florence Tarlow bounded and grinned, Mae West-like, to Al Carmine's music in Ruth Krauss's "This Breast." It was glorious, and looks it too in Ruth's *There's a little ambiguity over there among the bluebells*. Count the colors in the book, by the way. They're all made from blue and yellow, but because of tints and secondary reflectances they make ochres, blacks, even a brown at one point. Cloth, $3.95.

Technically, historically, it is said, Eugen Gomringer (a Bolivian Swiss living in Germany) is the papa of Concrete Poetry, and that his "Constellations" series is the beginning of the medium. Actually his *Book of the Hours and Constellations* is so gentle, so unpretentious that it's hard to realize one is reading a historic work. Seems too perfect for that. And hats off to Jerome Rothenberg for his selection and translation. Cloth, $4.50. Paper, $1.95.

What do Columbus, Melville, and Carl Mills (the kidnapper) have in common? Well, for one thing they're all in the sentence you just read. And they're all obsessional personalities—documented and reacted to—in Paul Metcalf's GENOA, published by Jargon and available through the SMALL PUBLISHERS COMPANY, 175 Park Avenue South, New York, N. Y. 10010. It's the most exciting big prose work I've come across, since, well, since Afghanistan.

CAMILLE GORDON

Camille's Reports #2

Ay-o's down at the University of Kentucky at Lexington this year. That's one bunch of colonels who won't be sitting back with their mint juleps ever again.

On the wall facing my door there hangs a poster, Robert Filliou's *L'Immortelle Mort du Monde* (in English, in spite of the name). Not only is it really pretty, but I have yet to see a visitor to my place come or go without noticing it and maybe doing a brief performance from it. The Press sells it, hand-colored in 10 colors, for $5.00.

246 Little Clouds, Diter Rot's newest book—his first published here—is a very cloud colored object. Grey top, grey pages, grey cloth, grey everything. Probably a surprised reader will think he has a defective copy when he first picks it up. But no, it's the style, and no, it's not all grey: Diter's drawings and handwritten texts are often sunny. It's a beaut! Clothbound, $5.95.

Remember *Poor Old Tired Horse?* The most exciting little mag on the Scottish scene in years? Seems Ian Hamilton Finlay signed a contract with a New York publisher to reissue the whole series, but ill health and a number of moves have destroyed his records of just who he signed with. Ian says he just can't find it. We'd like to know so we can find those mags around again. They're still very fresh eggs.

It took over 1400 letters to settle all the rights and permissions questions in John Cage's new *Notations*, ready in December. A very interesting book could be made of all that correspondence!

CAMILLE GORDON

Something Else Newscard #5

We'd hate to lose a nickle for everyone who is claimed to have originated happenings, each in his own way. The latest is Red Grooms, (The Village Voice, July 15th). Our interest is in the namer and systematizer of the concept, Allan Kaprow, whose masterwork on the subject, *Assemblage, Environments and Happenings* is being published by Harry N. Abrams, Inc., 6 West 57th Street, New York 10019, on November 22nd.

Philip Corner, Spades in *The Four Suits*, is in Meridian, Mississippi with the Movement. Al Hansen's First World Congress of Happenings at Provincetown, Mass. was a resounding success. Among those attending was Eric Andersen, the terror of Copenhagen, who is best known for having cut off the head of the little mermaid. Camille Gordon is writing a sexy detective novel: her hero's name is Bobsy Kamp. Dick Higgins has a new graphic arts camera, on which we will do all our own halftones and illustrations. This should give us spectacular quality control.

Jackson Mac Low's *Stanzas for Iris Lezak and Other Works* will be one of our next winter titles. Wolf Vostell will do the design. Mac Low is also the author of the very interesting jacket copy on Fillou's *Ample Food for Stupid Thought*, now available as a book for $5 or as a handsomely boxed set of postcards for $9.

Something Else Newscard #8

The millenium has arrived! *The Four Suits* and Al Hansen's *Primer of Happenings & Time/Space Art* are ready at last! To say nothing of our muchly fun catalog, which you should receive shortly; [text struck through and illegible]

Roll out the beer, boys, Great Bear Pamphlets are born—the best (and least expensive) small documents on the new art. Order, through us, "by Alison Knowles," which has all her performance pieces to date (40¢), Dick Higgins' "A Book About Love & War & Death, Canto One," a 60¢ round robin intended only for reading aloud, with each reader picking up where the previous one cracked up laughing or roaring, and George Brecht's "Chance Imagery" (80¢), the best essay on the subject. Future Great Bears will be by Oldenburg, Hansen, Rothenberg, etc. Please include 10¢ handling charge for each pamphlet ordered by mail.

Al Hansen, the well-known rocketeer, is going to do a "visual-visceral happening environment," *A McLuhan Megillah*, in his huge loft Time/Space Theater late in January and in February. Interested in further details? Drop a self-addressed postcard to Al Hansen, Time/Space Theater, 119 Avenue D, New York, N. Y. 10009. Put him on your mailing list too: there are very few things he's not interested in.

Camille Reports #3

From Afghanistan: "The cat ate it, all three pounds of it," she said. Nasrudin put the cat on the scales. It weighed three pounds.

"If this is the cat," said Nasrudin, "where is the meat? If, on the other hand, this is the meat, where is the cat?"

Alison Knowles, James Tenney and the Siemens 4004 computer came together, and the result is an edition of 500 different fifteen-page poems, all entitled *A House of Dust*. Four categories of lists of elements are joined in random juxtapositions by chance operations. Over 10,000 combinations are possible for each stanza. Imported from Verlag Gebr. König, but auf Englisch. $6.50 per original 15-page printout.

Merce Cunningham's *Changes: Notes on Choreography* goes to press finally. Put together by Frances Starr from Merce's notebooks, articles and notations, the structure of the book, the placement of texts and illustrations, parallels the forms of Merce's dances. None of that static memorabilia stuff more suited to the biography of an industrialist than an artist. This one really reads like a dance. The book will be manufactured by the beginning of the summer, for September 1, 1969 pub date. You can order in advance, $8.95.

Guess who else has been through changes? Daniel Spoerri's back from Greece, after his *Petit Colosse de Simi* episode. Back to Düsseldorf, that is. And what's he got there? A gourmet restaurant that sells such goodies as elephant steaks and curried cutlets, but where the real tour de force is—hamburgers. Well, that's to be expected since he's written a book on the subject which is to be part of a big book we're doing of his this coming fall.

"The constellation is a system....It disposes its groups of words as if they were clusters of stars." Eugen Gomringer's *The Book of Hours and Constellations*, translated and presented by Jerome Rothenberg, will take you someplace else. Jerome Cushman, in *Library Journal*, said various kind words about the book, including that it "is recommended for any library, including high school, because it is the work of a founder of a significant poetry movement." Personally I just think it's groovy. Available in cloth, $4.50 and paperback, $1.95.

"There's no satisfying the people!" he claimed.

"Now, now, my friend," intervened the Hodja, "Don't rush to false conclusions! Whoever heard of anybody complaining about the sweet spring weather?"

We're scrapping our Max Bense reader. It was to be the deepest statement of the philosophical bases underlying "primary cool." Alas, the book has minimalized itself out of existence. The ironic fulfillment? Only 306 days to 1970.

Our *Something Else Newsletters* have gone fishing. We'll be doing more of them, but not for a while. They've gotten pretty expensive to do. And right now we're concentrating on doing books. But if you liked the old newsletters, all those articles Dick Higgins wrote for the newsletters will be included in his new book, *FOEW&OMBWHNW* (say that again, will you?), due out in May. Just in case you're missing any issues. It'll cost $5.95, and will look just like a prayer book.

SOMETHING ELSE NEWSLETTER, SOMETHING ELSE NEWSCARDS and CAMILLE'S REPORTS

Something Else Newscards

Nos. 1–9 (1965) issued as cards; nos. 10–13, 15 were issued as part of the *Something Else Newsletter*.

No. 10 appears on last page of the *Something Else Newsletter*, vol. 1, no. 1
No. 11 appears on last page of the *Something Else Newsletter*, vol. 1, no. 2
No. 12 appears on last page of the *Something Else Newsletter*, vol. 1, no. 3
No. 13 appears on last page of the *Something Else Newsletter*, vol. 1, no. 6
No. 14 not issued
No. 15 is the *Something Else Newsletter*, vol. 2, no. 3

Something Else Newsletter
"Sent to the complete mailing list of about 6000" (SEP&S)

Vol. 1, no. 1   "Intermedia" (Feb. 1966) includes *Newscard,* 10
Vol. 1, no. 2   "Games of Art" (Mar. 1966) includes *Newscard,* 11
Vol. 1, no. 3   "Intending" (Apr. 1966) includes *Newscard,* 12
Vol. 1, no. 4   "Serious Gabcard" (Aug. 1966)
Vol. 1, no. 5   "Serious Gabcard #2" (Feb. 1967)
Vol. 1, no. 6   "Against Movements" (May 1967) includes *Newscard,* 13
Vol. 1, no. 7   "Chatter Letter" (Jan. 1968)
Vol. 1, no. 8   "Structural Researches" (Apr. 1968)
Vol. 1, no. 9   "Boredom and Danger" (Dec. 1968)
Vol. 1, no. 10   "Camille Reports Again" (Nov. 1969)
Vol. 1, no. 11   "Towards the 1970s" (Dec. 1969)
Vol. 1, no. 12   "Camille Raps" (Feb. 1970)
Vol. 2, no. 1   "Blank Images" (Apr. 1971)
Vol. 2, no. 2   "About Bern Porter and his *I've Left*" (Dec. 1971)
Vol. 2, no. 3   "Newscard No. 15" (Apr. 1972)
Vol. 2, no. 4   "Why do we publish so much Gertrude Stein?" (Sept. 1972)
Vol. 2, no. 5   "Seen, Heard and Understood" (Sept. 1972)
Vol. 2, no. 6   "Camille's Column" (Jan. 1973)
Vol. 2, no. 7   "Distributing Books" (Apr. 1973) [Not distributed]
Vol. 2, no. 8   (Feb. 1983)
Vol. 3, no. 1   Not issued
Vol. 3, no. 2   "Mediocracy: Getting the Arts Past the 1980s" (Oct. 1983)
Vol. 3, no. 3   "A [very short] Autobiography of Originality" (Nov. 1983)

Camille's Reports

Camille's Reports, nos. 1 and 2 were issued as cards in 1967 or 1968
Camille Reports, no. 3 was issued as a folded sheet in 1969
"Camille Reports Again" is the *Something Else Newsletter*, vol. 1, no. 10 (1969)
"Camille Raps" is the *Something Else Newsletter*, vol. 1, no. 12 (1970)
"Camille's Column" is the *Something Else Newsletter*, vol. 2, no. 6 (1973)

L'IMMORTELLE MORT DU MONDE

THE DEATHLESS DYING OF THE WORLD

BY ROBERT FILLIOU

Five Emotions Corresponding to Five Sounds:

Suffering: performer contradicts his initial statement (eg., "Man is not good.")
Confusion: initial statement, or its negation, preceded by "maybe..." (eg., "Maybe man is (not) good.")
Guilt: initial statement, or its negation, preceded by "I'm sorry that..." (eg., "I'm sorry that Man is (not) good.")
Shyness: initial statement, or its negation, preceded by "I wish..." (eg., "I wish Man were (not) good.")
Joy: initial statement preceded by "Thank goodness..." (eg., "Thank goodness Man is good!")

RED:	I've known for a long time that...	I'm happy to learn that...	I deny that...	Why complain because...	Let's form a committee and decide if really...	Who told you to say that...	Descartes first said...	Kiss my ass if you want to know for sure if...	Does it make you happy to say that...
OLIVE:	I disagree but I'll defend your right to maintain that...	I'm not going to cry because...	It's very American to say that...	Go tell a cop that...	It's the government's fault if...	I'm mad at the thought that...	How stupid to believe that...	I suspected that...	Why be good if...
YELLOW:	It's so unfortunate that...	It is evident that...	It's your fault if...	In our time it's normal that...	Only a very original mind could grasp that...	Negroes deny that...	After death do you still feel that...	Of course...	I pity you if you believe that...
DARK BLUE:	It's not my fault if...	How do you know that...	Should I commit suicide because...	Why have children if...	It saddens me to think that...	What's life about if...	I was wondering, myself, if...	I don't give a shit if...	You must live as if you didn't know that...
GREEN:	I forbid you to say that...	It is meaningless to say that...	You mustn't tell de Gaulle that...	Why talk if...	I wish it were true that...	You must be mad to believe that...	It's so strange that...	A good metabolism is more important than knowing that...	You should confess to a priest that...
SKY BLUE:	To know that "......" has cosmic significance.	Since ends justify means it's normal that...	It's not Mom's fault if...	Who has told you that...	You're very lucky to believe that...	You'll be shot if you keep maintaining that...	Learning that "......" will demoralize the country.	It's the first time I've heard that...	I confirm that...
ORANGE:	I'll repeat to my wife that...	Shit, why say that...?	The Chinese don't give a damn if...	I doubt that...	What to do if it's true that...	Ask God whether...	Do your duty instead of telling everyone that...	I'll kick the hell out of you if you repeat that...	You must have read McLuhan to know that...
BROWN:	Shakespeare denied that...	A few centuries ago would you have said that...	Since you know it, you should keep it to yourself that...	In this country you'll be sent to jail if you say that...	I must think it over before deciding if...	What do you want me to do if...?	We went to war because...	I know that...	I'm flabbergasted to learn that...
PURPLE:	I've read in the newspapers that...	Write to the Beatles that...	I'm delighted to see that...	You have no perspective if you insist that...	It makes me laugh when you say that...	It's impolite to say that...	Only an insane man would proclaim that...	It's nice to believe that...	Sleep over the idea that...
PINK:	How disgusting to say that...!	I'm fed up to hear you repeat that...	I congratulate you for confessing that...	You should be televised while saying that...	OK! OK! "......"	Thank you for informing us that...	I was expecting you to say that...	No wonder you're a failure if you tell everyone that...	Love more and worry less if...

Vertical Instructions

The ten colors represent ten performers, numbered from 1 to 10. The performers come onstage one by one, asking one another: "What are we doing here?" According to random selection (looking up the last number of a dollar bill, for instance), one performer comes forward and gives a commonplace explanation for his presence onstage (eg., "I'm here because I'm a man. Man is good.")

He will modify his explanation according to the spreading out of 5 readily-identifiable random sounds provided by the sound track. Each sound is associated with an emotion. For instance, when suffering is struck, the performer contradicts himself (eg., "Man is not good.") A sixth sound means that the performer forward is replaced by the performer immediately behind him, who then proceeds to give his own explanation for his presence onstage.

Horizontal Instructions

The 9 performers move at random behind the performer standing forwardmost. They make comments about what he says, either in words or with gestures. Each performer's comments depend upon the color of the performer immediately to his right on the stage. For instance, red (supposing pink is forward) will comment, if olive is to his right, "I've known for a long time that man is good." But if blue is to his right he will say, "I deny that man is good." The comments on this poster merely indicate.

Performers may improvise, or, as said above, replace comments by gestures, dance steps, faces, sounds, etc. The performance continues for any length of time.

This "auto-theater" poster may be used for advertising the performance by simply gluing over this portion of it a band giving names of performers, credits, composer, locale, etc.

Dedicated to Daniel Spoerri
Paris, September 1960

L'Immortelle Morte du Monde by Robert Filliou.

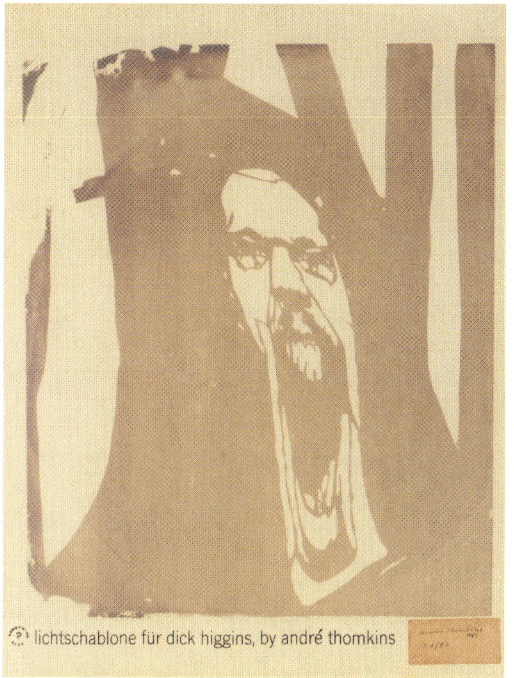

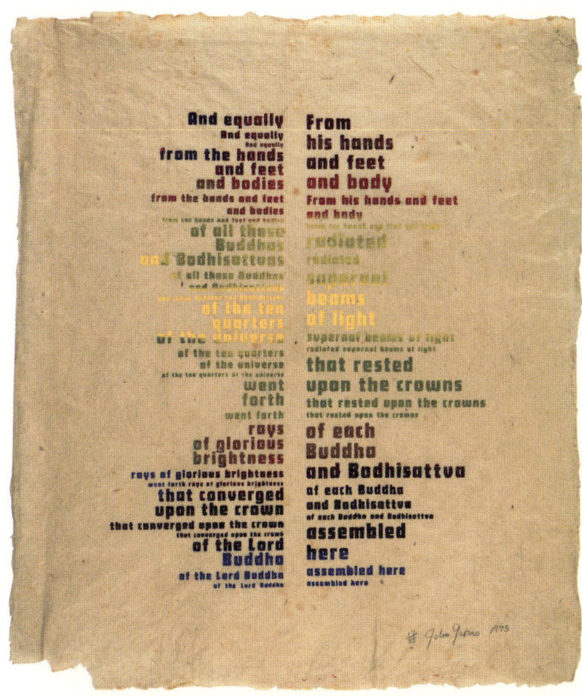

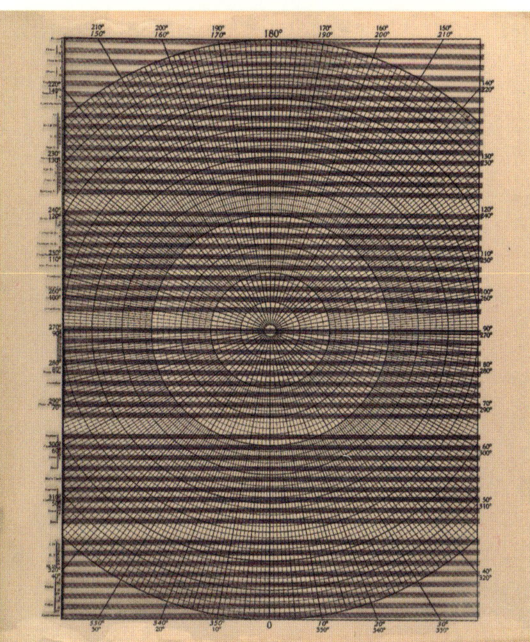
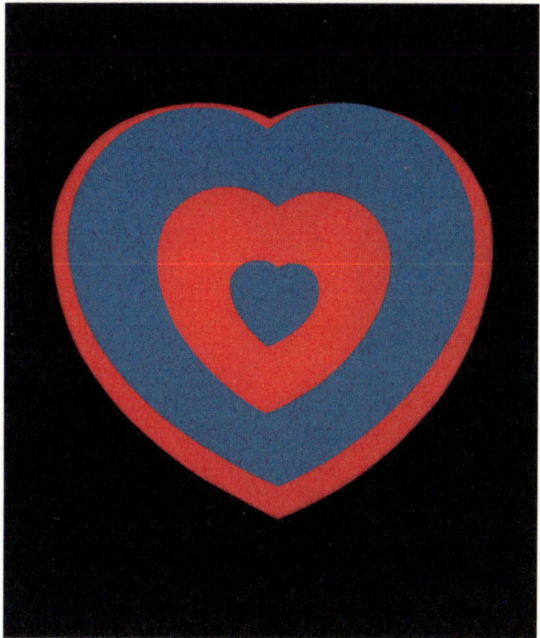

Clockwise from top left: *Lichtschablone für Dick Higgins* by André Tomkins, *[From the Book of the Dead of John Giorno] [Rainbow Buddhas & Bodhisattvas]* by John Giorno, *Graphis #144* and *#143 . . .* by Dick Higgins, and *Coeurs Volant* by Marcel Duchamp.

GRAPHICS

Dick Higgins. *Graphis #144 Wipe-Out for Orchestra* and *Graphis #143 Softly, for Orchestra.* **New York, 1967.**

Printed card stock (19 ⅞ x 23 ⅞ inches) and printed overlay (19 ¾ x 23 ¾ inches). Edition of 100 numbered and signed on the verso.

When the acetate is placed in any position over this diagram and when the resulting notation is performed by an orchestra large enough to play most though not necessarily all the parts and when everything from solos to tuttis is played as loud as the instrument is capable and when the notation is interpreted in any consistent way, you will hear Dick Higgins's *Graphis #144: Wipe-Out for Orchestra* (July, 1967).

But when the acetate is placed over anything else perhaps a newspaper or a poster, a drawing or a photograph and the parts are played consistently as above in a manner appropriate to the title, you will hear Dick Higgins's *Graphis #143: Softly, for Orchestra* (July, 1967). (Higgins, from Colophon)

Marcel Duchamp. *Coeurs Volants.* *[Fluttering Hearts.]* **New York, 1967.**

From the 1936 original. 24 x 18 inches, edition of "twenty-six copies, sold for $50." (SEP&S) We are aware of two copies, both from an edition of twenty-four numbered, signed, and dated in pencil by the artist.

Robert Filliou. *L'Immortelle Morte du Monde.* *[The Deathless Dying of the World.]* **New York, 1967.**

Translated into English by the author. 21 ¾ x 28 ½ inches. Black and white and ten colors hand-colored, 300 copies.

Robert Filliou, action poet, is best known to the English-speaking audience for *Ample Food For Stupid Thought.* This is a poster event. 100 squares, each with a comment to be enacted, are outlined in diagonal rows with ten brilliant handpainted colors, one for each performer. (ANM)

André Tomkins. *Lichtschablone für Dick Higgins.* **New York, 1967.**

Printed white on white. 22 ½ x 29 ¾ inches, fifty copies signed and numbered on a paper label affixed to the lower right-hand corner of the front of the print.

A disappearing work, which only becomes visible when held up to the light. (TAGT)

John Giorno. [*From the Kama Sutra of John Giorno.*] [*Black Cock.*] [Barton, VT, 1973.]

Printed silk-screen in black ink on glossy black card stock. 23 ½ x 38 inches, edition of twenty-five. Originally printed by John Giorno in New York in 1967 in an edition of fifty copies, this poem was reprinted in Vermont in 1973 in an edition of twenty-five. According to the poet, the Something Else Press half of the edition was lost in a flood.

John Giorno. [*From the Book of the Dead of John Giorno.*] [*Rainbow Buddhas & Bodhisattvas.*] [Barton, VT, 1973.]

Printed via silk-screen with Alison Knowles in her Vermont studio, in four colors on Nepalese eucalyptus paper. 23 ¾ x 28 ½ inches, edition of twenty-five numbered and signed.

DELUXE EDITIONS

Allan Kaprow. *Calling*. New York, 1967.

Five pages plus front and back cover. Printed on 23⅜ x 20 inch unbound sheets of heavy grade clear vinyl with wood cover printed on both sides and unprinted white, heavy vinyl rear cover. Held together with a sturdy cloth belt and metal buckle. Edition of twenty-five numbered and signed copies. Frank identifies the title of this work as *Calling (A Big Little Book)*. Press literature refers to the work sometimes with and sometimes without (*A Big Little Book*); however, this portion of the title does not appear on the piece itself.

Calling, a Happening by Allan Kaprow performed in and out of New York in the summer of 1965, is one of the landmarks of the form, and its scenario typifies the poetic ritual style he has developed. This present graphic representation, however, began as an improvisation when Kaprow, playing with a set of rubber stamp letters, stamped out each word of the scenario on a separate index card. I continued the game by assembling the cards on the copyboard of a graphic arts camera and shooting them and by adding an element of color play. The resulting object is not, however, a final one in any sense. While the original scenario may be read by starting from bottom to top, right-hand column to left hand, on the silver, blue, red, yellow and finally, brown sheets, there are other stories which the reader is invited to tell, other games for him to play. —Dick Higgins, New York City, September 26, 1967 (Colophon)

Alison Knowles. *The Big Book*. New York, 1967–68.

Eight pages, 96 x 48 inches. Unique object (two versions).

Alison Knowles' *The Big Book* (eight feet tall and four feet wide, fully electrified and equipped for Modern Living) was shown at the Phase Two branch of the Pollack Gallery in Toronto, and then was the sensation of the opening exhibition of Chicago's new Museum of Contemporary Art. Although this is the Press's largest publication, it is doubtful it will be seen in New York before it sails off for Europe, where it will presumably remain. (SEN, vol. 1, no. 7)

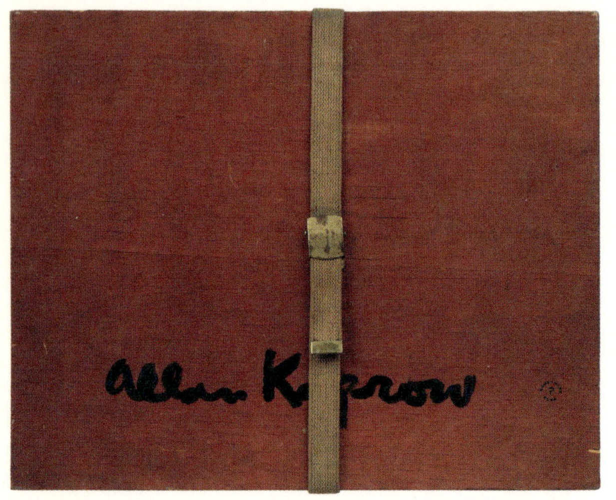
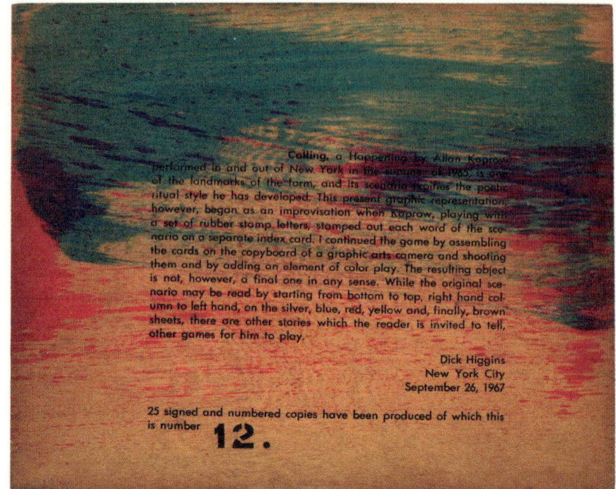

Calling, a Happening by Allan Kaprow performed in and out of New York in the summer of 1965, is one of the landmarks of the form, and its scenario typifies the poetic ritual style he has developed. This present graphic representation, however, began as an improvisation when Kaprow, playing with a set of rubber stamp letters, stamped out each word of the scenario on a separate index card. I continued the game by assembling the cards on the copyboard of a graphic arts camera and shooting them and by adding an element of color play. The resulting object is not, however, a final one in any sense. While the original scenario may be read by starting from bottom to top, right hand column to left hand, on the silver, blue, red, yellow and, finally, brown sheets, there are other stories which the reader is invited to tell, other games for him to play.

Dick Higgins
New York City
September 26, 1967

25 signed and numbered copies have been produced of which this is number 12.

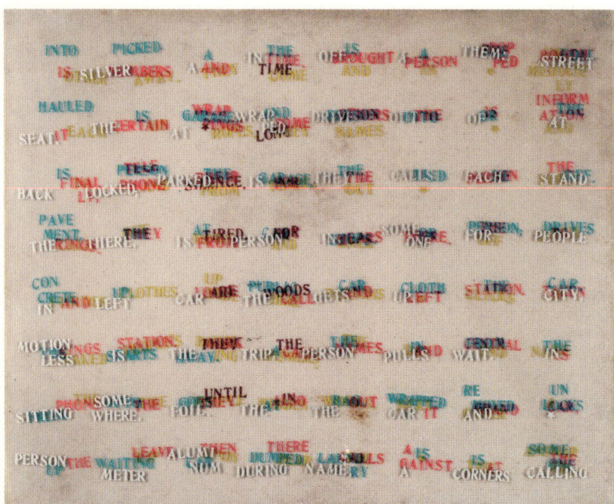
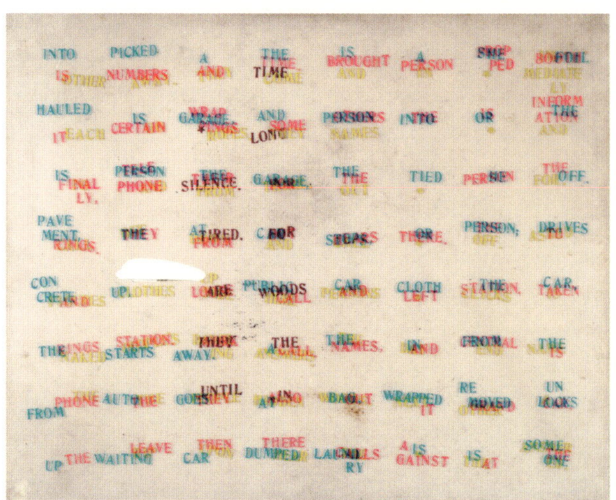
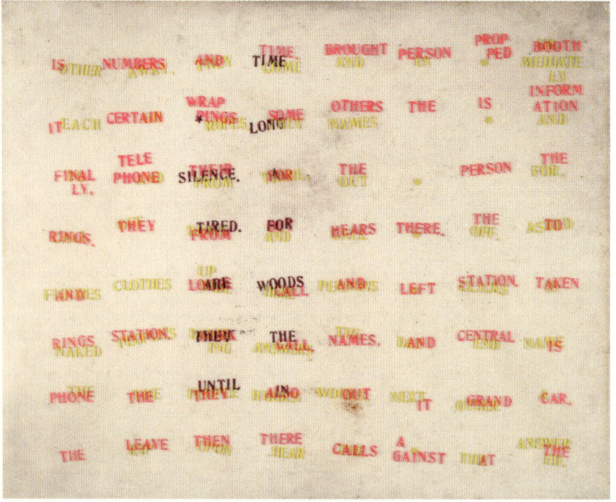
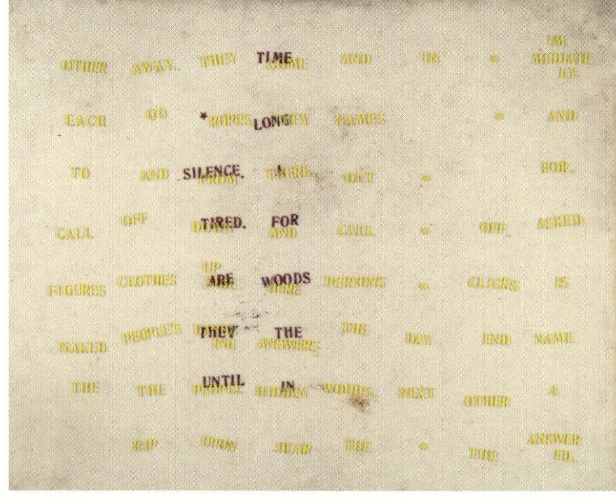

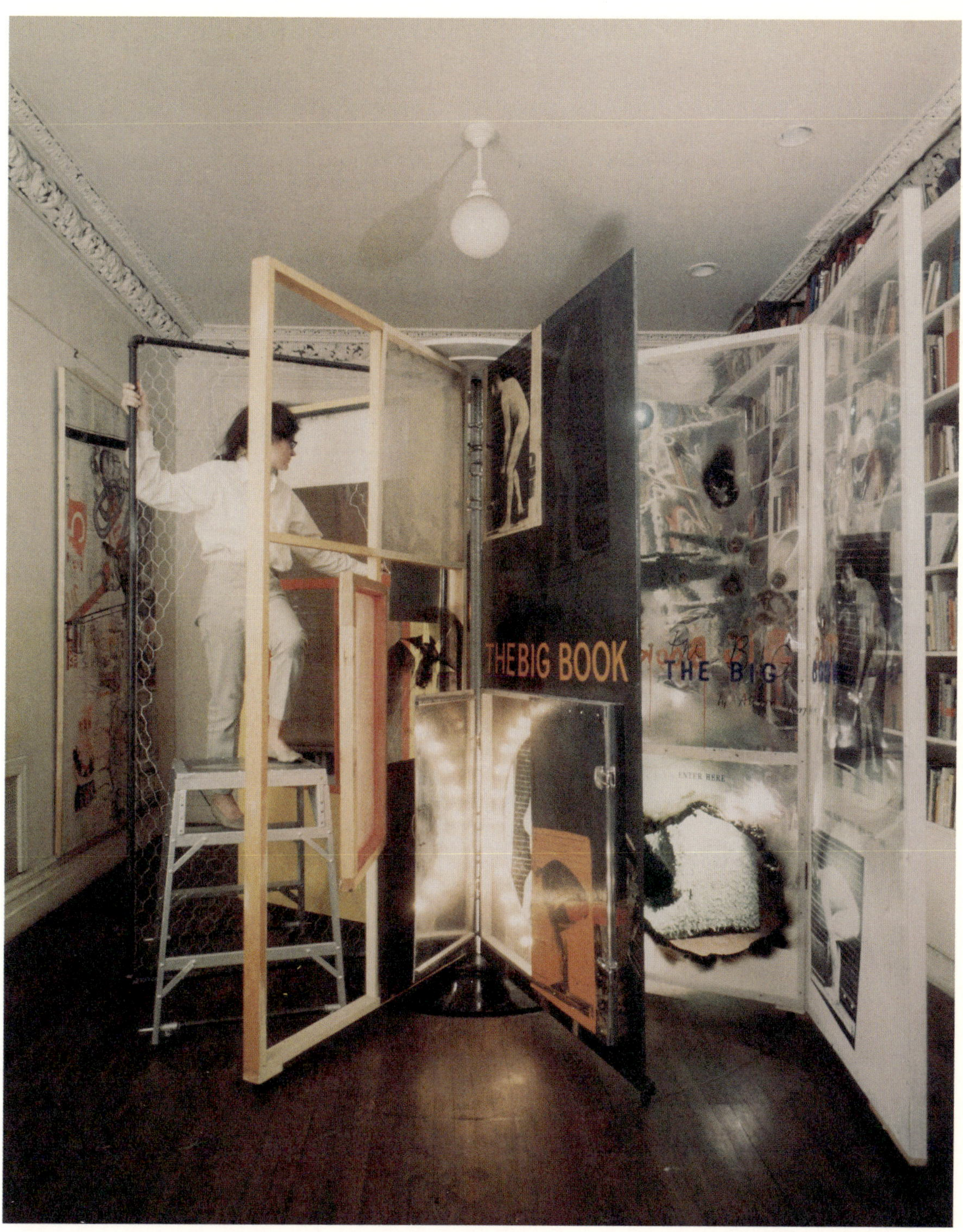

Opposite—Details from *Calling* by Allan Kaprow. Above—Peter Moore's photo of *The Big Book* by Alison Knowles.

GALLERY ANNOUNCEMENTS and POSTERS

The Something Else Gallery hosted a discrete series of four exhibitions during the spring of 1966 that were advertised and documented with three folding posters. These formal exhibitions were followed by approximately nine events including exhibitions, piano concerts, a reading, and a benefit. The events took place at 238 West 22nd Street in New York on the ground floor of the home of Dick Higgins and Alison Knowles, with the exception of "Technological Oak Tree" by Wolf Vostell, which took place in West Glover, Vermont. —SC

"Object Poems"

(April 16–27, 1966; opening April 15). 29½ x 21¾ inches. Printed on one side, includes a statement by Dick Higgins. Artists represented in the exhibition include George Brecht, Philip Corner, Carl Fernbach-Flarsheim, Robert Filliou, Ian Hamilton Finlay, Peter Green, Al Hansen, Dick Higgins, Alison Knowles, Jackson Mac Low, Diter Rot, Carolee Schneemann, Gertrude Stein, Wolf Vostell, Emmett Williams, and others.

"Intermedia"/"The Arts in Fusion"

(April 30–May 11, 1966; opening April 29) / (May 14–25, 1966; opening May 13). 21⅜ x 29⅜ inches. The two shows announced with a single poster. Includes the essays "Intermedia" by Dick Higgins (a brief discussion of intermedia in the work of Alison Knowles, George Brecht, and Joe Jones) and "The Arts in Fusion" by Carl Fernbach-Flarsheim. Current and forthcoming Something Else Press books listed on verso.

"Dogs and Chinese Not Allowed" by Wolf Vostell

(May 28–June 8, 1966; opening May 27; dé-coll/age-happening May 21). 21¼ x 29⅜ inches. Distributed press Typos Verlag titles listed on verso.

Exhibitions, Concerts, and Other Events

["Intermedia"] (April 30–May 11, 1966; opening April 29). Supplementary flyer for the "Intermedia" exhibition (see above) featuring Alison Knowles, George Brecht, and Joe Jones. 8½ x 11 inches.

"Piano Music of Charles Ives" (May 1966). 8½ x 11 inches.*

"Piano Music of Erik Satie" (June 18, 1966). Includes marathon performance of *Vexations*. 8½ x 11 inches.

"Alice Hutchins" (February 1968). 8½ x 11 inches. Black on pink paper.

"Marathon reading of the complete *Finnegans Wake*" (June 1969).*

"Something Else Gallery Benefit for The Land Fall Press" (October 1969). 8½ x 11 inches.

"Ruth Waldinger" (February 1970). 8½ x 11 inches. Black and white on card stock.*

"Wolf Vostell: Technological Oak Tree" (August 1972). 17 x 11 inches black and white, folded to make a four-page 8½ x 11 inch pamphlet. Includes "Vostell's T.O.T." by Dick Higgins and "T.O.T. (Technological Oak Tree) An environment: consciousness = art" by Wolf Vostell.

"Music of John Cage." (n.d.) 8½ x 11 inches.*

"Piano Ragtime." (n.d.) 8½ x 11 inches.*

*(FRANK)

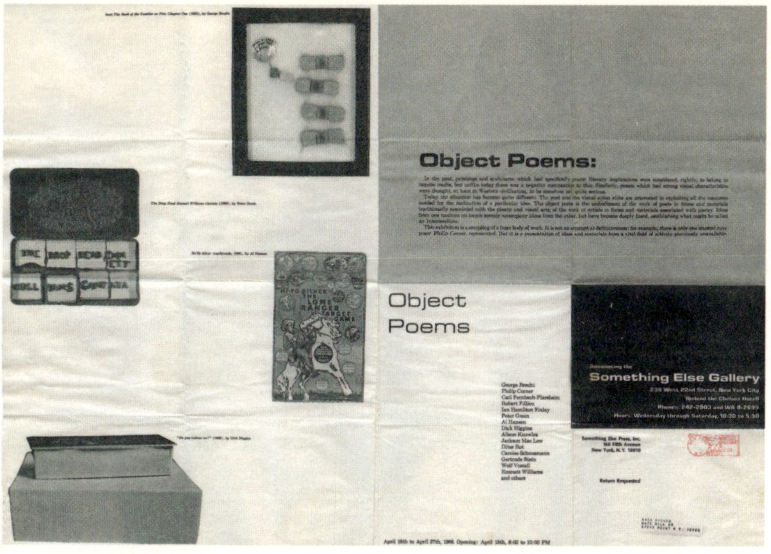

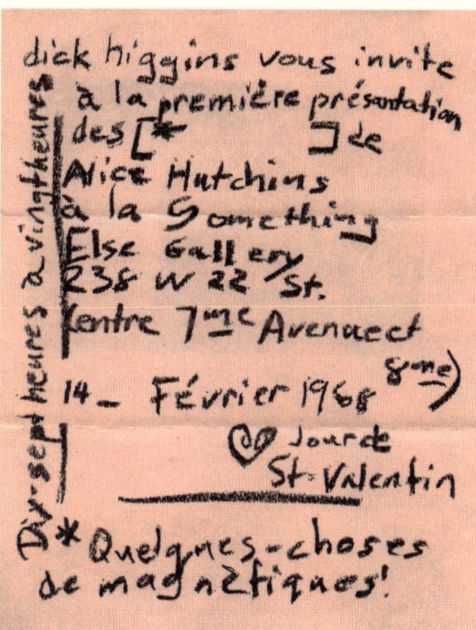

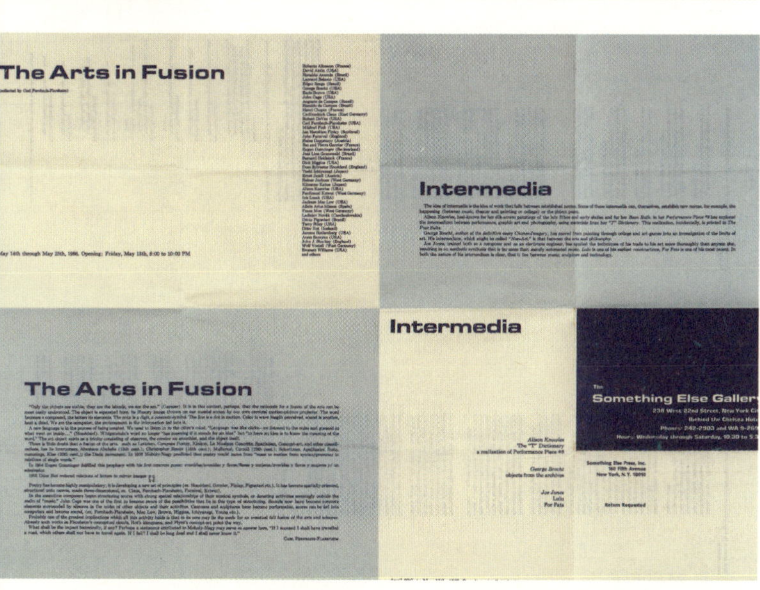

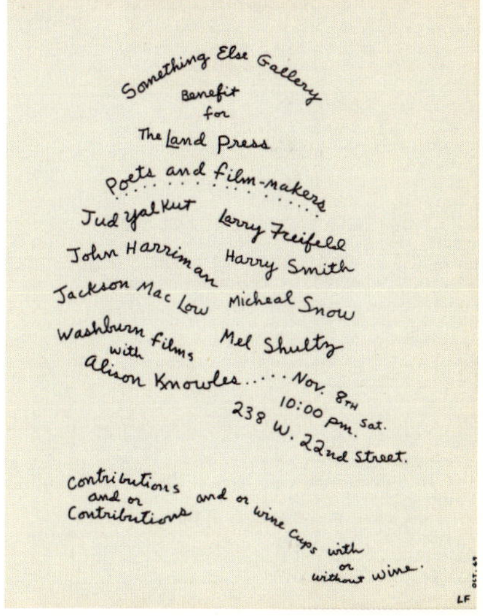

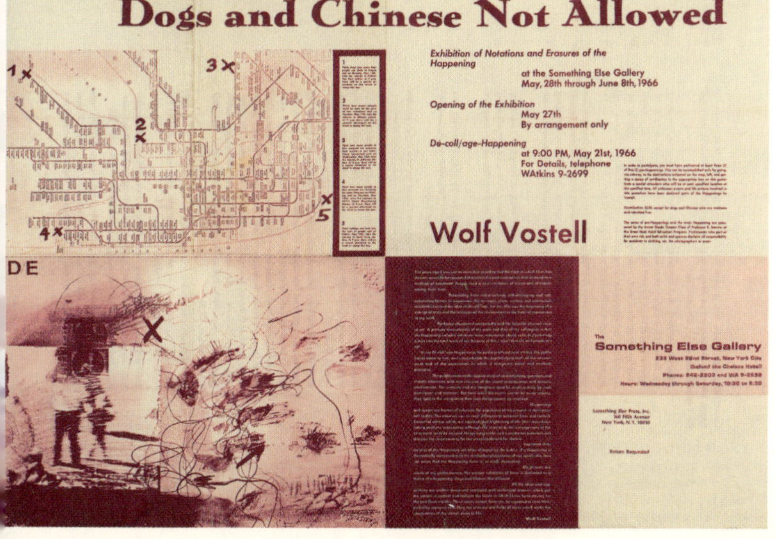

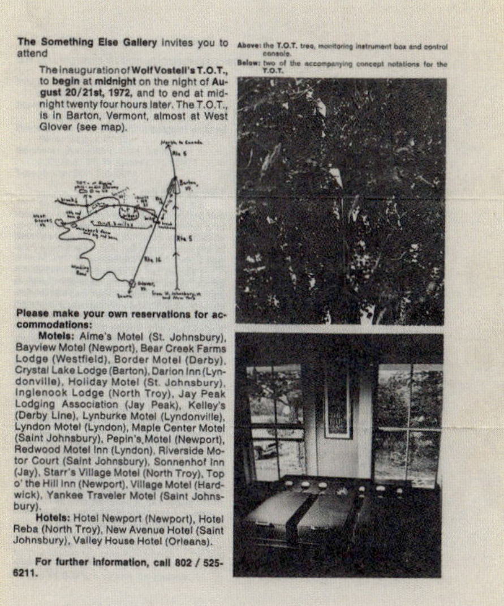
The Something Else Gallery invites you to attend

The inauguration of **Wolf Vostell's T.O.T.**, to begin at midnight on the night of August 20/21st, 1972, and to end at midnight twenty four hours later. The T.O.T., is in Barton, Vermont, almost at West Glover (see map).

Above: the T.O.T. tree, monitoring instrument box and control console.
Below: two of the accompanying concept notations for the T.O.T.

Please make your own reservations for accommodations:

Motels: Aime's Motel (St. Johnsbury), Bayview Motel (Newport), Bear Creek Farms Lodge (Westfield), Border Motel (Derby), Crystal Lake Lodge (Barton), Darion Inn (Lyndonville), Holiday Motel (St. Johnsbury), Inglenook Lodge (North Troy), Jay Peak Lodging Association (Jay Peak), Kelley's (Derby Line), Lynburke Motel (Lyndonville), Lyndon Motel (Lyndon), Maple Center Motel (Saint Johnsbury), Pepin's Motel (Newport), Redwood Motel Inn (Lyndon), Riverside Motor Court (Saint Johnsbury), Sonnenhof Inn (Jay), Starr's Village Motel (North Troy), Top o' the Hill Inn (Newport), Village Motel (Hardwick), Yankee Traveler Motel (Saint Johnsbury).

Hotels: Hotel Newport (Newport), Hotel Reba (North Troy), New Avenue Hotel (Saint Johnsbury), Valley House Hotel (Orleans).

For further information, call 802 / 525-6211.

SOMETHING ELSE PRESS, INC.

238 West 22nd Street, New York, NY 10011 (offices)
(mail) P. O. Box 523, Old Chelsea Station, New York, NY 10011
(212) 924-3975   (212) 924-3976

Regular Editions

§ **John Cage, Notations.** A cross-section of the varieties of musical notations of our times, with nearly three hundred reproductions of manuscripts, and with an accompanying mosaic text by the composers supplemented by John Cage and Alison Knowles. *Hardcover, $15. Paperback, $4.50.*

Philip Corner, Alison Knowles, Benjamin Patterson and Tomas Schmit, The Four Suits. A strikingly handsome collection of intermedia performance art researches. *Clothbound, $5.00.*

§ **Merce Cunningham, Changes: Notes on Choreography,** ed. by Frances Starr. Pages from the notebooks of the dancer and reflections on his art. *Clothbound, $8.95.*

William Brisbane Dick, Dick's 100 Amusements. Delightful "parlor game" 19th-Centuriana and pre-Happenings. *Illus., Clothbound, $4.50. Paperback, $2.25.*

Robert Filliou, Ample Food for Stupid Thought. Poetic questions that provoke not-so-stupid answers. *Hardcover, $5.00. Postcards, $5.00.*

Robert Filliou and George Brecht, Games at the Cedilla. Proposals for performance and other aesthetic researches into the bases of aesthetic communications. *Clothbound, $5.95.*

Eugen Gomringer, The Book of Hours and Constellations, translated and selected by Jerome Rothenberg. Masterworks by a founder of Concrete Poetry. *Clothbound, $4.50. Paperback, $1.95.*

§ **Walter Gutman, The Gutman Letter,** presented by Michael Benedikt. Whether or not an artist in the stock market is like a bull in a china shop, Gutman's fantasies, his "letters" issued by a major brokerage house over a period of years, his life and loves make up a fabulous self-portrait of a very interesting artist. *Clothbound, $6.95.*

Al Hansen, A Primer of Happenings & Time/Space Art. A delightful introduction to the Happening as an art form. *Hardcover $4.50. Paper, $2.25.*

§ **Dick Higgins, FOEW&OMBWHNW.** Essays, poems, speculations and performance works running concurrently by the well-known artist-critic. *Bound like a prayer book, $5.95.*

Dick Higgins, Jefferson's Birthday/Postface. Two books bound as one, the former a collection of performance and other work from 1962-1963, the latter Higgins' memoire of the beginnings of Happenings and Intermedia. *Clothbound, $5.95*

Dick Higgins, What Are Legends. Published with Bern Porter (and with his illustrations and design), this 1960 text speculates on how legendary images work. *Paper, $1.25.*

Richard Huelsenbeck, ed., Dada Almanach. The key document of early Dada, in type facsimile of the Berlin original, mostly in German. *Clothbound, $4.50.*

Ray Johnson, The Paper Snake. Visual and verbal stimuli by the famous collagist of the New York Correspondance School (sic). *Clothbound, $3.47.*

Ruth Krauss, There's a little ambiguity over there among the bluebells. Poem-plays and play-poems by the beloved Off-Broadway writer. *Clothbound, $3.95.*

Marshall McLuhan et al, Verbi-Voco-Visual Explorations. The major statement by McLuhan to date on the arts. *Hardcover, $6.95. Paperback, $2.95.*

Claes Oldenburg, Store Days, ed. by Emmett Williams. Notes, sketches, photos and scenarios from the exciting beginnings of Pop Art. *Clothbound, $12.95.*

§ **Diter Rot, 246 Little Clouds,** translated by Emmett Williams. Fascinating poems, graphics and drawings by one of the major figures in German art. *Clothbound, $5.95.*

Daniel Spoerri, An Anecdoted Topography of Chance, ed. by Emmett Williams. The most readable of all *nouveaux romans*, a novel by accumulation. *Hardcover, $5.00.*

Gertrude Stein, Geography and Plays. A collection, long out of print, of short works and plays by the discoverer of "subjective realism." *Hardcover, $6.95. Paper, $2.95.*

Gertrude Stein, The Making of Americans (complete version). This is a facsimile of the famous classic in its long-unavailable, unslashed state, six times as long as the more familiar abridged edition—and worth every word of it. *Hardcover, $10.95.*

Wolf Vostell, Dé-Coll/age Happenings. Texts of all Vostell's Happenings to 1966, oversize black-and-white scores for them, objects selected by the artist and an original, signed and numbered "mini-notation," all in a wooden box with a plastic top. *$15.00.*

Emmett Williams, ed., An Anthology of Concrete Poetry. The largest and most thorough collection to date of this increasingly popular format of visual literature. *Clothbound, $10. Paperback, $2.95.*

Emmett Williams, Sweethearts. The full text of this major erotic concrete poem cycle, with an authorized reproduction of Marcel Duchamp's *Coeurs Volants* on the cover. *Hardcover, $6.95. Paperback, $2.95.*

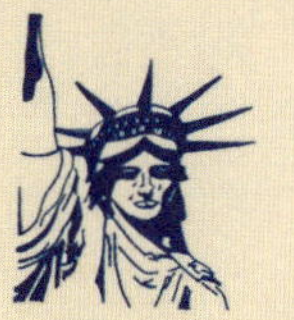

Posters

Robert Filliou, L'Immortelle Mort du Monde. A brilliant drama in poster format, translated into English by the author. *Hand-colored, $5.00.*

Dick Higgins, Graphis 144 "Wipe-Out for Orchestra" and Graphis 143 "Softly for Orchestra." Two instrumental scores using common graphic elements. Acetate overlay and paper structure, *signed and numbered, $5.00.*

André Thomkins, Lichtschablone für Dick Higgins (1966). A disappearing work which only becomes visible when held up to the light. *Signed and numbered, $5.00.*

Deluxe Editions

Marcel Duchamp, Les Coeurs Volants. The corrected edition of this poster-format work, in an edition of 24 signed and numbered copies. One to a customer, no discount to the trade on this one, *$125.*

Allan Kaprow, Calling. The text of the Happening Calling made into a color game portfolio. Vinyl, wood and plastic panel, *$100.*

Alison Knowles, The Big Book. A gigantic electrified object-book, equipped for living, presently on tour. Edition limited to one copy, *$11,000.*

Forthcoming in 1969

Max Bense, A Bense Reader
Henry Cowell, New Musical Resources
Abraham Lincoln Gillespie, The Collected Poems
Jackson Mac Low, Stanzas for Iris
Richard Meltzer, A Sequel: Tomorrow's Not Today
Gertrude Stein: How to Write
Wolf Vostell and Dick Higgins, eds., Fantastic Architecture

§ 1968 title, ready by the end of the year. All other titles are in stock.

Prices quoted are USA prices, FOB New York.

All personal orders must be prepaid but will be charged neither sales tax nor shipping.

Orders from countries for which we have representation will be forwarded to our representatives there.

Orders from countries for which we have no representation should be sent to the nearest representative geographically to prevent damage in the mails.

CATALOGUES

Dick Higgins. *What to Look for in a Book—Physically & Catalogue 1965–66*. New York, 1965.

Saddle-stitched wrappers. 5¼ x 7 inches, 16 pages. Also issued as a single 8½ x 11 inch sheet that prints the text of the essay though not the catalogue of books.

— *German Avant-Garde Publications & 1967 Catalogue*. New York, 1967.

Saddle-stitched wrappers. 4 x 5½ inches, 16 pages.

— *The Arts of the New Mentality / Catalogue 1967–1968*. New York, 1967.

Saddle-stitched wrappers. 4 x 5⅜ inches, 48 pages.

— [Untitled catalogue in poster format]. New York, 1968.

20 x 28¾ inches, folds down to 10 x 7¼ inches for mailing. [Image at left.]

— *Catalog 1969–1970*. [New York], n.d.

Saddle-stitched wrappers. 4 x 9 inches. 16 pages.

— *Foreign Imports/Futura Object Books 1969*. New York, 1969.

9 x 14 inches sheet, folded into thirds to make an eight-panel 3½ x 9-inch pamphlet, lists Futura and Object Books from Germany.

— *Foreign Imports 1969*. New York, 1969.

9 x 14 inches sheet, folded into thirds to make an eight-panel 3½ x 9-inch pamphlet, lists books from the German avant-garde.

— *Tomorrow's Avant Garde Today . . . Catalogue 1970*. New York, 1970.

Saddle-stitched wrappers. 3⅞ x 9 inches, 16 pages.

Dick Higgins and Jan Herman. *Catalogue Fall/Winter 1973–1974*. Barton, VT, 1973.

Perfect bound. 3½ x 8¾ inches, 48 pages.

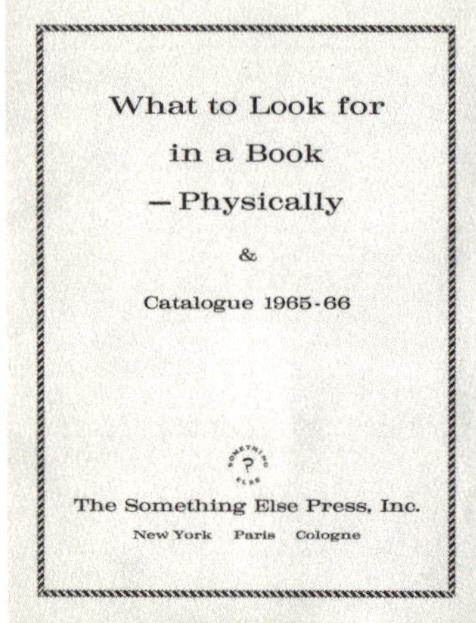

What to Look for
in a Book
— Physically
&
Catalogue 1965-66
The Something Else Press, Inc.
New York   Paris   Cologne

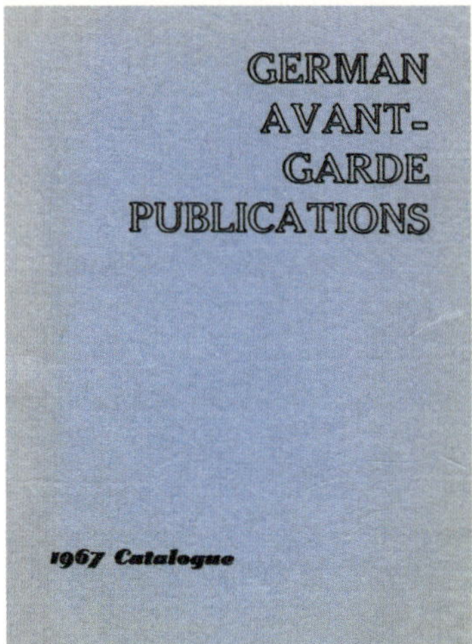

GERMAN
AVANT-
GARDE
PUBLICATIONS
1967 Catalogue

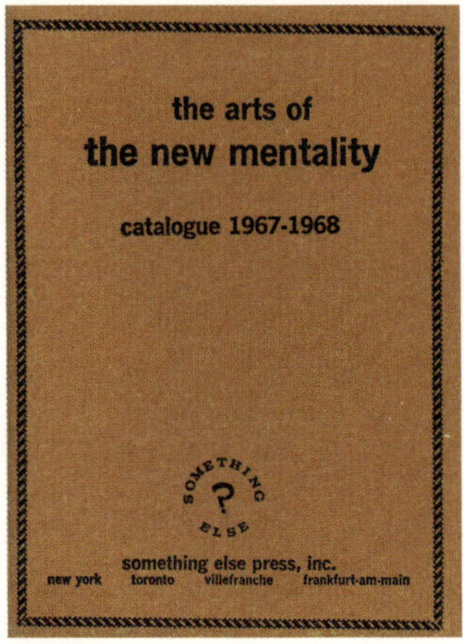

the arts of
the new mentality
catalogue 1967-1968
something else press, inc.
new york   toronto   villefranche   frankfurt-am-main

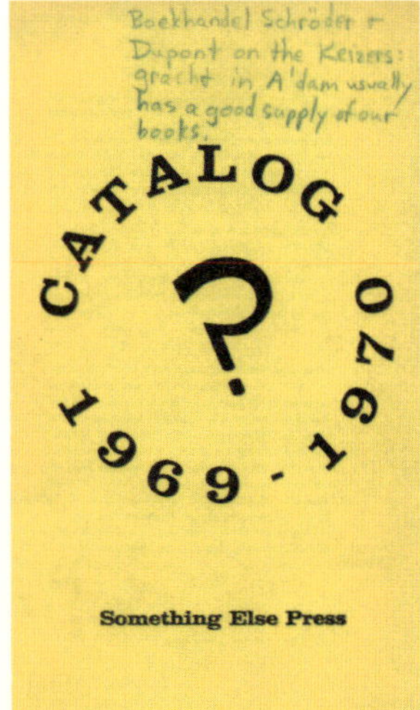

Boekhandel Schröder +
Dupont on the Keizers-
gracht in A'dam usually
has a good supply of our
books.
CATALOG
1969 - 1970
Something Else Press

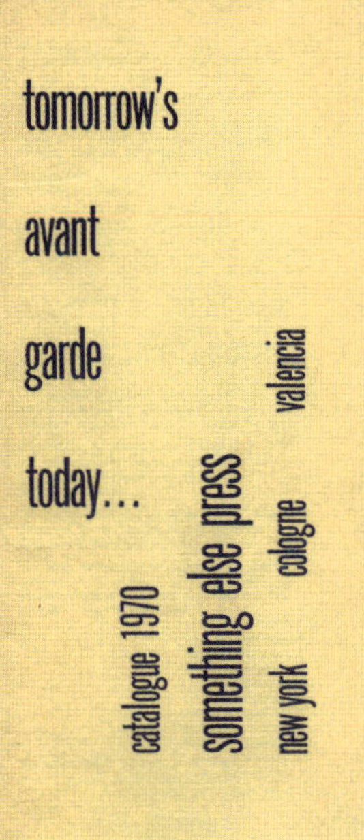

tomorrow's
avant
garde
today...
catalogue 1970
something else press
new york   cologne   valencia

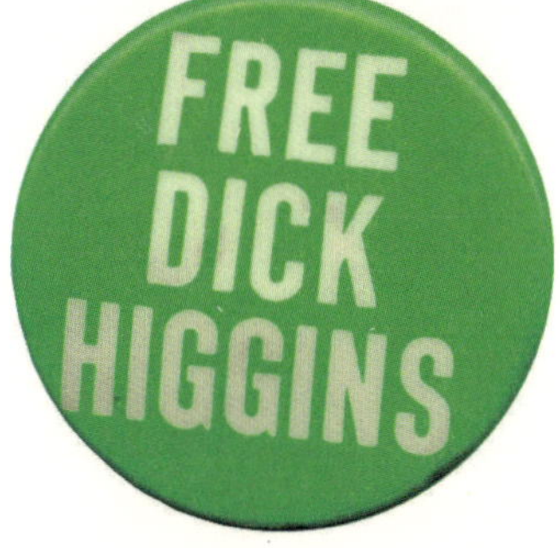

SOMETHING ELSE PRESS
SOMETHING ELSE PRE
SOMETHING ELSE PR
SOMETHING ELSE PF
SOMETHING ELSE P
SOMETHING ELSE
SOMETHING ELS
SOMETHING E
SOMETHING
Futura
Object Books
FOREIGN
FOREIGN II
FOREIGN IMI
FOREIGN IMP(
FOREIGN IMPOF
FOREIGN IMPORT
FOREIGN IMPORT!
FOREIGN IMPORTS
FOREIGN IMPORTS '
FOREIGN IMPORTS 1!
FOREIGN IMPORTS 19
FOREIGN IMPORTS 196
FOREIGN IMPORTS 1969
Catalogue
Fall/Winter
1973-1974

FREE
DICK
HIGGINS

if you can't
do it twice
you haven't
really done it

ASSORTED OBJECTS and OTHER PUBLICATIONS

Buttons, Balloons, Cookies, and Ephemera

5-inch rubber balloons in various colors, with a verbal/graphic imprint announcing *The Four Suits* [1966].*

4-inch rubber balloons in various colors, sent with the 1967 catalog, proclaiming "concrete poetry is something else" (and subjecting that slogan to a visual permutation), advertising the *Anthology of Concrete Poetry* [1967].

1-inch green and white pin-back button that reads: "Free Dick Higgins" [1969].

The main promotion for Dick Higgins's FOEW&OWMBWHNW ($5.95) is enigmatic, like the title. It's not even an ad. It's a green and white button, given out free on request, that says FREE DICK HIGGINS in big caps. A kiss from me will be the price in this year's Camille Gordon Literary Contest, whose alternate subjects are "What does the FREE DICK HIGGINS button mean?" or "Why did Dick want his book bound like a prayer book?" All entries should be three hundred words or more, and the best will be published in this newsletter. —Camille Gordon (SEN vol. 1, no. 10)

Something Else Fortune Cookies distributed at the Modern Language Association Convention [December 1972].*

1⅝-inch green and white pin-back button that reads: "If you can't do it twice you haven't really done it." [1974]. This button prints one of Dick Higgins's mini-manifestos; technically not a Something Else Press publication.

"Up to 1970, all of the major publications of the Press were advertised with folded broadsides and cards reproducing jacket blurbs, selections, and bibliographic listings, and occasionally choice graphic images. Such 'laundry tickets' were printed more intermittently after that."*

*(FRANK)

DISTRIBUTED PUBLICATIONS

As early as 1966 the Press was listing and distributing Dick Higgins's first book, *What Are Legends?* (Bern Porter, 1960). By 1967 the Press was importing and distributing works from important European avant-garde publishers including Edition Et, Edition Hansjörg Mayer (including the *Futura* series), Thek/Mat-Mot, and Typos Verlag. The 1973–1974 catalog announced distribution for several American publishers including Something Else Press editor Jan Herman's Nova Broadcast Press, John Giorno's Dial-a-Poem Poets, and the magazine *Source: Music of the Avant-Garde*. The Press also distributed *How to Make a Happening* by Allan Kaprow. —SC

Dick Higgins. *What Are Legends?* Calais, ME, 1960.

Wrappers.

Actually published in 1960 by Bern Porter jointly with the author (who subsequently turned over his stock to the Press), this is a poetic statement of the "legending effect" used not only in Higgins's suspension plays but in the large unpublished series of works to which this was intended to serve as introduction, *Legends and Fishnets* (1958–1960). (ANM)

Published with Bern Porter (and with his illustrations and design), this 1960 text speculates on how legendary images work. (TAGT)

Allan Kaprow. *How to Make a Happening*. New York: Mass Art, 1966; Something Else Press, 1967.

33 RPM LP record album with silk-screened cover with a photograph by Sol Goldberg from Kaprow's *Happening Household*, Cornell University, 1964. Mass Art went out of business soon after *How to Make a Happening* was published and consequently the album was not properly distributed. When Something Else Press took over distribution in 1967 the album was placed into a sturdy vinyl sleeve with the title of the work silk-screened in red ink on the front by Alison Knowles. The Primary Information reissue in 2008 was created using vinyl sleeve art from a copy supplied by the Allan Kaprow Archive; it includes the title in red ink along with the artist's name and the Something Else Press logo printed in purple ink. Although copies with the red title appear on the market from time to time, we have not seen additional copies with the artist's name and Press logo.

This is a Pandora's box of incendiary ideas, masquerading as a cool, formal lecture, straight from the horse's mouth since Kaprow is the man who gave Happenings their name. Originally published by Mass Art Inc. in 1966, this record has never actually been distributed until now. (TAGT)

Rule no. 1: Forget all the standard forms—don't paint pictures, don't make poetry, don't build architecture, don't arrange dances, don't write plays, don't compose music, don't make movies and above all don't think you'll get a happening by putting all these together. —**Allan Kaprow**

ANNOUNCED, PROMISED, and/or ALLUDED TO
THOUGH NEVER PUBLISHED

Like any publisher, large or small, Something Else Press planned a number of projects that were never completed. Very few were provided an explanation in print as to their demise; they just dropped from sight. Not all were simply left over when the Press closed in 1974; in fact, a good many were cataloged and discussed time and again. For example *Abraham Lincoln Gillespie: The Collected Poems*, edited by Hugh Fox, was listed as forthcoming for most of the Press's history. (Poet, writer, editor, and scholar, Hugh Fox wrote *An Analytical Checklist of Books from Something Else Press*, published in *Small Press Review*, vol. 6, no. 1. March 1974.) Over the course of doing research for the Something Else Press checklist, we accumulated a list of titles that made an appearance in the catalogs, newsletters, and other announcements but were never published. We've included catalog descriptions for several titles that seemed on the verge of release, a notice for those barely mentioned, and reference to their eventual publication, if known. —SC

Max Bense. *A Bense Reader.*

Translated by Polly Williams in Pfungstadt, Germany. Announced as a winter, 1968 title.

Although Max Bense is one of the most stimulating, widely read and celebrated of the German postwar philosophers, he has been, until this book, unrepresented in the U.S.A. This volume has been compiled to reflect the range and depth of his thought. 192 pp., illus., hardcover, $6.95. (ANM)

William S. Burroughs. *The Book of Breething.* (CAT 73–74)

Published by Edition OU in 1974 as the *Book of Breething,* and again by Blue Wind as the *Book of Breeething* in 1975.

Clark Coolidge. *The Maintains.* (CAT 73–74)

Published by This Press, 1974.

Philip Corner. *Starting with the Piano and Not Necessarily Stopping There.*

The book starts as notes on a piano-playing technique based on balance, spills over the keyboard and out into the streets to become a political philosophy of the world. Corner, one of the most revolutionary and imaginative of the avant-garde composers makes a statement "Limits are henceforth of vision never of permission," and illustrates it. (ANM)

Abraham Lincoln Gillespie. *The Collected Poems.*

Edited by Hugh Fox. Originally titled in 1966, *Abraham Lincoln Gillespie: The Collected Poems*, then changed, c. 1973, to *The Collected Writings of A.L. Gillespie*. Published as *The Syntactic Revolution*, edited by Richard Millazo, by Out of London Press, 1980. [See pages 232–233.]

Gillespie, the American avant-garde poet writer (1898–1950), was concerned, like Gertrude Stein, with language as material. His process of "disintergramarising" to obtain a "phraseMomentUnity" evolved virtually a whole new language. This volume contains all the surviving works: poems, essays, pre-happenings, criticism and other experimental pieces. (ANM) has announced it's going to sell seeds for a new tomato in 1973 that weighs up to three pounds each! Heaven only help the poor actor who gets one of those thrown at him.

Why did the Knox County Regional Planning Commission (in Rockland, Maine) surpress the Bern Porter-authored **Regional Report 69** and **Regional Summary 69?** Is this an example of political corruption? Or merely short-sightedness. Anyway, you can get Bern's **Found Poems** from us —crazy almost Duchampian investigations they are too—for **$10.00 cloth** or **$3.45 paper.** It's a whopper of the book world, and I'd much rather be hit with the tomato above than the Porter tome below.

If you run out of silver polish for your shoe-buckles, try using toothpaste. For years I've been told this was so, and occasionally I've tried it. Results: indifferent. But I keep on trying, because I've been told it works so long that I can hardly believe it doesn't. Marriage, anybody?

Gertrude Stein's **Matisse Picasso and Gertrude Stein** seems to be turning into Something Else Press's all-time best seller, in spite of the rough style and the unorthodox subject matter. I have to disagree with the male reviewer from **Gay Liberator** (Detroit) who said that **A Long Gay Book** (one of the three novellas in the volume) is about "gay" joviality, not the "gay life." Read deeper, sir. Anyway, it's a great book and you can get it from us for **$10.00 cloth** or **$3.95 paper.**

We're also doing Gertrude Stein's **How to Write,** which has the reputation of being the toughest to read of all her main books. 'Tain't so, not at all. The original edition was set in mini-type, so only a fly could read it. If you believe in learning by doing, its her most instructive statement of what makes her style tick. **Cloth, $10.95** and **Paper, $3.45.**

And while we're still on Stein, for goodness sakes don't miss Leon Katz's adaptation of **The Making of Americans,** with Al Carmines' music and Larry Kornfield's directing. If you can sneak away to NYC while it's still on—at the Judson Memorial Church's Judson Poets Theater—you'll never feel badly for doing it. And nobody who cares about Stein can possibly forgive themselves if they miss it. All the Stein mayhem with families comes through crystal clear, as does the

from our

upcoming (1974)

Anthology of

Amateur Graphics

(62 BC to 1973 AD)

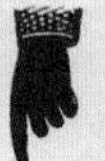
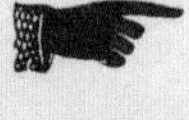

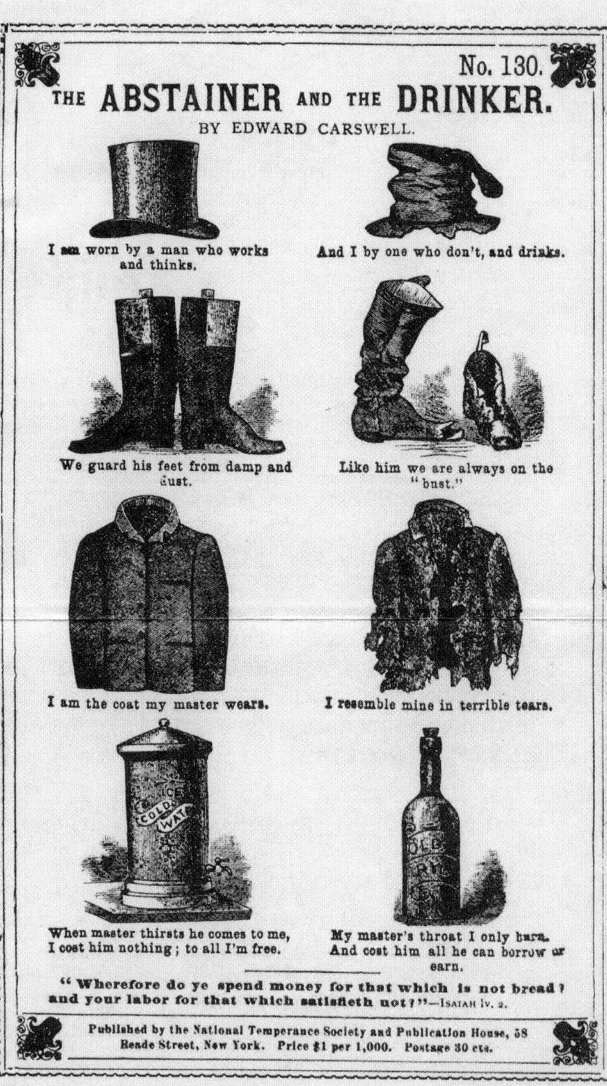

John Giorno. *John Giorno's Anthology of New York Poetry.*

John Giorno's at work on an anthology, *John Giorno's Anthology of New York Poetry.* The cover's being done by Les Levine, and each of the six poets included will have his section on a different-colored stock. So it oughtta be out of sight, visually. (SEN, vol. 1, no. 10)

[*John Giorno's Anthology of New York Poetry*] Off to be typeset . . . (SEN, vol. 1, no. 12)

After the Central Park Poetry Events in September 1968, I had the idea of doing a book of six of the nine poets: Vito Acconci, Emmett Williams, Jackson Mac Low, Anne Waldman, Hannah Weiner, John Giorno. *Dial-A-Poem* started in December 1968, and I became overwhelmed by it, not doing the book. —John Giorno (Email, March 31, 2018)

Camille Gordon. *The Golden Armadillo.*

Originally announced in *What to Look for in a Book—Physically & Catalogue 1965–66.* Camille Gordon, of course, was the Press's alter ego at large, under whose name any number of staff, perhaps wishing to preserve their anonymity, might contribute to the newsletters or even conduct correspondence; particularly, according to Dick Higgins, if they were a well-known artist working for the Press as a day job. Over the course of the years Camille developed a curious and sometimes dramatic backstory, for example in *Newscard,* no.12 we learn that she "was killed on Route 1 when her car smashed into a chicken truck." Not to worry: "It isn't true. She's gone to Afghanistan, to Mazar-i-Sharif, with her fiancé, a folk song collector. We don't know how the tribesmen will feel when they see her shoe buckles, but we're awfully glad to hear she's okay. (SEN, vol. 1, no. 7) Sometimes Camille was replaced by "Charles Gagnon" whose initials are also C.G. and for Dick Higgins sound like the French adverb *ci-gît,* which means "here lies."

Jan Herman, editor. *Yearbook 1975.* (CAT 74–75)

Dick Higgins, editor. *Anthology of Amateur Graphics (62 BC to 1973 AD).*

Forthcoming (1974) mentioned with illustrations. (SEN, vol. 2, no. 6) [See facing page.]

Richard Huelsenbeck et al. *A Dada Reader.*

The Dada Almanach, translated by Benjamin and Pyla Patterson. Announced as a winter, 1968 title.

This translation of our earlier facsimile edition of *The Dada Almanach* will mark the first time these documents contributed by Dadaists at the height of the movement are available to the English audience in complete form. 192 pp., illus., hardcover. $6.95. (ANM)

Richard Kostelanetz, editor. "A collection of experimental essays." (CAT 73–74)

Published as *Essaying Essays: Alternative Forms of Exposition,* Out of London Press, 1975.

Alvin Lucier with Douglas Simon. *Chambers: Interview on Music and Environment.* (CAT 73–74)

Eventually published as *Chambers: Scores* by Alvin Lucier. Wesleyan, 1980.

The Collected Writings of A.L. Gillespie

Paris. The 1920's: American expatriate artists. To most of us this brings to mind a time of tremendous ferment, achievement and experimentation in the arts. In literature we think of Stein, Joyce, Hemingway, *transition* magazine "and *others*." *Others*, the man who as much as the Jolases gave *transition* its yeasty quality—"Linc" Gillespie, black sheep of a main line Philadelphia family, who originated a highly original panoramic or contrapuntal style that looks like prose but reads like poetry.

Nobody appreciated him but the big ones: Pound, Joyce and, after his return to the *Amerikaka* of his writings, Kenneth L. Beaudoin. A diabetic, Gillespie was finally picked up by some policemen while on a brief visit to Philadelphia, on September 10, 1950, who mistook his illness for intoxication. He died in a sobering-up pen, screaming for medicine. And the county lost one of its great writers at the age of 55. Nobody appreciated him but the big ones: Kay Boyle, in her *Being Geniuses Together*, for instance, describes him as speaking very strangely, and attributes his style and his various artistic insights to a traffic accident he had. And which did, in fact, provide him with a convalescence full of reading time, at which point he clarified his thinking on many things—his style, his career, his own role. It was then that he left for Paris, arriving rather late in the twenties, in the heyday of the *transition* group, and only returned to the United States in the late 1930's. Many of his works appeared in now-defunct and vanished Philadelphia newspapers, though his main dwelling place was New York: we have been unable to locate a single one except for *The Shaper*, a souvenir of his activities on the part of Henry Wallace's 1948 Presidential Campaign. Five years of research and inquiry on the part of Hugh Fox, the editors of the Something Else Press (especially Dick Higgins) and our various friends (and Gillespie's) failed to reveal more than the contents of this very little book. If any of our readers can help, we'll be delighted. But I'm afraid it's as Freda Douglas (Gillespie's sister)—through whose courtesy and permission this book appears—"Whatever we had got lost in the mail when my sister sent it to me from Brooklyn. I'm afraid there just isn't any more." For instance—there exists no known photograph of Gillespie, even as a child, let alone in *transition* days. No photograph. No juvenilia in stanzaic forms, for instance.

Just an incredibly terse, tightly written body of work that has to be compared with the tiny corpus by Anton Webern in music to find a real analogy. Each of the pieces means a great deal. Each is unique: there is no duplication. Many works anticipate later developments in North American arts and in Germany: *Amerikaka* is a pre-happening, a sort of Andy Warhol pageant. Some of the structures anticipate Bill Bissett or d.a. levy. The common denominators are the sound, the contrapuntal, many-layered ways of using words, in different sizes: this anticipates even concrete poetry. And let us not forget Gillespie's radical world-outlook. It provides the justifying ideology. Of Pound, Joyce and Stein, the "other"—Abraham Lincoln Gillespie— was the only one who really belonged to the Left in all respects. (JC)

… PHILÓ LOGICALLY SOUND. ITS ALERTÉXCELLENCE-WORKR …
ONEY NAMEGIV APPELLATIVES … PAG… OGIC 4
EXPLOSE SHOW UP REACTIONARY "SQUAVRTS" … ONEY & WHENOVER N
NA KENS FREE ENTERPRISE … WITH A "BYBY "FLABUY?"
RLDEMERGING IM MA:SAPIENS. FOR, ONCE THIS COVINCVE
ACTITUDING, MENSCHAPURJ WIL LINGUÁ:L SHAPURITY.
MOURE INDIGNITY). [LATER TO FELLOW: SHAPEX] 6
SWETc 7
OUTLI:NE THE SHAPEWEORL'S STRATA-WORKSHAPERS.

The Collected Writings of A.L. Gillespie

The Collected Writings of

A.L. Gillespie

5

edited and with an introduction by Hugh Fox

Kurt Von Meier et al. *A History of Rock and Roll.*

This book remained unpublished at the time of Von Meier's death in 2011. The Kurt Von Meier website states: "Kurt spent a number of years focused on Rock and Roll. He saw it as an authentic artistic expression and began work on a book, despite it being only the mid-sixties, he planned to call *The History of Rock and Roll.* He accumulated a large collection of vintage 45's (current location unknown) but a few . . . remain among his files. There is a fat folder of rejection letters among his records; at some point he gave up on the idea of getting the book published and moved on to other things." N.b. A portion of the manuscript is available on the Kurt Von Meier website.

Exploding on the page in picture text type collages with the same immediacy that it catapults out of and into our lives are the individuals Presley Dylan, groups Beatles Rolling Stones, roots r&b c&w, events Newport, phenomena 45s Allan Freed, that made rock and roll the most popular of the pop art forms. (ANM)

Orson K. Miller. *General Symphony of the Fleshy Fungi* (tentative title). (CAT 73–74)

Published as *Mushrooms of North America.* Plume, 1977.

Claes Oldenburg. *Selected Poems.*

Announced as a winter, 1968 title.

Many of the images and ideas that appear and develop in the sculpture, theater pieces and fantasies of Claes Oldenburg, one of the prime movers in the pop art movement, are embodied in these poems composed since 1958. 192 pages., illustrated, hardcover, $5.95. (ANM)

Erik Satie. *Collected Writings.*

Published as the *A Mammal's Notebooks: The Collected Writings of Erik Satie.* Atlas Press, 1996.

With great pride—and some amazement that it has never been done before—we will present this, to our knowledge, complete and certainly definitive collection of the writings, most of them unpublished, almost all of them inaccessible. This key figure in the Dadaist and Surrealist movements remains one of the prime forces in contemporary music, one whose influence is still gaining momentum. (ANM)

Cary Scher. *Fruits, Berries, and Other Good Things.* (CAT 73–74)

Gertrude Stein. *Before the Flowers of Friendship Faded Friendship Faded.* (CAT 73–74)

Announced as illustrated by Wolf Vostell in *Catalogue Fall/Winter 1973–74.* We find no evidence of such an edition being published.

Emmett Williams. *The Selected Shorter Poems.* (CAT 73–74)

Published by Edition Hansjörg Mayer in 1974 and New Directions in 1975.

With an introduction by Dick Higgins. These are landmarks in concrete and other poetries, collecting as much of Emmett Williams' early work as appeared in out of the way places since he began writing. That Emmett Williams was an originator of concrete poetry is more or less well known by now. But that his work covers the scope it does is not yet widely appreciated. Here's the remedy. It is also a mere sampling: the complete Williams poems to date would have to be about six volumes. And since many of the visual poems require color and are as much paintings as poems, it would be a mammoth undertaking. In Emmett Williams' works, a large part of America previously unspoken for, has found its voice. Pub. October 1973. 320 pages, 13 ½ x 20 ½ cm, illustrated, 8 pages in color. (CAT 73–74)

A few wisps:

We'd love to receive small and marvelous facts, remarks, enigmas, proverbs, family and regional traditions, birthday news and so on for a *Diary* we're thinking of putting out for 1968. (SEN, vol. 1, no. 4)

We'll also do the first supplement to *An Anecdoted Topography of Chance* and will, briefly, convert this *Newsletter* into a *Newspaper.* (SEN, vol. 1, no. 7)

Speaking of sound poetry, we were thinking of doing a couple of records of it. Any number of poets seem to be doing it, and since they have no outlet so far here [U.S.] besides readings, they might like to send us stuff suitable for an anthology of short things. Let's hear tapes, shorties, preferably technological but not necessarily, and we'll consider them and send back the ones we can't use. It should be a marvelous double album. (SEN, vol. 1, no. 12)

The Something Else Press is preparing for publication *A Dictionary of the Avant-Garde.* The dictionary will be an international work of reference in which innovators in all the arts, their principal works, and any special terminology used in their work, as well as relevant isms, schools and movements, will be listed alphabetically, described and/or defined.

Emphasis will be placed on developments in the arts since 1960. (Flyer on Something Else Press letterhead)

III

The Constant Dialectic

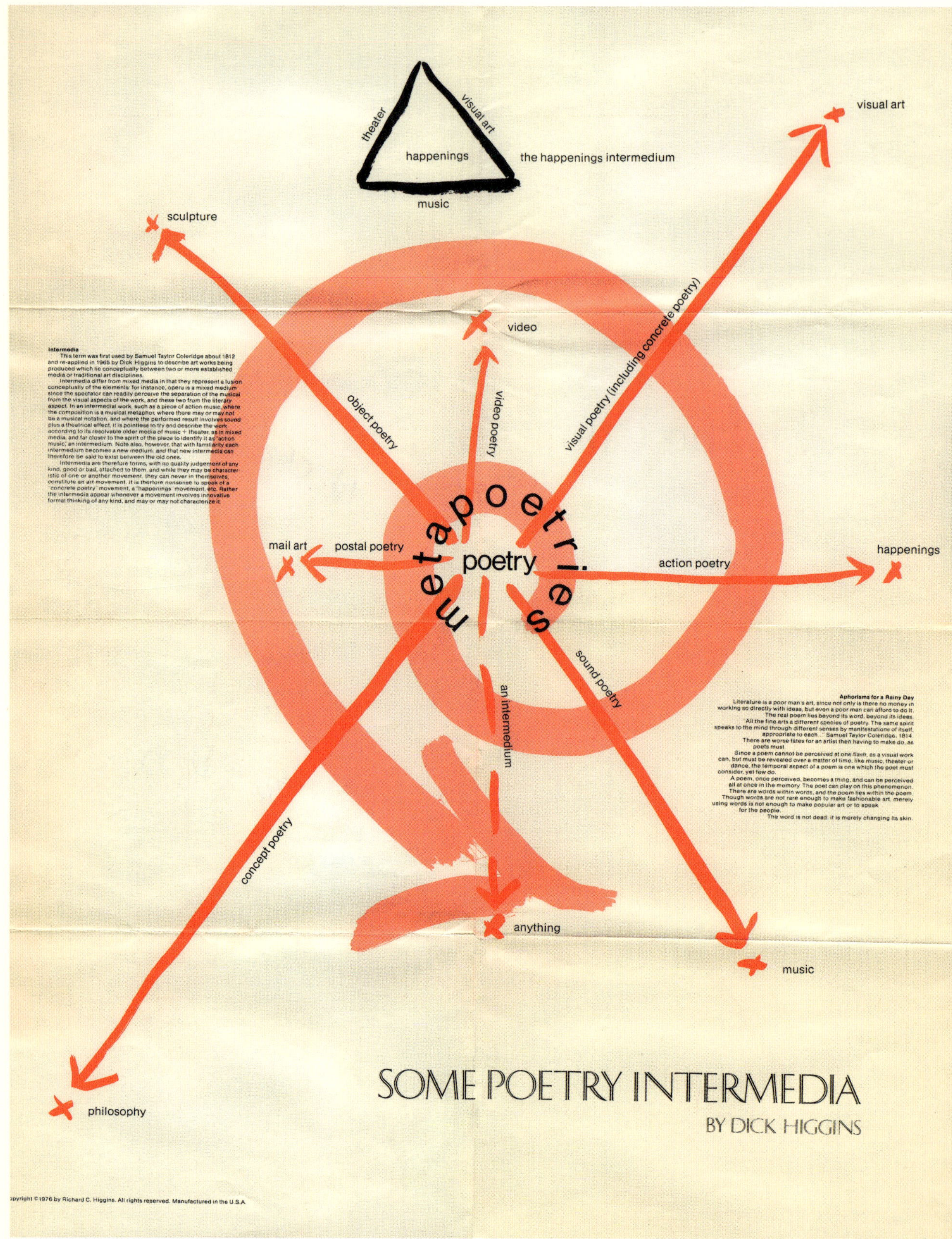

SOME POETRY INTERMEDIA

BY DICK HIGGINS

Five Traditions of Art History, an Essay
by Dick Higgins

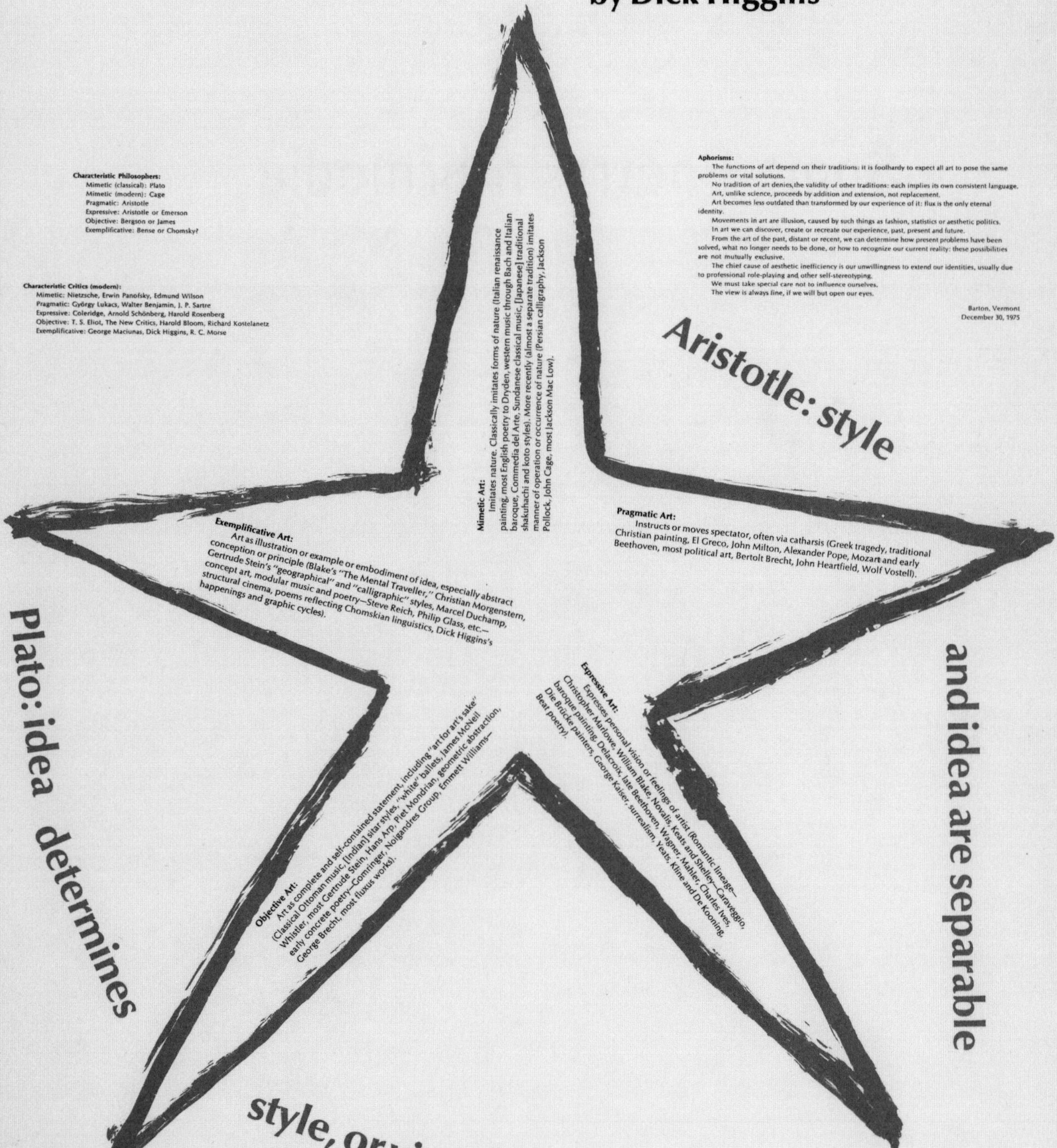

Characteristic Philosophers:
Mimetic (classical): Plato
Mimetic (modern): Cage
Pragmatic: Aristotle
Expressive: Aristotle or Emerson
Objective: Bergson or James
Exemplificative: Bense or Chomsky?

Characteristic Critics (modern):
Mimetic: Nietzsche, Erwin Panofsky, Edmund Wilson
Pragmatic: György Lukacs, Walter Benjamin, J. P. Sartre
Expressive: Coleridge, Arnold Schönberg, Harold Rosenberg
Objective: T. S. Eliot, The New Critics, Harold Bloom, Richard Kostelanetz
Exemplificative: George Maciunas, Dick Higgins, R. C. Morse

Aphorisms:
The functions of art depend on their traditions: it is foolhardy to expect all art to pose the same problems or vital solutions.
No tradition of art denies the validity of other traditions: each implies its own consistent language.
Art, unlike science, proceeds by addition and extension, not replacement.
Art becomes less outdated than transformed by our experience of it: flux is the only eternal identity.
Movements in art are illusion, caused by such things as fashion, statistics or aesthetic politics.
In art we can discover, create or recreate our experience, past, present and future.
From the art of the past, distant or recent, we can determine how present problems have been solved, what no longer needs to be done, or how to recognize our current reality: these possibilities are not mutually exclusive.
The chief cause of aesthetic inefficiency is our unwillingness to extend our identities, usually due to professional role-playing and other self-stereotyping.
We must take special care not to influence ourselves.
The view is always fine, if we will but open our eyes.

Barton, Vermont
December 30, 1975

Mimetic Art:
Imitates nature. Classically imitates forms of nature (Italian renaissance painting, most English poetry to Dryden, western music through Bach and Italian baroque, Commedia del Arte, Sundanese classical music, [Japanese] traditional shakuhachi and koto styles). More recently (almost a separate tradition) imitates manner of operation or occurrence of nature (Persian calligraphy, Jackson Pollock, John Cage, most Jackson Mac Low).

Exemplificative Art:
Art as illustration or example or embodiment of idea, especially abstract conception or principle (Blake's "The Mental Traveller," Christian Morgenstern, Gertrude Stein's "geographical" and "calligraphic" styles, Marcel Duchamp, concept art, modular music and poetry—Steve Reich, Philip Glass, etc.— structural cinema, poems reflecting Chomskian linguistics, Dick Higgins's happenings and graphic cycles).

Pragmatic Art:
Instructs or moves spectator, often via catharsis (Greek tragedy, traditional Christian painting, El Greco, John Milton, Alexander Pope, Mozart and early Beethoven, most political art, Bertolt Brecht, John Heartfield, Wolf Vostell).

Expressive Art:
Expresses personal vision or feelings of artist (Romantic lineage— Christopher Marlowe, William Blake, Novalis, Keats and Shelley, Caravaggio, baroque painting, Delacroix, late Beethoven, Wagner, Mahler, Charles Ives, Die Brücke painters, George Kaiser, surrealism, Yeats, Kline and De Kooning, Beat poetry).

Objective Art:
Art as complete and self-contained statement, including "art for art's sake" (Classical Ottoman music, [Indian] sitar styles, "white" ballets, James McNeill Whistler, most Gertrude Stein, Hans Arp, Piet Mondrian, geometric abstraction, early concrete poetry—Gomringer, Noigandres Group, Emmett Williams— George Brecht, most fluxus works).

Footnote:
Mimetic, Pragmatic, Expressive and Objective traditions were first identified for poetry by M. H. Abrams in *The Mirror and the Lamp* (1954). I have extended the identifications to other arts, identified the modern subset within Mimetic traditions, and identified Exemplificative traditions. Others surely exist or soon will.—D. H.

Some Poetry Intermedia

[Reproduced on page 238.] Published by Unpublished Editions, New York, 1976.

Intermedia

This term was first used by Samuel Taylor Coleridge about 1812 and re-applied in 1965 by Dick Higgins to describe art works being produced which lie conceptually between two or more established media or traditional art disciplines.

Intermedia differ from mixed media in that they represent a fusion conceptually of the elements: for instance, opera is a mixed medium since the spectator can readily perceive the separation of the musical from the visual aspects of the work, and these two from the literary aspect. In an intermedial work, such as a piece of action music, where the composition is a musical metaphor, where there may or may not be a musical notation, and where the performed result involves sound plus a theatrical effect, it is pointless to try and describe the work according to its resolvable older media of music + theater, as in mixed media, and far closer to the spirit of the piece to identify it as "action music," an intermedium. Note also, however, that with familiarity each intermedium becomes a new medium, and that new intermedia can therefore be said to exist between the old ones.

Intermedia are therefore forms, with no quality judgement of any kind, good or bad, attached to them, and while they may be characteristic of one or another movement, they can never, in themselves, constitute an art movement. It is therefore nonsense to speak of a "concrete poetry" movement, a "happenings" movement, etc. Rather the intermedia appear whenever a movement involves innovative formal thinking of any kind, and may or may not characterize it.

Aphorisms for a Rainy Day

Literature is a poor man's art, since not only is there no money in working so directly with ideas, but even a poor man can afford to do it. The real poem lies beyond its word, beyond its ideas.

"All the fine arts [are] a different species of poetry. The same spirit speaks to the mind through different senses by manifestations of itself, appropriate to each . . ." Samuel Taylor Coleridge, 1814.

There are worse fates for an artist then having to make do, as poets must.

Since a poem cannot be perceived at one flash, as a visual work can, but must be revealed over a matter of time, like music, theater or dance, the temporal aspect of a poem is one which the poet must consider, yet few do. A poem, once perceived, becomes a thing, and can be perceived all at once in the memory. The poet can play on this phenomenon. There are words within words, and the poem lies within the poem. Though words are not rare enough to make fashionable art, merely using words is not enough to make popular art or to speak for the people.

The word is not dead: it is merely changing its skin.

Five Traditions of Art History, an Essay

[Reproduced on page 239.] Published by Unpublished Editions, New York, 1976.

Characteristic Philosophers:
Mimetic (classical): Plato
Mimetic (modern): Cage
Pragmatic: Aristotle
Expression: Emerson
Objective: Bergson or James
Exemplificative: Bense or Chomsky?

Characteristic Critics (modern):
Mimetic: Nietzsche, Erwin Panofsky, Edmund Wilson
Pragmatic: György Lukács, Walter Benjamin, J.P. Sartre
Expressive: Coleridge, Arnold Schönberg, Harold Rosenberg
Objective: T.S. Eliot, The New Critics, Harold Bloom, Richard Kostelanetz
Exemplificative: George Maciunas, Dick Higgins, R.C. Morse

Aphorisms:
The functions of art depend on their traditions: it is foolhardy to expect all art to pose the same problems or vital solutions.

No tradition of art denies the validity of other traditions: each implies its own consistent language.

Art, unlike science, proceeds by addition and extension, not replacement.

Art becomes less outdated than transformed by our experience of it: flux is the only eternal identity.

Movements in art are illusion, caused by such things as fashion, statistics or aesthetic politics.

In art we can discover, create or recreate our experience, past, present and future.

From the art of the past, distant or recent, we can determine how present problems have been solved, what no longer needs to be done, or how to recognize our current reality: these possibilities are not mutually exclusive.

The chief cause of aesthetic inefficiency is our unwillingness to extend our identities, usually due to professional role-playing and other self-stereotyping.

We must take special care not to influence ourselves.

The view is always fine, if we will but open our eyes.

Barton, Vermont
December 30, 1975

Aristotle: style and idea are separable
Plato: idea determines style, or vice versa

Mimetic Art:

Imitates nature. Classically imitates forms of nature (Italian renaissance painting, most English poetry to Dryden, western music through Bach and Italian baroque, Commedia dell'arte, Sudanese classical music, [Japanese] traditional shakuhachi and koto styles). More recently (almost a separate tradition) imitates manner of operation or occurrence of nature (Persian calligraphy, Jackson Pollock, John Cage, most Jackson Mac Low).

Pragmatic Art:

Instructs or moves spectator, often via catharsis (Greek tragedy, traditional Christian painting, El Greco, John Milton, Alexander Pope, Mozart and early Beethoven, most political art, Bertolt Brecht, John Heartfield, Wolf Vostell).

Expressive Art:

Expresses personal vision or feelings of artist (Romantic lineage—Christopher Marlowe, William Blake, Novalis, Keats and Shelley—Caravaggio, baroque painting, Delacroix, late Beethoven, Wagner, Mahler, Charles Ives, Die Brücke painters, George Kaiser, surrealism, Yeats, Kline and De Kooning, Beat poetry).

Objective Art:

Art as complete and self-contained statement, including "art for art's sake" (Classical Ottoman music, [Indian] sitar styles, "white" ballets, James McNeil Whistler, most Gertrude Stein, Hans Arp, Piet Mondrian, geometric abstraction, early concrete poetry—Gomringer, Noigandres Group, Emmett Williams—George Brecht, most fluxus works).

Exemplificative Art:

Art as illustration or example or embodiment of idea, especially abstract conception or principle (Blake's "The Mental Traveller," Christian Morgenstern, Gertrude Stein's "geographical" and "calligraphic" styles, Marcel Duchamp, concept art, modular music and poetry—Steve Reich, Philip Glass, etc.—structural cinema, poems reflecting Chomskian linguistics, Dick Higgins's happenings and graphic cycles).

Footnote:

Mimetic, Pragmatic, Expressive and Objective traditions were first identified for poetry by M.H. Abrams in *The Mirror and the Lamp* (1954). I have extended the identifications to other arts, identified the modern subset within Mimetic traditions, and identified Exemplificative traditions. Others surely exist or soon will.

—D. H.

An Exemplativist Manifesto

Published by Unpublished Editions, New York, 1976.

i—the model

The artist, the notation and the work, and the audience—these are three separate settings or complexes, normally separate though in some specific works or media they may converge upon each other.

The audience constructs, by means of the notation and work, an image of the set of possibilities intended by the artist. Any realization of such a set will necessarily be to some extent arbitrary, and is therefore an example rather than a fixity. For this reason, such art can be called exemplative. The emphasis rests on precisely that which the work is an example of, and not on the precise structure or realization of the work.

ii—the dialectic

In exemplative art, the action is always between: it cannot take place at any one pole without the conception of another. It is therefore

> between the heart and the mind,
> between the personal and the objective,
> between the unitary and the general,
> between the warm and the cold (as Af Klintberg put it),
> between the water and the stone.

The idea is developed through its embodiment in the actual work, and thus the work is an instrument for conveying a thought-and-feeling complex by implying a set of examples of it. The audience perceives the work, not merely as an end in itself, but as a communication of the entire range of possibilities of an aspect of reality. The profundity of such a work cannot be merely profundity of thought or irony, as in most recent art (since Eliot and the neoclassics in poetry, the antiromantic reaction in music—and ranging up through the recent structuralist movements in all the arts), but will also have to reflect the profundity of feeling as well.

iii—the artist

Because of the sterility of most recent art, in which innovation has been purely a technical matter, the artist has become dehumane-ized, and has experienced deep ambiguity about how he or she should behave—leading, in some cases, to despair and inactivity or to a failure to escape from a mold, to a cookie-cutter approach to art (for instance, the music of Morton Feldman) where the artist acts like a robot and grinds out endless replicas of his once-strong works—for fear of losing his identity. That we are living at the end of an age (the normative and usually pessimistic view) is an illusion caused by the passéist habit of cannibalizing works of the past, including of the artist's own past. What the new artist will cannibalize is sher own life

An Exemplativist Manifesto

80¢

i-the model

The artist, the notation and the work, and the audience—these are three separate settings or complexes, normally separate though in some specific works or media they may converge on each other.

The audience constructs, by means of the notation and work, an image of the set of possibilities intended by the artist. Any realization of such a set will necessarily be to some extent arbitrary, and is therefore an example rather than a fixity. For this reason, such art can be called exemplative. The emphasis rests on precisely what the work is an example of, and not on the precise structure or realization of the work.

ii-the dialectic

In exemplative art, the action is always between: it cannot take place at any one pole without the conception of another. It is therefore

> between the heart and the mind,
> between the personal and the
> objective,
> between the unitary and the
> general,
> between the warm and the cold,
> (as Af Klintberg put it)
> between the water and the stone.

The idea is developed through its embodiment in the actual work, and thus the work is an instrument for conveying a thought-and-feeling complex by implying a set of examples of it. The audience thus perceives the work, not merely as an end in itself, but as a communication of the entire range of possibilities of an aspect of reality. The profundity of such a work can not be merely the profundity of thought or irony, as in most recent art (since Eliot and the neoclassics in poetry, the antiromantic reaction in music—and ranging up through the recent structuralist movements in all the arts), but will also have to reflect the profundity of feeling as well.

iii-the artist

Because of the sterility of most recent art, in which innovation has been purely a technical matter, the artist has become dehumane-ized, and has experienced deep ambiguity about how he or she should behave—leading in some cases to despair and inactivity, or to a failure to escape from a mold, to a cookie cutter approach to art (for instance, the music of Morton Feldman) where the artist acts like a robot and grinds out endless replicas of his once-strong works—for fear of losing his identity. That we are living at the end of an age (the normative and usually pessimistic view) is an illusion caused by the passéist habit of cannibalizing works of the past, including of the artist's own past. What the new artist will cannibalize is sher own life (his or hers), and this is always fresh and changing. The old artist worries who he is: the new one observes shemself among the shoes, and makes a work of it. For the new artist, the past lives in the present, and works from the past take on new meaning as models of present experience. One finds Goethe in the post office and brings him home for dinner. We—the new artists—are our own people—neither in competition with our ancestors, nor responsible either for their sins or their greatnesses. We are pan-tribal, pan-professional. No single identity can suffice for the new artist whose eye is on sher (his or her) life and not on inherited or arbitrary boundaries.

We **are** according to what we do, not according to the bounds of the roles that limit our fathers' views of themselves. We epitomize the world, and by so doing we come to epitomize ourselves—becoming both ever more deeply ourselves and ever embodied in the world, and are thus unalienated from our brothers and sisters: when we offer ourselves, it means. It is not the passéist participation in a professional charade.

We enact: we do not act in the sense of playing roles, but stress the interplay among many roles and ourselves. One role could never be enough for this—roles become media for developing ourselves and our work.

The art form, par excellence, of the passéist—of what I call the "cognitive" person (named for sher psychological attitude) —is the fiction, the illusion. For the cognitive person, reality must be interpreted and colored—it has no place, raw, in art.

Our arts, on the contrary, seem always to involve some aspect of performance—

> we enact,
> we do,

we perform or commit aesthetic acts.

We commit an act of education when we teach or when we present our live manifestations. Even our most static works are the result of such acts and, thus, have a performance aspect—the poem, the painting, the collage and the photograph, the unnamed complex work that lies in the intermedium between these—there is always interaction among

> their elements,
> their elements perform roles—

the action of the artist (what it involved for the artist to produce the work) is always sensed in the work, and so the work can never be a fixity. Like life itself, our works are impure—always the centers of emanations of experience.

iv-the work

Our art is always the center of an emanation of experience, unlike cognitive art, which embodies statically and without implications, except for other cognitive works. It revels in its virtuosity and attempts perfection. But perfection, while not to be despised (unless it is merely an end in itself), is only one of the possibilities. In place of perfection we offer implicativeness as a goal—the work has not only its own integrity but suggests a whole vast range of further possibilities. The dancerly dance is always deadly—but the dance of life is very rich. We do not love a Gertrude Stein play or a Shakespeare sonnet or a recent John Cage orchestra piece because it is perfect—but because we feel our lives in these works. They do not symbolize life (which would be just another form of static embodiment), but they actively reflect it—suggest and propose things about it.

Such works cannot be ends in themselves. Instead they always participate in the ongoing process of sharing an experience. Among the criteria for evaluating such works must always be the efficiency and force of their suggestion and proposal.

Since this process stresses not the single realization as the work, but the dialectic between any single realization and its alternates, for many exemplative works the method and format of the notation are far more crucial than in the works of the cognitive past. The look of the written text, the (his or hers), and this is always fresh and changing. The old artist worries who he is; the new one observes shemself among the shoes and makes a work of it. For the new artist, the past lives in the present, and works from the past take on new meaning as models of present experience. One finds Goethe in the post office and brings him home for dinner. We—the new artists—are our own people—neither in competition with our ancestors, nor responsible either for their sins or their greatnesses. We are pan-tribal, pan-professional. No single identity can suffice for the new artist, whose eye is on sher (his or her) life and not on inherited or arbitrary boundaries.

We *are* according to what we do, not according to the bounds of the roles that limit our fathers' views of themselves. We epitomize the world, and by so doing we come to epitomize ourselves—becoming both ever more deeply ourselves and ever embodied in the world, and are thus unalienated from our brothers and sisters: When we offer ourselves, it means. It is not the passéist participation in a professional charade.

We enact: We do not act in the sense of playing roles but stress the interplay among many roles and ourselves. One role could never be enough for this—roles become media for developing ourselves and our work.

The art form, par excellence, of the passéist—of what I call the "cognitive" person (named for sher psychological attitude)—is the fiction, the illusion. For the cognitive person, reality must be interpreted and colored—it has no place, raw, in art.

Our arts, on the contrary, seem always to involve some aspect of performance—

> we enact,
>
> we do,
>
> we perform or commit aesthetic acts.

We commit an act of education when we teach or when we present our live manifestations. Even our most static works are the result of such acts and, thus, have a performance aspect—the poem, the painting, the collage and the photograph, the unnamed complex work that lies in the intermedium between these—there is always interaction among

> their elements;
>
> their elements perform roles—

the action of the artist (what it involved for the artist to produce the work) is always sensed in the work, and so the work can never be a fixity. Like life itself, our works are impure—always the centers of emanations of experience.

iv—the work

Our art is always the center of an emanation of experience, unlike cognitive art, which embodies statically and without implications, except for other cognitive works. It revels in its virtuosity and attempts perfection. But perfection, while not to be despised (unless it is merely an end in itself), is only one of the possibilities.

In place of perfection we offer implicativeness as a goal—the work has not only its own integrity but suggests a whole vast range of further possibilities. The dancerly dance is always deadly—but the dance of life is very rich. We do not love a Gertrude Stein play or a Shakespeare sonnet or a recent John Cage orchestra piece because it is perfect—but because we feel our lives in these works. They do not symbolize life (which would be just another form of static embodiment), but they actively reflect it—suggest and propose things about it.

Such works cannot be ends in themselves. Instead they always participate in the ongoing process of sharing an experience. Among the criteria for evaluating such works must always be the efficiency and force of their suggestion and proposal.

Since this process stresses not the single realization as the work, but, the dialectic between any single realization and its alternates, for many exemplative works the method and format of the notation are far more crucial than in the works of the cognitive past. The look of the written text, the graphic element of the musical notation, the prescription for the dramatic presentation—in exemplative works, much of the meaning interfaces here with the work as the final audience will see it. In fact, in such a system all form is a process of notation, among other things. The audience sees or senses the bare bones of the work along with the flesh, so the clarity with which these bare bones are assembled becomes a criterion of the value of the work. And the act of such assembling is part of the work—another performance aspect of it, even if, for instance, the finished work is a painting and thus immobile. A truly exemplative fugue or sonnet would have to imply the essence of many fugues and sonnets, all of them, even. This emphasis on the form-notation complex leads to a sense that, if any notation is a prescription for action (or from action), and if the action of any work should tend to be unique (since every group or individual experience is somehow unique), then each form should tend to be unique for each work. The vision of the artist seeks some unique embodiment—suggesting in the particular the whole set that is exemplified. In exemplative art, then, the artist will always be involved in an ongoing process of inventing new forms—his works and styles will seem, to a cognitive observer, to be terribly chaotic and inconsistent. To us there will be a consistency; however, it will lie in the kinds of materials that are chosen to express and epitomize the artist's reality, and in the things about the forms that he invents which stay the same—the artist of the goat, the artist of the shoe, the artist of the small. This may well lead to a new imagism.

But make no mistake here: Neither the process nor the notations are ends in themselves in being fixities. A notation made to be a notation, for instance, without its being specified what or how it notates, is not a fixity (like a painting one painted merely to paint a painting)—because it implies not one but an enormous variety of possible interpretations.

The question for an audience to ask, then, when confronted by an exemplative or other non-cognitive work, is not the usual "Who did this and why," but the newer "What is this, and how does it work?"

v—the audience

Each member of the audience can answer these last questions (and so get beyond the questions to actual enjoyment) only by asking three further questions:

1) *What is the artist sharing*? This corresponds to—but does not equal—subject matter in our traditional arts.

2) *What possibilities does this form make actual*? In practice this may well be the first question asked—confronted by a work, most of us have to discover a motivating process before we can tell what we are supposed to enjoy. Few of us are satisfied entirely with our own interpretations, which may miss possible areas of enjoyment—("I like that dance because I like to watch fat women move" sounds strange and incomplete).

3) *For whom and what, and to whom is the artist speaking*? This seems secondary, but in practice it is a necessary stage in incorporating a work into one's own reality—"Is this for me, or is it for someone else? Is it part of my world, or is it academic to me?"

The audience that asks such questions would be the perfect one—the one the artist must always use in sher model, mentally, since it can gain the maximum impact from sher work. Though artists (especially composers) like to claim they cannot predict an audience and therefore must ignore the question, who would want to do a work that nobody, even oneself, could be aware of? Can an art exist like a tree falling in the wood with nobody to see it? Wouldn't it, too, seem incomplete? Thus an artist's conceptual model always includes an ideal audience, usually a projection from one's own experience—"I write for myself and others" was Gertrude Stein's formula, written in her notebooks. And by identifying these key questions, which an audience for exemplative or other non-cognitive art should have at hand, the artist and educator are able to begin to deal with the problems of developing such an audience.

vi—the psychology

Traditional psychology in Western art is geared
        to winning,
        to moving,
        to convincing,
        to delighting,
        to amusing,
        to impressing, and
        to the common denominator of all these, to controlling the audience.
Thus the artist in any medium becomes as much a strategist as he is an artist. Thus

he or she becomes sher own fiction, with sher eye on shemself and on sher role and its potential—it is in this sense that I have called any such artist "cognitive." This was true of virtually all Western art between the Renaissance and the late 1950s, when the social and cultural revolutions of our century finally broke our historic mentality down—precipitating a time of tremendous ferment, from which only now are some of the clear outlines of things to come emerging.

Many of us—increasingly, most of us—are post-cognitive or even non-cognitive in our outlook: this is a dominant phase of the postmodern experience. Obviously it isn't just the artists but almost every person who has come of age since the late 1950s (and many of those who came of age before that watershed time) who revels, for instance, in the affirmation of sher identity through doing a vast variety of things, conducting multiple careers and taking on many more roles than our parents would have dared. In our organizational structures—in our sexual politics and means of earning a living, for example—we have looked for and often found far more flexibility than our parents would have felt comfortable with. Communes, the hippie movement, the cult of the unwed mother—these are only very superficial and, usually, middle-class expressions of a need that goes far deeper and cuts across all classes and sexes—to increase the options open to us. We would feel utterly stifled—in fact, some of us do—if we had to live up to the roles our parents knew. Their fears of going beyond themselves, their guilty feelings about survival and their successes and failures—we understand them (though perhaps our children won't), but they are not ours. We have no fear of becoming; our thought processes are meditations (for our parents, the purpose of meditation was medicinal—it was to clear the mind and restore perspective. It had to be slow, for fear of losing control. But we begin where they left off—we need not control in order to experience, so we can meditate at any speed and virtually in any situation)—"meditations," they are, in the sense that they are liberated processes of thought and feeling, as opposed to directed ones. We are quite capable of experiencing these as emptiness and beyond concrete conceptibility. All this adds up to a new mentality, at least for the Western world.

Exemplative art is merely the first art to reflect this new mentality. It is not done only by self-proclaimed exemplative artists—the only one of those, to date, is myself, since I coined the term. But I coined it to describe what many of the new artists are doing—and if some of these choose to use the term, fine, I'm glad it's useful. But other arts with other names will come along, reflecting the new mentality, the movement into which is irreversible—we cannot erase, even if we want to, what we know (and know we know). There have been other arts reflecting this new mentality—but not in Western culture, at least in recent times. The search for siblinghood, rather than some naive, Luddite search for an innocent nature or some quest for the exotic, explains the new centrality, among us formerly privileged Westerners of this world—among white males, especially, it's interesting to note (how few female contributors there are in *Alcheringa*, the main art magazine expressing this search!)—the new centrality of the arts of ancient times, other cultures and the tribal societies. This is no mere exoticism: nothing stays exotic when it has been experienced for any length of time. Rather it is a movement away from the negativity and fear and guilt of our parents and into new alliances and less alienated relationships—by means of the arts as media for exchange. Our involvement as Westerners in such an exchange involves a new dialectic, which we then project onto our whole aesthetic experience—we must learn in order to teach, we must teach in order to learn. This explains the didactic element so common in post-cognitive art.

vii—some conclusions

Should a list be prepared of exemplative artists? I see no need for one. Such artists, reading this text, will recognize themselves—and non-artists, thinking of what I have said, will recognize exemplativism in art that they already know, especially in very recent art. A list would seem definitive—and one would wonder who had been left out. Manifestos of the past were written as part of the journalism of launching a career or a movement—but this one is to call attention to what is involved in a new mode of work which has already been under way for some time—to mark and hail the value of a groundswell that has developed into a huge wave.

But there are still cognitive people around, and for them exemplative art will remain bewildering, uncohesive, insubstantial. Though we can understand and appreciate them, they cannot appreciate us, at least on the gut level. They copy our rhetoric to seem far-out—they trope their tropes and take themselves very seriously indeed. But it's the seriousness of a terminal disease—not the seriousness of a prisoner writing his first sonnet or a composer working out some new form for epitomizing sher deepest sonic experience. Far-out toward what? Toward eccentricity and alienation—no wonder, then, that they speak of "late poetry" of art as clinamen and misprision. It's all they dare accept of themselves.

But such people control the media: we do not. They thus are in a position to determine the economics of our lives, which we are not. Our strategy must therefore be geared toward our survival—the rest can come later.

This means that we must use the pudgies' resources when these are offered, but we must also remain independent of them, since they can be withdrawn at any time. If we teach, it must be without the sense of being confined to a teacherly role—it must be with some degree of contempt for the limitations of the teacherly professions. If we work in the art industries—in publishing, in museums or galleries, for printers—we must similarly maintain our independence from the assumptions that the pudgies—the cognitives—would like to force on us, and must move wherever possible toward more open-ended roles for these organizations. We must gear ourselves for the conversion, ultimately, of all professions into media.

Beyond such oblique cultural guerrilla warfare, our strategy must be such that we gain, from every act of art that we commit, some tactical advantage, even if it is only among ourselves (which gives freedom to breathe). When we make our own organizations—magazines or publishing, for instance—we must not overexpand beyond our actual audiences, or beyond our ability to reach those audiences. This is an age when the dinosaurs are dying, and the future belongs to the warm-blooded little mammals. Most of our work, for now, should be designed so that even if it were not paid for we would not be financially ruined. Survival is among our moral obligations, so long as it is distinguished from cowardice. Thus any economic benefits that come to us from our activities—splendid! But let's remember how passing these can be and, again, maintain our independence of them. We should not risk our future freedom (on which our identity depends) by making too great commitments in the present for us safely to sustain. Pudgy believes in Santa Claus: we can't afford to.

Next: cognitivism—cognitive attitudes, taken collectively—creates the illusion that there are movements when what there is are slight shifts of popular style and format. Thus, for a cognitive person, the arts must always belong to the world of fashion—one movement is in, then another comes along to replace it—while our innovations, instead, simply accumulate and add to the possibilities. The cognitive artist is always in danger of being replaced, so he or she experiences great anxiety from every change. We merely include each new development in our present bag of tricks—we don't have to worry so much about our image as poor Pudgy does. If fashion changes and we have to work more modestly for a while, very well, we'll enjoy our privacy. If we were to be as professional as Pudgy or as the pudgies, and were therefore always to work for those who paid us the most, we would be working most of the time for and among people who were not interesting to us—and, in due course, our arts would suffer. We would, if we did that, no longer be sharing our experience so much as exploiting it—and exploitation, in the long run, always hurts the personhood of the exploiter. We must always, therefore, act like dedicated amateurs (even when we are lucky enough to benefit in a major material way from some work we have done)—devoted to our freedom enough to participate only when and where it seems appropriate to do so. The pudgies' institutions are our compost heaps, good for our roots' tendrils—the source of a little dollar fertilization. But we need not take them seriously. They can mirror our light, but can't originate it. The pudgies sit on each others' boards, swapping compliments and insults, impressing each other. We don't. Nor do we

scream,

yell,

cheer, or

regurgitate exclamation points when there are envelopes to lick and seal. We need no prizes to show when we have done something beautiful. We know the dancer from the dance. No external uniform or costume is necessary to identify what we are doing. A truth that must be shouted (like an art idea that must be proved) is probably academic: Pudgy can make a career, shouting and proving—but ours is the art of vanilla ice cream. How can you prove the taste of vanilla ice cream? Can you argue that it is not peppery? Or isn't it, perhaps, better to see, by comparing the taste with our experience of the peppery—to see that it is something else?

The pudgies are losing—fewer and fewer take them seriously. Their English departments are being dismantled, merged with speech, dramatic arts and linguistics. Good riddance. Nobody—seldom even the contributors—reads their magazines, most of which therefore cannot survive except through massive grants—and they have almost no private readers, only institutions. *Antaeus, Tri-Quarterly, Poetry Magazine, Arts*—who reads such things? Who could? Mostly only the table of contents gets perused, and the magazine goes back to the shelf. Pudgy's point in writing for such a magazine, or in having a picture of his art, was really just to be included—any ideas or opinions beyond the standard, professional ones would therefore be beside the point, threatening.

Pudgy the critic knows the horses but only dares to ride the ponies. He insults the horses—but it's done from fear. He would mount one if he dared, but he's too self-conscious to manage to balance. Still—in his dreams, when his truth comes out, it's the horses he rides, not the ponies. And in time, then, he is fickle—and forgets the ponies as he stares at the horses.

Pudgy the artist is no different. He knows what needs doing—but is afraid to seem unprofessional, so he doesn't do it. Deeper and deeper his despair grows—and hollower and hollower his work.

Meanwhile the exemplativists are happily swimming—probably in the raw. It seems more natural that way. The water's fine and the tide is theirs—ours. "Come on in," they—we—yell to Pudgy. Who is it that stops Pudgy from coming along in for a dip?

The water we swim in is our life—and swimming is an art. Any art (from Latin: *ars* = skill) is tested here by how it works in the water. The rest is dross: "gaudyverse," the romantic poets called it. Our world is vast and growing; we always knew it, but now we're acting upon it, trying to be as complete as each of us uniquely can. We are trying to be altogether together. As the old joke says, the whole of the doughnut is its most valuable part.

—for his brothers and sisters:
Barton, Vermont, August 26, 1976

The Strategy of Each of My Books

Originally published in *Horizons: The Poetics and Theory of the Intermedia*, Carbondale: Southern Illinois University Press, 1984.

What Are Legends (1960), my first book, is the theoretical text which goes with *Legends and Fishnets* (1958–60, 1969; published in 1976). It exemplifies my near-obsession with unifying my theory and practice, written as it is in my "legend" style; this style uses few verbs in the indicative mode, substituting participles wherever possible, in order to get a pictorial effect in words. Important conceptual models to me were certain late Latin poems in which strings of participles provide the movement of the poem (e.g., the "Stabat Mater") and the last part of the De Quincey "English Mail Coach," as well as the obvious modernist texts by Gertrude Stein and others. I printed it myself when I was at the Manhattan School of Printing, using a handlettered text and found-illustrations by Bern Porter, a highly original graphic artist and writer from Maine whose work I have admired for many years.

Jefferson's Birthday/Postface (1964) is two books, bound back-to-back. *Jefferson's Birthday* includes all the texts which I composed between April 13, 1962 (Thomas Jefferson's birthday) and April 13, 1963. The book came about when George Maciunas, the organizer of fluxus, offered to publish all my texts. I said it would be a monstrously big book, decidedly non-commercial. He then suggested that he publish a year's worth of my writings, which would then provide a cross section of my work. I was delighted with the idea and proceeded to finish all texts begun during that year (which I seldom do). It is, in fact, representative of my work from that time except that it includes no long texts. The resulting manuscript then lay on his desk for several months, while he tried to make the peace with it.

His studio was downstairs from mine, and every few days I would drop by and ask him what was happening with it. He would stall and groan—it was much bigger than he had expected. Finally he told me that it would be ready "a year from next spring." That was too late, I said—I needed the books for acting scripts, etc. He said there was nothing he could do about that. I then went to the bar downstairs and had a few drinks, went back up to his studio, removed my manuscript and took it upstairs to my studio, returned to the bar and had a few more drinks. I then went home to Alison Knowles, a fluxus artist to whom I was married at the time.

"Alison," I said, "We've founded a press."

"Oh really," Alison said, startled. "What's it called?"

"Shirtsleeves Press," I said.

"That's no good," she said. "What don't you call it something else?" I thought about that, and the next day I wrote the "Something Else Manifesto," in which I promised always to publish "something else," different from whatever was in vogue at the time.

Postface is a rather personal memoir of the early days of happenings and fluxus in which, as I said before, I was active. I was aware that the pieces in *Jefferson's Birthday* would seem strange to most readers, so it was important to me to provide a context for those pieces—the essay is a little thin on theoretical content, but as narrative and polemic (attacking alternative, conventional modes of working) it was valuable enough that it will now (1981) be reissued by another publisher.

As for Something Else Press, it lasted from 1964 to 1974 (I left it in 1973), and one aspect of it too was to provide a context for the understanding of my works—I always thought of it as a big collage with many contributors.

Throughout the later 1960s I brought out rather few of my own books—only the first canto of *A Book About Love & War & Death* (1960–70), which appeared in Something Else Press's inexpensive Great Bear Pamphlet series, as a sort of work-in-progress publication—more of that in a minute. Most of my creative work was in film, photography, and performance at that time, and a lot of my attention was devoted to working out a theoretical position which would be more appropriate to the avant-garde than the conventional, Aristotelian models with their emphasis on power (especially catharsis). The preliminary texts in this direction, such as the essay "Intermedia" (1963–64) which revived that term from Samuel Taylor Coleridge, were published and sent out free to friends of Something Else Press in the *Something Else Newsletter*. One of these essays from the *Newsletter* appeared also as a pamphlet, *Towards the 1970's*, with another small press in 1969; in it I tried to predict (with mixed success) what would be of importance to those who followed the new arts in America in the 1970s—notably "a revolution in subject matter" which came true with the obsession with subject matter/meaning/narrativity in structuralism and semiotics (to which I was only partly sympathetic), and the new centrality of the dance to our arts (Meredith Monk and Trisha Brown, for example).

But by 1969 it was clear that I had to do a new cross section of my work and to reissue the texts which had appeared in the *Newsletter*, some issues of which were becoming scarce. I therefore did *foew&ombwhnw* (1969), which is, ironically, bound as a prayer book. The book is in four columns. The left-hand column continuously features long works, mostly for performance, such as the *Danger Music* series or the long aleatoric play *St. Joan at Beaurevoir* (1958–59) with its long phonemic speech structures. The second column includes short plays and graphics. The third column is poetry, and the fourth column is essays—not only the *Newsletter* texts but also, for example, a long account of the *Graphis* series (1958–), a series of graphical notations for musical, theatrical, and other performances which is still a preoccupation of mine now, nearly a quarter century later. The design of the book reflects the McLuhanesque preoccupations of the time, with its simultaneities, but is also, to some extent a book about making a book, reflecting my experience doing almost all the design work for the Something Else Press.

Also in 1969 I brought out *Pop Architektur* with a trade publisher in Germany, a collection co-edited and designed with Wolf Vostell, a colleague from happenings and fluxus; the English text, slightly expanded, appeared in 1970 with Something Else Press as *Fantastic Architecture*. It is an anthology of ideas by artists and composers and writers about the elements of architecture—space, construction, environment—some practical and some fantastic, and with commentaries on some of the ideas of the artists or on the elements of architecture, printed on translucent sheets bound into the book; my commentaries are in the *Legend* style to make them literary works and not just traditional captions. Again, it was a matter of combining Theorie and Praxis in the German sense.

The same small press which had done *Towards the 1970's* also did two more pamphlets, *Die Fabelhafte Geträume von Taifun-Willi* in its original mixed German-and-English text (an all-German translation was done in 1969 by a small press in Stuttgart) and *Computers for the Arts*, both in 1970. *Willi* is the first of my radio plays—a supposed tape-recorded dialogue between two reporters at an impossibly large happening—and reflects my love of radio as a medium; I love the way radio allows us to imagine the visual element (which television so imperfectly realizes), providing us with a literature which one can experience while doing something else, while driving a car, for example. *Computers for the Arts* is a polemic in favor of the artist being his or her own technician; as information it is now very much out of date, but the point remains important to me, that collaboration often leads to diffused works with diluted personality.

By 1972 Something Else Press was no longer a small press. Two of its books had sold well over ten thousand copies, and I was running myself ragged raising funds to do new books, which was ruining my health. The history of Something Else Press is not a subject to investigate in depth here; I have told my side of the story in two long accounts in the *New Lazarus Review* (1979 and 1980) and there are two books about Something Else Press, Hugh Fox's *An Analytic Checklist of Something Else Press* (1974) and the much more comprehensive Peter Frank book, *Something Else Press: An Annotated Bibliography* (1983). What I missed was the flexibility of Something Else as a small press. So in 1972, at the suggestion of my friend and co-worker Nelleke Rosenthal, I started Unpublished Editions, in order to make model editions of my books, which would, hopefully, be reissued in time by trade publishers.

The first book from Unpublished Editions was *amigo* (1972), a series of gay love poems; it was also my first book of just poems as such, with no theoretical texts included.

Also in 1972 there appeared my last Something Else Press book, the complete *Book About Love & War & Death* (1960–70). As I mentioned before, the first canto had already appeared in 1965, and also the second and third cantos appeared with a small press in California, Nova Broadcast Express, which was edited by Jan Herman, my successor at Something Else Press. With half the work in print, it seemed desirable to do the rest of it, so I did. It is my largest published prose work, a sort of aleatoric novel with sections in poetry after the manner of some of the romantic writers of Germany, who have been a lifelong interest of mine; more of that presently.

The next Unpublished Editions book was *The Ladder to the Moon* (1959–63, rewritten and published in 1973), my largest work for the theater to date. It is a very opulent, romantic piece with sections (e.g., the "Tiger Lady Episode") in which the normal time progression is suspended; all my experience in happenings and fluxus is included in that work, and I will write no more large-scale theater works until *The Ladder* has been performed—I can't.

Also in 1973 Unpublished Editions brought out *For Eugene in Germany*, a sort of sequel to *amigo* but, somehow, dead; it is the only book I have done which I regret. In the same year two small publications appeared with small presses in Europe: *Gesehen, Gehört, und Verstanden*, from Reflection Press in Stuttgart (which had done the German version of *Willi*), which is a translation of an issue of the *Something Else Newsletter*, "Seen, Heard, and Understood," a praise of the literary medium, and also *Le Petit Cirque au Fin du Monde*, a radio play in my French, which is pretty bad, a sort of homage à Jean Cocteau (whose "Le Printemps au Fond de la Mer" is a favorite of mine). Its only performance to date happened when it was on the desk of Jean-Jacques Lebel, a teacher at the University of Paris at Vincennes in May 1968 when the students seized the university; they broadcast it over the university intercom during the insurrection.

For me the big event of 1973 was finally leaving Something Else Press. I celebrated it by setting to work on a huge cycle of prints, *7.7.73*, which eventually numbered more than eight hundred graphic works, mostly silk-screen, but which also extended into different media—sculptures and environments and even a visual diary which is, as yet, incomplete. The cycle was organized to follow the seasons of the year, and the climax was the spring, since I felt that I had reached a new springtime in my life. For the springtime I also took some of the better visual images, printed them onto plastic, and made up a set of shadow puppets and a nonstory to go around them. For these puppets I composed an opera, the libretto of which was published in 1973 (well before the cycle was complete) as *Spring Game* by Unpublished Editions.

Finally in 1974 there was the Unpublished Editions *City with All the Angles* (written in 1970–71), a radio play which satirizes Los Angeles where I was living (if it can be said that anyone really lives there) at the time I wrote it. That completed the cycle of radio literature which I wanted to make. I have written other works for radio, but they belong to another world. For example, there is the presently unpublished *Ebb Tide* (1975), but it belongs to the cycle of *amigo* and *For Eugene in Germany*.

In 1975 I collected my aleatoric and other system poems together, destroyed many of them, and published or republished the rest as *Modular Poems* with Unpublished Editions. Many of these had appeared in mimeographed form earlier, and others had been in little magazines, but I needed a substantial book of such poems to complement the more prose-oriented *Book About Love & War & Death*, if there were to be a cycle of aleatoric works that would be in any way a balanced statement by one artist of the possibilities in that area. Collecting these poems stimulated me to compose a new aleatoric cycle of poems, conceived as a set, so I wrote "The Colors" in March 1975; in 1977 it was accepted for publication by an Italian publisher, but it has never appeared. I feel this non-publication as a gap.

My interest in languages other than my native English had been an ongoing preoccupation from the beginning, as the reader can see from the list of books to date. But I also, therefore, felt that I should extend this into a single work in two languages, punning back and forth between the two. So it happened that in 1976

I wrote and Unpublished Editions published *classic plays*, which is in French and English throughout, and the title of which is an ironically pretentious reference to *word*plays as well as an allusion to its story, the Persephone myth, which it tells by allusion and reference, following an idea of Augustus Wilhelm Schlegel, one of the Jena group of early German romantics, of whom more in a moment.

As yet, I had published rather few works of fiction, and so it was now time to bring out the whole set of works, *Legends & Fishnets* (1959–69) to which *What Are Legends* (1960) had been the prefatory statement. This Unpublished Editions did in 1976. At the same time a small press in California, Tuumba Press, brought out *Cat Alley,* a very short novel which is in some ways a counterpart to *amigo* and which tells the story of an imagined affair between a married man and his secretary; it is the same story that is told in "Moments in the Lives of Great Women," the longest poetic work in *foew&ombwhnw* (1969).

Returning to the language investigations again, in 1977 Studio Morra in Naples, Italy, where I had a show of ceramic shards on which their texts were drawn in calligraphy, brought out *The Epitaphs/GliEpitaphi*, satirical epigrammatic poems in Latin, French, German, and Swedish. It is poorly edited but handsome.

But apart from 7.7.73, the decade of the 1970s was, for me, principally my decade as a poet. I therefore decided to publish two books of poems, the first a miscellany and the second a more concentrated, highly visual selection. The first was published by Unpublished Editions as *Everyone Has Sher Favorite (His or Hers)* (1977), and it ends with a story showing my poetic techniques applied to fiction. The second, *some recent snowflakes (and other things)* (1979) ends in the same way, but we shall get to it in due course.

In 1974–75 I suffered a severe nervous breakdown which left me without much sense of who I was. I therefore enrolled in the Graduate English Department at New York University in order to inventory the English-language literature which was of interest to me, to find my roots and precedents, and to improve my scholarly habits. One preoccupation which emerged from this investigation was old visual poetry—the ancestors to the concrete poetry of the 1950s and since, and of which I have been a desultory practitioner since the early days. I assembled a tremendous collection of such texts, nearly a thousand items from ca. 500 B.C. to A.D. 1900, my arbitrary cutoff date, in Greek, Latin, Hebrew, Arabic, Turkish, Chinese, Gujarati (an Indian language), Russian, Polish, German, Swedish, Czech, Serbo-Croatian, French, Dutch, Spanish, and Portuguese (among others), as well as English. Virtually no scholarship existed in this area, which flourished up to the end of the baroque period, and then "went underground" into folk and comic poetry, during the period of neo-Aristotelian art (ca. 1660–1960) until, at the beginning of this century, it began to come back into vogue with the works of Mallarmé, Apollinaire, the futurists, constructivists, and dadaists, etc. There was no way that I could focus upon this entire field—to do an anthology of all my findings was far beyond my means—so I instead concentrated upon some of the currents of the field that relate to the great English poet George Herbert (1593–1633), and in 1977

Unpublished Editions brought out my *George Herbert's Pattern Poems: In Their Tradition*, a scholarly monograph whose bibliography, while itself quite selective, at least includes enough materials to suggest to comparative literature scholars what a lot of work has yet to be done in this very fertile field.

The Unpublished Editions project had been so successful for me that in 1975 I was joined in it by Alison Knowles, and in 1978 by John Cage, Philip Corner, Geoffrey Hendricks, Jackson Mac Low, and Pauline Oliveros (in 1980 Jerome Rothenberg also joined the group); the group, however, chose to change the name from Unpublished Editions to Printed Editions, which is its present monicker.

The strategy of the books remains the same, however—to bring out model editions of one's less commercially viable work (which includes, evidently, virtually all of mine, according to the trade publishing establishment) and to sell them through a common catalog; someday, hopefully, the books will be reissued by commercial publishers. I still try every year to get such publishers interested in my work, but it never happens. The last time I did this, the trade publisher told me his sales force had estimated that they could sell perhaps 600 copies of a manuscript-book that I had offered him; and since, with (now) Printed Editions I can usually sell 1000–1500 copies of whatever I produce, this did not seem like a wise way to proceed.

Thinking about these problems induced me to write *The Epickall Quest of the Brothers Dichtung and Other Outrages*, my first Printed Editions book for 1978. The title story is the result of first writing a long essay on the narrative theory of two of the Jena group of German romantics, Friedrich and Augustus Wilhelm Schlegel while, simultaneously, reading John Bunyan's *Pilgrim's Progress*. I realized that there were probably only a dozen or so people in the world who would understand my essay, so I discarded it: but its traces remained in my mind. So I wrote, instead, a satirical novella about the American literary scene, interspersing many of the Schlegel brothers' ideas, and giving the whole the picaresque plot of two brother poets wandering towards Mount Parnassus. Also in the book is an account of European history seen in the microcosm of the croissant. My friend from fluxus, Ken Friedman, provided me with some delightful line drawings, and the result was one of my most accessible works.

But my most serious work for 1978 was the other Printed Editions book, *A Dialectic of Centuries: Notes Towards a Theory of the New Arts*. By now the *Newsletter* essays were out of print, and I had broadened my understanding of the dynamics of the new arts of which I was a part, by the ideas of exemplativism (the notion that a work can be a more or less arbitrary example chosen by the artist from a range of possibilities inherent in its conception), which attacks the idea, so prevalent till now, of definitiveness, and of the allusive referential, the concept that the displacement of what we actually hear or see from what we expect to hear or see can be a factor in giving the work its emotional context. It was therefore desirable to collect my present theory texts together in a book, which I therefore did. However it sold much better than I had expected, and I found myself virtually out of stock on it. At the same time, the original printing had been rather shoddy and there were a few inconsistencies in my thought which bothered me, so in 1979 I brought out a second, revised edition, which is where that book can stand. I will not reprint those *Newsletter* essays again, although ideas from them will surely reappear in later theoretical formulations.

Part of my desire to call attention to the new relevance of German romanticism was incomplete: many of the texts were unavailable in modern translations. In 1977, as part of my studies at New York University I was obliged to pass an examination in a foreign language. I chose German, and to brush up on my language, I made a translation of Novalis's *Hymne an die Nacht*, one of the masterpieces of the Jena phase of the movement. This was published by Treacle Press in 1978; there are, however, a few inaccuracies in it, and also I would like to complete my work in this area by making available some of the texts by the Schlegels which are the basis for my insistence on their relevance, so that is a project which is at hand. Making available key works from the past, taking them away from the heavy hand of the specialists and bringing them into the light of the day—this is an ongoing theme in my literary activity. I had done it in Something Else Press days by republishing rare classics—the *Dada Almanach* (because so many people accused me of being a dadaist without having any idea what the dadaists had actually achieved), the more experimental works of Gertrude Stein (which were, in the 1960s, more "talked about than read," as she had once lamented during her lifetime)—we published *The Making of Americans, Lucy Church Amiably, Matisse, Picasso, and Gertrude Stein* (also known as *G.M.P.*), *How to Write, Geography and Plays*, and *A Book Concluding with As a Wife Has a Cow*—and, of interest to music people, Henry Cowell's very prophetic *New Musical Resources*. But this work was also incomplete; even though I had no ambitions as a scholar, it was necessary to establish my own context. So I decided to work on Giordano Bruno, and to translate some of his Latin writings, which are more interesting to the cultural historians than are the more familiar Italian ones, but none of which have been published in any modern language although Bruno died over 380 years ago. I did this in collaboration with Charles Doria, a classics scholar and poet, starting with his striking sixteenth-century semiotics, *On the Composition of Images, Signs, and Ideas*. Selections from our translation have appeared in a California magazine, *Wch Way*, but the whole work will not be finished for several years more. One aspect of Bruno's work which is relevant to my own is his assertion of the idea of intermedia (in the above-mentioned work): "True poetry is at the same time music and philosophy. True poetry and music are in a manner divine wisdom and painting." And so on, including painting (and, by implication, all visual art) in the mix.

Speculating on Bruno and poetry led me to start a new cycle of poems, the snowflake poems in what I call "snowflake form" because of their visual symmetry. Elements of these poems had been in my work for a long time, but the first full-fledged and conscious use of the visual cancrizan was in my poem "the snowflakes of giordano bruno," which I printed first as a Christmas card in 1978 and then, together with twenty-one other such snowflakes or sets of snowflakes, in the 1979 Printed Editions book *some recent snowflakes (and other things)*. It also includes some translations by sound rather than sense, a kind of work which had preoccupied me for years, and which led me also to do another translation project in collaboration with Steve McCaffery and bpNichol of Canada. In 1967 Robert Filliou had written a set of rock and roll lyrics which, however, proved too risqué for commercial broadcasting; so he published them with English translations by George Brecht and German ones by Diter Roth. In due course the book went out of print. We now (1978) published, with Membrane Press in Milwaukee, our "homophonic" translations, with myself translating Roth, Nichol (who speaks almost no French) doing Filliou's original French, and McCaffery doing a "homolinguistic" (his term) translation of Brecht's English into punned English. The result, *Six Fillious*, makes a handy paradigm of such things; but one book which is still needed, to establish the field, is an anthology of homophonic translations by many poets.

Way back in the start of my creative life I had thought of myself as primarily a musical composer, had studied with Henry Cowell and John Cage (among others), and music was still very much a part of my artistic consciousness. I continued to compose music through the 1960s and 1970s, and I strongly felt the need to create a body of music which would reflect the same concerns as I was working with in my writings and visual art. I therefore decided that the next focus for my publishing activity should be music. Naturally, I first submitted my music to conventional publishers, and after five or six rejections, it became clear that Printed Editions would have to undertake some music publishing. A suitable starting place seemed to be to do a collection of short piano pieces, which, in due course, materialized as *Piano Album: Short Piano Pieces, 1962–1984* (1980). The reason for the 1984 date in the title was that I wanted to make it clear that I was not going to compose some avalanche of piano pieces, opportunistically, for everyone who asked for one, that I would publish no additional short piano pieces until 1984 or later.

A short digression about printers seems necessary at this point. I had studied offset printing in the early 1960s, had worked in printing shops before I went into publishing, and, in the years when I was running the Something Else Press, I did most of the sophisticated camera work that was needed in our publications on a camera which was located wherever I lived at the time. I also designed a good many books for other publishers. Though I was not tempted to print our books myself—the ownership of this or that kind of press would have made me feel obliged to use this or that format for most of our books, as each press is most suitable for only a small number of possible formats. Even so, working closely with the printers that we used was the only way to achieve the results that were wanted, and we simply could not have afforded to buy some of the special effects I called for in my designs from outside sources. In the early 1970s I had settled "permanently" (as I hoped) in a small village in northern Vermont, which happened to be near the legendary Stinehour Press, the finest letterpress book printer in North America. Thus the presence of Stinehour Press is a factor in some of the editorial decisions of what book to do and what not to do. They printed classic plays, *Everyone Has Sher Favorite (His or Hers)*, *George Herbert's Pattern Poems: In Their Tradition* and *some recent snowflakes (and other things)*. Their offset division also printed *Piano Album*. But that book includes a couple of graphic notations which, like most of my graphics, use the human nude. They had troubles with this. I was also then planning out *of celebration of morning*, which is in part a celebration of the body of its young protagonist, Justin. When they set the type for that book, there was no problem. But when they actually saw the mechanicals for it with all the photographs, they decided not to do the book. So I realized it was time to find another printer—and therefore, presumably, another home for myself.

A poet friend of mine, George Quasha, had started a small printing firm in the mid-1970s called Open Studio, which specialized in artists' books and literature. As the public funding for such work dried up at the turn of the decade, while other printers went under or searched more desperately for grants, Quasha decided instead to move into the area of commercial viability, specifically into the field of high quality printing. He therefore seemed like an appropriate neighbor and so I bought a small church, parsonage, and parish house up the hill from his home and editorial and art facilities. That is where I and Printed Editions now reside, and, except for *celebration*, he has printed all the recent books, not just for myself but for the other Printed Editions authors as well.

If *foew&ombwhnw* is a sort of summing up of whatever I had achieved up to 1969, then *of celebration of morning* (1980), my most complex single work to date, sums up my experience of the 1970s. On the one hand it is a story: the homoerotic (if not necessarily homosexual) celebration by an older man (not necessarily myself) of a younger one, who dies at the end of an overdose of heroin. The story is told in a cycle of poems which moves through the year from August to July, most of them in my snowflake form and following the theory of narrative I have referred to before, as one finds it in the Schlegel brothers. It also uses the same cyclical temporal structure as *7.7.73* and celebrates nature (including the human figure) in the same way. It also uses a thematic set of photographs, almost all of Justin, some of which have poems, mostly in snowflake form, written after the photographs. Most photographic images are presented in several forms, as line drawings or as photo-derivations, in one form or another. The styles of these visual materials are more appropriate to the narrator (unnamed) than to myself—which is to say that they are more like snapshots than like traditional art photographs; similarly, the line drawings are not of a fine art type but are more like comic book illustrations. The layout of the book is mostly off-square, askew, like a scrapbook rather than an art book. There are other strands to the braid too—a set of I Ching trigrams and hexagrams, providing a second cycle. Each page is called a "world"—"world 1," "world 2," and so on. A second, less systematic arrangement of the pages was determined by chance operations, giving an aleatoric factor: this sequence is given by the instruction on all pages (except page 60, where the printer left it off by mistake) to "Go to World 35," for example, and on "World 35" one is instructed to "Go to World 3." The poem on the month of May is nonexistent: its place is taken by a piece of music, "Long Arch," which is in snowflake form, a cancrizan. At every stage, all the elements interpenetrate—like a braid, as I said before. All in all, it is a "polysemiotic fiction" (my phrase on the title page) in which each element points to the others. There are also questions on every page, mostly chosen from remarks which the model said at one time or another, others which seemed suitable for the narrator, and few which deal with the fact that this is, in various ways, a book about a book— it is not "a celebration of morning" but "*of* celebration of morning"—or perhaps "of celebration of *mourning*," since there is little question but that this young man is in some way doomed, either to grow old (and to become himself like the narrator?) or, as it happens, to die. It is a complex book but, I hope, not indecipherable; I could not have achieved my desired result in a simpler way. The reader simply takes the work and makes what he will of it—a perfect work for my new audience-centered theoretical focus, of which more momentarily. It was also a suitable goodbye to my literary emphasis in the 1970s, since it was clear to me then that I must explore the implications of my work in music in a more rigorous way.

The reason for doing ambiguous work of this sort is to allow the participants—performers or readers or whatever—to use their own experience and capabilities in developing the eventual meaning of the work. This is nowhere more true than in my next Printed Editions book, *Ten Ways of Looking at a Bird* (1981), whose title is a playful variation on the name of a poem by Wallace Stevens whose work I have always admired, though, goodness knows, there is no modern poet more different from myself. This is a piece for violin and harpsichord; the harpsichord part is developed in "live time" (that is, during the performance) from what the violinist is doing, according to a set of rules. The violinist uses musical staves set over a set of ten blue photographs of the same model that I used in *celebration*; each movement uses a different gamut, or set of up to seven notes, which he may use in any octave or transposition, but which are the *only* notes he uses in any performance of that movement. Just *what* notes he uses is determined by his own skills and unique abilities—no "fully composed" realizations could take advantage of all the skills of all violinists—but there are also rules for using the photographs.

Twenty-Six Mountains for Viewing the Sunset From (1981) is for a small ensemble, including three dancers. It is a different kind of notation, not using photographs but using an indication of what kinds of textures and patterns are desired. The title comes from a trip I took late one night with a teenager from Vermont, who brought me to some of his favorite places to view the sunset from; it was magical evening, and I wanted to celebrate it in this twenty-six movement piece, each movement of which is characterized, somehow, by a fanciful description of a mountain which might or might not be spoken aloud at the time of the performance.

Sonata for Prepared Piano (1982) is a short work which, again, uses photo-derivations as parts of the notation—this time nature with incomplete figure photographs, mostly obscured by the natural objects around them.

Variations on a Natural Theme (1982) is a large orchestral work, in some ways a companion to the *Ten Ways*, since this time it uses gamuts (in this case selected by the individual musicians) and photo-derivations made from a female model; she was insistent that she not be recognizable, since she was a teacher and was afraid that it would be damaging to her professionally if it were known that she had posed for figure photographs. This was fine by me, since it fitted in with my plans to use very extreme derivations which are, at times, difficult to relate to the human figure at all. If performed, the work would sound rather like the *Ten Ways*. Socially the work interests me too, since it means that each musician must act creatively to work out his or her part and must therefore take the responsibility to make it sound according to his vision. Most musicians in most performances are near-automatons, and that does not accord with how I think human beings should be, especially in artistic situations—they should be (and the audience as well) as alert as the spectators at a boxing match, empathizing with each thrust and event, seeing where it all goes, and fitting into their own roles appropriately.

With *Variations* I have created musical paradigms to accord with my musical and visual art practice, and so my musical publishing can now become more intermittent. But what is next to do?

The theory that I set forth in *Dialectic of Centuries* lacked a teleology—I needed to state what the purpose of my practice (and the practice of many of my contemporaries) is and to suggest what was offered to the recipient of the work—performer, audience, reader, viewer, and so on. This lack was made up in an essay, "Horizons," which focuses on the fusion that occurs when the horizon of the recipient meets the horizon of the creator, myself or otherwise. I also needed a taxonomy of the works of my contemporaries, in the intermedia (visual poetry, sound poetry, etc.) and otherwise. This makes manifest the need for a second theory book, presumably to be called "Horizons," to develop these areas and to complete the critical system into which my work and that of so many contemporaries falls. Otherwise our learned brethren will come along and say, "This work does not do what X does (Beethoven, Pound, the structuralists, Picasso, whoever); therefore it is boring and not good." It is my task to point out not only wherein it is not boring but where the pleasure lies—an erotic of the new work is needed, and also, in such a taxonomy, to deal with the historical problems of such work, that they have a pedigree as old as that of mankind itself.

It would also be appropriate to prepare a collection of my early works, since few of these were collected into *foew&ombwhnw*; many of them were published in mimeographed booklets as acting scripts and suchlike. I should show the steps which led me to what I subsequently did, as parallel to the ratiocinations and inner arguments which philosophers use, to establish not only the validity of their points but as part of the points themselves; it is sometimes as important to show the paths one did not take as to show the course that one followed.

The collection of early visual poems and the homophonic anthology, both already mentioned, are well worth doing; I cannot afford to do them with Printed Editions, but perhaps some trade publisher would like to do them some day.

The Bruno translation should be completed, and "The Colors" should be published as what it is—the keystone cycle of my aleatoric texts. Perhaps my early novel, "Orpheus Snorts," should be published—it too relates to all this, since it follows a geometrical structure as well as its plot and is therefore in some sense an intermedial work.

What I do *not* want to do is to have a career, in the sense of filling commissions that do not tie in with my actual interests, to get my name into print "in all the right places" and anthologies; there are quite enough of those already (and of course these have their role, but not in the sense of keeping me from doing what only I can do—my real work). My real career should be, as I am currently fond of saying, a trajectory of satisfactions. And in that trajectory, each book should define a necessary and inevitable point in the trajectory as a whole, clearly related to the other points in the trajectory. Or perhaps, in my case, a better analogy would be to a "braid" of themes and interests, since I have chosen all the arts as my media or intermedia; each strand of the braid moves in a parallel direction to the others, intertwined with it and making up the characteristic quality of the whole. Make no mistake: no work was ever worth reading/watching/seeing/hearing *because* it was intermedial—many wonderful artists cannot, with integrity, move in more than one medium. My work is only intermedial because I am a child of my time, and because I am who I am—it is simply my nature to be that way.

A Book

Originally published in *New Wilderness Letter*, no. 11, 1983.

A book. Consider a book. Before one can consider a book, one must consider what it is to have a text. A text is an array of words on paper. Or, if not words, others things that are to be read. One can have a text with no words at all—music or visual entities or symbols.

But when we are talking about art—an art book, the art of language and not just information that is to be used for something other than the experience of being oneself—one must have a self or selves. One need not dwell upon it. But we are all complexes of past experiences and knowledges, each unique unto itself. One need not ask oneself, at the outset, "What is this self? Who is this me that I am being?" One needs no particular ego to experience art. But one does bring a certain horizon to the experience of a book which is its own past and complex of tastes and non-tastes, desires and non-desires, beings and non-beings. Like a ship moving towards a horizon, that horizon always recedes, no matter in what direction one moves. The complex of what one knows and what one does not know and what one knows without consciously considering it, that horizon is always in motion. And the text that is a work of art brings its horizon to us. The horizons intersect and interpenetrate.

Authors make texts when they offer us arrays of words which generate horizons that interpenetrate with ours, when they displace ours in the course of this interpenetration. The author is supremely unimportant while we are studying a text. If we want to know about apples, if we want to study why apples are as they are, *then* we must study about appletrees. But when we are hungry, we do not study about apples. We eat them. So it is with texts and authors. When we are hungry to experience our horizons in motion, the author is beside the point; here it is the text which the author has made that is important. For us it is our experience of the text which we are living with, not the text which the author thought he made. When Samuel Richardson wrote *Clarissa*, he thought that he was making a series of morally exemplary letters—prudish, perhaps. Instead he created what we experience as one of the most erotic novels in our language, erotic in its curious horizon of dwelling forever upon the sexual innuendo. Lately most criticism has dwelt upon the linguistics of the text, upon the structure and *langue* and *parole* and semiotics of the work. But judged as experience, that is relatively unimportant, since it is the effect of the style which is so crucial, the phenomenon of the generation of the horizons of Clarissa and her circle and how they fit and do not fit with ours. Same with Gertrude Stein, whose focus is upon the language of her horizon and ours: it is displacement. A structuralist and a semiotician would go mad trying to explain why Stein works when "it" (her work) works. For us, enjoying the diplacements of our horizons of language by hers, there is no problem. We each have our own horizons, our own hermeneutic for this (our own methodology of interpretation). I can document mine, and each human being who reads a Stein can learn to document hers or his. But the gut feelings that the work generates, the emotional and connotative and phatic elements, these do not come from what she says but from the process of matching how she says it with our own horizons.

A text can be spread over space without becoming a book. We can write it on a scroll and experience it as never-ending, unbroken. Most texts seem to have been written for experience upon scrolls—perhaps their authors think of life as scrolls. In point of fact, of course, scrolls have their own interesting qualities, their physicality and their unique continuity.

But a book, in its purest form, is a phenomenon of space and time and dimensionality that is unique unto itself. Every time we turn the page, the previous page passes into our past and we are confronted by a new world. In my *Of Celebration of Morning*, my book qua book which uses these ideas most purely, I even called each page "world 1," "world 2," and so on through the eighty pages. The only time a text exists in a solid block of time is when we are no longer reading it, unlike, for example, a single painting which is all present before us when we consider its presence physically. In this way a book is like music, which is only experienced moment by moment until it, too, is past and remembered as a whole. But the space of the book, even when it is not self-consciously shaped and patterned (as in visual novels or concrete poetry or comic books), is part of the experience. *Alice in Wonderland* written out by hand is a different work from *Alice in Wonderland* set in type; set in Baskerville, even, it is a different entity from what it would become set in some barely-legible but beautiful Old English blackletter face. It is, as it were, translated when it is set from one face to another, just as surely as if it had been paraphrased into another language. All literature exists only in translation for this reason—it is displaced from the author's intention, displaced visually by being presented to us upon the page, displaced by us conceptually every time we experience it by reading it, displaced according to our horizons at the moment. One time we read a text with passion, one time coolly, one time in a desultory way, one time with great attention to the characters and gestalts generated by the text, another time with our eye on the horizons of our language and that of the text.

The book is, then, the container of a provocation. We open it and are provoked to match our horizons with those implied by the text. We need not consider ourselves to do this; but the more vivid our horizons and the more vivid the gestalts and horizons in the text, the more vivid the displacements and coincidences of these horizons. And therein lies the true pleasure of the text, the true erotic of literature. Criticism which ignores this does so at its peril—it may be fashionable for a moment, but it will die. Great criticism always keeps its eye on the horizons of work at hand and so, like Coleridge's lectures on Shakespeare, always exists upon three horizons of time—its subject's, the critic's and ours. Perhaps that is the crucial difference between criticism and poetry, for example—the first has three horizons, the latter has two to offer. Not that "the more the merrier," of course. Two horizons can be plenty. But the book that is clear upon what horizons it can offer up for our experience (whatever nonsense its author may have intended it to be), that book is well upon its way to matching its horizons with our and is, thus, on the tract of potential greatness.

There is no need to bother with the rest.

274

Letter to Steve McCaffery

Originally transcribed, typeset, and published in *Horizons: The Poetics and Theory of the Intermedia*, Carbondale: Southern Illinois University Press, 1984. This is the first facsimile publication and comes from the correspondence between Higgins and Steve McCaffery that began April 17, 1976 and continued until Higgins's death in 1998. Steve McCaffery (b. 1947) was then a central figure in the Toronto literary avant-garde. Transcribed and annotated, the correspondence exists as a 525-page manuscript in the Steve McCaffery Archive.

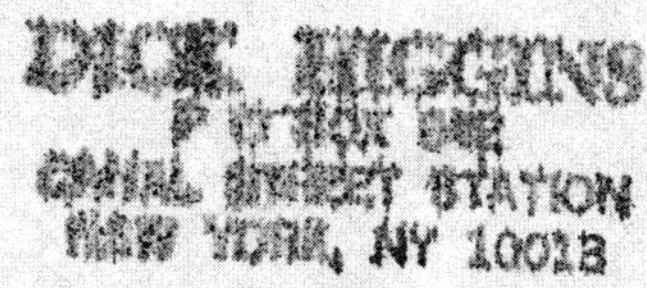

3 October, 1977

Ah, Caro Stefano---

        Many thanks for your sharp response-- that's just what
I needed for the TELEOLOGY paper. It didn't feel right to me,
as I'd been working it up: thus I typed it out and sent you
the carbon. But sent out no other copies. I did show it to
Alison, who noted its sketchy writing: but she didn't identify the
really weak parts of my discussion.

        I do not agree with your defense of Derrida but am
very interested by it: I've looked through a copy of GLAS
but haven't gotten one for my very own chewing. As for his
vocabulary, if I say

                THIS SENTENCE IS INCONSISTENT

                                        does that
either make it inconsistent? Or does it make some discussion
of which it is a part <u>more</u> consistent? True, I like the paradox
involved in saying such a thing. But I don't think it solves
any of the problems.

        Where can I get the Lucette Finas texts to which you
refer?

        Probably I should simply postpone (again) any discussion
on my part of the Paris Mafia-- I do think the concept is useful
and not just amusing or satyrical: for the last year I've been
reading bushels of books in the area-- the two fine Jonathan Culler
books, Bense and Heissenbüttel (have you seen his three little
lollypops from <u>Diana's Bimonthly</u> (71 Elmgrove Ave., Providence,
RI 02906: "Novel," "Schematic Development of Tradition," and
"The Dilemma of Being High and Dry"-- $1 each)), Jakobson-- part
of whose theory I like,-- and Barthes, Eco, Derrida, Lacan and
Lyotard, among whom familiarity brings an increasing perception of
similarities. I agree that the implications of these gents for
new art and writing haven't been followed through except in a minor
way (eg., Maurice Roche), but to do so would seem to me very after-
the-fact-- "thin-making," to allude to your phrase in the letter.

        But ah, to sign the sign (and humanize it), to stress
the direct and indirect signified-- you are quite right, that is
the teleology of my a.r. idea, and should be the purpose of my

paper, not to fret over the teleological confusion of the
Parisian Brethren. (Notice: no women? Why?) Furthermore,
you've pointed up some confusion of my own, for which I thank
thee.

Do I see a structural primacy in my poems, you ask: no, I see
a constant dialectic on as many levels as possible. Hence my
attraction to Ramus and Bruno. Hence my "intermedia" notion.
Hell, it even affects my sexuality. I am attracted and moved
by multi-hattedness. And the forms I use reflect this. Eg.,
in classic plays and in the new everyone has sher favorite (his
or hers) and elsewhere there are many poems in what I call my
"snowflake" form-- visually symmetrical, with the visual structure
tied to the semantic sense and thus in constant interplay.
example:

                    those pieces

                              that move like this

                    those pieces

                                        i say

                                              are snowflakes

                                        i say

                    those pieces

                              that move like this

                    those pieces

They are symmetrical visually and conceptually: the form falls
apart (ie., it seems silly) when it is used abstractly-- either
non-semantically or acoustically a la sound-poetry (it seems
arbitrary), but when the snoflake is in dialectic with content,
it tends to feel quite natural. Similarly, there's a form I've used
a lot since moments in the lives of great women and before (in
foew&ombwhnw) where the form is simply a triangle or pair of triangle

                    a short
                    line must be
                    followed by much longer
                    lines until a strong visual shape results

the triangle or triangles can go either way:

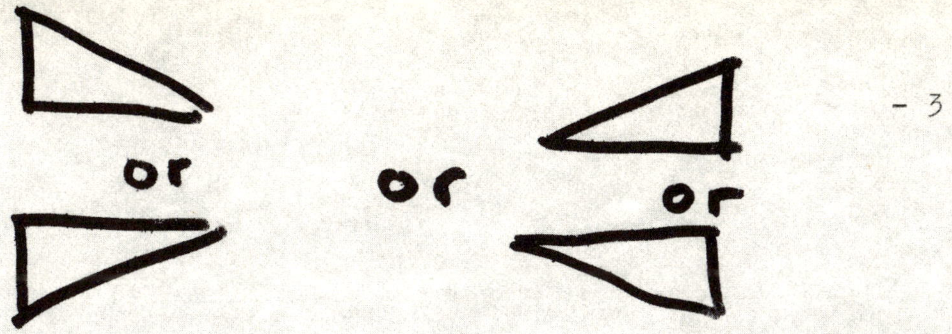

Of course, my example is just that: I almost never carry an
idea from one idea into the next line except for variation
or to create momentum-- I like to use the length for its own
sake, certainly a la George Herbert in <u>Easter Wings</u> and a la
one kind of W. C. Williams.   The triangle form inplies two kinds
of rectangles also:

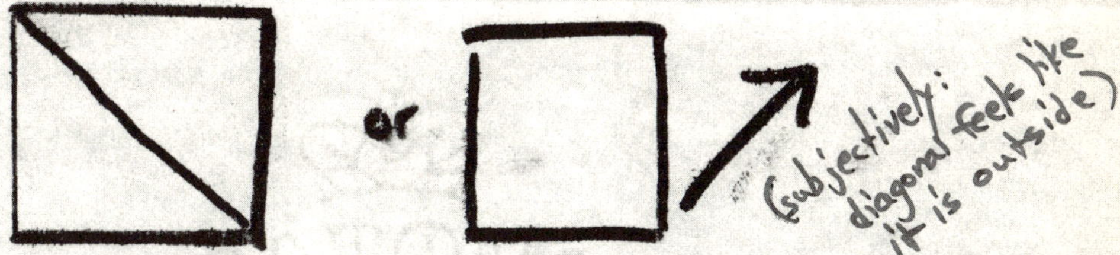

The two triangles form one, and the exact repeats form another.

```
abbbbbbb                the long one is very clear
aabbbbbb                is the short?
aaabbbbb        or      is the short?
aaaabbbb                is the short?
aaaaabbb                is the short?
aaaaaabb                is the short?
aaaaaaab                is the short?
                        the long one is very clear
```

The stasis of the second kind seems to work best when it is in
contrast with something quite different before or afterwards.

Finally, the triangles can align to form a rhombus:

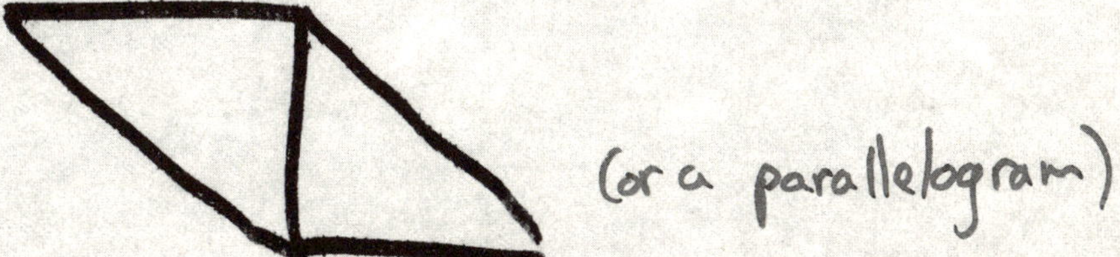

And/or the rhombus can be presented or imitated with right angles
only (which relates to the second kind of rectangle also), or a
series of these kinds of structures can be nested, giving a sort
of caryatid which could in most cases project into infinity a la
Brancusi.

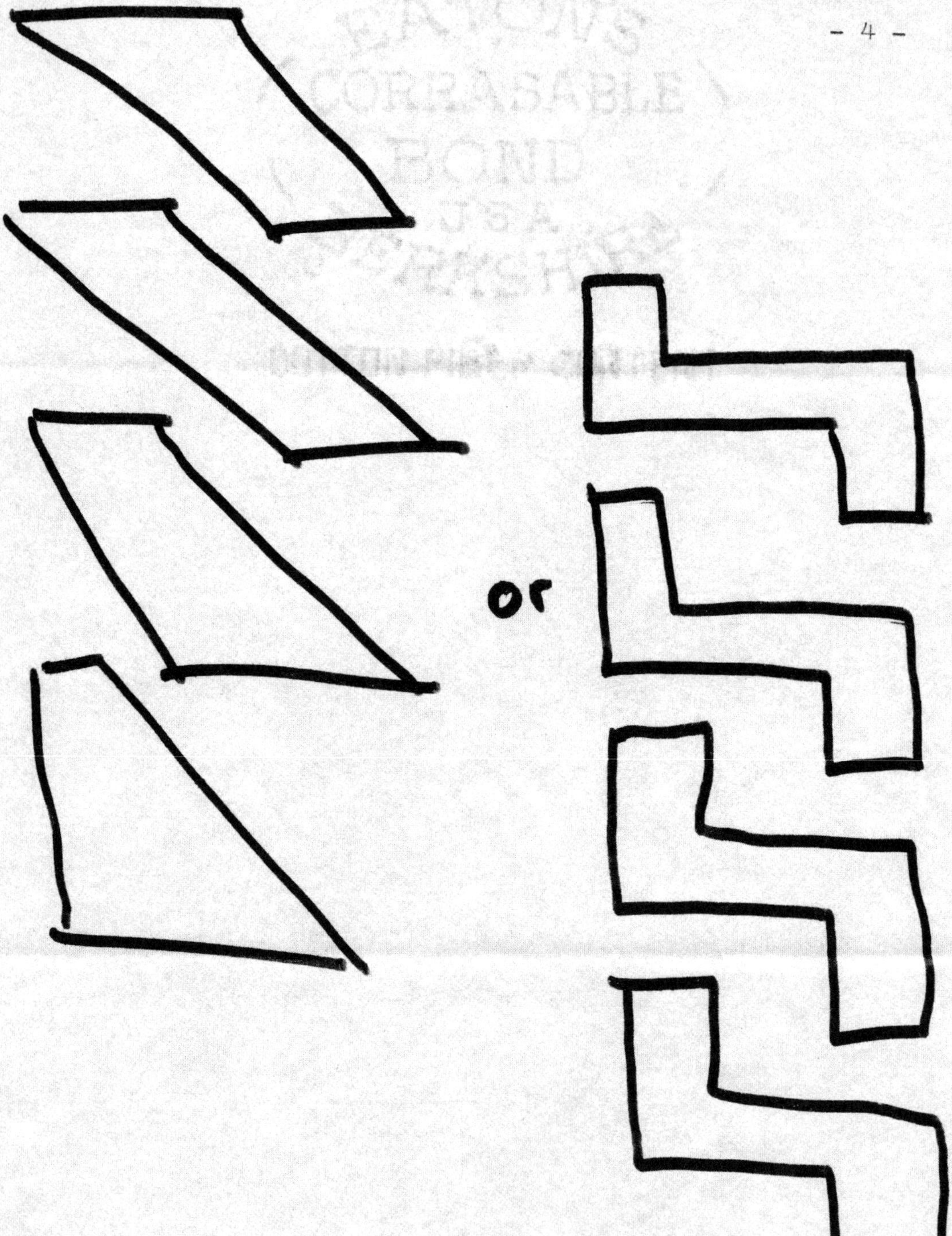

or

Obviously such caryatids can either repeat the same form
exactly (as in the right hand example) or they can follow
some modular progression of their own (as in the left hand
example). So: as the term "structure" is used by traditional
literary critics, those shapes aren't structures. As "structure"
is used by art historians-- eg. Michel Seuphor in his critiques
in the 1940's and 50's of geometric abstract painting-- they
are indeed structures. And in terms of the Paris brethren,
they imply structures though they aren't structures. So,
am I structure oriented? Among other things, yes. But I
don't think it's as meaningful to call me that as process-
oriented-- the process of allusion and reference interests me
far more than either signifier or signified (or any other thing),
and the active process of relation between language and meaning,
form and content, structure and reference is much more interesting
to me than either polarity. I just ain't the pure type.

        As for McCaffery in NYC-- I'd welcome you any time,
but late December sandwiched among the usual deluge of Christmas
visitors and, in my case, term papers-- alas, I fear 'twould be
a horrific disappointment. BUT please let me urge you to visit in
mid-or-late-mid January (ideally anytime between January 19th and
29th)-- at that time you could stay with us, I'd be relatively
unscheduled (and thus free to take you hither and yon and to
talk and think with you in a more leisurely way than December
would offer)-- surely we could set up a reading for you: I'm sure
Charles Bernstein would be so glad to hear you were coming too--
I passed a very interesting evening with him last weekend-- fine
guy. What're the chances?

        And so-- onwards-- besides the Parisian affliction I'm
enjoying some folkloristic/culturo-historical cure in the form of
a yard or so of books by Mercia Eliade-- oh so rich (especially
NO SOUVENIRS)--

                        As ever

IV

Pattern Poetry, Visual Poetry, Sound Poetry

A Short History of Pattern Poetry

Originally published as the first chapter of *Pattern Poetry: Guide to an Unknown Literature*, Albany: State University of New York Press, 1987.

Once upon a time there was a form that wasn't a form; perhaps it was a tribe. The story of pattern poetry is, in fact, not the story of a single development of one simple form, but the story of an ongoing human wish to combine the visual and literary impulses, to tie together the experience of these two areas into an aesthetic whole. Pattern poetry did not originate in any one simple situation or even century, as, for example, the opera did in the late sixteenth century in Florence and elsewhere in Italy. It is, rather, a maze within a maze covered over with obscurity, an attempt which recurs century after century to make the synthesis, in almost every Western literature and many Eastern ones. To those who attempt this synthesis, something of the picture of the whole seems crucially important. A visual poem has always suggested its own traditions, but to make a tradition the artist cannot feel that he or she is operating without any precedent—there must always be a trajectory through time, even when the entire story is not known. So it is that in the 1950s and 1960s the concrete poets were intensely conscious of their antecedents in dada and futurism, and, for all their apparent anti-intellectualism, the dadaists and futurists felt themselves in an iconoclastic tradition which included visual poetry somewhere in the background. For example, Waldemar Deonna, who wrote one of the early studies of pattern poetry in 1926, also published a good number of works in futurist publications. And each wave of pattern poets drew on at least some knowledge of earlier pattern poetry. Even those works which appear to come at the very beginnings of pattern poetry cannot be stated definitely as being beginnings; we can only say that no earlier ones have survived.

Pattern poetry is extremely hard to define, since it is no one thing. But it is, at least, both visual and literary art—visual poetry. The visual poetry of the twentieth century is rather well known, and its subclasses—concrete poetry, *poesia visiva, parole in libertà*, etc.—are fairly clearly defined. For the moment it will suffice to define pattern poetry in very general terms as visual poetry from before the twentieth century but in any Western literature. That there is visual poetry in non-Western literatures is not surprising, since, as I have mentioned, it seems to be so universal a tendency to attempt the synthesis of visual and literary experience.

Pattern poetry is itself a fairly modern concept; the origin of the term is unknown, but it appeared sometime in the nineteenth century, along with the synonymous term, "shaped poetry." How the earlier pattern poets felt about their work, how they saw it as fitting into the whole of literature or art, is largely unknown, though we shall deal with this too in due course. But it seems unlikely that the renaissance or baroque poets would have been happy with simply isolating what we call pattern poems from their cognates in sound poetry and analogous forms. The forms associated with pattern poetry—leonine verse, proteus poems, and various kinds of inchoate sound poetry, for instance—are not always visual. But in many cases, the poets who did them composed pattern poetry as well. They seem to have had some sense of these being alternate forms of poetry, intended to enrich the fabric of poetry as a whole (and perhaps of visual art). In addition, the distinction between poetry and prose is not always a binding one. Thus, there is a tradition

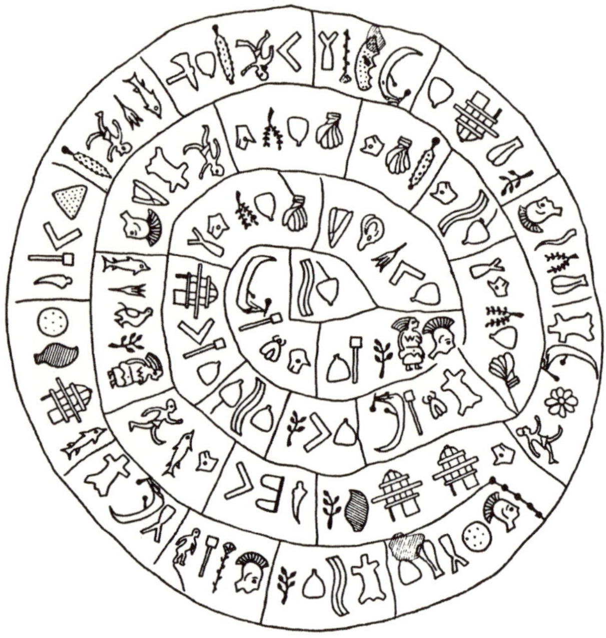

Figure 1: The "Phaistos Disk."

of shaped prose as well as of shaped poetry. And there are even graphic musical notations—one would be tempted to call them pattern notations—which are part of the picture of the analogues of pattern poetry.

Too, the terminology associated with pattern poetry is hard to make consistent; it is unfamiliar enough that virtually every critic who has attempted to describe pattern poetry and its subforms means something different from every other critic using the same terms. But we should repeat once more that there is, in fact, no consensus on what the terms mean. I have tried to use a common sense approach in this regard, inventing no terms of my own but repeating a sort of statistical averaging of what others seems to mean by this or that term.

The theoretical implications of pattern poetry and the questions which it raises, the problems of what our ignorance and understanding of the subject mean—these things cannot really be dealt with until enough material has been gone over to make our theorizing appropriate. The questions cannot be posed in vacuo without seeming more abstruse than they are or quite irrelevant; or, equally bad, "for specialists only," which is damning in a subject in which there are almost no actual specialists and in which the work should be of interest to anyone who wishes to understand whatever it is about our visual and literary experience which pattern poetry can explain.

And if this book makes anything clear, it is that pattern poetry is far, far more widespread than most people realize. One hears it said that there are, perhaps, one hundred pattern poems. But everyone who knows any of them seems to know a different hundred from everyone else. The French scholar knows the French materials, the German scholar the German ones, and, while most scholars know at least the most famous group of pieces, those that have come down to us from Hellenistic times, in the medieval collections known as the "Greek Anthology" or the "Planudian Manuscript," most scholars do not know many pieces apart from their various individual disciplines. And almost nobody seems to know very many of the pieces in the largest group of all, that in Neo-Latin poetry. In fact, we have collected some fourteen hundred or so pieces in the various Western literatures.

The story of pattern poetry is, as I have said, a complex and ambiguous one, complicated by its overall obscurity. The story has been told mostly without regard to the field as a whole, by specialists of one kind or another, in spite of the fact that the larger public, when confronted by some actual pieces, tends to find them interesting or at least exciting.

The earliest known pieces that are possibly pattern poems are the two texts on the faces of the "Phaistos Disk," a modest-sized grey disk from roughly 1700 B.C. (see fig. 1) which is in the Heraklion Museum on Crete. These are certainly spiral-shaped and they are certainly texts, but are they poetry? Since they are written in Minoan A, which has not been deciphered, this question cannot be answered with any degree of certainty. However, one can say that it is unlikely that they are prose in any mundane sense, business letters for instance, since it is most improbable that straight prose would be arrayed in a spiral form. Furthermore, the distinction between prose and poetry is not always applicable to very early writings. For example, the Hebrew Bible is often poetic prose to the extent of seeming like what we today call prose poems. So it seems to be with many such early texts. Another thing which should be noted about the Phaistos Disk is, however, that its origin is uncertain. Nothing is known from Crete which resembles it, thus raising the possibility that it was brought, at some unknown point, to Crete from wherever it was made. Therefore, it is best thought of as some sort of enigmatic forerunner of a more substantial group of pieces.

These are the six Hellenistic Greek patterns, evidently composed between 325 B.C. and A.D. 200, and shaped as two altars, an egg, a pair of wings (see fig. 2), an axe, and a syrinx. Very little is known about the poets, though none is anonymous; only Theocritus is at all well-known, and the dates of the others remain somewhat controversial. Furthermore, the pieces have never been truly unknown to those who would seek them out. One does not feel, when one reads them, as if they were innovative or avant-garde in their time. Rather, they seem like surviving texts from a

ΠΤΕΡΥΓΕΣ ΕΡΩΤΟΣ

Λεῦσσέ με τὸν Γᾶς τε βαθυστέρνου ἄνακτ', Ἀκμονίδαν τ' ἄλλυδις ἑδράσαντα,
μηδὲ τρέσῃς, εἰ τόσος ὢν δάσκια βέβριθα λάχνᾳ γένεια.
τᾶμος ἐγὼ γὰρ γενόμαν, ἁνίκ' ἔκραιν' Ἀνάγκα,
πάντα δὲ Γᾶς εἶκε φραδαῖσι λυγραῖς
ἑρπετά, πάνθ' ὅσ' ἕρπει
δι' αἴθρας.
Χάους δέ,
οὔτι γε Κύπριδος παῖς
ὠκυπέτας οὐδ' Ἄρεος καλεῦμαι·
οὔτι γὰρ ἔκρανα βίᾳ, πραϋλόγῳ δὲ πειθοῖ·
εἶκε δέ μοι γαῖα, θαλάσσας τε μυχοί, χάλκεος οὐρανός τε·
τῶν δ' ἐγὼ ἐκνοσφισάμαν ὠγύγιον σκᾶπτρον, ἔκρινον δὲ θεοῖς θέμιστας.

Figure 2: Simmias of Rhodes, "The Wings" (ca. 325 B.C.).

lost tradition of some kind. This does not seem unlikely, since they all come down to us from the "Greek anthology," which was compiled sometime in the early Middle Ages by unknown editors as poems which were acceptable to the church, probably to be used as reading materials for those few who studied Greek at that time. Except for the piece by Theocritus, the poems are all religious, perhaps intended to serve some mystical or magical function. It has been speculated that these five were originally texts intended to be inscribed on sacred objects.

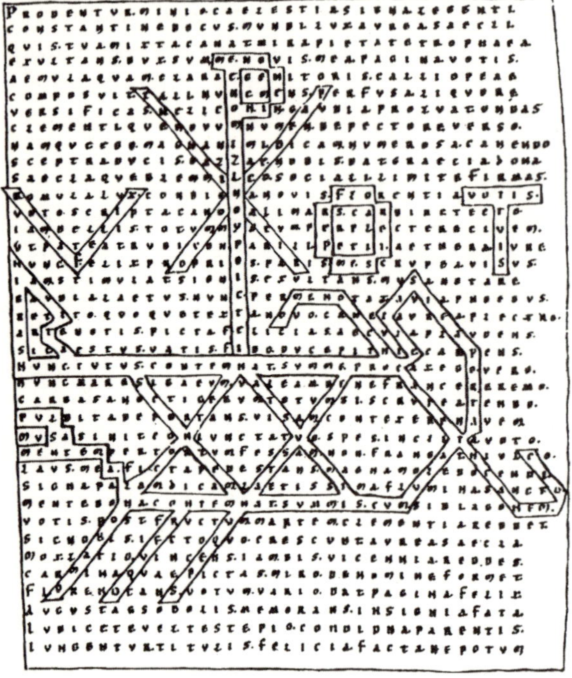

Figure 3: Optatian, "Carmen XIX," the trireme, folio 7 of the Paris Manuscript, in "Ein Fulder Miniturhandschrift der K. K. Hofbibliothek" (1892).

The fact that we have no entire pattern poem from Classical Latin literature does not mean that none existed, merely that none has survived. In fact, Laevius (first century A.D.) is known to have written a phoenix-shaped piece which only survives in a fragment quoted in a later work. In addition, there are several pieces in Greek, but from Rome, carved in marble between 50 B.C. and A.D. 50, known as "tabulae iliacae" because their faces depict scenes from Homer's *Iliad*. Nothing is known about the sculptor but his name, Theodoros, which appears on one of the pieces. The texts, which appear on the backs, are permutational, evidently intended to serve some magical function. They closely resemble cabalistic texts that date from a much later period.

But there are twenty-five pattern poems by Optatian (fl. A.D. 325), rectangles for the most part, sometimes called "carmina quadrata," with secondary texts within the body of the main one, cancelled out from the background (so that they are also "carmina cancellata"); because these texts include other texts, the interior texts are also called "intexti" or "intexts," and they are also "mesostics" in that some inner array of letters forms such an intext (see fig. 3). As for Optatian, he probably came from Africa, and his poems are panegyrics, praises of Constantine the Great. They must have pleased the Emperor because he appointed Optatian to be his court poet around A.D. 325.

We now come to one of the typical aspects of pattern poetry, which is its characteristic function of serving very specific social purposes as occasional verse. Occasional verse has a bad reputation, since most of us assume that poetry is intended only to serve eternity. But the very fact that a pattern poem is visual, that it evokes shapes which are suitable as commemorative objects, means that it was recognized as adding to its subject in some way a visual dimension which is perhaps comparable to the function of allusion that is so much at the heart of our traditional verse. It somehow reduces the sense of datedness and triviality which occasional verse is apt to evoke. We will see this again most notably when we get to baroque pattern poetry. Nobody would argue that Optatian was one of the great

Latin poets; he simply isn't. His language is rather flat and extravagant, his imagery opaque. But that he is remembered at all is probably due to his visually striking works. In their original form, according to the scholia in the Kluge and Polara editions, the pieces were executed in precious metal letters on dark blue or purple backgrounds. But unfortunately they have not survived in that form, so that the extent of their visual appeal in their original form cannot be measured. Rather, they survive in several manuscripts of a much later date. And even here, our usual experience of the pieces is similarly inadequate, because usually we see the poems in typeset versions which are less visually striking than they would be in manuscript. Thus, the extent of their visual effectiveness is difficult to measure, and it is unfair to judge them by their literary quality alone. One of the pieces, "Carmen XIX," (see fig. 3) is a carmen cancellatum of a trireme with sailes; what can it have looked like in the original? "Carmen XX" is an organ, with its right-hand side forming a sort of syrinx effect. "Carmen XXVI" is an altar. Do these last two indicate that there was any degree of consciousness on the poet's part that the Hellenistic Greeks had found the syrinx and altar suitable shapes for their own pattern poems? We can only speculate, but it could form the evidence of a tradition.

The cross in Gardthausen (see fig. 4), probably from the fifth century, is the earliest known cruciform poem. There are also a goodly number of anonymous Greek and Latin minor pieces from the early Christian period. But the next major pattern poet is Venantius Fortunatus (ca. 540–600), one of the principle writers of the Merovingian Frankish kingdom. He composed three surviving rectangular carmina cancellata, and one cruciform poem in which the text seems to be only a formality needed to flesh in the whole as a symbolic or ceremonially evocative entity; that the piece has come down to us as one of the most consistently popular of pattern poems, surviving into the nineteenth century in German where it was worn as a good luck talisman and called the

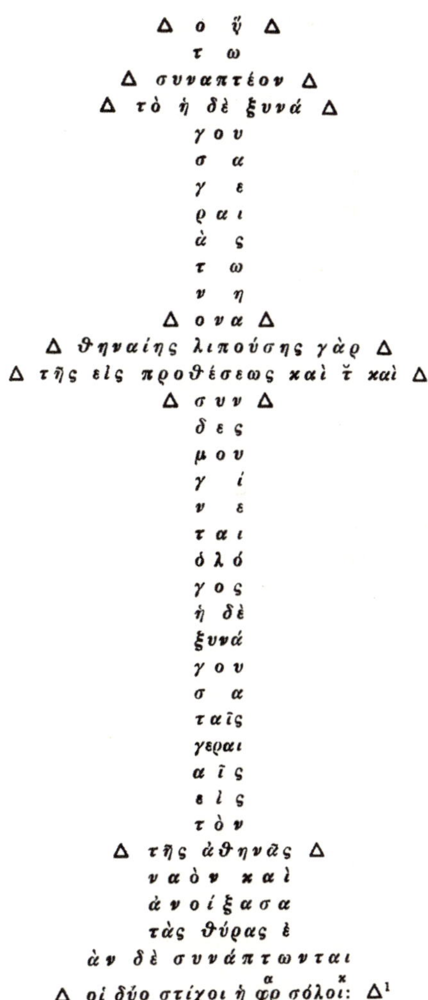

Figure 4: The earliest known cross-shaped poem. From Viktor Gardthausen, *Griekische Paläographie.* Leipzig: Verlag von Viet, 1913.

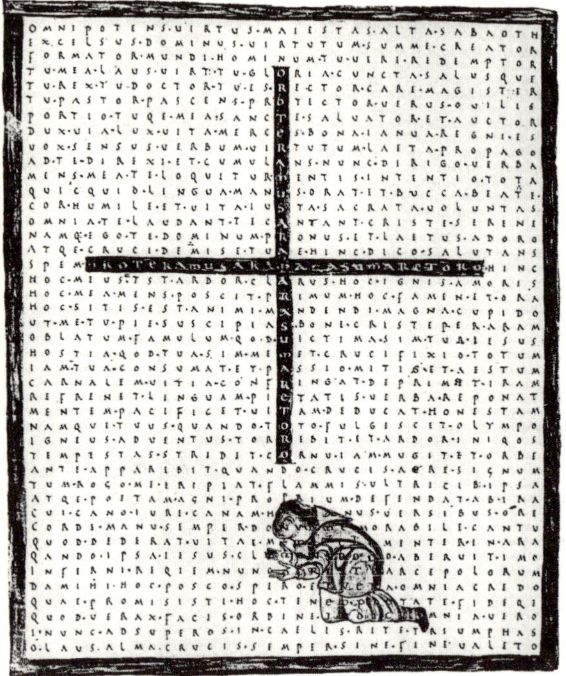

Figure 5: "Poem XXX" from Hrabanus Maurus, *De laudibus sanctae crucis* (ca. 845), "Codex Vinobadensis 652."

"Thomaskreuz." Since Venantius is also the author of other, more traditional hymns and poems which show an excellent poetic sense, it is not reasonable to suppose that he did not know what he was doing when he departed from normative poetry into pattern poetry; and since the poetry of his time is virtually all extremely conservative, one suspects he knew many pattern poems which have not survived. Venantius is also the first pattern poet whose works do *not* display any reference to the Hellenistic Greek pieces. Of course, he may well have known some of them; but his shapes do not duplicate theirs, though they do seem somewhat similar to Optatian's. In Venantius, we really enter medieval literature.

Passing over such minor works as a carmen cancellatum by Winifried (St. Boniface, 680–755) and a modest cruciform poem by the Lombard poet and historian Paul the Deacon (ca. 720–97), the next important group of pattern poems comes from the Carolingian period, by Alcuin (775–804), Charlemagne's tutor, by Josephus Scottus (ninth century); and others. The first highlight of this body of materials is the *De laudibus sanctae crucis* of Hrabanus Maurus (784–856), abbot of Fulda and a formidable poet, who wrote the Roman Catholic hymn for Pentecost, "Veni creator spiritus," whose ecstatic flavor Gustav Mahler catches perfectly in his setting of it in the first movement of his *Symphony No. 8.* For those familiar with this setting, the quality of Hrabanus's thirty carmina cancellata in the *De laudibus* will come as no surprise. They are joyful meditations covering the principal points of the Christian faith as Hrabanus saw them. The intexts are rather simple, almost in the nature of inscriptions and formulae; the poetry is in the field texts from which the intexts emerge, and in the relationship between the two (see fig. 5). In addition, the original work survives in at least three exquisite manuscript versions, both equally valuable. Unfortunately, many people know these pieces only from typeset versions in which the visual dimension is greatly reduced; thus, we should be extremely skeptical of criticism of the pieces which does not reflect some knowledge specifically of one or the other manuscript version, two of which have been published, the one in facsimile and the other in black and white.

Following Hrabanus's time, carmina cancellata slowly wane, with only a very few pieces being known from the tenth century, though these include the exquisite pieces by a monk from Riojas province in Spain, Vigila de Albeda (= Vigilán), who made five magnificent carmina cancellata that are almost unknown; fortunately, they have been reprinted recently.

The eleventh century is close to being a void, with only one Latin piece by Pierre Abèlard, plus a Greek one for the Emperess Eudocia Macrenbolitissa. However, the gap begins to be filled in the twelfth century with the first known Hebrew pattern poems, the tree by Abraham ben Ezra (d. 1167) and the pieces by the two Abuláfias, Abraham ben Samuel Abuláfia (1240–ca. 1291) and Tadros Abuláfia (d. after 1298), the latter of whom composed another tree, while the former wrote a series of circular pieces which are cabalistic permutations of a simple text. With the appearance of the trees we have the first natural form that we know definitely to have been introduced since the Greeks. One might speculate that this is due to the influence of Hebrew micrographic texts, a genre of work which was new at that time. These are pieces in which a text is chosen, usually from the law or some other part of the Jewish Bible, and is then shaped into a brilliant visual display, with phoenixes, dragons, knights and other beings—or sometimes simply ingenious geometrical formations. These works cannot be considered pattern poems, since either the poet was not responsible for the visual element or the artist was not responsible for the poem. But the works are splendid in their own right. The tradition appears to have originated in the levant in the ninth century and to have spread westward through Italy, finally dying out in the sixteenth century in Spain and Portugal. Also in the thirteenth century we find a copy of Hrabanus Maurus's "De laudibus" was made by the Nürnberg scribe Berthold, indicating that the knowledge of earlier visual poetry remained alive. This is important if one wishes to argue for the continuity of pattern poetry.

Now we come to Nicolò de' Rossi (ca. 1290–ca. 1348), who wrote what may be the earliest pattern poems in any modern language, his "Canzone 247" and "248." While it would be foolish to assert that the two pieces are definitely influenced by Sanskrit citra-kāvyas, still the special characteristics of the pieces are significant enough and similar enough to these that they are at the very least a remarkable instance of parallel development. In Western pattern poetry, the poem normally stands alone; in the citra-kāvyas, the piece is usually given twice, once visually and once in a linear transcription—as are de' Rossi's. The shapes of the poems suggest a necklace and a fourteen-spoke wheel, both unknown in pattern poetry but both common in citra-kāvyas. De' Rossi says in his scholia that the pieces represent a star and an arch, but they do not look like either. While direct cultural influence on Italy from India was minimal at this time, we might speculate that the poet saw some manuscript which worked its way to Italy, recognized the pieces as interesting, even if he could not read what they said, tried his hand at similar pieces, and then, concerned that they not be acknowledged as pagan, might have called them whatever images seemed most acceptable. Poets have been doing such things since time immemorial. And, even if the pieces are not influenced by the citra-kāvyas, they are at least very strikingly parallel.

Later in the fourteenth century we find the florid and startling poetic experiments of Iacobus Nicholae de Dacia (Jakob Nielsen, fl. 1363–79), a Dane who, around 1363, produced the "Liber de distinccione metrorum." This work, which exists in two manuscripts, "Ms Cotton Claudius A XIV" at the British Library and "Ms Latin 10323" at the Bibliothèque Nationale in Paris, and which was published in 1967 in an edition by Aage Kabell, includes a triangle, a series of concentric squares, a geometrical construction on squares, a complex star, and a wheel with concentric circles—all new shapes to pattern poetry. The work also includes some startling experiments in alliteration which approach being sound poetry. The whole work revels in novel forms. The fourteenth century was a time of great change in the arts, with the *musica antiqua* being gradually replaced by the *musica nova* and with the earliest graphic musical notations also dating from this time, with medieval painting being replaced by renaissance painting, and it is not surprising that Iacobus should participate in this change. Also during the fourteenth century, one finds some magnificent shaped prose, such as the anonymous "Clm 7960" manuscript in the Bayerische Staatsbibliothek in München, which include six similar urns or jars and one archway, meditations on the John ii, 6 in the New Testament.

The fifteenth century was perhaps less inclined towards formal innovation than the fourteenth, and, correspondingly, there are almost no known pattern poems, only the "Litera Pythagora" by Janus Pannonius (1432–72), a Y-shaped poem, and perhaps Eneo Silvio Piccolomini's labryinth (if it *is* authentic), but rather little else in actual poetry. However, a good deal of shaped prose was produced during this time, such as, at the end of the century, the *Hypnerotomachia Poliphilis* of Francesco Colonna (d. 1527), which was first published by the great printer Aldus Manutius in 1497 at Venezia.

However, shortly after the beginning of the sixteenth century we find the start of the largest body of pattern poetry of all, which continues through the baroque and into the eighteenth century. That such a convergence of the visual and literary as pattern poetry should occur here is not surprising, since, as Robert J. Clement makes clear throughout the first chapter of his book *The Peregrine Muse* (Studies in Romance Languages and Literatures, Chapel Hill: University of North Carolina Press, 1969, 13–42), literary and fine art theory were extremely close at that time, to the point that painting was sometimes thought of as "silent poetry," and poetry as "blind painting." What else are we to make of such a passage as the following by Giordano Bruno (1548–1600), in his *De imaginum, signorum et idearum compositione* (1598, bk. 1, pt. 2, chap. 20; in Bruno, *Opera latine conscripta*, ed. V. Tocco et al, 1889, vol. 2, pt. 3, 198):

Alibi dixi de cognatione quadam mira, quae est inter veros poetas,
qui ad eandem speciem referuntur atque musici, veros pictores et
veros philosophos; quandoquidem vera philosophia musica seu

poesis et pictura est, vera pictura et est musica et philosophia, vera poesis seu musica est divina sophia quaedam et pictura.

Elsewhere I spoke of a marvelous kinship that exists among true poets, who are to be referred along with musicians to the same species, that exists as well between true painters and philosophers since true philosophy is music as well as poetry and painting, true painting is also music and philosophy, true poetry and music are a kind of divine wisdom and paint painting. (Translated by Charles Doria)

Most of the early pieces among the renaissance pattern poems are in Latin, such as the wings, birds in flight, "Song for Priapus," and undulating acrostic which may be either hills or wings, by Laurentius Curtius (= Lancino Curzio, d. 1511) in his *Epigrammaton libri decem* (1521). A wing-shaped poem (it looks more like an axe, but see fig. 6) from France in Latin, is found in the *Epithalamion liber . . .* (1531) of Salmonius Macrinus [Jean Salmon Maigret, 1490–1572], while a third one was composed in French by Melin de Sainct Gelays (1481–1558) to celebrate the recovery of the queen mother from an illness. There are, in fact, quite a few French pattern poems of the sixteenth century by François Rabelais (1494?–1553), Jean Antoine de Baïf (1532–89), and Simon Bouquet (n.d., but sixteenth century), among others. One set of pyramids that is of strikingly high quality is the set of four inverted pyramids by Jean de Boyssières (1555–ca. 1583) in *Les troisièmes oeuvres de Boyssières* (1579); these are not occasional verse but very intense and inspired poetry, in which the emotional curve of the poem follows the shape of the lines in a deep way.

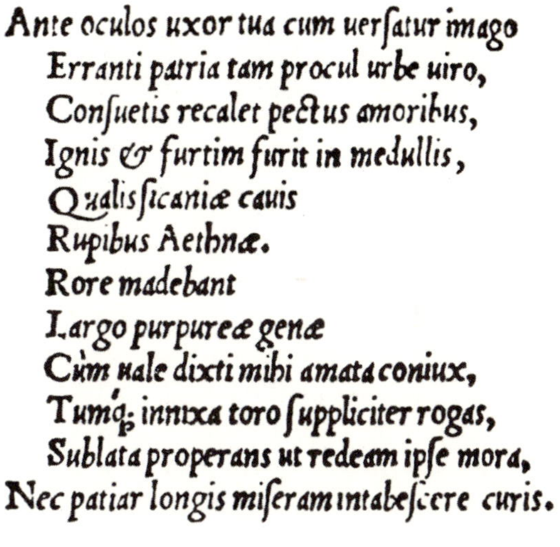

Ante oculos uxor tua cum uersatur imago
Erranti patria tam procul urbe uiro,
Consuetis recalet pectus amoribus,
Ignis & furtim furit in medullis,
Qualis sicaniæ cauis
Rupibus Aethnæ.
Rore madebant
Largo purpureæ genæ
Cùm uale dixti mihi amata coniux,
Tumq̲ innixa toro suppliciter rogas,
Sublata properans ut redeam ipse mora,
Nec patiar longis miseram intabescere curis.

Figure 6: A wing-shaped poem from the *Epithalamion liber . . .* (1531) by Salmonius Macrinus (Jean Salmon Maigret, 1490–1572).

British pattern poetry begins in the last quarter of the century with eight Latin pieces—an altar, a sword, an egg, a pear, a syrinx, a set of wings, an inverted pyramid, and an axe—in the *Poematum liber . . .* (1573) of Richard Willis (ca. 1545–1600), a pillar-shaped love poem in English by Thomas Watson (155?– 92) in the *'Ekatompathia* (1582), and an acrotelestic monument by King James VI of Scotland (I of England, 1566–1625) in his youthful work *The essayes of a prentise, in the divine art of poesie . . .* (1585). It has been claimed that a poem by Stephen Hawes (d. 1523) in *The convercyon of swerers* (1509) is a pattern poem, but for reasons we discuss

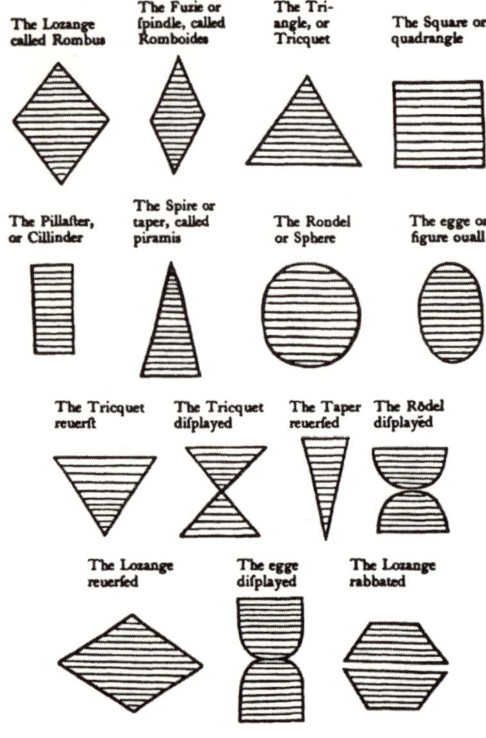

Figure 7: These are the shapes which George Puttenham (d. 1590) considered suitable for pattern poetry, from his *The arte of english poesis* (1587).

in our English section we cannot accept this. What is most striking about the English materials is their formal conservatism. Probably 85% of the pieces are in shapes known from the Hellenistic Greek pieces, supplemented by a few additional ones, such as columns and some geometrical forms, prescribed in one of the earliest works on poetics which describes pattern poetry, *The arte of english poesie* by George or Richard Puttenham. Puttenham suggests fifteen shapes as suitable for pattern poems and gives several examples using these (see figure 7). Interestingly, he does not list the cross among his prescribed shapes, although the cross continued popular among both protestants and Roman Catholics into the eighteenth century. The English materials are also, typically, contained in books, as are the French; very few broadsides and pamphlets are known to include pattern poems, unlike the situation in German, Neo-Latin, and Central European pattern poetry. Also, the percentage of occasional verse is lower than with these other literatures.

At some time in the sixteenth century the labyrinth became a popular form. The question of the origin of literary labyrinths will probably never be resolved satisfactorily, just as a precise definition or classification of them seems unlikely. Labyrinths are, by their nature, somewhat mysterious—they are poems to be solved; one looks at what typically is an arbitrary and unconventional array of letters, and discovers its process, after which the piece is simple or even simplistic at times. Labyrinths may have evolved out of cabalistic texts—Christian caballism evolved out of Jewish caballism in the fifteenth and early sixteenth centuries, and became quite widespread later in the century—or the growing popularity of caballism may simply have preconditioned readers to appreciate labyrinthine texts. The most ambitious work on the subject in general, Hermann Kern's massive *Labyrinthe* (1983), does not even attempt to speculate on the origins of the literary labyrinth; it may equally well have evolved out of sources other than caballism, perhaps from texts like those in the *tabulae iliacae* or out of the carmina cancellata (Hrabanus's *De laudibus sanctae crucis* was published early in the sixteenth century). They are especially popular in Neo-Latin, Portuguese, and Polish literatures, but at least a few labyrinths are known from almost every European literature in which pattern poems are found, though they are rather rare in the Scandinavian literatures and in English.

In German there is a spiral piece carved around 1510 by Erhard Falkener (n.d.) in a choir stall in the St. Valentine's Church in Kiedrich in the Rheingau, but this is an isolated occurrence. The large body of German pattern poetry begins with the lozenge-shaped poem in the *Teutsche Grammatik* (1573) of Laurentius Albertus (Lorenz Albert, n.d.), is joined by four more pieces during the century, and then the flood begins with something like two hundred pieces dating from the seventeenth century alone, if one includes the pieces in German from Scandinavian, Polish, and Czech literatures. This is not astonishing, since nearly half of all known pattern poems date from the seventeenth century. The German pieces cover the full range of pattern poetry from the devotional cross of Catherina Regina von Greiffenberg (1633–94), to the pastorales of Johann Helwig (1609–74), Georg Philipp Harsdörffer (1607–58), Johann Klaj ("Klajus," 1616–56) and their circle, to the many chalices ("Pokals") and hearts composed for weddings and crosses for funerals, some of which are, from a literary point of view, about on the level of greeting card poetry, but some of which are fine and sensitive verse; even those which are inferior poetry are often of linguistic or social interest, as documents of the language and formal sensibility of their times or as indicators of the poetic taste of the middle class, since, especially in Germany, the taste for pattern poetry was not confined to the literati or upper classes but was a bourgeois phenomenon as well.

In the Slavic literatures, Polish and Czech literature have the most pattern poems. Most of the Polish materials are in Latin, most of the Czech ones in German or Latin, reflecting the preferred languages of the elites in those countries. But there are also pattern poems in Russian and Ukrainian; in the latter, notably a small number of extremely fine pieces by a mystical poet, Ivan Velićkovskij (1687–1726) who demonstrates his awareness of earlier pattern poetry traditions by including, on the cover of one of his manuscripts, the "Enigma of Sator," an anonymous Latin word square probably dating from the second century A.D. which was often treated as a pattern poem rather than as a charm (as which it may have been intended).

The Jesuit order had a long-standing tradition of supporting pattern poems; there are collections of them published or collected by Jesuit academies in Neo-Latin, such as the *Carmina libri quatuor discessuro Lemensium comite . . .* (1616), the Polish Latin pieces for Henryk Firley "Leopardus" (1624), and the Neo-Latin and Neo-Greek pieces in *Sylvae . . .* (1592) from France. The tradition continued into the late eighteenth century with the "Necrologbücher" from Hungarian literature. These were books in which the deaths of students in the Jesuit schools were recorded, and pattern poems were occasionally written into these in their memory, presumably by their fellow students.

In Italy, most of the pattern poetry was written in Latin—for example, the most famous Italian piece of the sixteenth century, the pear-shaped poem of 1549 (see fig. 8) of Giovanni Pierio Valeriano Bolzano (1477–1558), known as "Pierius" (which resembles "pirus," the Latin word for "pear tree")—so that the body of pieces

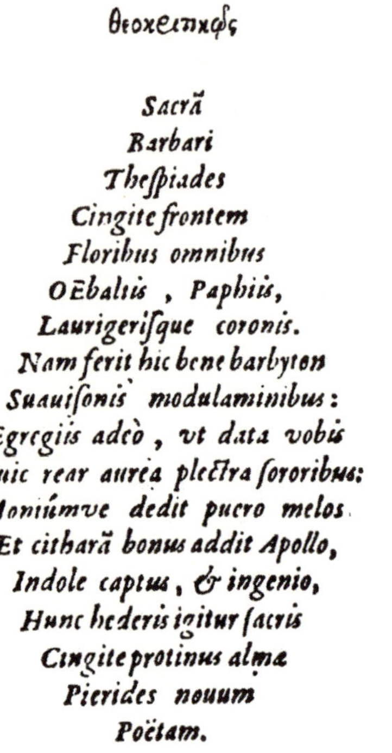

Θεοχριτικῶς

Sacrā
Barbari
Theſſiades
Cingite frontem
Floribus omnibus
OEbaliis , Paphiis,
Laurigeriſque coronis.
Nam ferit hic bene barbyton
Suauiſonis modulaminibus:
Egregiis adeò , vt data vobis
Huic rear aurea plectra ſororibus:
Aoniúmve dedit puero melos.
Et citharā bonus addit Apollo,
Indole captus , & ingenio,
Hunc hederis igitur ſacris
Cingite protinus alma
Pierides nouum
Poëtam.

Figure 8: The pear-shaped poem of Giovanni Pierio Valeriano Bolzano (1477–1558), known as "Pierius" ("the poet") but which suggests the word "pirus" ("pear tree")—thus the shape of the poem. This is the piece against which Gabriel Harvey (1550?–1630) ranted and raved. Note, however, that the poet's title means "Egg in dactyls."

in Italian itself is rather scant. Most important, however, are two actual groups of pattern poets. One was in the north, in the Veneto in the 1620s, and it included Bonifacio Baldissare (ca. 1570–1625), Fortunio Liceti (1577–1654), and their mycaenas, Domenico Molino. Baldissare's pieces based on the Molino coat of arms are of very high quality, and, while Liceti wrote rather few pattern poems himself and these of indifferent quality, he wrote a number of extraordinarily detailed books on most of the Greek and Latin pattern poems, comparing surviving versions and, in general, offering a startling hermeneutic analysis of the pieces.

The second group developed at Rome in the middle of the century, and it included Francesco Passerin (1619–95) and Juan Caramuel de Lobkowitz (1602–82), a Cistercian monk, born of a Spanish father and a Bohemian mother, who lived most of his life traveling for his order and inspecting buildings. Most of his published works deal with ecclesiastical architecture, but the two *Primus calamus* books are linguistic or aesthetic studies. The second of the two is less interesting from our point of view, dealing as it does with a proposed synthetic and universal language. But the first, known as the "Metametrica," which is short for its title *Primus calamus ob oculos ponens metametricam, quae variis currentium, recurrentium, abscendentium, descendentium nec non circumvolantium versuum ductibus, aut aeri incisos aul buxo insculptos aut plumbo infusos multiformes labyrinthos exornat* (1663), contains more than twenty rectangular or circular poems which Caramuel sees as labyrinths (see fig. 9), as well as descriptions and speculations on all the sorts of unusual forms of verse he can find out about—leonine verse, anagrams, echo poems, and so forth. He even proposes some poetries which did not then exist—spherical and cubical verse, for instance. This work is the high point of the various poetics which discuss pattern poetry, such as those by Julius Caesar Scaliger (1561), Etienne Tabourot (1588), and George Puttenham (1587, this last already discussed), or the many German poetics which prescribe shapes and sometimes give examples.

Such groups were not unknown elsewhere in Europe either; we have mentioned the group in the mid-seventeenth-century Germany—Harsdörffer, Helwig, Klaj[us] et al. Another such group developed in Danzig, modern Gdańsk, and elsewhere in Prussia.

Pattern poetry receded in popularity in the face of neoclassic taste. It was associated with baroque (or earlier) poetry, and, as the heroic couplets and alexandrines become predominant in poetry, the pattern poems become fewer. One might speculate that the neoclassic arts were suitable for the grand mercantilism and colonialism of the time, while pattern poetry was specifically unsuited for an art that was based upon power. But that is not for us to say. Suffice to say that it was never the predominant mode and that there were violent attacks upon it in each age in which it occurred; furthermore, since the history of any poetry is always to some extent the history of responses to it, the antagonism which it aroused continued greatly during the colonial era, so that it fell into disrepute in one literature after another, eventually, by the nineteenth century, surviving only in comic, folk, or popular verse.

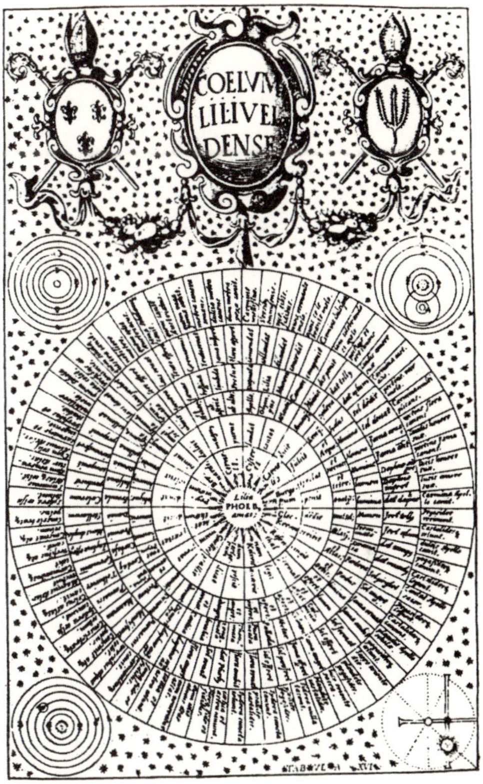

Already in the sixteenth century Michel de Montaigne (1533–92) attacked pattern poems in his "Des vaines subtilités" (*Oeuvres complètes*, Paris: Éditions du Seuil, 1967, 136):

Figure 9: A permutational, circular labyrinth by Juan Caramuel de Lobkowitz (1606–82), pl. XVI of his so-called *Metametrica* (1663).

> *Il est de ces subtilités frivoles et vaines, par le moyen desquelles les hommes cherchent quelquefois de la recommandation; comme les poètes qui font des ouvrages entiers de vers commençant par une même lettre; nous voyons des oeufs, des boules, des ailes, des haches façonnées anciennement par les Grecs avec la mesure de leurs vers, en les allongeant ou raccourcissant, en manière qu'ils viennent à représenter telle ou telle figure. Telle était la science de celui qui s'amusa à conter en combien de sortes se pouvaient ranger les lettres de l'alphabet, et y en trouva ce nombre incroyable qui se voit dans Plutarque . . .*

There are some subtleties which are frivolous and vain, by means of which poets who compose whole works in which every verse begins with the same letter; we see eggs, balls, wings, hatchets, shaped by the Greeks of old time with the measure of their verses,

> by lengthening or shortening some lines, in such a manner that they come to represent this or that figure. Such was the knowledge of that man who amused himself by counting in how many ways he could arrange the letters of the alphabet, and so one finds that incredible number which one sees in Plutarch . . .

And, roughly at the same time, one finds in the *Letter Book* of Gabriel Harvey in England (1550?–1630) (*Elizabethan Critical Essays*, edited by George Gregory Smith, Oxford: Clarendon Press, 1904, vol. 1, 126) real invective against them:

> Folishe idle, phantasticall poet (and deviser) madd gugawes and crockchettes . . . of late foolishely reuiued by sum, otherwise not vnlearnid, as Pierius, Scaliger, Crispin and the rest of that crue. Nothinge so absurde and fruteles but being once taken upp shall have sume imitatoures . . .

One thing that is interesting in Harvey's remarks is to see just who he chooses to attack—Julius Caesar Scaliger, already mentioned as a great humanist, Pierius (already mentioned), and Crispin, who was one of the great French humanist scholars. Notice that Harvey does not attack the Greeks, and notice also his patronizing remark, "otherwise not unlearnid," and the assumption that these men formed a "crue" (crew), which is absolutely untrue—all they had in common was their reverence for culture. This says more about Harvey than about those he attacks.

Also in the sixteenth century, Ben Jonson (1573–1637) dismissed pattern poetry as "a pair of scissors and a comb in verse" (*Handy-book of Literary Curiosities* by William Shepard Walsh, Philadelphia: J.B. Lipincott, 1925, 271).

In the seventeenth century Samuel Butler (1612–80) attacks the pattern poet Edward Benlowes (1603–76) in his "Character of a small poet" (in Butler 1970, 89–90), the royalist essayist Thomas Hobbes (1588–1672) attacks pattern poetry as such but especially George Herbert in *A discourse upon Gondibert* . . . (1650, 126), and we even have the spectacle of John Dryden (1631–1700) attacking pattern poetry in general in "Mac Flecnoe" (*Selected Works*, edited by William Frost, New York: Holt Rinehart & Winston, 1959, lines 202–8).

It is interesting that there are no eloquent defenders of pattern poetry as such. The subject is generally covered in the various works on poetics, especially in Germany and Poland, as one of the standard forms of poetry which every would-be poet ought to be able to master, but with little or no attention being given to the theoretical intricacies and potentials of pattern poetry as a visual or conceptual hybrid.

In the eighteenth century, Joseph Addison (1672–1719) provides a similar attack in *Spectator* 58, which Richard Owen Cambridge (1717–1802) carries on in passing and in a light-hearted way in *The Scribleriad* (*The Works*, edited by George Owen Cambridge, London: T. Cadell and W. Davies in the Strand and T.

Payne at the Muse Gate, 1803, book 2, lines 152–84) later in the century. English pattern poetry, unsurprisingly, wanes in the late seventeenth century, and there is none known at all from the eighteenth.

Even in Germany, where pattern poetry was far more common than it ever was in Britain, by the early eighteenth century we find the rhetorician Johann Bernhard Frisch (1666–1743), in his *Schlspiel*, objecting to the "verworfnen Unsauberkeit der falschen Dicht- und Reim-kunst." However, Frisch attacked pattern poetry in part by doing it, and the resulting pieces are the only pieces by him that are remembered today—especially the one that is shaped like the Bear of Berlin, which can still be bought in souvenir stalls in that city. Evidently the learned Dr. Frisch's attack backfired.

In the nineteenth century, Jean-Jacques Barthélemy (1716–95), in his *Travels of Anacharsis the younger in Greece* (London: C. and J. Rivington, 1825, 6, 182), carried on the attack, calling the poems in the *Greek Anthology* "puerile and laborious." In *The Improvisatore* (1835), his first novel, Hans Christian Anderson (1805–75) criticizes his hero's teacher, a Christian arab named Habbas Dahdah, for his taste for pattern poems, saying Dahdah could not accept truly emotional poetry. Hippolyte Taine, perhaps more thoughtful than some others, says, in the discussion of medieval literature in his *History of English Literature* (New York: Holt and Williams, 1872, vol. 1, 54), precisely what offended him in pattern poetry:

A few, like Aldhelm, wrote square acrostics, in which the first line, repeated at the end, was found also to the left and right of the piece. Thus made up of the first and last letters of each verse, it forms a border to the whole piece, and the morsel of verse is like a morsel of tapestry. Strange literary tricks, which changed the poet into an artisan! They bear witness to the contrareity which then impeded culture and nature, and spoiled at once the Latin form and the Saxon genius.

However, the most impassioned negative response to a pattern poem, quoted to me in a letter of 24 July 1984, from Dr. Kilián István of the Hungarian Academy of Sciences, was a letter by the famous poet Petöfi Sándor (1823–49) to the editor of the newspaper *Hazank* who on 27 March 1847 had printed a rather innocuous cross-shaped poem by Bulyovszky Gyula (n.d. but nineteenth century):

Amennyire telik, örizkedjél olyan égbekiáltó silány portékákat közleni, mint a minap Bulyovszky és Halha vagy ki a fene versei voltak. Amint elolvastam hát fosást kaptam, okádtam, a hasamba kólika jött, aszkórságba estem és három izben ütött meg a guta. Ha kedves elötted az életem, válogasd meg jobban a verseket. Inkább semmit, mint rossz verset. Isten veled; csókol igaz barátod Petöfi Sándor.

If possible, for goodness sakes don't bring out such heaven shriekingly bad stuff as the poems of Bolyovszky and Halha or whoever the author of the poems was. When I read it, I had diarrhea, vomited, and became consumptive. If my life is dear to you, please choose your poems better. Rather none than such wretched poems. Goodbye; your true friend Petöfi Sándor kisses you.

By no means is this list an exhaustive one, but it will suffice. Interestingly, Kalanath Jha, the main authority on the citra-kāvyas of Sanskrit and the other languages of India, has written complaining that the response to visual poetry in India has tended to be similar to these attacks in the West.

As we have already noted, the works on poetics which describe or advocate pattern poetry, from Scaliger to Caramuel, do not match the passion and intensity of the attacks on it. They usually simply state what pattern poetry is, give some brief history of it, and then recommend some shapes as being suitable to it. Sometimes the history is erroneous, such as Puttenham's claim that "pattern poetry comes from the east, from Tartary"—in fact, by "Tartary" he seems to mean Central Asia, from which no pattern poetry is known, although there do exist a few Persian pieces. Of course, by "Tartary" Puttenham might have meant China and could have been referring to the hui-wen.

The criticism of pattern poetry only begins with Boissonade's writings in nineteenth-century France. It continues very scant—a piece here, a piece there, a little historical narrative in this or that journal, usually intended for bibliophiles or graphic arts specialists more than for literary scholars—until the 1970s, following the appearance of concrete poetry during the preceding two decades. At this point several collections appear, Massin (1970), Peignot (1978), Dencker (1972), and Bowler (1970), by no means scholarly works but at least responsible ones. This made substantial numbers of the works available together for the first time, sometimes only intended as a background for twentieth-century visual poetry, but at least clearly presented and sometimes well documented. This, in turn, leads to the appearance of two substantial works on the subject, Giovanni Pozzi's *La parola dipinta* (1981), already mentioned, and Ana Hatherly's *A experiência do prodigio*, which deals with Portuguese materials, especially labyrinths, and which helps demystify the relationship of pattern poetry and cabbalism. Apart from an excellent dissertation by David W. Seaman, published as a book, *Concrete Poetry in France* (1981), the rest of the materials on concrete poetry are articles, usually only on very specific aspects of pattern poetry. Only very recently has genre criticism begun to appear, such as the articles by Ulrich Ernst, especially his "Europäische Figurengedichte in Pyramidenform aus dem 16. und 17. Jahrhundert" (1982), which traces the relationship of text and pyramid shape, and the associations and traditions of the latter. Apart from these few works, almost all the rest of the critical materials in our large bibliography are either extremely specific, scattered, or ephemeral, displaying an insufficient knowledge of the body of pattern poetry as a whole to enable the critic to place the works he or she is discussing into perspective. This in turn leads to amusing opinions, such as one critic's discussion of George Herbert's magnificent pattern poem, "Easter Wings," which concludes that it shows a "dangerous preoccupation" with the visual element; or even such a strange omission as the fine critic Helen Vendler's discussion of the same poem, (in Vendler, *The Poetry of George Vendler*, Cambridge: Harvard University Press, 1975, 145–6), who prints and analyzes it without even noting its visual aspect, let alone its tradition (the parallel with the Hellenist Greek wings of Simias, etc.) In fact, even in such works as Gustav René Hocke's *Manierismus in der Literatur: Sprach-Alchimie und esoterische Kombinationskunst* (1959), a study of literary mannerism, where one might have expected to find a discussion of pattern poetry, even if a negative one, the subject is unmentioned. Incidentally, "mannerism" in art history and in the continental European critical tradition is not the perjorative term that it is in the colloquial English-speaking world, so that is not the point so much as that the existence of a substantial body of visual and visual-related literature and cognate arts was as forgotten to large, mainstream, public. The critical literature from Boissonade to the late 1960s is for the most part quite obscure, as even a cursory glance at those titles from that period which are listed in our bibliography will show. Only when the collections already mentioned—of Dencker, Peignot, etc.—appeared, placing pattern and concrete poetry into a continuum (which is not quite proper), did the world open up for the criticism of pattern poetry as such.

However, it remains that pattern poetry disappeared in the face of the change to neoclassic taste and harsh criticism, though not everywhere at the same time. In France it disappeared from serious literature fairly early in the seventeenth century but was used in comic verse in the eighteenth and nineteenth century, in the work of Charles-François Panard (1689–1765), Pierre-Adolphe Capelle (1772–1824?), and a small handful of others.

In Spain and Portugal, it continued through the eighteenth century; and in Spanish Latin America, into the nineteenth century, especially in the works of the Uruguayan poet Francisco Acuña de Figueroa (1791–1862), who wrote twenty-seven pattern poems, including twenty-two glass-shaped pieces; almost all his pieces were occasional verse, written for the autograph or poetry albums of his friends (or, once in a while, for more serious situations). Also in the nineteenth century, the Spaniard José González Estrada (ca. 1830–83) and his circle attempted to create a whole world of poetry that was based upon the acrostic family, which, for them, included pattern poetry. To this end they maintained a fascinating literary journal, *El piston*, sometimes charming or naive, which lasted for twenty-four issues in 1864. The end of this period is described in Bohn (*The Aesthetics of Visual Poetry, 1914–1928*, Cambridge: Cambridge University Press, 1986, 85–6).

In Germany, the late eighteenth century is when pattern poetry disappeared, except for a very few pieces by Joseph Gutsmüthl and some comic verse.

In Wales, the only known pattern poems are from the nineteenth century. They are serious verse, not comic; however, they seem a little anachronistic.

In England, pattern poetry disappears in the eighteenth century, though it is used in the nineteenth century for comic verse, as in the familiar "Tale of the mouse" in *Alice's Adventures in Wonderland* by Lewis Carroll (1832–98). In American literature, there is only one baroque piece, by Edward Taylor (1642–1729), but a form of pattern poem called "lovers' knots" was popular until the mid-nineteenth century; thereafter pattern poetry was used only for comic verse, as in England.

In the Scandinavian literatures, it disappears altogether; only two Swedish pieces are known from the nineteenth century, and none from elsewhere in Scandinavia.

In Serbo-Croatian and Russian literature, where the baroque style lasted longer than in most other places, there are a few eighteenth-century pattern poems, but these too vanish late in the century. There are some early twentieth-century pieces in the old tradition, however. One piece is known in Slovenian.

There are only two pattern poems known from Canada: a rather serious piece in French from the end of the nineteenth century, by Albert Ferland (1872–1943) of Montréal, and the Bean gravestone in English from the mid-century.

We could go on describing other late materials, but the pattern is well established from what we have said, and we would merely duplicate ourselves. Both pattern poetry and the knowledge of its traditions gradually disappeared in the eighteenth and nineteenth centuries—that is the fact.

The stage was then set for others to act upon the natural human impulse to combine one's visual and literary experiences, and this began to happen with the 1897 publication of Mallarmé's "Un coup de dés . . ." followed soon after by the publication of the various futurist *parole in libertà*, the works of Marinetti and Cangiullo, the dadaists, and so on. Most of these new works were made without any deep knowledge of the earlier works of pattern poetry or with any knowledge of the pattern poetry traditions of the specific literatures. The new poets found new forms and styles independently of these, starting, as it were, from a blank page, rather than working with given materials or evoking old traditions.

The Strategy of Visual Poetry

Three Aspects

Originally published in *Precisely*, nos. 3–5, 1979.

A s soon as the visual aspect of a poem becomes not just incidental but is actually structural, the strategy of a poem is affected in several ways: (1) The momentum of a linear thrust is broken, since the eye must stop and take note of the shape. A static element is thereby introduced. (2) The idea of the work is less exclusively dependent upon the words of the text and can even become somewhat transcendent to the verbal text. (3) In the case of visual poems which are primarily visual and only lesserly textural—the verbally poetic visual piece—a similar metamorphosis occurs: the verbal aspect becomes transcendent to its visual embodiment, and a kinetic thrust becomes possible in a way that very few visual artworks can have. To make a few beginnings and substantiations of these observations is the purpose of this paper.

The Breaking of the Linear Thrust

Among the traditional thoughts of a poem which a poet tends to keep as a paradigm in his mind is the idea of the poem that "catches you up, and won't let go of you until you have finished reading the poem." In our Western culture this is almost the normative view. It is the source of "power" in a poem. There is an element of compulsion which leads ultimately to catharsis, the touchstone criterion which Aristotle attributed to the tragedies of Sophocles. But Aristotle belonged to a time in Greek culture when it was no longer possible to rest content with the earlier civic virtues and the mental and poetic culture of the previous generation. Greek civilization was becoming obliged to conquer or to be conquered: and the linear philosophy which he developed was geared toward proof and demonstration, ultimately toward power. The aim of his rhetoric is to persuade. The goal of our rhetoric today is far less to persuade than to develop the mental or perceptual resource, to share the experience. Applied to rhetoric, this means that our goal is less to persuade (at least by logical means) than to show in such a way what it feels like to think this or that, what happens if one does think this or that way, and to clothe the thought, therefore, *in the most vivid and memorable embodiment possible* rather than the most logically defensible one. The linear expression of an Aristotelian logic is apt to be left to lawyers: the artists have other concerns.

But the normative taste has been, in poetry, for the powerful poem. The poems that reject this have been damned as decadent, feeble or impotent. Even our occidental lyricism has been power-oriented. As I've noted elsewhere, Shelley's "Ode to a Skylark" seems to be more about a fighter plane than about a bird. Yet each generation must reinvent its arts in its own image; that is the inner drive toward realism, and to go against it can only lead to an art of shallow and hollow gesture. As power is removed from our options, it can be replaced with new criteria that were always there but were undervalued—truth, serenity, harmony. The work which is *forced* to be only one thing, because serious works are thought to be only one thing, may be logically defensible, but it will tend to be experientially

[1] Dick Higgins, *George Herbert's Pattern Poems: In Their Tradition* (West Glover, VT: Unpublished Editions, 1977), pp. 17–19. Hereafter cited as Higgins, 1977.

[2] Giordano Bruno, *Jordani Bruni Nolani Opere Latine Conscripta*, 3 vols. in 8 pts. (1891; Bad Cannstatt b. Stuttgart, Friedrich Frommann Verlag, 1962), vol. 1, pt. 3, pp. 87–318, esp. 197–99. In collaboration with Charles Doria I am currently working on the first English translation of this text.

[3] Isabel Frith, *Life of Giordano Bruno, the Nolan*, ed. Prof. Mauriz Carriere (Boston: Ticknor, 1887), p. 16. What Ms. Frith has done is to assemble a montage here of passages from the section referred to in fn. 2.

inadequate. Thus the drive to make works which are conceptually intermedial—whose essence lies between the traditional media—gathers momentum today as part of a great variety of what passes for "movements" on our cultural scene, though without being a movement in its own right. Many times in history intermedia have appeared—in India following the Hindu revival (and again following the Moslem conquest), in Italy at the end of the Renaissance[1]—and in many other times and places as well. But we see some Italian instances of this drive toward intermedia in the literary and emblematic painting of the late sixteenth century, the many pattern poems of the period (of which more presently), in the emblematic imagery of such works as Giordano Bruno's *Degli Eroici Furori* and in his almost semiotic ideas of syncretic imagery in such later Latin writings as his *De Imaginum, Signorum, et Idearum Compositione* (On the composition of images, signs, and ideas) of 1591,[2] and even in the appearance of the opera, which is, however, more of a mixed medium than an intermedium, since there is no conceptual fusion between text, music, and mise-en-scène; the components of a mixed medium remain separate though simultaneous. However, the syncretism of the following quotation from Bruno could equally well serve to describe the theoretical underpinnings of many artists' work since the late 1950s:

> Therefore, and in a certain measure, philosophers are painters; poets are painters and philosophers; painters are philosophers and poets. He who is not a poet and a painter is no philosopher. We say rightly that to understand is to see imaginary forms and figures; and understanding is fancy, at least it is not deprived of fancy. He is no painter who is not in some degree a poet and thinker, and there can be no poet without a certain measure of thought and representation.[3]

Thus, returning to the visual poetry of today, it is easy for us to see how the syncretism of a Bruno fits well with the formal syncretism of recent visual poetry and parallel art forms—conceptual art, fluxus performances and happenings, for instance—and indicates the synchronic appropriateness of it, given our cultural milieu. Of course the pattern poem of the past tended to be strongly mimetic—to take the shape of a natural object rather than a geometrical or other schematic form. Figure 1, for instance is a very typical pattern poem of this sort.

Of the roughly 1100 pattern poems that I have collected from before 1900, probably eighty-five percent are representational in the sense of the example

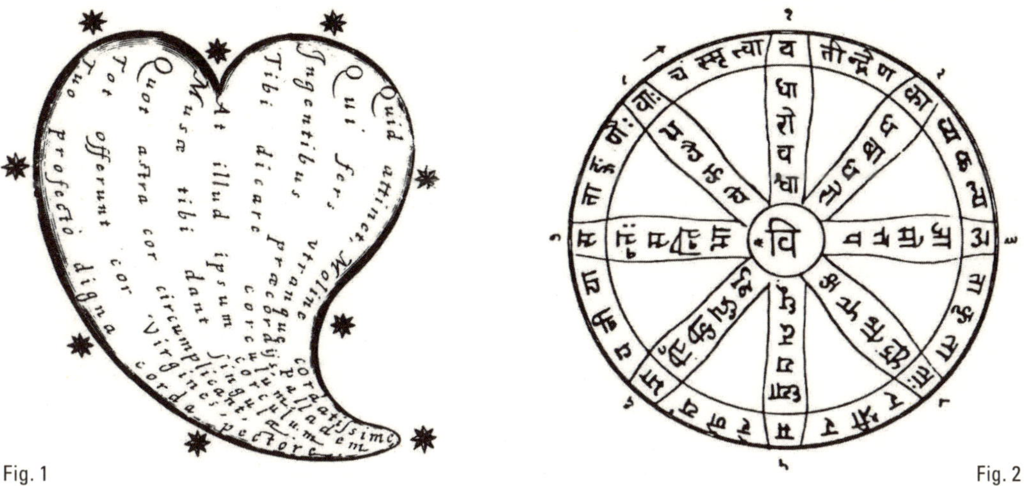

Fig. 1
Fig. 2

Figure 1: Bonifacio Baldessare, from *Musarum Libri* (1628). This heart-shaped poem has a text which falls quite naturally into its shape: many similar pieces do not, but rather the text seems forced into a visual form, like a Procrustean bed. But many traditional poems, too, seem forced to *remain* nonvisual when the natural thing for them would be to take shape and fly, if only they were to follow their own inner logic.

Figure 2: Amaracandra Sūri, from the *Kāvyakalpalata* (ca. 1297 A.D.). The Latin Middle Ages abound with cabalistic arrays of letters into grids, moving metatactically from magic into art, whose "inscriptions" can also be rearranged readily into traditional poetry. Several examples will be found in my book on pattern poems, cited in the footnotes. But just to show how universal this phenomenon is, here is an example in Gujarati, an Indian language from the area north of Bombay. This is one of many examples collected by Professor Hiralal R. Kapadia and printed in various issues of the *Journal of the University of Bombay* in 1954 and 1955 and elsewhere. Professor Kapadia gives written-out versions for this text and others, which would otherwise appear to be simply diagrams.

[above], and only about fifteen percent are as schematic as the one given in figure 2, as an example of the other type.

Modern visual poetry tends, however, to be far less mimetic. The visual element is often purely expressive and improvised, in the manner of an abstract expressionist painting. Or it is clean and geometrical. Or its forms are not those of natural objects, but of the ways and processes of nature. Thus the familiar Apollinaire rain calligram shows the words scattered down the page as rain falls, and not spread out into a lattice on the page, as if the falling raindrops could be photographed with a time-stop mechanism. The array of words may be schematic or linguistic; it may resemble the flow charts of a computer programmer's diagram. But what it always does is follow some sort of spatialized method which requires, for the fullest enjoyment of the piece, that we become sensitized to the spatial aspect of the piece. The space is not just a notation, at best a stand-in for time, as is the tendency in traditional poetry. Rather, it is a structural unit which may serve a large variety of purposes.

The Poem Transcends the Verbal Text

Perhaps at this point the concept of metataxis should be introduced. This is a term used in anthropology to describe the shift in function (which determines a shift in identity) of an object from one situation to another. A horse, once a means of transportation, becomes a symbol of status or leisure. A bow and arrow, formerly an instrument of war or a hunting tool, is metatactically altered into being a child's toy. Elsewhere I have pointed out how magical and cabalistic devices, originally intended as metaphors for a hidden truth, became instead metaphors for an aesthetic truth; this explains the art forms of some of the earlier pattern poems.[4] A similar process seems to be involved, as one looks at the role of text in the concrete poems of the 1960s and before, and as one compares them with the *poesia visiva* works of the 1970s.[5] These former usually consisted of arrays of letters or words, while the latter are for more visual than verbal or textual: many consist of photographs of people carrying words or even letters, others show something happening to the words or letters—a process of erasure, metamorphosis, dissolution, or reconstruction.

For anyone who has followed visual poetry or concrete poetry for any length of time, this distinction which I am making between the more text- or letter-oriented sort and the more purely visual variety will come as no surprise. Most of the works in the two major anthologies of the 1960s, those edited by Emmett Williams (*An Anthology of Concrete Poetry*, 1967) and by Mary Ellen Solt (*Concrete Poetry: A World View*, 1968) are of the first sort, while those in more recent books, such as those edited by Jean-François Bory (*Once Again*, 1968) and by Klaus Peter Dencker (*Text-Bilder: Visuelle Poesie International*, 1972) include many examples of the latter. A number of the informal magazines devoted to the most visual sort of work have come out of Italy, and so this sort has come to be known by an Italian term for "visual poetry," *poesia visiva*. Some writers such as Klaus Peter Dencker have tried to make a qualitative distinction and a hard line between concrete poetry and "visual poetry" (by which he means *poesia visiva*) and Dencker is currently at work on a large anthology of *poesia visiva* through the centuries—sculptural poems and object poems from the past, up to the most current sort of photographic poems. A hard-line qualitative distinction is, in my opinion, not possible, but a general quantitative one, based on the degree within the intermedial polarity between text or visual orientation, is useful for taxonomic purposes. Anyone who wants to distinguish and verbalize the differences between the concrete or verbal sort, as in the works of Eugen Gomringer, Mary Ellen Solt, the earlier Ian Hamilton Finlay, or Jonathan Williams, and the new works by Finlay (the sailboats), Alain Arias-Misson, or Thomas Ockerse, will find this distinction useful. For those photographic sequence-works of *poesia visiva* that are extremely close to some works of concept art, such as some pieces by

[4] Higgins, 1977.

[5] Christian Wagenknecht, "Proteus und Permutation: Spielarten einer Poetischen Spielart," in *Text + Kritik*, heft 30 (1970), pp. 1–10.

Robert Smithson, it is almost impossible to get a sense of text when one reads the work. In a piece by Jean-François Bory, one sees photographs of a book left on the sand, the tide comes in and bears it away—and it sinks. There may have been words in the book. But does it matter what these were? The criteria for evaluating the nature and impact of such a work are those which would be used for photojournalism or for a performance—in fact, such a work tends to feel like the documentation of a performance which one is to imagine, but which may or may not have taken place. Not only the grammar of the text is gone, but the words as well. Because there is so much of this *poesia visiva* being done right now, one is apt to forget that it has been done for a long time. It is nearly twenty years since Emmett Williams's "Poetry Clock" (1959) was made; it appeared in his anthology. And, in a sense and to a degree, many of the geometric paintings of the Swiss school of the postwar years, which are historically ancestral to the term "concrete poetry," can be regarded as wordless poems. I mean of course paintings by Richard Löhse, the early Karl Gerstner, and Max Bill, the last of whom called many of his works which appeared to be physical realizations (concretizations?) of an intellectual principle or progression "Konkretionen," which we would translate as "concretions." His secretary in the early 1950s was Eugen Gomringer, to whom the term "concrete poetry" is usually attributed, and who used the term by analogy to Bill's works. Many works by Bill and Löhse and others of that group consist of series and progressions and even permutations, and the progressions of shapes or colors are analogous to the behavior of verbal elements in what are sometimes referred to as "Proteus poems" after a famous poem by Julius Caesar Scaliger. In the paintings, the progression is one of verbal units. Here are two examples, the first from Scaliger's "Proteus" (ca. 1561):[6]

[6] Etienne Tabourot, *Les Bigarrures du Seigneur des Accords* 1597/1866: (Gèneve: Slatkine Reprints, 1969), p. 113.

[7] Wagenknecht, 1970.

> Perfide sperasti divos te fallere Proteu
> Perfide te divos sperasti fallere Proteu
> Perfide te sperasti divos fallere Proteu
> Perfide te Proteu sperasti fallere divos
> Perfide sperasti te divos fallere Proteu

And here is a brief passage from Jackson Mac Low's "Jail Break (for Emmett Williams & John Cage) September 1963, April & August 1966":[7]

> Tear now jails down all.
> Tear all now down jails.
> Tear now all jails down.
> Tear jails now all down.
> Tear jails now down all.

The relation of such "Proteus poems" to concrete poetry is that what syntax there is is geometric rather than, as in traditional poetry, algebraic—cumulative rather than linear. The elements taken separately have no particular power or impact. But each line gets nearly all its meaning from its relation to the others, where in traditional poetry the lines normally make some sense even when isolated. In a geometric painting, shapes get their relevance from their relation to other shapes, and in a "Proteus poem" the pattern of the components is far more important than just what they happen to be.

In fact, in many cases the pattern is made clearer and more vivid by using elements that relate to words but are not words—numbers, the letters of the alphabet, or visual vocabularies. I made a series of one-of-a-kind (mostly) silk-screen prints using a vocabulary of 300 elements, repeated and juxtaposed in a variety of ways to make almost 900 different works. There is no need for the viewer to see all the works in this series, which is called *7.7.73*; there is just enough information to establish the pattern in a clear and indelible way. Each work in the series is analogous to a line in a poem—and in a "Proteus poem" there is seldom a need to go through every possible line, every possible permutation. The lines of such a work tend to be synecdochal—the parts of the work can stand for the whole. Many of Emmett Williams's pieces in his *Anthology of Concrete Poetry* will serve as examples of the alphabet-poem genre, and the number poems of Richard Kostelanetz or Ladislav Nebesky can illustrate this latter category. Some works of visual art are analogous to these poems—especially certain paintings by Jasper Johns and Robert Indiana. But these latter seem, for the most part, geared to a luxury market and not to the page or the poor connoisseur's library: for social reasons, one would tend, then, to class these last as paintings more than as poems.

The Transcendent Text

In the works which I have discussed up to now, the effect has been seen of the introduction of spatial considerations and visual elements into verbal materials, progressively, until their structure is no longer dependent upon any verbal text, though something of a verbal method of experiencing the work remains—the process of reading, of abstracting a sort of verbal pattern from the work and subsumption of the visual dimension into that verbal framework. But of course the opposite is true too—that there can be visual works whose impact depends upon their association with the word, the *logos*. This is true of many religious works. There can be a metataxis from a religious or mystical perception into a political one, as in the case of the highly emblematic iconography of many works from the period of the French Revolution and the Napoleonic era. Or there can be (and this is what concerns us more here) an emblematic array of images which embody a verbal message. In its extreme, this could be the rebus, taken as an art form (as it was, for instance, by the French Renaissance poet Clement Marot). Or it could be simply the emblem literature of the late Renaissance and baroque, the emblem books of Francis Quarles and others, or even the works of William Blake, such as *The Marriage of Heaven and Hell*. For these, the grammar and pattern of literature are not superimposed over the visual art base, necessarily, but rather the verbal image and often the word itself is included. This would be the case with a good many advertisting illustrations, obviously. But it is also the area, conceptually, of the calligraphic text, the "drawing of words." This has not been a very productive area for avant-garde visual poetry, just now. The highest products of this have been the calligraphic poems of Paul Reps, or the various collaborations between abstract expressionist painters and poets in the 1960s, between Larry Rivers and Frank O'Hara, for instance. In such work, one tends to abstract from the whole not so much a reading as a number of discrete words or images, to notice the pattern and then let the work go as a whole. Put linguistically, one sees the *langue* incompletely because one is not caught up by the component *paroles*.

Yet, to put the question philosophically, could there not be a work of this sort which was independent of the words which comprised it? A work of pure form, a matrix into which anything which was put comprised the realization of the work? This is a question which any translator must face: but often it is faced, now, by the artist or poet or concrete poet. How can I "translate" my work from text into music? From one realization of a work into another? In such pieces as *The Twin Plays* (1963) Jackson Mac Low used an identical matrix of action, sentence structure and so on, to make two different stage works; one set of verbal events was made from all the sounds and syllables in the proper name "Port-au-Prince" and the other came from a list of sayings and proverbs recorded in Adams County, Illinois. A similar assumption is at work in Stephen McCaffery's "homolinguistic translations"—systematic puns from given texts to new ones. The potential here for visual poetry is equally great. It seems likely that blank works will come to exist, which one fills with words, and that these will be a new category in visual poetry. Prototypes have been made already by myself and others. Novels which come on cards which one is expected to shuffle and then read aloud (often with materials which the reader also contributes) have some of this character. But as a genre, the area is yet unexplored.

Conclusion

Just as one might imagine from the quotation I gave from Giordano Bruno, there are analogous interfaces and intermedia that are similar to the visual poem in poetry/music (sound poetry), poetry/philosophy (concept poetry), even poetry/technology (what Bern Porter calls "sciart" poems). These too are very much in need of classification, with an accepted taxonomy. It is very difficult to enjoy a work fully before one has made some mental classification of it, and yet the hermeneutics of such classification are very difficult owing to the lack of any consensus.

But without the classification, one is ill at ease with a work, unable to relax and live with it. Thus the real need, in understanding visual poetry right now, is not for a dualism of good and bad or true and false, but for an overall teleology of the work which can serve as the basis for both a taxonomy and hermeneutic. For instance, in this paper we have dealt a little with a teleology of visual poetry. But what does this imply for sound poetry? Many sound poems are being distributed on tape cassettes; but one plays a cassette more than once, usually, in a great variety of situations. One hears the cassette at home, and one plays it in one's automobile when one is driving: how does this affect the poem? And in any case, while a traditional poem was made to be witnessed from beginning to end in a book—and was usually designed for its maximum impact to be on first reading (which later readings reevoke), what is the effect of a sound poem in which one assumes the cassette will be played over and over and over again? The text must be designed for reexperiencing. It must "wear well." Similarly, few traditional poems were designed for putting on one's wall and for living with. Yet many visual poems are designed for just that purpose. How does this affect their nature? These are questions which have not yet been answered in any satisfactory way, so far as I know.

But to sum up: the potential for visual poetry lies in its introduction of space and visual shape—at the cost of momentum and kinetic inertia. A visual poem, if it has power, will not gain it from the sequence of verbal images in the same way that Virgil's *Aeneid* did but, rather, in the way that the powerful anti-Hitler graphic photomontages of John Heartfield do. And in any case, the medium seems more suitable for the achievement of lyrical and analytical effects than for the mighty impact that western poetry sought for during the imperial era. We need not be like Joseph Addison, the Aristotelian critic in the eighteenth century, who, in the *Spectator*, denounced all visual poetry as "false wit," because he was unable to see that this loss of power and momentum was accompanied by a holistic realism that would make the visual poetry medium suitable for qualities that he did not associate with poetry. Rather the best strategy for the visual poet consists of matching the natural potentials of the medium (or of the intermedium, depending on how one wishes to look at it) with whichever of his or her notions and projections seem most suited for it, and not to try and force it to do something of which it is not capable. The audience, then, sees this process of matching, identifies it, relaxes and enjoys the process. Which is what happy audiences have always done anyway.

Points Toward a Taxonomy of Sound Poetry

Originally published in *Precisely*, nos. 10–12, 1981.

For Starters, a Subhistory

Most sound poets and observers of the contemporary scene approach sound poetry as if it were a purely contemporary phenomenon, but this neoteric view simply does not hold up. It is true that some kinds of sound poetry are new in the sense of being without formal precedent. But just as "concrete" and other recent visual poetries have their analogues going back into folklore or into (for example) the Bucolic Greek poets, so sound poetry too has its close analogues. This is natural, since it is natural for anyone who is interested in poetry to try, at some point, isolating the sounds of poetry from other aspects of it and to try out the making of poems with sounds more or less alone; only if such an experiment were totally artificial could something so basic as a poetry of sound alone be entirely without precedent. But, to start our investigation, let us consider sound poetry not (as might be tempting) by some tight definition that gave a climactic structure to the argument of the critic or poet who offers it—the revelation-of-the-heretofore-unknown-truth kind of discussion—and simply use "sound poetry" as, generally, poetry in which the sound is the focus, more than any other aspect of the work.

Three basic types of sound poetry from the relative past come to mind immediately: folk varieties, onomatopoetic or mimetic types, and nonsense poetries. The folk roots of sound poetry may be seen in the lyrics of certain folk songs, such as the Horse Songs of the Navajos or in the Mongolian materials collected by the Sven Hedin expedition.[1] We have some of this kind of thing in our own culture, where sound-poetry fragments are apt to be used at the ends of stanzas, such as the French "il ron ron ron petit patte à pont" in "Il était une bergère," or the English "heigh down hoe down derry derry down" in "The Keeper." Similarly, in black American music there is a sound-poetry tradition, possibly based originally on work calls, which we find metastatized into the skat singing styles of the popular music of the 1930s, in the long nonsense-like passages in Cab Calloway's singing of "Minnie the Moocher," for example.

[1] Henning Haslund-Christiansen, *The Music of the Mongols: Eastern Mongolia* (1943; New York: Da Capo Press, 1971).

In written literature, by contrast, most of the sound poetry fragments are brief, onomatopoetic imitations of natural or other sounds, for example the "Brekekex ko-ax ko-ax" of the frogs in Aristophanes' drama, or the "jug jug jugs" of the birds among the Elizabethans. This use of sound has no semantic sense to speak of, although, on occasion, its freshness consists of possible overlaps between nonsense and sense. Even some recent sound poetry has an onomatopoetic element. For example, my own *Requiem for Wagner the Criminal Mayor* is above all a structural piece, but its sounds resemble the fighting of cats and also the so-called Bronx cheer of traditional calumny.

Some of the most interesting sound poetry is the purely nonsense writing of the periods in Western literature when nonsemantic styles and forms were not supposed to be taken in full earnest. One of their delights is the art with which they parody the styles of their authors' native tongues. Try this English example, for instance, from the Victorian, Edward Lear:

> Thrippsy pillowins,
> Inky tinky pobblebookle abblesquabs?—
> Flosky! beebul trimple flosky!—Okul scratcha bibblebongebo,
> viddle squibble tog-a-tog, ferrymoyassity
> amsky flamsky ramsky damsky crocklefether squiggs.
>> Flunkywisty poom.
>> Slushypipp.[2]

While not set up as verse and therefore not exactly sound poetry, this text is from the period when prose poems were redeveloped, and it tropes the style of a conventional polite letter of its period quite admirably. Another well-known example from its time would be the nonsense words in Lewis Carroll's "Jabberwocky"—"Twas brillig in the slithy toves" and that kind of thing. The protagonist is equipped with a "vorpal" sword, and speculation on that kind of sword has been abundant ever since. When I was a child I had a science fiction magazine in my possession—long since vanished—in which two genius children invented a "vorpal" sword to protect themselves against an invasion of creatures from another dimension, and there are currently even a literary magazine in California and an art gallery in New York City named—what else?—*Vorpal*. Thus though no meaning has ever been assigned definitively to "vorpal," the word has become familiar as a sort of empty word, significant for its lack of meaning and for its harmony in a sentence of other, more semantically significant English words.

Similarly, in Christian Morgenstern's "Gespräch einer Hausschnecke mit sich selbst," from the famous *Galgenlieder*, a snail asks if it should dwell in its shell, but the word fragments progress and compress into strange, decidedly ungrammatical constructs; these use a sort of inner ear and inner grammar of the German language which reveal a great deal about the sounds and potential of that language:

> Soll i aus meim Hause raus
> Soll i aus meim Hause nit raus?
> Einen Schritt raus?
> Lieber nit raus?
> Hausenitraus—
> Hauserans
> Hauseritraus
> Hausenaus
> Rauserauserauserause . . .[3]

[2] Edward Lear, *The Complete Nonsense Book* (New York: Dodd Mead, 1934), p. 10.

[3] Christian Morgenstern, *The Gallows Songs* (Berkeley: University of California Press, 1966), pp. 28–29.

Which Max Knight has translated as follows:

> Shall I dwell in my shell?
> Shall I not dwell in my shell?
> Dwell in shell?
> Rather not dwell?
> Shall I not dwell,
> shall I dwell,
> dwell in shell,
> shall I shell,
> shallIshellIshallIshellIshallI . . .

Of course in German the last five words can be perfectly compressed into one invented word each, which cannot be done to the same extent in English. This illustrates not only the uniqueness of the German language but also the unique relationship between successful sound poetry and the effective use of the linguistic potentialities in *any* given language.

When Sound Poetry Becomes Conscious of Itself as Just Another Genre

At some point around the time of the First World War it ceased to be assumed that sound poetry could only be used for light or humorous works or as interludes in otherwise traditional pieces, or as something so unique that each poem appeared to be the first sound poem in history—assumptions that seem to underlie most early sound poems. The sense of pioneering was replaced by the sense of potential mastery, and a tradition of sound poetry was precipitated. Implicit in this development is the even more radical aesthetic shift which seems to have begun at this time (and to have become even more pronounced recently, since, say, the late 1950s) that it is no longer *de rigeur* that a poem must attempt to be powerful, meaningful, or even necessarily communicative (a main assumption of the eighteenth and nineteenth century poetries). I have developed this observation more fully elsewhere,[4] but basically my argument is that poetries which used means which, while not unknown, were not usually taken seriously in the West, especially visual as well as sound poetry,[5] could now be accepted as valid possibilities and genres.[6] Thus the *parole in libertà* (1909) of the futurist T. F. Marinetti or the dada *laut-gedichte* of Hugo Ball (1917), both of which flourished at this

[4] I have developed this argument more fully in three parts of Dick Higgins, *A Dialectic of Centuries: Notes towards a Theory of the New Arts.* 2d ed. (New York: Printed Editions, 1979), pp. xi, 3–9, 93–101, and also in Dick Higgins, *George Herbert's Pattern Poems: In Their Tradition* (New York: Printed Editions, 1977), pp. 18–19.

[5] The early history of visual poetry is my subject in the work listed in fn. 4, above. Its bibliography will also be useful for anyone seeking to explore the matter further. For a similar discussion of sound poetry, but one which continues into modern times as well, the best such article in English is that of Stephen Ruppenthal and Larry Wendt, "Vocable Gestures: A Sound Poetry," in *Art Contemporary* 5 (1978); 57–8, 80–104. A large study of the subject by Henri Chopin was recently published in France, which should help fill in the gap in historical scholarship in sound poetry.

6 For an example of a naive attack on visual poetry, see Hippolyte Taine, *History of English Literature* (New York: Holt & Williams, 1872), 4:54. Another such attack is in Joseph Addison, *Spectator* 58, many editions.

7 The Talking Heads' "I Zimbra" is on their album, *Fear of Music* (New York: Sire Records, 1979), SRK 6076.

8 Many excellent examples of such work are given in Eugene Jolas, "From Jabberwocky to *Lettrisme*" in *Transition Forty-Eight* (1948), v. 1, n. 1, pp. 104- 120.

time and both of which, while they may include elements of humor, are not particularly intended as *divertissements* as is, for instance, the Edward Lear piece I cited. The cycle since then is a sort of arc of increasing acceptance of these genres as our mentality has shifted from the normative art of power in the late nineteenth century toward an art of experience and paradigm today. As a measure of just how much a Ball *lautgedicht* (a work which probably seemed quite esoteric at the time of its composition) is accepted, one can point to the use of Ball's "I Zimbra" in its surprising appearance as the lyrics to a recently popular song by the punk rock group, The Talking Heads.[7] The punk rock song, like Ball's poem, opens with "Gadji bera bimba clandridi," which is not even anchored in the parody of any *one* language but is purely without reference to any known language. This in turn evokes the possibility of an artificial invented language, an idea which was also explored at this same time in the Russian Iliazd's "zaoum" or the German Stefan George's "lingua romana" pieces. In our taxonomy, then, works in an artificial or nonexistent language will be the first class of modern sound poems.[8]

A second class comprises works in which the joy or other significance of the work lies in the interplay between the semantically meaningful lines or elements and those which are probably nonsense. It is thus related to the first class, and such pieces often use found materials collaged into the text, as it were, so that one gets either a shock of recognition or a momentarily heightened sense of immediate, concrete reality. These works parallel, conceptually, the early collages of Picasso or Braque with their inclusion of newspaper fragments among the forms on the canvas, or the use of photographs by the dadaists and such Bauhaus figures as Moholy-Nagy, or the *objets trouvés* of Marcel Duchamp. That traditional critics can still be puzzled by such works is indicated by the titles of the contributions to a 1972 issue of *Text+Kritik* devoted to the writings of Kurt Schwitters, the German near-dadaist who flourished in the 1920s and later. Sample titles: "Kurt Schwitters' Poem 'To Anna Blume': Sense or Nonsense?" or "On the Function of the Reality Fragments in the Poetry of Kurt Schwitters," etc.[9] Another such device,

9 *Text + Kritik* 35–36: (1972), 13 and 33.

though not one that fits into sound poetry, would be the "newsreel" passages of John Dos Passo's *USA* trilogy, which I only mention as a parallel paradigm.

A third class might be called "phatic poems," poems in which semantic meaning, if any, is subordinate to expression of intonation, thus yielding a new emotional meaning which is relatively remote from any semiotic significance on the part of words which happen to be included. If, for example, one were to wail the words "blue" and "night" repeatedly over a period of time, the initial function of those words to establish a frame for the wail would soon become unimportant by comparison with the musicality of the wail itself and residual meaning of the two words would come to seem more like an allusion than a conveyor of meaning. One would have, in effect, an invocation without anything specific being invoked. This is precisely the effect which one gets from the recently rediscovered recording by Antonin Artaud of his "Pour en finir avec le jugement de dien," which was originally recorded in the late 1940s a short time before the poet's death, broadcast (causing a great scandal), and then lost for many years until Arrigo Lora-Totino unearthed it in the archives of Radiodiffusion Française.[10] Here Artaud uses more or less conventional words, but they are, as I have suggested, essentially allusions—or perhaps illusions, since so few can be understood anyway. Instead Artaud's emphasis is on high sighing, breathing, wheezing, chanting, exclaiming, exploding, howling, whispering, and avoiding.

Poems without written texts constitute a fourth class. They may have a rough schema or notation that is akin to a graphic musical one (and there are those who regard a magnetic tape as a sort of notation), or there may be some general rules, written out like those of a game, which, if followed, will produce a performance of the work. But by comparison with the role of the written text and the heard result in traditional poetry or in the previous sound poetries that we have discussed (except, perhaps, the previous class, the phatic poems), they are relatively unnotated. Highlights in this class would be Henri Chopin's explorations of the voice by means of microphone and tape recorder, François Dûfrène's very phatic *crirhythmes* series (which, perhaps, constitute a transitory class between the phatic poems and the unwritten-out ones), or the highly sophisticated tape-recorded poems produced in the recording studio by such artists as the Swedes, Bengt Emil Johnson, Sten Hanson, and others.[11] A very large portion of the recorded literature of sound poetry, especially in Europe, is of this type, presumably because of the inherent close connection between such works and audio recording as an industry.

Although this is also the class in which most American sound poetry falls, the American literature tends to be aesthetically naive by comparison to the European (and Canadian) works. The artists seem ill at ease with the very "performance" of their "texts." For example, there are some ten records in the Poetry Out Loud series, edited by Peter and Patricia Harleman, which seem somehow like an extension of the beat poetry of the 1950s with its heavy jazz influence, its antiformal bias, and its dogmatic insistence upon the freshness of improvisation.[12] There exist also similar records edited and produced independently by John Giorno, whose work tends to sound improvised even when it is not. These have isolated fragments of rich material, but most are heavy-handed in their unformed iconoclasm. Fortunately, even in

[10] Arrigo Lora-Totino, editor, *Futura /Poesia Sonora* (Milano: Cramps Records, 1979), 5206 304. This seven-record set contains a large program book with many materials that are unavailable elsewhere.

[11] Recordings of highlights of seven of the International Sound Poetry Festivals, held at Stockholm from 1968 to 1975, can be found on five records from Sveriges Radios Förlag, RELP 1049 1054 1072 1073 and 1074, and on two from Fylkingen Records, RELP 1102 and 1103.

[12] *Poetry Out Loud* (St. Louis, Missouri: Out Loud Productions, 1971 to 1977).

zweiter chor	hol ihn doch	hol ihn doch	hol ihn doch
	hol ihn doch	hol ihn doch	hol ihn doch
	willst du nicht	hol ihn doch	hol ihn doch
willst du nicht	willst du nicht	willst du nicht	hol ihn doch
willst du nicht	willst du nicht	willst du nicht	

	hol ihn	hol ihn	hol ihn
dritter chor	hol ihn	hol ihn	hol ihn
	hol ihn	hol ihn	hol ihn

	hol hol hol hol hooo	
	hol hol hol hol hooo	
dritter chor	hol hol hol hol hooo	
	hol hol hol hol hooo	frau aber meine nähe nur
	hol hol hol hol hooo	

am samstag wenn ich an damals waren das die schönsten

stunden ich mag nicht mehr was ist die welt verrückt

und ohne dass der mensch was ändern mann hätten wir die

kinder nicht frau aber alle machens so und keiner sagt

mann die kinder haben uns frau wir machen uns was vor

Harig's *Das Fussballspiel* ("The Soccer Game") is, as its cover proclaims, "a stereophonic radio play," the word for which is, in German, appropriately enough, "hörspiel" or "hear-play." The resources called for on the depicted page alone are one chorus which evidently is working in unison here with a second and third chorus a man and a woman. The work was first broadcast by Südwestfunk in Stuttgart on April 11, 1966 (Ludwig Harig, *Das Fussbalspiel: Ein Stereophonisches Hörspiel* [Stuttgart: Edition Hansjörg Mayer, 1967]).

America, there are exceptions such as the works of Jackson Mac Low, Richard Kostelanetz, and Charles Stein, which are not of this sort.

The fifth class is the notated sound poem, which comprises the largest volume of sound poetry to date. By "notation" here I am referring to the normative sort of musical notation, in which there is some kind of correspondence between space, time, word, and sound and some form of graphic or textual indicator of those elements. Some of these notations closely resemble musical notations and have elaborate scores, such as the work in the 1940s of the *lettriste* Isidore Isou or the monumentally complex works that came out of Germany in the 1950s, such as Hans G. Helms's *Golem* or Ludwig Harig's *Das Fussballspiel: Ein Stereophonisches Hörspiel*, a page of which is reproduced herewith.

However, it could also be argued that any *text*, when it is taken as a work of art by a person who does not understand the meaning of its words, is conceptually transformed into a sound poem of this class. For example, in February 1960, during a now legendary performance of some "happenings" at New York's Judson Church, Claes Oldenburg (who later became celebrated as a pop artist) read aloud to his American audience from a Swedish translation of *The Scarlet Pimpernel*. Since Oldenburg's Swedish is excellent, what the audience heard was all the phatic and phonetic materials of the Swedish language. Once the spectator gave up trying to understand the semantic meaning of the words, the result was fresh and meaningful on another plane. Another such development is the use of a work which was presumably designed for an experience in some other medium in poetry, to produce a sort of intermedial translation. For example, there is the intertextual and intermedial relationship of sound poetry and concrete poetry. Concrete poetry is, quite roughly, the genre of visual poetry which uses writing or the letters of the alphabet presented visually or systematically, as opposed to visual poems which are photographic, environmental, conceptual, temporal, etc.[13] Concrete poetry became a widespread phenomenon in the late 1950s and 1960s. However, occasionally the need to perform concrete poetry "live" would arise. So when the poets would be asked to read their work aloud, they would often use the printed texts by analogy to musical notations, thus transforming them into notated sound poems. So close is the connection between sound poetry and concrete poetry, in fact, that many artists have done both and, in fact, one of the first phonographic recordings of sound poetry as such, the 1966 *Konkrete Poesie/Sound Poetry/ Artikulationen*, by its very title indicates the near-identity of sound and concrete poetry; some of the artists included, such as Ernst Jandl, Franz Mon, and Lily Greenham, are known in both areas, and Ms. Greenham has toured in Europe and North America with her live performances of concrete poetry translated into sound poetry.[14]

[13] I say "roughly" because, for purposes of discussion, I am ignoring that subgenre of concrete poetry which is either calligraphic or is written in nonlegible writing. Many fine anthologies of concrete poetry have appeared. For example, one of the largest, one which is technically out of print but which is often found, is Emmett Williams, ed., *An Anthology of Concrete Poetry* (New York: Something Else Press, 1967).

[14] Anastasia Bitzos, ed., *Konkrete Poesie/Sound Poetry/Artikulationen* (Bern: Anastasia Bitzos, 1966). Ms. Bitzos produced at least one other such record as well. There also are several records of Lily Greenham's sound-poetry translations of concrete, for example: *Internationale Sprachexperimente der 50/60er Jahre/International Language Experiments of the 50/60ies* [sic] (Frankfurt am Main: Edition Hoffmann, ca. 1970). Unfortunately there exists, as yet, nothing like a comprehensive discography of sound poetry.

Finally, within this fifth class there is another hybrid, sound poems which are also radio plays, or which seemed designed to be heard not as a unique experience but as part of something else, so that the sound of the words is accompanied by the meanings from some different area of experience. One hears the text with only half one's attention, as one hears most radio broadcasts with only half one's attention; this is more or less inherent in the nature of radio, that one plays it while watering the house plants, while driving through heavy traffic, or while sorting out the addresses in one's address book. My own *Le petit cirque au fin du monde* and *Ommaje* are of this subclass. The first is a "hear-play" written in French, a language I do not speak well, so that the errors in it are part of its texture, and it was broadcast repeatedly over the public address system at the University of Vincennes by Jean-Jacques Lebel's students during the May 1968 insurrection in France, a perfect environment for that piece.

These, then, are the five relatively modern classes of sound poetry: (1) works in an invented language, (2) near-nonsense works, (3) phatic poems, (4) unwritten-out poems, and (5) notated ones. Obviously, some of the modern works being generated today still fall within the three classes I described earlier in older sound poetry: (1) folk varieties, (2) onomatopoetic or mimetic pieces, and (3) nonsense poetries which trope their own languages. For example, there is no doubting the modernity or avant-garde credentials of the Toronto-based group, The Four Horsemen, whose members perform both separately and together. In their performances they allude constantly to folk or popular culture, to the extent of wearing the kind of elaborate, almost psychedelic clothes associated with rock and roll groups—and they even trope the style of rock and roll to the point of listening to each other take riffs and solos and playing off each other as any tight rock group would. Their presentations are deliberately popular and light-spirited in order to minimize the gulf that usually exists between performer and audience in the new arts. Yet, formally this work belongs to two of the oldest of sound poetry traditions—the folk and nonsense traditions. In no way does this work to the detriment of their achievement, but rather it serves to remind us of something very deep within us which sound poetry expresses clearly when it is at its best—the love of the sound of poetry.

Some Boundaries and Nonboundaries of Sound Poetry

Now that we have examined some eight classes of things that sound poetry is, it might be fruitful to turn our attention briefly to some things that sound poetry either is not, or is not *yet*.

One thing that sound poetry is not is music. Of course it has a musical aspect—a strong one. But if one compares typical sound poetry pieces with typical musical ones, music is usually the presentation or activization of space and time by means of the occurrences of sound. This is the nature of the most traditional Mozart piano pieces or Irish unaccompanied airs as of the most innovative John Cage musical inventions. But *any* poetry relates space, time, and sound to experience. Thus sound poetry points in a different direction, being inherently concerned with communication and its means, linguistic and/or phatic. It implies subject matter; even when some particular work is wholly nonsemantic, as in the microphonic vocal explorations of Henri Chopin, the nonsemantic becomes a sort of negative semantics—one is conscious of the very absence of words rather than, as in vocal music, merely being aware of the presence of the voice. Thus, for the sound poet certainly and probably for the audience as well, the creation or perception of a work as sound poetry has to do with questions of meaning and experience which are not essentially musical. We identify what we are hearing more than we would if we were listening to music. We are very concerned with just who or what is saying or doing what.

Some of the things that sound poetry has not yet become are intermedial. Intermedia are those formal, conceptual areas of the arts which fall between already accepted media, such as visual poetry falling between the visual arts and poetry. However there is always a tendency for intermedia, experienced with increasing familiarity, to become themselves new media. Thus, taking sound poetry no longer as an intermedium but as a medium, it would be exciting if the sound poets would explore these three new intermedia: (1) those between sound poetry and linguistic analysis; (2) those between sound poetry and sculpture, to produce profoundly three-dimensional poetic constructs and not merely analytical ones; and (3) those between sound poetry and the environment.

In the first of these new intermedia, we could use electronic means to apply the analyzed sounds of one language to the conceptual structure of another to see what aesthetic effects would be made possible. We could write English with the transformations of German. We could generate new categories of what the linguists have called "illegal" sentences—sentences that have no possible correspondences in the physical world (e.g., Noam Chomsky's famous "colorless green ideas sleep furiously"). All sorts of new macaronics would be worth exploring—puns and mixtures among different languages, not to be humorous but to expand our experiences.

In the second new intermedium poems would appear in situations and points of space, and would move toward other situations and points of space in an exciting way. Masses of sound and word, physical presence of more words—these things would enable new poetic structures to enter into our experience.

Finally, the third intermedium could exist in environments and situations which we do not normally regard as poetic. We could have poems for sauna baths, for sunsets, for the experiencing of elections from among the apple trees. We could use aspects of those places that would aestheticize our relationships to them, as traditionally, a prayer was supposed to spiritualize our relationship to its circumstances—a prayer for nighttime, a prayer for those who were lost at sea. There is a lot to be done in these areas and more.

The Golem in the Text

Originally published in *Poésies Sonores*, edited by Vincent Barras and Nicholas Zurbrugg, Geneva: Contrechamps Éditions, 1993.

Any old poem can have its music, just as any poem that is drawn, written, printed has its look. The study of this is "ekphrasis," and it is a useful area of inquiry, one that is being widely investigated today. Recently there was an issue of *Visible Language* devoted to it, and several of the panels at this summer's *Word + Image* conference at Zürich include papers on the subject.

But not all poems are illuminated by being described as "visual poems" or "sound poems." These terms should be reserved for pieces in which the work is as much visual or acoustic as literary or even all three of these, works that are truly intermedial. But among the intermedial poetries one sees that the works do not all behave the same way. A visual poem, whether a modern piece or a thousand-year-old pattern poem, is like visual art: it is seen all at once, one can let the eye return to a part of it, and though, like a painting, it can be read, there is always the potential for simultaneity, for seeing it all at once. It approaches, though it never quite achieves, an independence of time, perfect instantaneity. One sees its visual part when one first sees the text; the words seem somehow to fill the text in. The interaction of the two is usually easy to identify.

Sound poetry, on the other hand, needs *time* to reveal it—time to hear it and, like other poetries that are *not* intermedial, time to let the words enter the mind, by the eye and the ear, letting eye and ear penetrate into oneself, slowly discovering whatever is the essence of the piece. Thus it is that with a sound poem, a poem in which the sound or acoustic element is as much a part of the work as its semantic sense, it can be difficult to feel close to a notated work in which there are scored complexities, where the eye is asked to use its esemplastic, image-making function to deduce the presumed sounds of the piece. The reader tends to see the notation as a visual entity, to admire it and say to himself or herself, "This looks interesting. I will come back to it later when there is more time." Of course that moment seldom comes. Thus, one might offer a caveat to the poet who is making a sound poem that requires a complex notation of some kind—words scattered on a page, multiple voices to be sounded together, unfamiliar sounds and pitches—that he or she should not think of the notated version of the piece as the definitive one, while at the same time it should be clear that a notation can be useful if others are to make realizations of the poem, to see what they can bring to it, things the poet may not have thought of. Such works, it should be mentioned here, are known as "text-sound" pieces.

But let us think of a great traditional dramatic performance; more or less any will do. What the actor or actress does is to bring out something already living in the text, letting it come alive in some new way. The words are not just themselves. The performer may be a bore apart from the performance. But the performer is a medium, and the words are haunted by a ghost who comes to possess the performer, a sort of golem perhaps, who takes over and consumes the text. Olivier as Henry V, Brando in *On the Waterfront*, here the haunted actor is greater than the sum of his parts, than either Brando or Olivier (actors but mere mortals) or the simple character (a cipher on a page). The magic comes from the phenomenon of haunting, of the interaction between the performer and the piece generating a new identity. The process of haunting takes us beyond what we had thought were the possibilities of a story or a poem and into a process of comparing what we see with what we had imagined.

Think also of a puppet, especially of a complex one, a marionette. We see the doll limp on the wall. What might it do? Then it comes to life. We compare what we see with what we know and what we imagine; the puppet comments by its terms of existence on what we know and what we imagine. This is why puppet theater is so useful for satire. It is also why, for a puppeteer, the essence of puppetry, like that of dance, is movement. We can see from the limp puppet what the thing looks like, but the art begins when it moves, when it does something unexpected, with graces and styles we could not have anticipated.

Thus it is also with sound poetry. The poem can have a nonsemantic text, but its structure may rest with its sound; no, it *will* be with its sound. A poet can read his text and try to make it completely unstructured, but in vain. It will always be the poet's voice and the time of the performance. The poet cannot make the piece have happened the day before, nor can he or she suddenly become someone else reading it. Even if the poem is performed by a mechanical sound system—a tape recorder or a record—it is still being performed by a tape or a record. Thus, a truly unstructured piece is not among the options with a sound poem.

But the sound poem can do something else that is not obvious until one stops to think about it a while. That is, it too can play upon its nature as performance and do what the drama performances have been mentioned as doing. That is, it can generate a golem from within itself who can possess the performer in the mind of the listener.

This golem need not be a frightening creature. I prefer the word to "ghost" as being less loaded with supernatural associations for most of us. A golem is, after all, a homunculus in Jewish folklore, endowed with life by its maker. I can cite two examples of the process.

Meredith Monk's "Song from the Hills," a vocal piece, was performed in Milwaukee by her in 1977. In it she includes the sounds of cattle calling and street selling from long ago, digested and made her own. Her normal voice, both for speaking and singing, is rich and mellifluous, as those who know her records can attest. But here it was consistently tiny, nasal, shrill. What happened is that the piece we heard less as text ("Mikni minnikminni . . ." is not semantically rich) or music (as an *a cappella* piece with sliding tones it was not traditionally musical) than as a delightful process of character revelation—not Monk's character but that of a spirit, a golem—that lived only in her piece. What did its appearance suggest? A child, a rural spirit, a farm person by turns, someone half remembered but somehow familiar. One hoped the piece would last long, so one could watch the golem exist.

Another example is found in any typical work by Henri Chopin when he performs it live. He uses non-representational sounds of voice and microphone, and usually works by playing at least two tracks of highly complex recorded sound—often electronically manipulated and usually quite loud—over which he works, using voice and microphone, exploring the possibilities that can be generated. To help the audience concentrate on what he is doing, he works in semi-darkness with a spotlight on himself. He happens to be a small man, but he has great intensity. The result is that he seems to grow and grow and grow, to become a giant, and, because of the seriousness of his manner he suggests a vampire or a threatening spirit. The process by which this spirit emerges from his performance can be quite terrifying. Noticing the emergence was not akin to the naive viewer of an abstract painting, let us say, who says: "Oh, that piece of paint reminds me of my dog," because simply pointing to the possible resemblances holds a viewer in close connection with his or her memory and blinds him or her to what is actually being said, thus producing banality. Why? It is because the process is non-mimetic, based on something the performance artist, in this case Chopin, is actually doing. The emergence is inherent in the effective live performance of the material.

Of course, other personae can emerge from sound poetry, too, but these two brief examples will, I think, suffice. Something surprising about the appearance of these haunting golems is that they have been so little commented upon, for all that they are so obvious. After all, sound poetry is a form of performance poetry, like dance, drama, and puppetry. It is not just a hybrid of abstract acoustics and words but is art work in which the artist must take the responsibility for all the possibilities offered in a given piece. The artist is, among other things, an explorer of potentials. This or that element of a work can do this or that, and the artist, in realizing the work, brings out some of these.

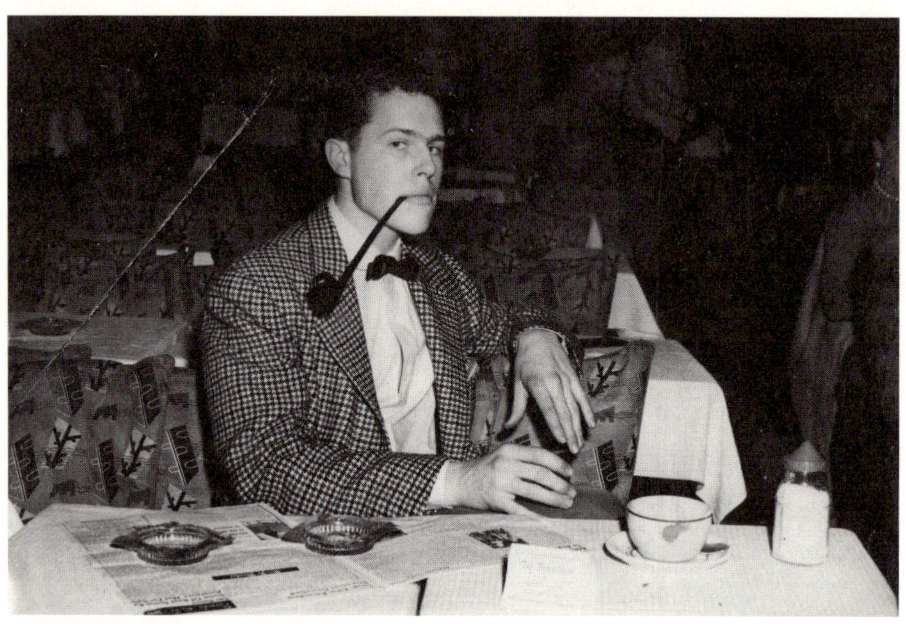

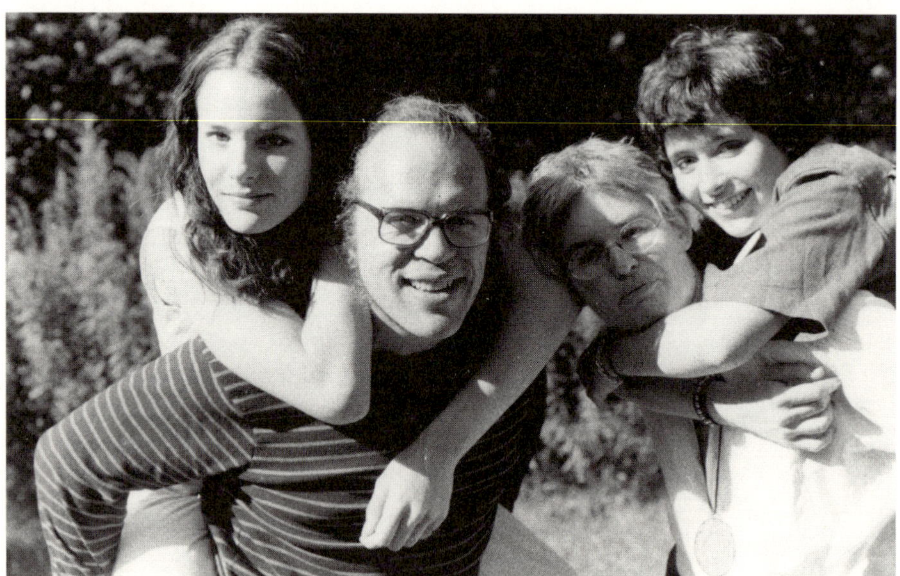

Top—Dick Higgins, circa 1962 (photographer unknown). Bottom—from left to right, Jessica Higgins, Dick Higgins, Alison Knowles, and Hannah B Higgins, 1980 (photographer unknown).

Eleven Snapshots of Dick Higgins
HANNAH HIGGINS

I suppose I'm part Emerson or Thoreau, and part Davey Crockett. For all my delight in other cultures and languages, my pleasure in digging gold nuggets out of bypassed selves, I'm still a crackerbarrel yankee at heart. I've whored, seduced, and gambled. I've been a precocious brat and a sedate businessman. I've been insane and sick. I've had enough fancy dinners to know that the best food is food for thought. I've worked in factories and universities enough to know that there's really precious little difference between them. I've tried to be a saint and found that wasn't me. —Dick Higgins[1]

We called him Pa or sometimes Pui (pronounced Poo-ee), Puter (an adaptation of the German Mutter), or Dick. As children, my twin sister Jessica and I (b. 1964) heard stories about our father's life that might shed some light on Dick Higgins, the apparently self-contradictory artist. In addition to those stories, I have relied on conversations with Dick's sister Lisa Null and my mother Alison Knowles, as well as his unpublished autobiography to fill in the details that he thought were either too insignificant to mention or that had been forgotten in the decades since then. This essay is not written as an art historian, though I am one. My expert's view of Fluxus can be found in my other books and articles on Fluxus. The context offered here seemed to be an occasion that required something else—something more lifelike, more conversational, more in the spirit of the day-to-day man that I knew as my father. These snapshots suggest some of the many dimensions of this man as we move forward and back in time.

As I knew him, he was 6' 2" tall and about 220 lbs., a large man by any standard. He sweated a lot, wore high-water pants (often white), and usually had some form of bauble around his neck. In the 1960s and '70s, these changed from neckties to wooden or turquoise necklaces and finally to those leather neckties with metal tips and a single bead worn by American cowboys. He smelled of garlic most of the time, even after a good slug of Listerine, but he was always clean. He often wore a moustache. His lips were full, and his table manners impeccable, except that he could clean a plate in a minute. The family was merciless about this last habit for good reason. He had stomach ulcers for the last twenty-five years of his life. He claimed he picked up the gobbling habit at boarding school, which brings us to the beginning.

[1] Dick Higgins, *A Life* (unpublished autobiographical manuscript), 1980, the Estate of Dick Higgins, 242.

I: The Family

In the 1920s and '30s, the Higgins homestead was a mansion surrounded by flowers and especially rose beds. These were prizewinning with the honors bestowed upon the home's mistress Clara Higgins. Each day she picked off the aphids and dropped them gingerly into a jar of kerosene. Manners were formal. Remnants of Victorianism clung fast to high society in the bustling New England manufacturing town of Worchester, Massachusetts, where the Higgins family was based. Clara's life was busy: a profound sense of social responsibility demanded her time as a volunteer as did carefully orchestrated social obligations, and her roses and horticulture.

Dick would recall a Friday afternoon concert of the nearby Boston Symphony, which he attended with his grandmother in about 1945, when he was seven. "There were surely twenty . . . aging, black-dressed dowagers, their eyes closed, being ravished by the music . . . breasts heaving . . . I decided then and there that I was for eyes-open music."[2] A small child in a scratchy suit, he sat, bewildered, beside them in his grandmother's universe. In later life, he loved to imitate them. Closing his eyes, sighing wistfully, and cocking his head, he'd gasp in feigned ecstasy and laugh.

But this caricature mightn't have been quite fair. This Clara Higgins, "who wanted to live a life from the old southern gentry," in Dick's words, also "studied piano with a student of Franz Liszt, and some of my earliest memories are of her playing Mozart."[3] She was, in fact, quite accomplished as a lay musician, studying throughout her life. In addition, having suffered post-partum depression, she developed an active interest in modern psychiatry, so much so that she would be chosen as Sigmund Freud's dinner partner when he came to Clark University on his one trip to the United States. No mere socialite, she was also an effective advocate and trustee at the Worchester Center for Crafts, where people of all stations had access to art education and was, likewise, very active in the Garden Club of America and at the nearby Silver Hill psychiatric hospital.

The Higgins family owned and operated a steel plant named Worchester Pressed Steel. The company held the patent on press-molded metal that could be used for tank parts, helmets and mess kits, as it was in World Wars I and II. Unlike other industrialists during the Great Depression and at great personal cost, the owner of the company, Dick's grandfather John Woodman Higgins, did not release workers to stem the flow of assets out of the company coffers. Of similarly social consciousness, John's son (Dick's father) Carter Chapin Higgins would later strike with workers against the family, as he was learning his way through the company.

The family traced its roots back to an Englishman Richard Higgins, who had come to the United States in 1633 and after whom Dick was named. The family genealogy *Richard Higgins*

2 Ibid., 8.
3 Ibid., 2.

and his Descendants includes amazing details of the lives of the family, making due note of its unorthodox strain, like the "sailor Yankee cousin who . . . shipwrecked near Mauritius, became a devout Muslim and founded a mudresseh."[4] John Woodman Higgins was likewise prone to such marvelous idiosyncrasy. In 1931, he built a glass and steel museum adjacent to the factory. The building's form resembled a medieval castle with sheer walls and narrow windows. This modern medieval castle, the Worchester Pressed Steel Museum, was later renamed the Higgins Armory Museum and held the largest private collection of armor in America. John Woodman Higgins could be found sometimes in full armor, distributing candy to children or simply walking about on the street near the museum or near his home, which housed a significant part of the collection. He was a kind of living exhibit extended into the streets of Worchester.

Dick's father Carter, on the other hand, had wanted to be an architectural designer of prefabricated housing but instead studied economics at Yale and Cambridge and returned to Worchester to run the family business in 1939. He was a deeply religious and socially conscious man, a deacon in the church, and a pacifist who registered as a conscientious objector until Pearl Harbor. His eye for art was excellent, and he built up a small but fine collection that included a Georges Rouault and, in the 1950s, Leon Feininger and Franz Klein. Carter would introduce Dick to much modern music in his own failed attempts to understand it. Put briefly, this was a society family, but one with some fascinating quirks. Grandfather might be found strolling the streets of Worchester in full body armor, while Clara, his wife, hosted a proper tea one day and volunteered her time the next, and the son invested in extremely modern culture.

Dickie, as his parents called him, was born in Jesus Pieces, England, on the ides of March, 1938. His parents Katherine Bigelow Higgins and Carter Chapin Higgins spent a year there before returning to the family homestead in Worchester. The Bigelows were a literary family of Calvinist ministers and missionaries. Katherine's mother Elisabeth MacDonald Bigelow, a.k.a. "Granan," ran a series of theater schools in New York City and frequently sang concerts in New York. Sinclair Lewis had once proposed marriage to this fascinating career woman. Katherine, or Kitsy as she was often called, was deeply intellectual as well; she regularly wrote poetry and read it to her son. The family was convinced Dick was a prodigy. As he was fond of saying, his first word was "hypotenuse."

---

[4] Ibid., 4.

II: Youth

The maternal grandmother Granan played a formative role in Dick's early life during her frequent visits to Worchester. Most importantly, she generated in him a love of theater and the arts as a vocation, not an avocation, as well as a transcendentalist sense of "nature as the hand of god."[5] Upon her death, she left Dick a bible with a quote in it from the 119th Psalm that read "The word is a lamp unto my feet and a light unto my path."[6] I think he took this quite literally. He remained close to the Episcopal Church throughout his life, periodically contributing to discussions at St. John the Evangelist Episcopal Church in local Barrytown, New York, where he attended Sunday service in the last decades of his life. In later life he would say he'd have liked to have been a minister. I'm not sure he had the patience for that although I think he loved using the bible to ask and answer moral and social questions. In his autobiographical notes, Dick wrote, "If I have to pray for help, I do not pray to some favorite saint, I pray to Granan."[7] She would die in Worchester of cancer in 1946.

Given the intellectual commitment of Granan, perhaps it was predictable that Katherine Bigelow would find life in Worchester among the roses stifling. She and Carter divorced in 1948, when Dick was ten. Nana, as my sister and I called her, would raise a second family with a Hungarian lawyer Nicholas Doman in New York City, providing Dick with two half-brothers, Danny (b. 1953) and Alex (b. 1955). Her studies continued throughout her life. She donated endless time and resources to the American Museum of Natural History and remained a strong intellectual presence for and confidant to Dick until her death in 1991. Carter remarried as well. His second wife Mary Bechold was a survivor of Auschwitz and Dachau and told stories of concentration camp life that Dick described as both "terrible and strangely beautiful when some act of incredible bravery or generosity was remembered . . . I decided then and there that I loved the Jewish people as no other besides my own."[8] Mary's experience exerted an enormous influence on her stepchildren. Dick would give my sister and me the Jewish names of Hannah and Jessica when we twins were born in 1964. His sister Lisa (b. 1942) described feeling socially alienated from Worchester society since she saw in their moderate anti-Semitism "the things that had created Auschwitz."[9] After having worked for Albert Schweitzer, Dick's brother Mark (b. 1940) died in the Congolese War of Independence in 1960, while he was on his way to Israel to work on a kibbutz.

In summary, all three of Kitsy and Carter's children were very close to Mary, even though she was "wildly manic-depressive. She could let you in and then turn on you in a rage."[10] She would commit suicide using sleeping pills in 1965.

[5] I loved this description when it came up in a fact-finding conversation with Lisa Null on July 24, 2003. It is consistent with my sense of how Dick understood nature.

[6] Higgins, *A Life*, 12.

[7] Ibid., 12.

[8] Ibid., 23.

[9] Conversation with Null, ibid.

[10] Ibid.

III: A Schoolboy's Laments

The first references to Dick's complex sexuality appear on the first pages of his unpublished autobiographical notes, when he was five or six years old. He wrote "We played doctor in curious 'grunt houses,' piles of furniture piled with blankets and rugs ... I found that I liked the girls better than boys as people, mostly, but that the boys bodies interested me more."[11] By Dick's account, he was therefore shipped off to weekly sessions with a child psychologist in Boston. By Lisa's account, however, the situation was quite a bit more complex than this. He was having trouble at the Bancroft School in Worchester, where he was bored as an early reader and, therefore, prone to outbursts, rages, and disappearances. His parents were informed that he suffered "gender identification" problems; they responded by hiring "male helpers"[12] for their summer vacations in Gloucester, where it was clear that these attendants were there to role model male behavior for the young man. Later, Dick would decide that he was sexually gay, for the most part, but enjoyed women as companions and even, occasionally, sexual partners. But that's later in our story.

Katherine looked hard for a school that could nurture her precocious and difficult son, who was already writing music and poetry. At eight, Dick was shipped off to Hickory Ridge School in Putney, Vermont. While the separation from his mother, Lisa, and Mark was painful at first, Hickory Ridge became the most congenial educational experience of his childhood. This little school was progressive in the extreme; teachers and students were known to skinny dip for exercise, read together by the fire at night as an English class, and hunt in the woods for living science specimens. Sexual experimentation among the students was tolerated, not punished. Dick would return to Vermont as an adult in 1971 in an effort, I believe, to recapture these times.

Among his friends at the school were Aubie Breton, daughter of the Surrealist poet André Breton, who educated him on the life of her father and on Surrealism in New York and Paris. Happy as Dick was to "have friendships that were based on interests in common," Hickory Ridge lacked discipline, as Carter's new wife Mary would have it. Dick was removed from the school before eighth grade and sent to Saint Paul's School, a conservative Episcopal boarding school of appropriately crusty pedigree in Concord, New Hampshire. In this school inhabited by "God's Frozen People,"[13] Dick "was proud to be a weirdo."[14] It was here that he began to write passionately and publicly across disciplines in a manner consistent with his future practice as an artist. Modernist poems in German and English, experimental plays, and literary and musical reviews appeared in *Horae Scholsticae*, the school newspaper, for which he was an editor.

[11] Higgins, *A Life*, 6.
[12] Ibid., 18.
[13] Ibid., 40.
[14] Ibid., 41.

Once, he and a friend wanted to run away. They needed money, and his "weir-do's" nose for rare books was fine enough for him to seek out good ones from the Saint Paul's library, peel off the school markings, and sell them to a rare book dealer in southern New Hampshire. He was expelled and attended Worchester High School, where he had "one of the richest six months of my life. Here I wasn't a weirdo anymore—I was a brain, instead."[15] After six months and, according to Dick, a stint in a local, gay motorcycle gang, he returned to St. Paul's. He graduated in 1955 and after not getting into Harvard, he grudgingly started his studies at Yale. Carter had been a football star there in his day as well as a member of the Whiffenpoof singers. Whether real or imagined, Dick felt his family expected the same of him.

IV: Thick Skin

Dick described Yale as "an education annex to a country club."[16] He simply didn't feel a part of the social order of that school but not for lack of effort. In addition to a full course load, he was active in the Dramatic Association, which attracted a few gay students, joined summer stock theater, and hosted a radio program of new music that aired John Cage, Karlheinz Stockhausen, Virgil Thompson, and others. This extraordinary level of activity taxed Dick psychologically and physically. In 1957, he "triggered an escape mechanism," stole some books, and tried to peddle them as he had at St. Paul's.

He was caught. Carter was notified and, rightly reading the symptoms of a nervous breakdown, took him to Silver Hill, the psychiatric hospital in New Canaan, Connecticut, where Clara was an active advocate for the mentally ill. Dick remained there for the winter of 1957–8. On that first visit, he described the depression like this: "My skin, I can remember, seemed thick like parchment. I imagined that I was very, very old in a world filled with laughing and sardonic puppets."[17]

V: Cage, Cowell, and The Beat Scene

Declining an invitation to reenter Yale following his departure from Silver Hill in 1958, Dick graduated from Columbia School of General Studies with an English major and a music minor in 1960. The Columbia years were happy ones, for the most part, as Dick immersed himself in the art world. He lived with his mother, stepfather, and their young sons on the Upper East Side of Manhattan. In 1958–9, he studied music with the modern composers Henry Cowell at Columbia and John Cage at the New School for Social Research. Both were important

[15] Ibid., 45.
[16] Ibid., 60.
[17] Ibid., 68.

experiences. Cowell composed using "tone clusters" and taught the first known courses on world music, an important collection of which Dick would amass and which would be donated to Williams College after his death.[18] Dick took Cage's now legendary course in Experimental Composition. That course, more of an exchange among peers directed by Cage's expert knowledge, was a hotbed of experimental art activity.

In the Cage class, compositional works using chance operations and other compositional experiments took the form of music, theater, and poetry and were performed on whatever instruments or objects could be found in a little closet adjacent to the classroom. Many artists associated with this class would become participants in Fluxus. In particular, the chemist George Brecht invented the Event type of performance that subsequently would be associated with Fluxus. Events are minimal, pared-down actions that make possible an aesthetic experience of everyday life. Among Dick's early Events was *Danger Music Number Seventeen* (May 1962), which reads "Scream! Scream! Scream! Scream! Scream! Scream!"[19]

Following one of the frequent, heated arguments at his mother's apartment between Kitsy and Nicholas, Dick punched his stepfather in the nose. It was determined that he should move, which he did, to Christopher Street in Greenwich Village. At about the same time (in 1958), fellow Cage-class student Al Hansen and Dick co-founded the New York Audio-Visual Group. This duo took the experimental attitude of the Cage class to Greenwich Village coffee shops and the street. The most important of these coffee shops was the E-pít-o-me Coffee Shop and Art Gallery, which was run by (among others) Lawrence (Larry) Poons, later of op-art fame, on then burgeoning Bleecker Street. The New York Audio-Visual Group would perform at E-pít-o-me with the Beat poets, and Dick's first professional appearance in print was in the now legendary *The Beat Scene* magazine.

In 1959 at the E-pít-o-me Coffee Shop, Dick met the collagist and mail artist Ray Johnson, after mistaking him for Jasper Johns. They "often wandered together through the Lower East Side, where he lived like a Troll under the Brooklyn Bridge investigating strange cheeses in jars or fishes in barrels."[20] Dick would go on to enjoy years of mail art exchanges with this founder of the New York Correspondence School and would publish Johnson's *The Paper Snake* many years later.

[18] At the time of his death, Dick was assembling a collection of Cowell's writings that has been published posthumously. *Essential Cowell: Selected Writing on Music by Henry Cowell*, ed. Dick Higgins. (New Paltz, NY: Documentext/ McPherson and Company. 2001).

[19] A full list of these Events can be found in *A Dick Higgins Sampler*, ed. Jeff Abell (Chicago, IL: Columbia College Center for the Book and Paper Arts. 2000), 9.

[20] Higgins, *A Life*, 78.

VI: Love Knots

In 1960, Ray Johnson's friend Dorothy Podber introduced my mother and father to each other. Dorothy brought Alison to a party "of mostly gay guys" at Dick's studio apartment on Christopher Street.[21] The party was running too loud and late, so Dick called the police on himself and hid under his bed until his apartment cleared out. Alison found him there, crawled under the bed with him, and stayed for three days. Expressing a love unbound by time, he symbolically tossed an alarm clock out the window. Just like that. Dick described his first sexual encounter with a woman this way: "Dorothy Podber had told her I was gay, but this didn't seem to bother her any. I decided to concern myself with the girl behind the eyes, and to let the plumbing take care of itself in its own way. So I lost my virginity with a woman, and, finding how much I cared for her, there didn't seem to be much point in going back."[22] She gave him her address and number and invited him to her industrial loft at 423 Broadway at Canal Street. There since 1959, she may well have been the first artist living in what would become SoHo. They were married in 1960, divorced in 1970, recommitted to their relationship in about 1974, and remarried in 1984.

Following the first divorce, Dick had two significant, gay relationships. Both were with alienated young men, whom Dick mentored. As far as I am aware, he never initiated a relationship with a man who could be called a peer, although in the later years at least one of his lovers certainly became one.

The first was Eugene Williams, the son of his good friend Emmett Williams. Dick and Eugene drove to Alaska together in 1971, and Eugene lived with us for a time in Vermont following that journey. Dick felt deeply for him. From my perspective, the relationship ran roughshod over Dick's parental responsibilities during this otherwise "strange and idyllic" period. That relationship would end (mercifully for Jess and me) in 1973 when Eugene married and had a daughter and Dick suffered a breakdown.

In 1983, Dick developed a committed relationship with a wispy and cerebral young poet Bryan McHugh. Bryan would later run a small press called Left Hand Books, which produced exquisitely crafted and designed books by both of my parents and by several interesting poets local to the Hudson Valley in Upstate New York. Bryan became very much a peer of Dick's and a part of the family, residing in a small apartment adjacent to the house until Dick's death in 1998.

For the family, this was Dick's most successful gay relationship, as it was a friendship able to allow for Dick's extremely deep feelings for and dedication to Alison, who was a close friend of Bryan's as well. In 1982, Dick wrote, "I've slept with sufficient men and women to know that love's more important than sex or gender."[23]

[21] Alison Knowles, in discussion with the author. July 24, 2003.

[22] Higgins, *A Life*, 94.

[23] Ibid., 242.

The relative domestic harmony and clarity of commitments that characterized the last decades of Dick's life model that principle.

VII: Happenings, or There About

Just prior to Dick and Alison's first wedding in 1960, Dick failed his military exams. Dick and Alison plotted that failure in what sounds, ultimately, like a parody of a Happening. Knowing he'd be nervous enough to vomit during the interview, Dick consumed several quarts of strawberries just before going to the recruiting center. These produced the desired volume of vomit upon his arrival. As he related the story to us, he said that he also was so nervous that he urinated each time he was asked a question, which must have been quite a sight in the long straight line of naked, would-be soldiers. As if this weren't enough, he was then removed to a side room and asked to write a few paragraphs on his relationship to his mother. After three hours of steady writing, the pile of pages was still growing. They took away the pencil and sent him home to Alison classified 3-F, "draftable only in case of a dire emergency."[24]

Performance and Happenings as well as the burgeoning experimental music scene had been going full force after 1958. Dick and Happenings artist Allan Kaprow had met and become friends in the Cage class, with Dick performing in Kaprow's first Happening by the name *18 Happenings in 6 Parts* in 1958. By 1960, Claes Oldenburg and James Dine had arrived from Chicago and were performing Happenings with Kaprow and the New York Audio-Visual Group duo Hansen and Higgins.

The resulting collaboration called the *Ray Gun Spex* series at Judson Church, host of much experimental work at the time including the famous Judson Dance group, was a huge success. Dine performed his famous *Smiling Workman*, which climaxed with a bucket of orange paint being tossed over his head. Popular success aside, Dick felt that his comparatively ascetic work was out of place with the Happenings format such that "fond as we might be of the individual artists . . . we refused to participate in further shows or performances with my Happenings brothers—now cousins."[25]

For some reason, the same wouldn't be true of Dick's performing relationship to Meredith Monk. After Meredith performed in several Happenings with Dick and Alison at the Cafe Au Go Go in 1964, Dick invited her to perform in his *Celestials* at the Sunnyside Boxing Arena. This "visual canon of activities" was, according to Monk, "one of the most beautiful works I ever encountered."[26] They later worked together on Eric Satie's *Relache*, where she was "a human wheelbarrow with Dick piling books on my back." Perhaps most memorably, however, Monk describes *Juice* (1969)

[24] Higgins, *A Life*, 96.
[25] Ibid., 105.
[26] Meredith Monk to the family, December 1998. Copy in my archive.

at the Guggenheim Museum: "The image of Dick painted red from head to toe dancing in large red combat boots remains indelible in my mind. That wonderful, generous body and extraordinary voice flowing with energy and commitment . . . with Dick anything was possible."[27]

VIII: Fluxus

Perhaps the most fortuitous event of 1960 was when the composer and Cage-class participant Richard Maxfield introduced a "cryptophilic designer" named George Maciunas to Dick and others in that social circle. Maciunas had "an art gallery and lots of ambition."[28] This Lithuanian-Georgian intended to introduce the Upper East Side to avant-garde work through his gallery called AG on Madison Avenue. He hosted shows by Yoko Ono and others and performances by La Monte Young, Ray Johnson, Henry Flynt, Richard Maxfield, Joseph Byrd (of later rock fame), and my father. The gallery failed a year later, but the voluntary alliance that would later become Fluxus had begun to form self-consciously for many of the artists.

After the collapse of the gallery, Maciunas collected notations for *Beatitude East*, a special issue of the West Coast magazine called *Beatitude*. Jackson Mac Low and La Monte Young later published these as *An Anthology* (1961), which contained scores by virtually every one associated with Fluxus in the United States and abroad.

The collection of new musical formats, performance, concrete poetry, and other experimental art might well be described as the first Fluxus collection and publication. Materials continued to arrive at Maciunas's doorstep, however. To address the volume, Maciunas "would issue a series of yearbooks as a periodical called *Fluxus*."[29] And so it was that the artists already associating with each other in New York came to be called Fluxus artists. These would include, but not be limited to, Brecht, Hansen, Mac Low, Ono, Young, and my mother and father from the greater context of the Cage class, as well as Joe Jones and Philip Corner.

Indeed, Maciunas would go on to be the most gifted organizer and designer of Fluxus activities and objects and would, thereby, be recorded erroneously in history as its founder. His significant role in co-founding Fluxus should not, however, be completely denied. Fleeing the U.S. because of debts incurred in relationship to his gallery, Maciunas headed to Europe, where he organized most of the relevant early Fluxus concerts, beginning with a series at the Wiesbaden Museum in Germany. These concerts established much of the content later used in Fluxus performance festivals and brought together Fluxus artists who had long admired each other's work but had

27 Ibid.
28 Higgins, *A Life*, 110.
29 Ibid., 112.

never met. In addition to Maciunas, Brecht, and my mother and father, these concerts included Ben Patterson, Emmett Williams, and Nam June Paik. These were followed by concerts at the Düsseldorf Kunstakademie, where Joseph Beuys met the artists, and in Paris and London, where the artists met French artist Ben Vautier and Danish artist Addi Køpcke. In November 1962, another Dane, the debonair and minimalist Fluxus artist Eric Andersen, who would remain among Dick's closest, lifelong friends, organized the first of the now famous Fluxus concerts in the seventeen-century Nikolajkirke in Copenhagen. Among the works performed at these festivals were several Events called *Danger Music* that Dick began writing in 1961. These were intended to place the performer at psychological or physical risk. For example, *Danger Music Number Nine* (for Nam June Paik) (1962) reads, "Volunteer to have your spine removed." Such an action is impossible and strangely violent. However, there are gentler ones as well, such as *Number Fifteen*, "Work with butter and eggs for a time," which results in squishy butter snakes and egg and butter flatulence.[30]

The most famous of these—*Danger Music Number Twelve* (1962), "Write a thousand symphonies"—resulted in a graphic work *The Thousand Symphonies* in 1968.[31] To produce the latter work, Fluxus artist Geoffrey Hendricks arranged to have a captain from the South Brunswick, New Jersey Police Department fire a 9mm MP40 Schmeisser submachine gun through pristine sheets of music paper. The hole-bitten sheets were then laid over one another and sprayed through with paint. The resulting dots and holes could be played, which they were in a concert at Rutgers University by Fluxus composer Philip Corner on December 9, 1968. Although Dick continued to produce the painted versions of them periodically, no new sheets of paper were fired through after the original "shooting."

It is relevant that this piece was written during the Vietnam era and suggests something of the other uses far from those merely destructive to which a gun might be put. Dick wrote of the *Symphonies* that "[at] that time the USA police seemed to have nothing better to do than to chase down teenagers for possessing miniscule amounts of marijuana and throwing them in jail, thus ruining their lives . . . I decided it could be more worthy if one could set all the policemen in the USA to composing symphonies themselves."[32]

[30] Abell, *Dick Higgins*, 9.

[31] Dick Higgins, "The Thousand Symphonies: Their Story" in *Critical Mass: Happenings, Fluxus and Performance Intermedia at Rutgers University, 1958–1972.* ed. Geoffrey Hendricks (New Brunswick, NJ: Mason Gross Art Galleries/Rutgers University Press. 2003), 102.

[32] Ibid.

IX: Intermedia and the Something Else Press

In 1960, Dick and Alison attended the Manhattan School of Printing. There he honed the skills he had picked up as a school newspaper editor, skills that very much would come in handy in the future. He got a job at Harding and Harding, a bank stationery and check production company on Prince Street. At that job, among other things, he designed checks for Elvis Presley. By 1963, Dick had developed an interest in publishing his own work as well as that of his friends in and around Fluxus. That year he founded the Something Else Press (SEP). It was incorporated in 1964.

The story of its naming has become something of a legend. Frustrated with Maciunas's slow progress in publishing a collection of Dick's writing called *Jefferson's Birthday*, Dick arrived home one evening to Alison and said, "We've started a press." She replied, "Oh, really? What's it called?" Prone to romantic visions of working-class life and communal culture, he answered "Shirtsleeves Press." "That is a terrible name," she said, "Call it something else." He did. The Something Else Press published short works by many artists, including my mother, as pamphlets called Great Bear after the water dispenser by the front door of their 22nd Street house in Chelsea, where Dick had been standing when he decided to publish such works. There would also be a newsletter and gallery given the name Something Else.

The following year, in 1965, Dick published an essay called "Intermedia" in the first issue of the *Something Else Newsletter*. Dick's revival of that term—originated by Samuel Taylor Coleridge in an 1812 essay—quickly filled a terminological void in the art world. Used to describe art that falls between media or between art and life, "intermedia" spread rapidly into use, since it could function as an umbrella term for much of the most interesting art of the period. "Much of the best work being done today seems to fall between media," he wrote. "This is no accident. The concept of the separation between media arose in the Renaissance."[33] Franconia College in New Hampshire designed an Intermedia Program, the New York State Council on the Arts established Intermedia grants, and Intermedia festivals were held around the globe. Today the term refers primarily to artists working with technology, multimedia, and, sometimes, mass media, yet even its current use has its origins in Dick's essay.

In the next nine years, SEP published first books by Mac Low, Oldenburg, my father, and others. It also published major books by Cage, Merce Cunningham, Robert Filliou, Ray Johnson, Jerome Rothenberg, Marshall McLuhan, and Daniel Spoerri, to name a few art world icons. The Press published several reissues of work then largely lost to the vicissitudes of time. Among these were the last known graphic work by Marcel Duchamp, *Flying Hearts* (1968),

[33] Dick Higgins, "Intermedia." *Something Else Newsletter*, vol. 1, no. 1 (1966). 1; reprinted in Dick Higgins, *Horizons: The Poetics and Theory of the Intermedia* (Carbondale, IL: Southern Illinois University Press, 1984), 18–21.

which was executed by Knowles, as well as Gertrude Stein's *Making of Americans* and Richard Huelsenbeck's *Dada Almanach*. All SEP publications were intended for mass consumption, and all hardcover publications were printed on and bound with the highest quality materials, including acid-free paper stock. Significantly, most were used, and those left undisturbed are still in perfect shape. The Great Bear Pamphlets occasionally even found their way into supermarkets, such as the Co-op in Berkeley, California.

In 1971, Dick and Alison were invited by their friend and Happenings cohort Allan Kaprow and by Paul Brach to teach at a new art school called Cal Arts in Burbank, California. We moved, press and all, to Newhall, California. Dick and Alison separated, and we girls moved in with him. Cal Arts was just getting on its feet, and for most of the faculty, who were excited about starting a school and rethinking creative art pedagogy, morale was quite high. Perhaps it was the freewheeling atmosphere of hippies, the endless banter of faculty meetings, or the increasing visibility of his art world peers in the commercial sphere, in any case, Dick quickly became unhappy there and was probably looking for a reason to leave. Fortunately, one materialized. Early one morning, Dick, astounded by the sudden silence of the birds, awakened and sat up. At that moment, his huge bookcase crashed onto the bed where he'd been sleeping (it could have killed him). A major earthquake was occurring. He swooped into our room and grabbed Jess and me in each arm, and we made our way to the swimming pool exit. There, as Dick later described it, we were astounded: "The water in the swimming pool . . . was standing on end, like a frozen sculpture about eight feet tall in the middle of the pool."[34] This description is consistent with how I remember our very own, private tidal wave. In 1972, Dick moved the Something Else Press as well as the family (sans Alison) to West Glover, Vermont.

The Press, whether in New York, California, or, after 1972, Vermont, was funded handsomely by Dick's inheritance from the Higgins fortune in 1964. In a cultural context that was actively hostile to experimental intermedia, this publishing venture stood alone in its brazen support of new and intermedia work. Through the Press, Dick gambled on the public interest in this work, faithfully relying on the public ability to know a good thing. He lost the gamble, spending nearly every cent of his part of the family fortune, and in 1973 suddenly withdrew his financial support for SEP, following which the Press was placed in the hands of editors who were understandably hamstrung without Dick's deep pockets and managerial authority. Not surprisingly, the Press collapsed in bankruptcy in 1974.

Perhaps the greatest loss associated with this collapse was that of Dick's closest friendship at the time, Fluxus artist, poet, humorist, and one of its best performers, Emmett Williams, who had moved his own family to Vermont to work for the Press. Williams had been the editor at the Press

<hr>

[34] Higgins, *A Life*, 159.

from 1966 until 1972, and his "fine hand," as Dick called it, can be felt in the books published during these years, the Press's most prolific. Indeed, much of its success is directly attributable to this one-time editor of the *Stars and Stripes* newspaper. In particular, *An Anthology of Concrete Poetry*, the Press's bestseller at 18,000, was edited by Williams and established the genre in the United States. In the early '70s as Dick declined into alcoholism and bankruptcy, it was this gentle humorist and Flux-poet who was left holding the bag, so to speak. In an inexcusable act of belligerence, Dick foreclosed on his obligations and effectively evicted this close friend from his life and home.

The brash provocateur and innovator, fully funded and financially secure for the future, had lost his steam as a public persona. His next publishing venture would be cooperative, with each author raising his or her own publication costs through grants and good will. This enterprise existed from 1972–85; initially called Unpublished Editions, in 1978 it was renamed Printed Editions, and it included on its board many of the most distinguished intermedial artists of that generation and many of the authors associated with the Something Else Press.

X: Arcadia

In Vermont, Dick tried to find the "god in nature" that he had so loved at Hickory Ridge School. He went back to the land, as it was called, hooking up with a network of communes that were very much in the tradition of his beloved school. He belonged to the tradition of American naturalism associated with some of his favorite writers, Henry David Thoreau and Ralph Waldo Emerson. Not coincidentally, Dick's former teacher John Cage likewise admired Thoreau and came north periodically for visits, as did Ray Johnson, Wolf Vostell, and Meredith Monk. Emmett Williams had relocated to Vermont in 1972 and moved into a log cabin up the hill from Dick's rambling farmhouse and barns that sat on a beautiful and remote piece of land in a part of Vermont, called the Northeast Kingdom. Dick dreamed of raising American bison on the huge swath of field that was our front and backyard. Instead he built a graphic studio, geodesic guest and dog domes, and an enormous addition that would serve as his office and library.

Beginning on July 7, 1973, Dick launched a major graphic series of unique prints based on chance operations. Completed in 1975 and consisting of perhaps a thousand prints, the *7.7.73* series brought together representations of nature's flora and fauna, with the chance operations of Cage's and Dick's experiments in the visual effects of language. The format would remain largely unchanged when Dick transitioned into painting, which would dominate his artistic practice for the last two decades of his life. Element, color, and placement were determined by a throw of the dice, and the world could be alternately quite spare or imagisticly dense. His description is worth repeating here: "My intention was to parallel pop art, which is usually urban, using rural materials and, in doing so, to imply a cycle of Arcadian life which I hoped to live. The cycle is organized into five seasons, each using materials that are somehow appropriate to them—summer, autumn, winter, spring and, between these two last, mud."[35]

In 1973, Dick, for a two-year period, suffered his second nervous breakdown, following the collapse of his financial fortunes and a bout of binge drinking during which he could "become quite belligerent."[36] As he described the beginning of the breakdown, one day when he woke up: "strange paisley patterns were all around me [and] what was even more frightening was the sound that I was hearing terrible, deep organ-like sounds that seemed like tuned earthquakes. I staggered to the window and looked out. Through the curtain of moving paisley insects I could see a cloud, and the cloud had a voice, the voice of Meredith Monk, whom I had not seen in years."[37] He spent a year and a half at Silver Hill being treated for alcoholism, returning to Vermont to build an indoor Olympic size pool that virtually bankrupted him, and then returning to Silver Hill to be treated for depression. "I felt that I was dead, or that I should be."[38] During these years, Dick took refuge in his relationship to my mother, "dear Alison," from whom he'd been divorced for four years and who would remain his love and anchor for the remainder of his life.

XI: Home on the Hudson

After the 1974 collapse of Something Else Press and his ensuing breakdown, Dick returned to academic life and New York City. In 1975, we moved in next door to Alison, who had a loft at 122 Spring Street, "not far from our old haunts at Broadway and Canal, in what is now called SoHo and which, mysteriously, had become quite chic."[39] In a gesture that realized a fantasy held by many children of divorced parents, the family was effectively reunited as a social unit, even if the parents had separate sleeping quarters. The big house in Vermont that had housed permanent residents, an enormous camera lab, and the SEP offices was sold off, and a small cabin up the hill from the press became Dick's respite from urban life.

Having spent his fortune running the Something Else Press, Dick was primarily interested in developing a means of earning a living. From 1975–79, Dick fought hard for advanced degrees from the conservative English Department at New York University. He received his Master's Degree there in 1977, but in 1979, he dropped out in protest after failing the comprehensive exams. This act of defiance cost him the PhD, and it was a bitter loss—

[35] Dick Higgins, archival notes regarding each series of work produced during his lifetime. Special Collections. Northwestern University Library.

[36] Dick Higgins, *A Life*, 184.

[37] Ibid., 186.

[38] Ibid., 192.

[39] Ibid., 197.

he was more accomplished than many of the professors. By 1979, he had published 146 articles and twenty-two volumes as a solo author, composer, or artist and had been written up in dozens of reviews, articles, and books.

At the same time, Dick became disillusioned with the business enterprise that the art world had become in New York in the 1960s and '70s. He came to see galleries as "emporia for the fashion industry's visual art adjuncts"[40] and felt himself unable to connect to the community of like-minded people that had once made the city tolerable for him. In a way, his presence was no longer necessary to that world, and he had lost his stature as pioneer. He briefly tried to relocate again to Vermont, but this put him too far from Alison, Jess, and me. At the suggestion of his friend George Quasha, who owned and operated the Station Hill Press with his wife Susan in Barrytown, New York, Dick purchased a small, white church and small house with green shutters near Bard College in the Hudson Valley in 1979.

The area offered him a combination of rural pleasures and intellectual outlets, "nearer New York without being in the whirl of Lilliputians."[41] The Station Hill Press was right down the street, and it had around it a circle of interesting poets, performance people, composers, and free spirits, many of whom Dick already knew. "Pauline Oliveros, one of my favorite composers," moved in nearby and remained among Dick's closest artistic and personal friends for the rest of his life. Unlike Vermont, however, Dick describes that "this time the idyll was unmarred. My relationships were real, not wishful thinking, as was the social and financial underpinning of my scene (in Vermont). Alison was there as often or as little as she chose, and that made for a more peaceful scene . . ."[42]

Perhaps most surprising to his friends, however, he began painting in earnest. His interests in historic, modern, and contemporary intermedial art forms found an unlikely, if appropriate, stage on canvas. While these paintings constitute Dick's single most concerted effort in materials and time, this work is virtually unknown. The work occurred in six cycles that addressed choreographic movement, cartographical history (how we represent the physical space of the world to ourselves), magic, religious and evolutionary history, and music theory and that took the form and title respectively of *Arrows, Maps, Brown Paintings, Cosmologies, Natural Histories,* and *Music.* It is a mistake to see the paintings as a repudiation of some imagined "critical" stance that he held before. Rather, they are explorations in paint of concerns that had long occupied him.

Not surprisingly, the art world, with its predilections for strictly stylistic categories, was unconvinced, and Dick had an almost impossible time showing and selling these later pieces. This caused him no small degree of anxiety and frustration. Relying on his reputation from the 1960s and '70s, Dick was able to lead workshops

[40] Ibid., 120.
[41] Ibid., 238.
[42] Ibid., 240.

in colleges and art schools periodically until his death in 1998. Unlike Dick's, Alison's individual art career advanced at that time. Nevertheless, his books continued to appear containing new poetry, plays, graphic musical notation, and art theory. These years also saw his greatest scholarly endeavors realized, such as his watershed collection of ancient to modern visual poetry called *Pattern Poetry: Guide to an Unknown Literature* and a translation with Charles Doria of Giordano Bruno's *On the Composition of Images, Signs and Ideas*.[43]

Imperfect as these years may have been from a professional and financial standpoint, they were important in other ways. Dick's relationship with Bryan McHugh was a great solace to him. The family, including Bryan, enjoyed time together as adults playing bridge, Scrabble, watching foreign films, and listening to Dick's wonderful record collection. Bryan's Left Hand Books publishing company kept a steady stream of new and innovative published material in the house, which took up some of Dick's interest in that end of things.

All this ended in the fall of 1997, however, when, on Station Hill Road, an oncoming car hit the car in which Dick, Alison, and Jessica rode. Alison went into the windshield, Jessica suffered a serious concussion, and Dick broke his leg in several places. Confined to bed for many months with pins and a halo, Dick then spent about six months in a wheelchair. A depression set in that seemed strangely justified. This lifted somewhat when he was invited by Richard Martel to participate in his Inter festival in Quebec, Canada. As the name suggests, the festival had its basis in the intermedia concept.

In Quebec, Dick had a high old time. On October 25, 1998, he was interviewed about intermedia and was honored, and he conversed with young people and contemporaries alike. I've seen the interview. It is haunting—he looked gray, like wet plaster, but seemed to be enjoying the conversation. That night he smoked the cigarettes that let off steam for him, since he couldn't drink socially anymore. He complained of feeling tired and went home early. The next morning he failed to show up for breakfast at the local diner. That was unlike him. His friend, Fluxus artist Larry Miller, who had been with him the day before, took off that morning to find him. He found him dead from a heart attack. Dick had been getting ready for bed. He was found nude on the floor, with a book about General Lee at his side. It was a great, if early, death that was commemorated in many venues, among them the Whitney Museum and the Judson Church. In August 2000, his ashes were laid to rest in Sag Harbor, Long Island, in the Knowles family plot. With children and grandchildren in tow, his family sang his favorite songs and put his favorite vanilla ice cream in with the ashes. My sister's husband Josh Selman had been wearing Dick's watch since his death. He spontaneously threw it in too. My youngest daughter

[43] Dick Higgins, *Pattern Poetry: Guide to an Unknown Literature* (Albany, NY: SUNY Press, 1987). Giordano Bruno, *On the Composition of Images, Signs and Ideas*. trans. by Charles Doria, edited and annotated by Higgins (New York: Willis, Locker and Owen, 1991).

Zoe, five at the time, spontaneously picked up a shovel and began the formal burial. It was perfect, as Dick would have wanted.

As Dick put it, "It's hard to say where a life begins (or ends)."[44] Dick's most engaged years with the art world occurred between 1958 and 1970, but in many of these years he was functioning as a publisher, which isn't how he ultimately saw himself. Then again, one might look to his most productive years of making his own art, which would pre- and post-date the Press, a sort of doughnut that doesn't really make sense either. If we're talking about painting, then the life really begins in 1979, when Dick was forty-one years old. We might trace an arc, a story of a life that ebbed and flowed in and around the arts. And then there's a quiet sense of order that people seldom find with themselves and with others. Perhaps he found that, and then it was over. Or his life may still be in occurrence, as publications, exhibitions, and collections continue to express the vitality of his work. Who knows or cares, really. What matters is that he had one, and it was a great one.

[44] Higgins, *A Life*, 1.

Index

This index primarily contains names and titles, with some conceptual analysis (e.g. see the Fluxus entry). Page numbers in italics indicate illustrations and photographs; page numbers with "n" indicate that the subject will only be found in a note on the page. Something Else Press is sometimes abbreviated as SEP. Dick Higgins is sometimes abbreviated as DH.

Copyrights and Permissions

Many of Higgins's texts were originally published by Something Else Press in newsletter, book or catalogue form. Others first appeared in small magazines, and a few were privately printed. Each text in this book is preceded by a note designating its original publication, if previously published. The excerpt from *Postface* is reproduced with slight alterations of the original publication for continuity's sake.

Several texts were later reprinted in two volumes of Higgins's writings. The following essays were published in *Horizons: The Poetics and Theory of the Intermedia,* Southern Illinois University Press (Carbondale, 1984) and the copyright holder, if different from the Estate of Dick Higgins, is noted: "The Strategy of Visual Poetry: Three Aspects" and "Points Toward a Taxonomy of Sound Poetry" © *Precisely*, Richard Kostelanetz, editor, 1979 and 1981; "The Strategy of Each of My Books;" and "Letter to Steve McCaffery" (published in typeset form), original letter courtesy of Steve McCaffery. The following essays were published in *Modernism Since Postmodernism: Essays on Intermedia*, San Diego State University Press (San Diego, 1997) with the copyright holder noted, if different from the Estate of Dick Higgins: "A Golem in the Text," © Contrechamps Éditions, 1993; "A Book," © *New Wilderness Letter*, Jerome Rothenberg and David Guss, editors, 1983; as well as "Fluxus: Theory and Reception" and "Two Sides of a Coin: Fluxus and Something Else Press." "A Short History of Pattern Poetry" is the first chapter of *Pattern Poetry: Guide to an Unknown Literature*, SUNY-Albany Press (Albany, NY, 1987). Thank you to the copyright holders for permission to reprint these texts here.

The Something Else Press checklist includes texts and images by artists and writers published by the Something Else Press. Reproductions appear with the permission of the copyright holders, as follows: pages from *The Paper Snake* by Ray Johnson (as well as "Letter to Ray Johnson," pages 173–74), © the Ray Johnson Estate; Jackson Mac Low's "Some Unsystematic Reflections for Filliou & Others," with permission of Anne Tardos, Executor of the Estate of Jackson Mac Low; "Preface" to *Notations* by John Cage, courtesy the John Cage Trust; *Coeurs Volant* by Marcel Duchamp, © the Association Marcel Duchamp/ADAGP, Paris / Artists Rights Society (ARS), New York; two graphic works, *[From the Kama Sutra of John Giorno] [Black Cock]* and *[From the Book of the Dead of John Giorno] [Rainbow Buddhas & Bodhisattvas]*, by John Giorno, courtesy John Giorno; *L'Immortelle Morte du Monde* by Robert Filliou, © Estate of Robert Filliou and Peter Freeman, Inc. New York/Paris; *Calling* by Allan Kaprow, © Allan Kaprow Estate and Hauser & Wirth; *The Big Book* by Alison Knowles, courtesy Alison Knowles; Peter Moore, photo of *The Big Book* by Alison Knowles © Barbara Moore/Licensed by VAGA, New York, courtesy Paula Cooper Gallery, New York.

An image from *Das Fussballspiel: Ein Stereophonisches Hörspiel* by Ludwig Harig, reproduced in Higgins's essay "Points Toward a Taxonomy of Sound Poetry," with permission from Edition Hansjörg Mayer.

We have attempted to contact all copyright holders for permission for works included in this book; however, we were unable to reach everyone. If you are a copyright holder who has not been reached and acknowledged, please contact the publisher at the address on the following page.

Cover design: Martha Ormiston
Book design and layout: Natalie Kraft
Proofreaders: Emily Gross, Julie Harrison, Lisa Pearson, and Elizabeth Zuba
Index: Victoria Baker

FIRST EDITION
ISBN: 978-1-938221-20-0
Printed and bound in China

siglio uncommon books at the intersection of art & literature
PO Box 111, Catskill, New York 12414 p 310-857-6935
www.sigliopress.com publisher@sigliopress.com

Available to the trade through Artbook.com/D.A.P.
75 Broad Street, Suite 630, New York, NY 10004
Tel: 212-627-1999 Fax: 212-627-9484